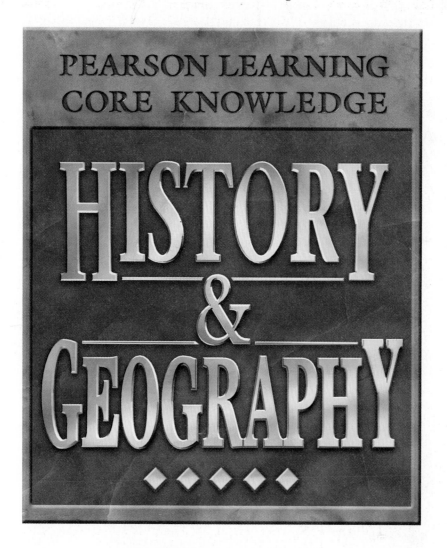

PEARSON LEARNING CORE KNOWLEDGE

HISTORY & GEOGRAPHY

Edited by E.D. Hirsch, Jr.

Pearson
Learning
Group

www.PearsonLearning.com

ISBN 0-7690-5026-3
Printed in the United States of America
   12 13 14 15 16 VO64 15 14 13 12 11 10

1-800-321-3106
www.pearsonlearning.com

CONTENTS

World Lakes

Contents

Lake Tanganyika Ready? Your air tank is strapped on your back and ready to go. Set? You make sure your scuba mask is snug on your face, covering your eyes and nose. Go! Your friend Stephanie gives you a smile and together you jump off the boat into the lake.

You're scuba diving in Lake Tanganyika (tan gun YEE kuh), Africa's deepest and longest lake. You've come to visit the home of many of the tropical fish you've seen in the aquarium in your school.

A cloud of shimmering colors swirls past Stephanie and then moves slowly toward you. Suddenly you're in the middle of shiny blues, bright golds, and neon greens sparkling all around you. You can practically hear Stephanie thinking one of her favorite words, "Unbelievable!"

You stop and watch a thousand tiny fish darting in and out. Most of them are only two or three inches long, as long as your finger. Some fish are covered with bold, black stripes, and others have polka dots on their backs and fins. These fish have strange names. Some are called giraffes, and others are zebras, daffodils, gold faces, and six-stripes. Because of the unusual beauty of these fish, people all over the world pay hundreds of dollars to buy only one or two of the rare ones.

You feel that you could watch for hours, but finally you glance over at Stephanie. She motions upward, as if to say, "Let's go back up to the boat and get on with our trip!" You use your flippers to help you swim to the surface.

Back on board the boat, you try to remember what else is unusual about Lake Tanganyika, besides its fish. A look at your map shows that Lake Tanganyika is one of a group of lakes that point like long fingers down the side of the map. A lake is usually described as a body of water that is surrounded by land.

"Do you remember why these lakes are so long and narrow?" you ask Stephanie.

"They're in those deep valleys, the **rift valleys**," she answers. You both look across Lake Tanganyika toward the shore, where mountains rise up from the water's edge.

Many centuries ago the earth's surface cracked and began separating between those mountain ranges. Gradually the edges of the cracks pulled farther and farther away from each other. Then the ground between the edges dropped down many hundreds of feet, forming deep valleys that filled up with water to form the lakes.

> **vocabulary**
> **rift valley** a long, narrow valley in East Africa

"Let's eat fish for lunch today," you suggest to Stephanie. You don't mean the sparkling green and blue fish; you mean the bigger fish that people catch to eat from this lake. Along the lake's shore are several small cities, with docks for ferryboats and fishing boats.

Fish are a valuable resource from Lake Tanganyika. Lake Tanganyika is a long lake and touches the boundaries of four different countries—Zaire, Tanzania, Burundi, and Zambia. This makes Lake Tanganyika a good transportation route.

"Fish for lunch, and then we go on to Lake Victoria," Stephanie says.

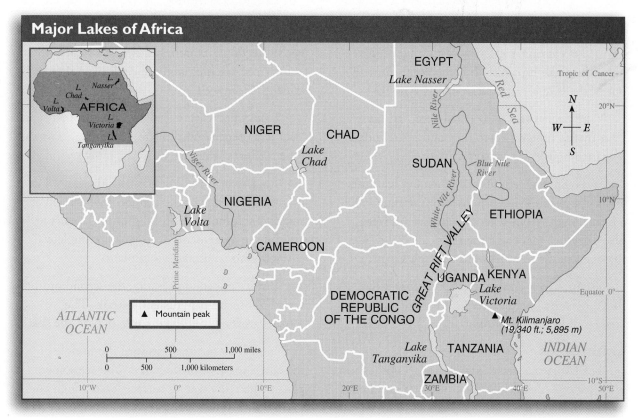

Major Lakes of Africa

Use this map to locate the three major lakes of Africa discussed in this lesson.

Lake Victoria

Africa has many other large lakes. Among these lakes are lakes Nasser, Lake Volta, Lake Chad, and Lake Victoria. We will explore Lakes Victoria and Chad on the following pages.

Lake Victoria, to the northeast of Lake Tanganyika, is the largest lake in Africa. You've decided to visit this lake because it is the source of the famous Nile River, which you studied in school. To get from Lake Tanganyika to Lake Victoria, you cross by land through the country of Tanzania (tan zuh NEE uh). First your jeep climbs up over the mountains along the edge of Lake Tanganyika. Then you cross the flat, grassy lands of Tanzania. As you pass through the many villages and towns here, the road is often quite crowded with people, bicycles, and motor vehicles. People are carrying bundles or babies, stopping to talk to each other, and busily doing errands.

Tanzania and its neighbor, Kenya, are famous for their **game reserves** and national parks. Tourists visit these parks to view elephants, giraffes, and other wildlife. Other tourists like to climb Mount Kilimanjaro (kihl uh mahn JAHR oh), Africa's highest peak. Even though Lake

Victoria is near these interesting places, probably few tourists see what you are about to see.

"We really want to see where the Nile begins," you tell your guide. "In school we learned about the Nile River and how the ancient Egyptians built the famous pyramids near the river."

"No problem!" he says. "Did you know that Lake Victoria is named for Queen Victoria of England? She was queen in the 1800s, when the first Europeans came to this lake," he continues.

Many beautiful islands dot this lake. Some of them are quite large. In one area steep cliffs rise from the shore. In another area the shore is more like a marsh or swamp. Finally you arrive at the place where water drains out of Lake Victoria.

"Is this the beginning of the Nile River?" you ask.

> **vocabulary**
> **game reserve** an area set aside by the government where animals are protected from hunters

"Actually, one of the small rivers that flow into Lake Victoria is the very beginning of the Nile River," he explains. "But the water flowing out of the lake is called the Victoria Nile River."

"The river is still quite small here," he says. "But by the time it gets to the country of Sudan, it's much bigger. It's called the White Nile there."

"Yes," Stephanie nods, "I remember learning about the White Nile. It joins with the Blue Nile, a river flowing from Ethiopia (ee thee OH pee uh). Together they form the river called the Nile, the one that flows northward through Egypt."

"Right," your guide says. "Don't forget that the Nile is the longest river in the world. Here you are only at the beginning of it!"

Lake Chad

The last African lake on your tour, Lake Chad, is in western Africa. Like Lake Victoria and Lake Tanganyika, Lake Chad is shared by several countries. Chad, Niger, Nigeria, and Cameroon each have part of the shore of Lake Chad.

"This is really different from the other lakes we saw," Stephanie says. "It's not mountainous here, and the weather is pretty dry." You look out across the land around the lake. It's mostly flat, with a bright sun overhead, making the air very hot, about 100°F.

"But don't forget," you remind her, "people have lived around this lake for at least a thousand years, perhaps even more."

Two men in a large flat boat stop to see if you need directions. They're brothers who make their living from catching and selling fish, so they know the lake well.

"Lake Chad is very shallow," one brother says. "But it is deeper from June to September," says the other. "That's when we have our rainy season."

"Look over there," the first brother says. He points to the edge of the lake near where you are standing. "It looks like solid ground, doesn't it?" You nod in agreement. That area is completely covered with reeds and other plants.

"But it's not solid ground," the second brother says. "Those are papyrus and cattails. They're actually growing in shallow water, right in the lake."

"Now look out there toward the middle of the lake," the first brother says. You see some places where the water's surface looks rough and lumpy, with spots of color. "What is that out there?" Stephanie asks.

"Waterlilies," says the second brother. "Hundreds of them. They're so crowded together that they form a mat that is almost solid."

Like the two brothers, many people make their living by fishing in the lake. Others have farms or graze livestock nearby. But it's fish that you see for sale everywhere—in the fish markets, on the docks, and along the streets—dried fish, fresh fish, salted fish, and smoked fish.

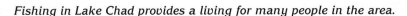

Fishing in Lake Chad provides a living for many people in the area.

Lake Titicaca Our train chugged and whistled across the flat plateau of southern Peru. Far in the distance were snow-covered peaks of the Andes in Peru and Bolivia.

People living near Lake Titicaca use boats made of reeds to travel on the lake.

I was writing postcards to friends at home after visiting Lake Titicaca (tiht ih KAH kuh), one of the world's highest lakes.

"Maybe you should tell them about the things we did here," my friend Ricardo suggested. "Tell about the cruise we took yesterday on Lake Titicaca and those ruins we saw."

Now that was interesting! Along the shore of Lake Titicaca are huge stone ruins of a civilization whose people lived in the area hundreds of years before the Incas. When I touched that ancient stone, I thought I could hear people whispering to me from thousands of years ago.

"And what about those llamas (LAH muz) we ran into?" Ricardo asked. Llamas are animals that are a little like camels but smaller. When I walked up to a llama, it looked me straight in the eye. They have really long necks, sort of like short giraffes. Farmers near Lake Titicaca raise llamas for their wool. They fasten ribbons or tiny bells in the llamas' ears to show who the owner is. Everywhere you go, people are selling colorful wool sweaters, scarves, hats, gloves, and blankets. They come in handy at night when it gets very cold.

"And tell them you ate a lot of *papas*," Ricardo continued. That's what they call potatoes in Peru and Bolivia. Around Lake Titicaca they grow a hundred different kinds of potatoes. The

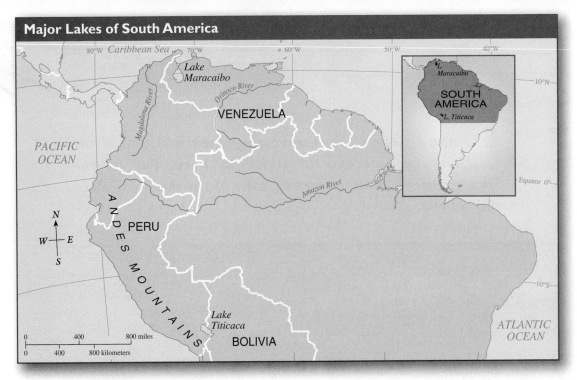

Major Lakes of South America

Find Lakes Titicaca and Maracaibo on this map. Notice that Lake Titicaca is completely surrounded by land, but Lake Maracaibo has an outlet to the Caribbean Sea.

cool climate near Lake Titicaca is great for growing potatoes.

The first potatoes in the world were grown in this part of South America. We wouldn't have the French fries all of us enjoy today if it weren't for potatoes or *papas*.

"And what about the lake?" Ricardo asked. When we took a short cruise on Lake Titicaca, we saw that people get practically everything they need from the lake. They get fish to eat, water to drink and for their crops. The reeds that grow in the lake are so strong that you can make furniture, roofs, and even boats with them.

Lake Maracaibo

On another trip, Ricardo and I visited Lake Maracaibo (mar uh KYE boh) in Venezuela, one of the most important lakes in South America. We discovered that Lake Maracaibo is not really a lake, because it is not completely surrounded by land. Instead, it is a **gulf.**

The area is rich with petroleum deposits under Lake Maracaibo's waters, along its shores, and out along the Atlantic coast. We saw oil **derricks** in the water, oil tankers on the water, oil storage tanks on the land, and oil company offices in many places.

"Tell your friends about how important the oil is in Venezuela." Ricardo suggested how I could write interesting postcards.

"I could tell them about the money Venezuela has made from selling oil and petroleum products and how big the city of Maracaibo has grown. After all, it's a huge city, with its own university and lots of different industries, mostly because of the oil."

"That's right," Ricardo agreed. "And petroleum is important to everyone, everywhere. Remember what we learned about the products that are made with petroleum?"

"Sure! Plastic and paint and gasoline and all kinds of things we use every day."

Lake Maracaibo is different from Lake Titicaca. Lake Titicaca is a quiet lake that seems to speak of the past, and Lake Maracaibo is a bustling trading hub of the present!

vocabulary
gulf a part of an ocean extending into land
derrick a framework tower that supports a drill over an oil well

A **Shipwreck** Icy winds roared across the lake. A huge ship as long as two football fields struggled slowly through enormous waves that washed over the ship's deck. Late in the afternoon the ship's captain radioed, "We are taking heavy seas over our decks; it's the worst sea I've ever been in."

The freighter **The Edmund Fitzgerald** *sank during a powerful Lake Superior storm in 1975.*

The crew of another ship nearby was keeping an eye on this ship, which was carrying thousands of tons of minerals. At 7:10 p.m. the captain radioed, "We're holding our own." But five minutes later the ship had simply vanished. Afterward, a rescue team found it on the floor of the lake, broken in half. The captain and all the crew members died.

This shipwreck occurred in 1975. People were shocked and asked how such a disaster could happen.

For one thing, the ship, *The Edmund Fitzgerald,* was sailing on Lake Superior, the largest lake in the United States. Lake Superior is a very pleasant place to sail and fish in the summer. But in winter this lake is famous for its wild storms and hurricane-force winds that can toss around even the largest and heaviest ships.

In fact, the area where the shipwreck occurred is sometimes called the Graveyard of Ships.

Investigators later decided that a cover door over the cargo area had collapsed. Then water from the crashing waves flooded the inside of the ship. The radar systems on the ship failed, and the captain could not get help fast enough to save the ship.

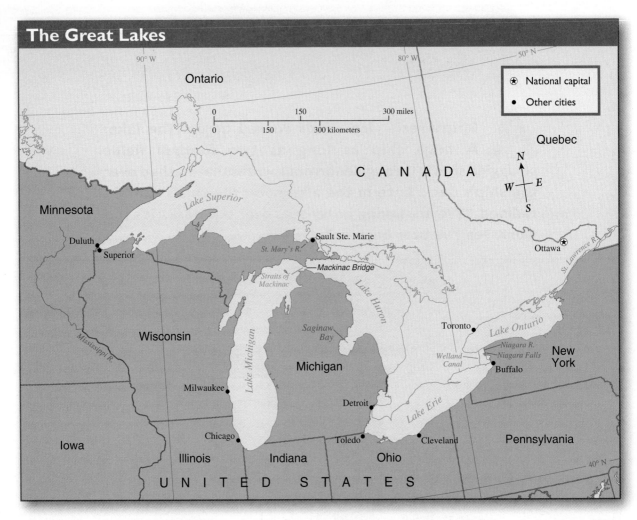

The Great Lakes

Ontario

Minnesota

Duluth
Superior

Lake Superior

Sault Ste. Marie
St. Mary's R.

Mackinac Bridge

Straits of Mackinac

Lake Huron

Saginaw Bay

Wisconsin

Lake Michigan

Michigan

Milwaukee

Chicago

Illinois   Indiana

Iowa

Detroit

Toledo

Ohio

Lake Erie

Cleveland

CANADA

Quebec

Ottawa ⊛

St. Lawrence R.

Toronto   *Lake Ontario*

Niagara R.
Welland   *Niagara Falls*
Canal
Buffalo   New York

Pennsylvania

UNITED STATES

N
W — E
S

⊛ National capital
● Other cities

0   150   300 miles
0   150   300 kilometers

90° W   80° W   50° N

40° N

Mississippi R.

The Great Lakes border eight midwestern states and provide a way for these states to ship their products by water.

Locks and Straits

What do the crews on ships like *The Edmund Fitzgerald* see as they cross the Great Lakes (Lakes Superior, Michigan, Huron, Erie, and Ontario)? To find out, we've asked the captain of a large sailboat to take us around the Great Lakes, five large lakes that are used for fishing, shipping, recreation, and drinking water. We ask him what places are the most interesting to see and learn about.

Each of these lakes is so large that when you stand along the shore and look out across the water, you cannot see the other side of the lake. It's almost like looking out at the ocean. The captain points far out across the water. We squint and look hard, and finally we can see a flat gray bump on the flat gray horizon. We might have never seen it if the captain hadn't pointed it out

to us. The captain says, "That little bump out there is probably a very large ship. A lot of huge cargo ships travel on the Great Lakes, carrying grain, iron ore, steel, timber, and all kinds of products to and from port cities along the lakes."

Sooner or later nearly all the big ships on Lake Superior have to go through Sault Ste. Marie (soo saynt muh REE), Michigan. That's where the ships use a **canal** to get from Lake Superior to Lake Huron. Our sailboat arrives at Sault Ste. Marie quickly because it's a very windy day. The canal there has a series of **locks,** sections of the canal that are closed off with gates. The captain explains how they work.

"Locks help a ship move from a lake where the surface of the water is high, such as Lake Superior, to a lower lake, such as Lake Huron," he says. Our sailboat leaves Lake Superior, and the captain tells us we're entering the first lock. The gates behind us shut. We feel a little nudge as our sailboat stops, and we hear a lot of water rushing somewhere. Then the sailboat begins moving downward very, very slowly.

"Don't worry!" the captain reassures us. "We're not sinking! Some of the water in the lock is being removed to lower the water level so that it matches the water level in the next lock."

Then the gates in front of us open and our ship moves into the next lock. After going through a number of such locks, our sailboat is in lower water, entering Lake Huron. The whole process only took a few minutes.

Next, the captain takes us to another interesting part of the Great Lakes, the Straits of Mackinac [MACK in awe]. (A strait is a narrow body of water that connects two larger bodies of water.) Ships and boats that want to get from Lake Huron to Lake Michigan have to pass through this waterway.

We want to see the straits from one of the most famous bridges in America, the Mackinac Bridge. This is among the longest and strongest bridges ever built. After all, it has to survive the ice and winter winds of the Great Lakes. The captain docks the sailboat, and we drive the five miles across the bridge. Out the window there's water, water everywhere. But we also see islands, a ferryboat, and some sailboats. The straits are not nearly as big as one of the Great Lakes, so ships have to move carefully through these waters.

A cargo ship passes through one of the canal locks at Sault Ste. Marie, Michigan, between Lake Superior and Lake Huron.

Sailing on Lake Michigan and Lake Huron

The captain has brought us to Lake Michigan because it's the only Great Lake that is entirely inside the United States. We head for the other end of the lake, to Chicago, Illinois. Trains, trucks, and barges carry grains and minerals from farms and mines in Illinois and many other states to Chicago.

With all the railroads, highways, and canals meeting in Chicago, the city is like the hub of a giant wheel. There the products are loaded on ships that carry them to other cities on the Great Lakes or out across the ocean.

After admiring the skyline of Chicago, we head north, pass under the Mackinac Bridge again, and enter Lake Huron. The captain asks us a question:

"Did you ever notice that the southern part of Michigan is shaped like a mitten."

We look at a map and sure enough, that's what Michigan does look like. Lake Huron has made that possible. The "thumb" and the "index finger" of Michigan are separated by a large bay of Lake Huron, Saginaw Bay. The main part of Lake Huron continues south toward the next of the Great Lakes, Lake Erie.

The captain has a riddle for us: "What is the only United States city on the Great Lakes from which you travel south to get to Canada?" We're puzzled at first but check the map again.

"Detroit, Michigan!" we call out. Detroit is a large industrial city built on the Detroit River, between Lake Huron and Lake Erie.

"Now, what's the nickname of Detroit?" the captain quizzes us. We remember that ships use the Great Lakes as a route to carry iron ore and steel. Many of these materials are shipped to the big Great Lakes cities, such as Chicago and Detroit. The automobile industry began near Detroit, and the city is nicknamed for that. "Motor City!" we shout. The captain gives up trying to stump us, at least for a while.

Two Lakes and a Waterfall

We've sailed past Detroit, and now we're in Lake Erie, the shallowest of all the Great Lakes. Along the shore are smokestacks, lighthouses, office towers, and loading docks. These are in some of the important industrial cities, such as Cleveland, Ohio. Finally we reach Buffalo, New York. Here we are to leave our sailboat for a day to visit the great Niagara Falls, which are among the world's largest waterfalls. The falls are created by the Niagara River, which flows from Lake Erie into Lake Ontario.

"How will you get the sailboat over Niagara Falls?" we ask the captain. He laughs and gets out the map again.

"Look, I'm going to take this boat around the falls, down the Welland Canal," he says. "If I went over Niagara Falls in this boat, you might never see me or the boat again!"

When we get to Niagara Falls, we can see what he means. A giant wall of water crashes over a huge cliff. The roar of the falls is so loud we can hardly hear each other. On our short tour-boat ride along the bottom of the wall of water, everyone is wearing raincoats, but the spray gets us wet anyway!

On Lake Ontario we again meet the captain and board the sailboat. The day is sunny, and the wind is brisk. We almost fly along the water, feeling the wind tugging at the sails. The captain points out rows and rows of trees along the shore. They are apple, peach and, cherry trees.

Finally our trip is over. The captain says that up ahead is the St. Lawrence River, which would lead us out to the Atlantic Ocean. Here, at this end of the river, are hundreds of islands scattered about. Called the Thousand Islands, they are very popular vacation places for camping, fishing, and boating in the summer.

We say goodbye to the captain. He's become our friend.

"The Great Lakes really are pretty great," he says. And we agree.

Lake Baikal

"Be careful! Don't lean over so far!" Valentin shouts. He is my guide on Russia's Lake Baikal (bye KAHL). "You'll fall out of the boat!"

Lake Baikal in Siberia is the deepest lake in the world.

"I just wanted to grab some of those little pebbles on the bottom of the lake," I explain to Valentin.

Valentin laughs: "You can't. Those 'pebbles' may look like they're just below the surface, but really they're many feet below the surface. And they're probably not pebbles.

The expression on my face tells Valentin I don't really believe him. So he explains. He tells me that Lake Baikal is a very deep lake—the deepest in the world—and also a very clear lake. Because it's so clear, things look like they're closer to the surface than they really are. It's an optical illusion.

"Those 'little pebbles' you saw are probably huge rocks," Valentin giggles. "But don't feel too

bad. Everybody makes this mistake when they first visit here."

Valentin tells us many interesting things about Lake Baikal. For instance, he tells us that this one lake contains enough water to fill all five of the Great Lakes until they overflow.

Lake Baikal is sometimes called the Pearl of Siberia. That's because it's located in a region of eastern Russia called Siberia. And, like a pearl, it's a great treasure to Russians. They also call this lake "the sacred lake" or "the sacred water" because it is mysterious, magical, and majestic. Lake Baikal is so deep that people imagine it has great mysteries tucked away down below.

The land surrounding Lake Baikal is also a great natural treasure. High cliffs and forest-covered mountains rise above the lake. Roaming the dense woods are reindeer, elk, deer, and bears. Wild rivers rush to empty their waters into the lake. Parks and game reserves around Lake Baikal protect the rivers and the animals. Many Russians feel that the beauty of nature around Lake Baikal is like magic.

Things may not stay this wild and natural forever. Timber companies are cutting down some of the forest to make lumber and paper. Ships are built on the lake's shore, and fishing boats come and go. A railroad connects mines and industries to the towns along the shore.

But for now, I am happy to breathe the fresh air and imagine the mysteries at the bottom of the world's deepest lake.

The Caspian Sea

Most of the world's lakes are freshwater lakes, but a few contain salt water. A lake has salt water if its water evaporates more quickly than rivers can bring in new water. When water evaporates, it leaves behind salts and minerals.

You can see how this works on a hot summer day. If you let the sweat on your arm or hand evaporate and then lick your arm, your skin tastes a little salty.

Although freshwater comes into the Caspian Sea from a number of streams and lakes, the sea has salt water because it has no outlet. And the Caspian Sea (which is really a lake in

Oil derricks are a common sight on the Caspian Sea.

spite of its name) is located in a very dry climate. So its water evaporates, leaving behind salt and other minerals. After thousands of years, a lot of salt has built up in the Caspian Sea.

The Caspian Sea is a very large body of water, and it has long been a good trade route. In the past, traders traveled between lands far to the east in Asia and lands far to the west in Europe. Many traders carried their goods by boat or ship across this lake during their travels.

When people discovered how valuable oil is, the Caspian Sea became more than just a trade route. Some of the world's largest oil deposits are located around and under the Caspian Sea.

The Aral Sea

From the Caspian Sea, we travel to the next stop on our trip, the Aral Sea. And we'd better hurry. This lake is shrinking. The volume of the Aral Sea has decreased by 75 percent in the past few decades. The Aral Sea is a salt lake in Uzbekistan and Kazakhstan, countries that were both part of the former Soviet Union.

In 1960 the Aral Sea was the fourth largest lake in the world. Now its shoreline has receded up to 75 miles in places; the sea level has dropped more than 50 feet. It is now about the tenth largest lake in the world.

We ask our guide, Kodir, what caused this.

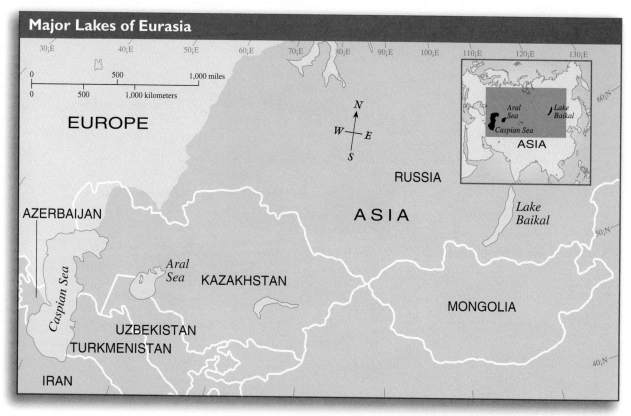

Major Lakes of Eurasia

EUROPE

AZERBAIJAN

Caspian Sea

Aral Sea

KAZAKHSTAN

UZBEKISTAN

TURKMENISTAN

IRAN

RUSSIA

ASIA

Lake Baikal

MONGOLIA

ASIA

Aral Sea

Caspian Sea

Lake Baikal

Use the scale of miles/kilometers on this map to measure the distance between the Caspian Sea, the Aral Sea, and Lake Baikal.

He replies, "Unfortunately this was not a natural change. The Soviets diverted rivers that flowed into the Aral Sea to provide water for cotton crops for export. A canal was planned that would eventually guide water from other rivers into the sea but the canal never was built."

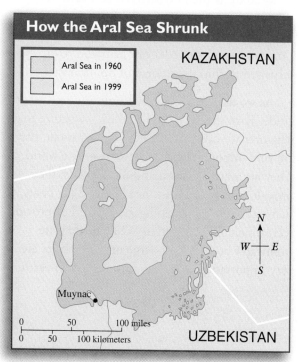

How the Aral Sea Shrunk

Aral Sea in 1960

Aral Sea in 1999

KAZAKHSTAN

Muynac

UZBEKISTAN

"How does the shrinking of the lake affect the people who live nearby?" we inquire.

Kodir replies, "It has made a big difference. For example, look at the town of Muynac. In the not-too-distant past. Muynac sat on the edge of the sea and attracted fishermen and tourists. Today the Aral Sea is a shrunken shadow of its former self, and Muynac is a desert town more than 60 miles from the sea. There are no tourists. Toxic dusts and salts spread across wide areas of central Asia when the wind blows, making life miserable."

Kodir tells us more alarming stories about the region around the Aral Sea. He explains that the loss of great parts of this lake has affected the climate. Snow comes earlier each year and spring comes later. The growing season is shorter. The people in the area suffer more respiratory diseases.

"What will happen to the Aral Sea and the region around it?" we ask.

"No one is quite sure what will happen,"

This map shows how the Aral Sea has shrunk from the fourth largest lake to the tenth largest lake in the world.

13

These boats were left high and dry on the Aral Sea as the waters in the lake receded.

Kodir replies, "There are now five Central Asian nations affected by the changes in the sea. First they need to agree on what to do. And then they must find the money to do it. It is a big problem."

What Is a Lake?

We have visited many large bodies of water, some called lakes and some called seas. Now we ask Kodir a question that has been on our minds for awhile: "If a lake can be salty like the Aral Sea or the Great Salt Lake, and a lake can be called a sea like the Caspian Sea, and a gulf can be called a lake like Lake Maracaibo in South America, then how can we recognize a real lake?"

Kodir laughs and says, "That is a really good question. Actually even the experts have some difficulty telling lakes from seas. One definition of a lake is a body of water surrounded by land. And yet the Great Lakes of North America are not completely surrounded by land. The St. Lawrence River connects them to the Atlantic Ocean. And if you think about it, both the Black Sea and the Mediterranean Sea are almost completely surrounded by land—and yet few experts would call these bodies of water lakes. So it's tricky to draw the line between lakes and seas. If you want to find out if a body of water is considered to be a lake by many experts, an almanac or encyclopedia can help you. Don't be surprised to find differences of opinion though."

As we think about what Kodir and our other guides have shown us and told us, we realize that whatever we call these large bodies of water, they are very important to people all over the world. They are sources of fish and other foods; they provide water for crops; they are used for boats that transport people and goods; and they provide recreational opportunities. Whether they are freshwater or salt water, large or small, lakes are very important geographic features of our earth.

canal a waterway made by people

derrick a framework tower that supports a drill over an oil well

game reserve an area set aside by the government where animals are protected from hunters

gulf a part of an ocean extending into land

lock a part of a canal that has gates for lowering and raising the water level

rift valley a long, narrow valley in East Africa

The Maya, Aztec and Inca Civilizations

Contents

The Vanishing Civilization Do you like mysteries? Try this one: More than a thousand years ago, a great civilization of American Indian people built cities across Mexico and Central America. They built temples and pyramids that rose far above the jungle treetops.

They discovered important mathematical ideas and studied the movements of the stars, producing a calendar almost as accurate as the one we have today. Then, after hundreds of years of prosperity, they disappeared. The people left the cities and seemed to vanish into the jungle. Their great civilization had mysteriously died.

This may sound like the plot of a science fiction movie, but it isn't. In fact, it is a short history of the Maya (MAH yuh), who lived in southern Mexico and Central America more than a thousand years ago.

Discovery in the Jungle

In 1839, two American archaeologists heard rumors about the ruins of a great civilization in the jungles of Central America and went exploring. They found the ruins of the city of Copán (koh PAHN) in the present-day country of Honduras. From the architecture it was clear that this was the work of an advanced civilization. After exploring some more, the archaeologists returned to the United States and wrote a book that became a bestseller. That was the beginning of our ongoing fascination with the Maya civilization.

For the past century and a half, archaeologists and other experts have devoted their lives to finding out more about these remarkable people. Recent breakthroughs in research have revealed just how much the Maya accomplished. Let's take a closer look at what we know about them and what still remains a mystery.

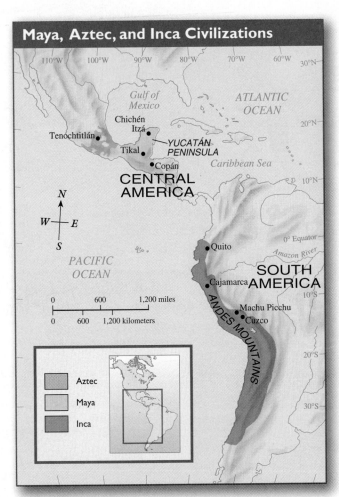

Three great civilizations flourished in Central and South America: The Maya, Aztec, and Inca.

The Maya controlled a large group of **city-states** on the Yucatán Peninsula in southeastern Mexico and in the modern-day countries of Guatemala, Honduras, and Belize. Archaeologists believe the Maya civilization was at its mightiest from about A.D. 200 to 900.

The largest buildings in Maya cities were pyramids and temples used for religious purposes. From the size of these buildings it is clear that religion was a very important part of Maya life. Maya pyramids rose high above the treetops of the surrounding rain forest. Indeed, these lofty pyramids remained the tallest structures in the Americas until 1902, when the Flatiron Building, a 22-story skyscraper, was built in New York City.

Mysterious Writing

Archaeologists found **hieroglyphs** (hye ur oh-GLIHFS) carved into Maya buildings and walls. In the city of Copán stands the Temple of the Hieroglyphic Stairway. A climb up this staircase is a journey back in time. Each of the 63 steps has a story to tell. Carved in the stairway, written symbols called glyphs name all the rulers of Copán and their victories. The staircase was found by the American archaeologists in 1839. The problem was they couldn't figure out what the symbols meant. Neither could many other expert archaeologists who visited the site.

Hieroglyphs are like a code. Once you figure out the code, you can read what they say. But Maya hieroglyphs were very complicated, with more than 800 different symbols. It wasn't until the 1960s, when computers were first available, that archaeologists began to crack the code. Since then we have learned a great deal more about the Maya.

Breath on a Mirror

What we have learned is that daily life for the Maya revolved around family, farming, and service to the gods. No individual or community made an important move without consulting the gods. Priests decided which days were favorable for planting a field, launching a war, or building a hut. The Maya believed that the gods were wiser than humans—much wiser.

According to Maya legend, the first people to be created could see everything. Then the creator gods decided that this gave people too much power. So the gods took back some of that power, limiting human sight and power. The Maya sacred book, the *Popol Vuh*, tells that the gods purposely clouded human understanding. It explains that a human's view of the world is unclear, "like breath on a mirror."

Serious Play

Breaking the Maya code also helped archaeologists understand the use of a kind of ball court found in many Maya cities. Archaeologists were puzzled about these ball courts, which varied in size. Some were the size of volleyball courts. Others were larger than football fields.

The Maya carved the names of the rulers of Copán in the Hieroglyphic Stairway.

Archaeologists now believe that a game called *pok-ta-pok* was played in these courts. They believe that the goal of *pok-ta-pok* was to drive a solid rubber ball through a stone ring. The ring was a target, somewhat like a basketball goal. However, it was no easy task to drive the ball through one of these rings, for the balls were large and heavy and the rings were only slightly larger than the balls. What's more, the players were not allowed to use their hands or feet! How do you imagine they drove those balls through the rings?

The court at the ancient Maya site of Chichén Itzá (chee CHEN eet SAH) is still visible today and is a popular tourist attraction. If you stand there and use your imagination, you can picture what a *pok-ta-pok* game might have looked like.

Imagine heavily-muscled *pok-ta-pok* players stepping out onto the field. They wear leather helmets and pads to protect themselves from injuries. You can also see that they are worried. They know that the stakes are high. *Pok-ta-pok* is a game with religious importance. The Maya think of it as a battle between good and evil, but the only way to find out who's good and who's evil is to see who wins the game.

Hundreds of spectators have gathered to watch an event that is not only entertainment but also a way of honoring the gods.

When the game begins, the sound of the bouncing ball is added to the cheers. *Pok, pok, pok!* goes the hard rubber ball as it hits the ground and bounces off the walls on the side of the court.

One player drives the ball downfield, banging it with his elbows, knees, and chest. Then, *whack!* Another player slams into him and knocks him to the ground. There is no whistle, or foul; there are very few rules in *pok-ta-pok!* The game continues until someone scores, which may not happen for quite a while. The side that scores wins the game.

The winners of *pok-ta-pok* games were considered to be the good ones. Sometimes they were rewarded with the clothing and jewelry of the noble spectators. Maya experts think it was not uncommon for the spectators to run from the stadium after a score, with the victorious player or players chasing them to get their clothing and jewelry!

But what do you think happened to the losers? They were considered evil, and experts believe that at least some of them were offered as sacrifices to the gods.

Human sacrifice was a part of the Maya religion. Maya priests sought to please the gods by offering sacrifices atop the pyramids. A typical sacrifice involved painting the captive blue, strapping him to a rock altar, and cutting out his still-beating heart with a stone knife. No wonder the *pok-ta-pok* players looked worried as they walked out onto the field!

Pok-ta-pok and human sacrifices are only two of the many aspects of Maya life that we understand better as a result of breaking the hieroglyphic code. In the next lesson you will learn about the scientific achievements and everyday life of these vanished people.

This is a statue of a Maya ballplayer.

Wisdom in the Sky The Maya may have believed that their gods gave them an imperfect understanding of the world and that their understanding was "like breath on a mirror." But archaeologists have discovered evidence that proves that the Maya understood some things very well.

Their understanding of astronomy, for example, is an impressive accomplishment when you consider that the Maya had no telescopes, no computers, and no satellites. They didn't even have the wheel. All they had were their own eyes, and yet they made incredibly precise observations of the stars.

Maya Calendars

We take it for granted that there are 365 days in a year, plus an extra day every fourth year for leap year. But these numbers were established after many years of close study of the sun and the seasons. The Maya, working without scientific tools, calculated that there were 365.2420 days in a year. Modern astronomers, using the latest technology, measure the year at 365.2422 days!

The Maya solar calendar, or calender based on the sun, is similar to our calendar but not exactly identical. We divide our year into 12 months, but the Maya divided their year into 18 months with names like *Pop* and *Zip*.

Besides their 365-day solar calendar, Maya astronomers produced another calendar called the Sacred Round. The Sacred Round was 260 days long and was used to keep track of religious holidays as well as other important events.

Because the Maya had two calendars, each day had two names. One name came from the Sacred Round and one from the solar calendar. This also meant that all Maya children had two birthdays.

Astronomy at Work

We can see the results of Maya astronomy in the location of important temples and pyramids in Maya cities. Temples were built in such a way that the sun would shine directly on the most important part of the temple on important days. In Chichén Itzá, for example, on the spring

THE MAYA MONTHS

POP UO

ZIP ZOTZ TZEC XUL

YAXKIN MOL CHEN YAX

ZAC CEH MAC KANKIN

MUAN PAX KAYAB CUMHU

Each glyph stands for one of the 18 months in the Maya calendar.

equinox and the fall equinox, the rising sun shines on a statue of a serpent at the base of the pyramid and casts a shadow on the steps of the pyramid itself. As the sun rises, it creates an image of the serpent slithering down the stairs of the pyramid.

Inventing Zero

The Maya also excelled at mathematics. They developed a powerful system of number symbols. A dot stood for one. A bar stood for five. A shell stood for zero. We all know that zero can stand for nothing, but when it comes to a system of numbers, zero means a lot! It enables us to write numbers like 20 and 201. Just as we use zero, the Maya used the symbol as a placeholder. In fact, the Maya were among the first people in the world to develop the concept of zero.

How They Lived

Most Maya people made their living as farmers. Their main crop was corn. One of their main foods was something you may have eaten—a flat bread called a *tortilla* (tor TEE uh). Farmers also grew beans, squash, sweet potatoes, tomatoes, and pumpkins.

Maya farmers lived in one-room huts made out of mud and grass. Families lived in walled compounds of several huts. Men and boys were responsible for the farming. Women and girls took care of the house, cooked, and made clothing and pottery.

Every culture has a few practices that seem odd to other people. The Maya did two things to their babies that may seem a little strange to you. They considered slightly crossed eyes a sign of physical beauty. So mothers would hang a bead from a baby's nose to help develop that condition. The Maya also considered a flat head a sign of physical beauty. So they would strap newborn babies to a board on their back. The board would flatten the baby's soft skull, giving the child the desired look.

Coming of Age

Before age five, Maya children had few responsibilities and were cared for by parents and other relatives. At age five they took on new responsibilities, such as helping their parents with farming and household chores. A boy had a white bead braided into his hair. A girl had a string tied to her waist with a red shell attached.

These symbols of childhood remained in place until children reached the age of 14, at which point an initiation ceremony was performed to mark their passage to adulthood. A priest would pick a day when the stars were favorable. Then the priest would cut the bead from the boy's hair. A girl's mother would cut the string from her daughter's waist. When these symbols of childhood had been cut away, the parents would have a celebration with family members and neighbors.

After these ceremonies, boys moved into a house for unmarried men and remained there until they got married. Marriages at that time were arranged. In the hard life of Maya farmers, marriages were seen not as romantic affairs but as business deals between families.

As with the initiation ceremonies, priests were consulted before a marriage date was set. Maya priests consulted the stars and the gods to find a day that would bring good fortune. However, no Maya couple expected married life to bring all good fortune. The Maya believed that every aspect of life was controlled by the gods. And, since some gods were good and some were bad, they expected life to be a mixture of joys and sorrows.

Where Did Everybody Go?

As you have read, the Maya were amazing people who built a great civilization. That alone would be reason to find them interesting. But one of the really fascinating questions about Maya civilization is what happened at the end.

Archaeologists believe that the Maya left their cities sometime in the 900s, possibly within the span of a few years. Until the 900s the Maya kept careful historical records. They used their hieroglyphs to carve names and dates on their pyramids and temples. Then in the 900s, the writing mysteriously stopped and the Maya temples and pyramids fell into disrepair.

So, what happened? Archaeologists have theories about what might have happened, but they can't find anything that would prove any one theory correct.

One theory suggests that farmers rose up against the priests and nobles. But scholars ask, "If that's so, what happened to the farmers?" There is no evidence of a new group of people replacing the old ones in power.

Some have guessed that disease wiped out the Maya population. But no mass burial grounds have been found. Archaeologists have found indications that some people in this area did die from diseases, but almost all of these deaths seem to have occurred after 1500, when the Spanish brought new diseases to America. The Maya had already disappeared many years before then.

Did disaster strike the Maya environment? Did a time of drought or heavy rainfall bring famine? Was there a major earthquake? Perhaps warrior invaders from central Mexico attacked the Maya. Could these invaders have toppled the civilization?

No one knows for sure. We only know that, whatever the cause, the once great Maya cities were abandoned and swallowed up by the jungle. The Maya scattered. But the people themselves did not disappear completely. Today, millions still speak languages derived from ancient Maya. These descendants of the pyramid-builders live in simple farming villages in southern Mexico, Guatemala, and Honduras. Although many of these people are poor, they have a rich heritage, one that we are learning more about with each passing year.

This pyramid still stands at Chichén Itzá. Twice a year, a shadow appears that looks like a serpent slithering down its steps.

The Eagle and the Cactus About 300 years after the decline of the Maya, another great civilization sprang up. This was the civilization of the Aztecs, in central Mexico.

According to legend, the Aztecs were originally a nomadic tribe. They wandered Mexico, camping here and there, fighting off unfriendly strangers, and surviving on a diet of snakes and lizards. Then one day the powerful god of the sun spoke to the people. "Search for an eagle perched on a cactus," commanded the god. "The great bird will hold a snake in its beak. Where you find the eagle and cactus, build your city."

The legend goes on to describe how the Aztecs searched for this sign and finally discovered it on a swampy island in Lake Texcoco (tesh KOH koh). On that day, the Aztecs' wandering ended. They settled down and began building a new city on the island. The Aztecs called their new home Tenochtitlán (tay noch tee TLAHN), which means "the place of the prickly pear" or "the place of the cactus." Even today the eagle and serpent are shown on the flag of Mexico.

Conquering City-States

Whether or not the myth is true, we do know that the Aztecs established Tenochtitlán in the year 1325. By the 1400s the Aztec civilization had begun to expand. The Aztecs proved to be

Bodleian Library

This Aztec drawing illustrates the legend of the founding of Tenochtitlán. Note the eagle standing on a cactus.

fearsome, ruthless warriors. One by one they conquered the neighboring city-states and incorporated them into their empire. At its height, in the early 1500s, the Aztec Empire included 400 to 500 city-states and controlled much of present-day Mexico. The Aztec emperor ruled more than 5 million people. Tenochtitlán alone probably contained between 150,000 and 200,000 people, making it one of the largest cities in the world at this time. Indeed, no city in the United States would grow so large until the 1800s.

The Aztecs grew strong and wealthy by conquering other people. When Aztec soldiers conquered a neighboring city-state, they forced the inhabitants to send gold, silver, jade, and turquoise to Tenochtitlán. If the conquered people didn't have such valuable items, they would be forced to send whatever they did have. People who lived by the ocean might send seashells, fish, or turtles. Those in agricultural regions might send corn, beans, peppers, squash, or fruit. A hunter might have to give animal skins and feathers, while a craftsperson might send pottery or woven blankets to Tenochtitlán.

The Legend of the Five Suns

Every empire needs supplies to grow strong. It needs food and building materials. What made the Aztec Empire different was its need for captured soldiers brought to Tenochtitlán.

Why did the Aztecs need captured soldiers? Because human sacrifice was the most important religious ritual of the Aztec people. To understand the importance of human sacrifice, we need to take a closer look at the Aztec religion.

According to Aztec beliefs, life was uncertain. The only thing that was certain was that the world would eventually come to a terrible, violent end. This sense of doom was based on a myth. The Aztecs believed that the universe and the sun had been created and destroyed four times in the past. Under the first sun a race of giants roamed the world. This world ended when a jaguar devoured the giants. The world under the second sun didn't do much better. Its people were swept away by wind. People under the third sun died in the fire and ash of volcanoes. Those living under the fourth sun drowned in floods.

The ancient Aztecs lived under the fifth sun. But they believed that this sun would also die: "There will be earthquakes and hunger, and then our end shall come," the priests told the people. The Aztecs took these myths so seriously that they planned their lives in response to them.

The Aztecs believed that the end of the world was sure to come, but they didn't know when. They figured the best way to guard against this disaster was to keep the gods happy.

The Aztecs believed the sun god had an awesome task. Each night he battled the forces of darkness. Each morning he had to find the strength to make the sun rise again. The Aztecs believed that they could help their god find that strength by offering human sacrifices on the altars of their temples.

But the Aztecs preferred to sacrifice someone other than their own family members and neighbors. Most of their sacrificial victims were foreign soldiers, captured in wars and sent to Tenochtitlán. Since Aztec priests believed that the heart was the most important thing to sacrifice, they preferred to offer up the strong heart of a soldier.

Human sacrifice was part of the Aztec religion. This illustration by an Aztec artist shows priests sacrificing prisoners at the altar of a temple.

Religious Sacrifice

The Aztecs held their sacrificial ceremonies on top of pyramids not unlike the Maya pyramids. A big drum would beat ominously as attendants led sacrificial victims to the top of the pyramid. Five priests with long, natty hair and faces painted black would lay a victim face up on a special altar stone. Two of the black-faced priests would hold the victim's legs and two would hold his arms. The fifth priest used a special necklace to hold down the victim's head. Once the victim's limbs were secured, a sixth priest would cut out the victim's heart with a razor-sharp stone knife. The priest held the still-beating heart up in the air, showing it to the spectators below and then offering it to the god. The victim's heart was burned on an altar; his body was allowed to tumble down the steps of the pyramid.

This process was repeated for each victim, until the top steps of the pyramid were literally covered with blood. When all the sacrifices had been completed, the victims' heads were placed on large racks and displayed in the plaza in front of the pyramid.

The Aztecs were fierce warriors ready to go to battle against their neighbors on a moment's notice.

The Aztecs believed that human sacrifices were necessary to keep the gods happy. They could even point to events in the past that seemed to prove that such sacrifices really did please the gods. Once, when a prolonged drought threatened to ruin the Aztec corn harvest, Aztec priests offered a number of human sacrifices in order to regain the favor of the gods. A day or so later, rain came. To us, this might seem like a pure coincidence, but to the Aztecs it seemed like a proof that human sacrifice worked: The gifts of blood had saved the corn crops. Experiences like this convinced the Aztecs of the power of human sacrifice and ensured that their offerings to the gods would be regular and generous.

Love of War

Aztec society was ruled by priests and soldiers. Priests used human sacrifice to deal with the gods. Aztec soldiers held the empire together and provided the victims for the sacrifices.

In Aztec society, as in many societies until recent times, people were born into a class and had little opportunity to advance. The army provided the one opportunity for brave men to better themselves. Success in battle was rewarded with advancement and honor. The Aztecs believed there was no greater honor than to die in battle.

No doubt about it— the Aztecs were fierce warriors. But their love of war and skill at fighting created a rich empire and a remarkable civilization. Read on to learn more about the civilization the Aztecs built and their fabulous capital city of Tenochtitlán.

Floating Paradise The first Europeans who came to America expected to find simple people living in mud huts. Imagine how surprised they must have been when they came upon the great city of Tenochtitlán, with its towering pyramids and its population of more than 100,000.

Tenochtitlán was unlike anything the Europeans had ever seen. The city was built on an island in the middle of a lake. Three wide **causeways** connected the city to the mainland, and a network of canals connected the various parts of the city. The Aztecs traveled around their capital in canoes.

City Tour

Imagine that you have hopped into a canoe to tour Tenochtitlán as it was in the early 1500s. First, you see the so-called "floating gardens" that ring the city. These gardens are not really floating; they just look like they're floating because they are surrounded on all sides by water. The Aztecs turned parts of Lake Texcoco into raised garden beds. They did this by digging up mud from the bottom of the lake and piling it up in shallow areas until the mud pile rose up above the waterline. Then they shaped the piles into long, narrow gardens. Because the gardens were surrounded by water, they stayed moist. The Aztecs also kept the soil fertile by scooping new mud onto the gardens every year. The rich soil was perfect for growing corn, squash, and beans.

> **vocabulary**
> **causeway** a raised road built over water to connect islands to a mainland

Aztec Home Life

As you glide toward the center of Tenochtitlán, you see Aztec men dressed in loin cloths and cloaks and women in long skirts, blouses, and ponchos. You also see hundreds of

This is a mural by Diego Rivera, a 20th-century Mexican artist. It shows the grand Aztec capital, Tenochtitlán.

one-room houses with thatched roofs and mud walls. Inside one, you meet two girls who are learning weaving from their mother. In another, a mother is punishing an unruly son. She throws a handful of chile peppers on the fire and holds the child near the smoking chiles. The chile smoke stings his eyes and makes him cry. This is his punishment for being disobedient.

A few houses away a wedding is taking place. During the ceremony the bride's blouse is tied to the groom's cloak. This tying together is a symbol of the connection between man and wife.

Suburbs and Schools

You also visit an Aztec school, where boys learn military drills and moral instruction. The students practice with miniature weapons. They throw spears and wield special wooden clubs that are studded with sharp pieces of black rock.

A visit to a school for the sons of Aztec nobles turns out to be a hair-raising experience. You quickly realize that the teachers in this school are Aztec priests. Although you've had some scary teachers over the years, you've never had one who painted his face black, refused to wash his hair for religious reasons, and performed human sacrifices on the weekend!

The priests train students to become priests and scribes. Students study Aztec religion and astronomy and learn how to read and write Aztec hieroglyphs. They also learn how to record information in a special kind of book known as a codex. The priest shows students a sample codex. It is a long strip of tree bark that folds up like an accordion. The pages of the codex are covered with pictures and pictograms. The priest explains that these folding codices (KOH duh seez) are used to make lists of rulers, record payments made by conquered people, and keep track of religious holidays.

The Market

The next stop on your tour is the central market. Here, people trade cacao (chocolate) beans and cotton blankets for other items. The sound of thousands of Aztecs trading in the open air creates a ruckus that can be heard a mile away.

In one corner of the market a man is offering to trade rabbits, deer, and small dogs that are bred for food. Across the way a woman displays pottery. You notice all sorts of other merchandise to be traded here, including sandals, feathers, seashells, turkeys, wood, corn, bananas, pineapples, honeycombs, and fabrics.

One section of the market is set aside for slave trading. Here you see slaves with wooden collars around their necks. Noblemen mill around, inspecting the slaves.

The Ceremonial Center

In the heart of the city is the ceremonial center. Here you find the largest temple in the city, the Great Temple. This massive pyramid is almost 100 yards wide at its base and rises almost 90 feet in the air. The top steps are stained with the blood of human sacrifices. Smaller temples surround the Great Temple, each dedicated to a particular god. In the plaza you also catch a glimpse of the gruesome skull rack displaying the severed heads of victims.

Not far from these religious buildings stands the palace of the Aztec emperor. You will have to admire the palace from the outside: Commoners are not allowed to enter. The palace contains hundreds of rooms and is staffed by more than 1,000 servants.

Montezuma II

In the early 1500s the Aztec emperor was Montezuma II (sometimes written Moctezuma). In the court of Montezuma II, no one was permitted to look the emperor in the eye. When Montezuma entered the room, even the nobles threw themselves face down to the ground. When he left the palace, he was carried in a fancy **litter**. When he wanted to travel on foot, nobles laid mats on the ground so he would not dirty his golden sandals.

During Montezuma's reign a number of unsettling things happened. There was a drought. A comet appeared in the skies. Lightning struck one of the temples in Tenochtitlán. All kinds of fantastic rumors began to circulate. One said that a ghostly woman was walking the streets of the capital at night, wailing, "My children, we must flee far away from this city!"

> **vocabulary**
> **litter** a chair attached to two beams and carried on the shoulders of several men

The Aztecs believed that the world might end at any moment. Montezuma and his priests worried that these strange events might be signs that the gods were angry with the Aztecs. They feared that doomsday might be near.

As it turned out, doomsday was coming, but it was not coming from the sky. It was coming from across the Atlantic Ocean. At that very moment, Spanish soldiers were sailing across the Atlantic in search of riches and glory. In the final lesson of this unit, you will learn what the arrival of these pale-skinned men meant for the mighty Aztec Empire.

Another mural by Diego Rivera shows the lively marketplace at Tenochtitlán where thousands of people gathered to trade.

Here Comes the Sun It is the year 1500. You are standing along a road in South America in a crowd of people. You seem to be at some kind of parade. You look down the road and see a gleaming, golden litter carried on the shoulders of four men. Inside the litter is a man wearing furs and golden jewelry.

As the litter gets closer, the people around you go down on their knees and touch their foreheads to the ground. Soon you are the only one still standing. Suddenly you notice several people yelling at you, though you can't understand what they're saying. An angry soldier is running at you with a raised club. You begin to run, and all of a sudden you wake up and realize you were having a dream.

It's a good thing you woke up. The people in your dream were bowing because the king of the Inca people, the Sapa Inca, was approaching. The Incas believed that the Sapa Inca was the living son of Inti, the sun god. No one was allowed to look at this powerful king—and you were staring right at him! If you had not woken up just in time, you would almost certainly have been killed by the soldier for being so disrespectful to the Son of the Sun.

The Empire of the Sun

Who were the Incas? They were people who built a great civilization on the western coast of South America. The first Inca people lived in the area around Cuzco in modern-day Peru.

This drawing, by an Inca artist, shows an Inca emperor on his throne.

In the early 1400s these people began conquering neighboring lands and extending their empire. They were so successful that by the time the Spanish **conquistadors** (kahn KEES tuh dorz) arrived in the 1530s, the Inca Empire was the largest in the Americas—larger even than the Aztec Empire had been.

The Sapa Inca gave orders to more than 12 million people. His territory stretched for more than 2,000 miles along the western coast of South America. The empire covered an area so large that today most of Peru and parts of Colombia, Ecuador, Bolivia, Chile, and Argentina would lie inside its borders.

This is a region of great geographical diversity. Arid plains stretch along the western coastline. This coastal region includes one of the driest deserts in the world—a place where not even a cactus can grow. Farther

> **vocabulary**
> **conquistador** the Spanish word for "conqueror"

east the twin ranges of the snow-capped Andes Mountains rise toward the skies. Between the ranges lies a high plateau, scorching by day, freezing by night. East of the Andes are thick jungles where heavy rains feed the mighty Amazon River. All these lands were ruled by the Sapa Inca.

Inca Life

The Incas were organized into tribal groups or clans. Every Inca family was part of a clan, and each clan was responsible for farming a piece of land. Families lived in windowless one-room stone huts with thatched roofs. Home, sweet home, probably didn't smell so sweet, since families sometimes burned dried animal waste as fuel. Parents and children slept together on animal skins spread on the bare floor. A few wall pegs were the only furnishings.

Boys followed their fathers' trades. Girls copied their mothers'. Farming was how most Incas supported themselves. They grew corn, squash, tomatoes, peanuts, cotton, and more than a hundred varieties of potatoes. The potato was an essential crop for the Incas because it could be grown at high altitudes, even on the slopes of the Andes Mountains.

Inca farmers also raised livestock, including guinea pigs, **alpacas**, and **llamas**. The guinea pigs were used for food. The alpacas were an important source of wool. The llamas were used for all sorts of things, but especially as pack animals.

The llama is truly an amazing animal. It is a smaller cousin of the camel, standing about 4 feet high at the shoulder and weighing about 250 pounds. Like its cousin the camel, the llama has greater strength and endurance than most other animals. Llamas can carry a load of 100 to 125 pounds for

15 to 20 miles a day. They will eat just about anything and can go long periods without drinking. Llamas are gentle animals, but if they are mistreated or overloaded, they will let you know it. A llama may simply sit down and refuse to move, or it may hiss and spit to make its point. When llamas spit, they don't just spit saliva; they spit hard pellets of partially-digested food, which can cause pain if they hit you.

vocabulary
alpaca a South American mammal valued for its long, woolly coat
llama a South American mammal valued for its endurance and for its woolly coat and meat

Today, people of the highlands of Peru need llamas much as their ancestors did.

The Incas used llamas to transport goods, but they also used the llama's wool for cloth, its hide for rugs and coats, its waste for fuel and fertilizer, and its meat for food. When a llama died, the Incas cut the meat into strips and dried these strips in the sun. They called these strips *charqui* (CHAHR kee), which is the source of our own word for dried meat, "jerky."

Inca women were master weavers. They made clothing from the cotton they grew and from the wool of their llamas and alpacas.

For the Good of the Empire

Inca families worked for themselves, but they were also required to spend part of their time working for the Sapa Inca and the empire. When they farmed, part of their time was spent raising crops for themselves and part was spent raising crops for the empire. Inca men also had to donate time by working on construction projects, building roads, or serving in the military.

For the most part, the Inca people seem to have worked willingly understanding that their labors were for the good of the empire. The Sapa Inca and the priests used only a small part of the goods produced. The rest was stored in warehouses and distributed to those who were too old or too sick to work. When crops failed and times were hard, food and goods were doled out to the working people, too. This system ensured that no one went hungry in the Inca Empire.

The rule of the Sapa Inca was absolute, and many government officials traveled throughout the empire to make sure his laws were obeyed. One of these officials was known as *He-Who-Sees-Everything*. He-Who-Sees-Everything was responsible for visiting Inca villages and making them pay their fair share of taxes. Oddly enough, he also served as a matchmaker.

He-Who-Sees-Everything would arrive in an Inca village every few years. When he arrived, he ordered the villagers to assemble in a plaza or field so that he could take a **census**. The more people in the village, the more the village would be required to pay in taxes.

Once the counting was over, He-Who-Sees-Everything asked all of the unmarried girls of marriageable age to step forward. The official interviewed each girl individually. If a girl was deemed especially worthy, she was sent to Cuzco to serve as one of the Sapa Inca's many wives.

Once these chosen few had been selected, He-Who-Sees-Everything called all the unmarried young men before him. He then proceeded to pair off young men and women, making dozens of marriages on the spot. No questions were asked. After all, He-Who-Sees-Everything was a servant of the Sapa Inca, and the marriages he was arranging were for the good of the empire.

> **vocabulary**
> **census** a count of the number of people living in a certain area

The Inca Empire lasted only a century, from the beginning of its expansion in 1438 to the Spanish conquest in 1532. But it was a century of towering achievement. The Incas did not just conquer people. To keep their empire unified, they changed every place they conquered. Read on to find out how the energetic Incas changed the face of South America.

The Royal Road It's one thing to conquer many lands. It's another thing to keep everything together once you've finished conquering. Remember how the ancient Romans held their empire together? They built roads all across their empire.

The roads made it possible for government officials to travel around the empire. They helped make trade between parts of the empire possible. But most important, the roads enabled the army to travel quickly to outlying territories to put down a rebellion and enforce the emperor's rule.

The Incas knew nothing of ancient Rome. But they too were incredible road builders. Their main road, known as the Royal Road, stretched for more than 2,000 miles, from the northern end of the empire to the southern. It was the longest road in the world until the 1800s.

The Royal Road was 24 feet wide for most of its length. Although it crossed mountains, valleys, deserts, and swamps, long stretches of the road were straight as an arrow. Markers measured distances along the road. Trees gave shade and a canal provided water for travelers. There were even roadside storehouses where travelers could stop at the end of a day's travel and get food.

Parts of the Royal Road were made of packed dirt, and other parts were paved. Inca engineers fitted the paving stones together like pieces of a jigsaw puzzle. Modern builders use mortar, a cement-like material, to keep stones together. But the Incas did not have any kind of mortar. Instead, they cut each paving stone so exactly that it fit snugly and stayed together without mortar.

The Royal Road is an impressive achievement of Inca engineering. We need to remember that the Incas had no earth-moving machinery. They did not have horses or oxen to pull wagons. They did not even have the wheel. Everything was done by hand. And yet the end result was a road so sturdy and well designed that not even torrential rainstorms and flash floods could destroy it.

This road is part of the ancient Royal Road that connected all parts of the Inca Empire. It stretched for more than 2,000 miles.

The Royal Road was the most important Inca road, but there were many others. At every valley, east-west roads crossed the Royal Road. The Royal Road was like the spine, and these secondary roads were like the nerves that branch out from the spine. This network of roads held the Inca Empire together.

Bridges Built for the Centuries

In order to build roads across the mountains, streams, and canyons of South America, the Incas had to build lots of bridges. Like the roads, these bridges are marvels of engineering. A bridge built over the Apurímac (ahp uh REE mahk) River in Peru is especially interesting. It was built over a steep river gorge by the Incas in 1350. The bridge was a hanging suspension bridge, held together by enormous strands of rope. The rope strands needed to be replaced every two years.

What is amazing is that the bridge was in service from 1350 until 1890! For more than 500 years, the bridge was maintained and used, first by the Incas, then by the Spanish, and finally by the independent people of Peru. It is one of the greatest achievements of the Inca engineers, and it gained additional fame when it was featured in a classic novel, *The Bridge of San Luis Rey*, by the American writer Thornton Wilder.

Mountain Staircases

The Incas also used their engineering know-how to help them farm in the mountainous Andes. Farming on a mountainside is almost impossible; the steep incline makes every task— plowing, planting, and harvesting—terribly difficult. Hillside farming is also bad for crops. In the heavy downpours, water runs downhill and washes out crops.

The challenge was to find a way to grow crops on the sides of the Andes. The solution was to cut **terraces** into the sides of the mountains, creating flat farm fields that could be planted and harvested just like valley fields. The Incas also built irrigation systems to bring water to these terraced fields.

> **vocabulary**
> **terrace** a flat piece of land carved out of the side of a mountain or hill

Keeping It All Together

The Incas may have had an advanced road system, but they had no written language. How could they possibly run an empire that spanned the length of a continent and included 12 million people without writing?

An Inca noble receives a report from one of his officials who holds a quipu.

The Incas came up with some clever strategies. For instance, they invented a device for counting and record-keeping called a *quipu* (KEE poo). A quipu was a piece of string from which dangled shorter strings of various colors. Government officials would tie knots on a quipu to record how many warriors were headed for a village or how much corn was in a storehouse.

The Incas also used messengers trained to run short distances at great speeds to carry news throughout the empire. Since the Incas had no written language, these messengers could not carry a written note. Instead, a runner memorized his message and sprinted to a rest station, a mile or so away, where the next runner was waiting. Without slowing the pace, the first runner recited the message, and, running alongside, the relief runner repeated it. Then the first runner dropped out, and the new messenger continued on.

The system was fast! A message could travel 150 miles in a day, and all the way from Quito (KEE toh) to Cuzco in a little over a week, which was very fast for the time. In the 1860s the famous pony express riders of the American West were only able to cover about 200 miles a day—and they rode on horseback!

City in the Clouds

Another marvel of Inca engineering is the famous city of Machu Picchu (MAH choo PEEK choo). Machu Picchu is a mountain fortress located about 50 miles northwest of Cuzco. It sits in a high valley, between two peaks of the Andes.

In the center visitors can see ruins of an open plaza, a temple, and a palace where archaeologists discovered Inca skeletons. The surrounding hillside is terraced for farming.

Archaeologists estimate that Machu Picchu was built in the mid-1400s. For years it was a vacation spot for the Inca emperors. Today it is the leading tourist attraction in Peru.

Because Machu Picchu is more than 7,000 feet above sea level, it is not an easy place to visit. Tourists now take a railroad partway up the mountain and then follow a steep, twisting road to the top. Energetic hikers can walk on an old Inca trail that climbs up the steep slopes of the Andes.

Expanding the Empire

Like the Aztecs, the Incas built their empire by conquering other people. And, like the Aztecs, they are known to have sacrificed human beings for religious purposes. However, human sacrifice seems to have been less widespread in the Inca Empire. The Incas seem to have placed less emphasis on sacrificing conquered people and more emphasis on having those people become loyal Inca subjects.

When the conquered people in a particular region were cooperative, the Sapa Inca made few changes. Inca architects and managers came to the region to supervise the building of roads and temples. The Incas taught their language to the local people and asked them to worship the sun god Inti. However, the worship of local gods was allowed, and sometimes those gods were even made part of the Inca religion.

However, if the people were uncooperative, the Sapa Inca moved swiftly. He shipped trouble-makers out to villages where they were surrounded by loyal Inca citizens, and he shipped loyal Inca citizens in to live among the conquered people. In this way, in a short time, the Sapa Inca was able to build an empire that was enormous and yet unified. This empire would endure until the Spanish conquistadors made their fateful appearance.

The city of Machu Picchu is located high in the Andes Mountains, about 50 miles northwest of Cuzco.

he Question An Aztec poet once stood atop the Great Temple and boasted of the greatness of the Aztec capital, Tenochtitlán. He asked, "Who could conquer Tenochtitlán? Who could shake the foundation of the heavens?" You are about to learn the chilling answer to that poet's questions.

The Answer

In 1519 the Aztec emperor Montezuma II ruled a mighty empire. Then one day a messenger arrived in Tenochtitlán. He had walked all the way from the Gulf of Mexico, and he brought astonishing news. "My lord," the exhausted man told Montezuma, "it was a mountain, and it floated on the water!"

What was the weary traveler talking about? The emperor's men were not sure, so they journeyed to the coast themselves. They returned with tales of white men with thick beards. Like the first messenger, they saw a "floating mountain," but they also saw other wonders, including "magic sticks" that belched smoke and "enormous dogs" with flat ears and long tongues.

The "floating mountain" was actually a Spanish ship anchored along the coast. The magic sticks were cannons, and the giant dogs were horses. The Aztecs had never seen horses or cannons, and they knew nothing of sailing ships or Spaniards, so they had to guess who these strange beings might be.

Montezuma remembered the ominous events of recent years and guessed that the strangers might be gods come down to Earth. He sent golden robes and other gifts fit for the gods. When the Aztec messengers reached the coast, they presented these gifts to the leader of the Spanish expedition, Hernán Cortés (er NAHN kor TEZ).

Hernán Cortés

Cortés was a Spanish explorer who had taken part in the conquest of Cuba a few years earlier. In 1519 he set sail from Cuba to search for riches in Central America. Montezuma's gifts aroused

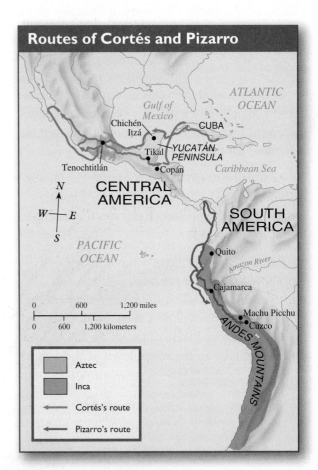

This map shows the voyages and marches of Cortés and Pizarro.

Cortés's interest. He recruited a translator and led his men toward the Aztec capital.

As he journeyed west, Cortés marched through areas that had been conquered by the Aztecs. The people in these areas had been forced to give money to the Aztecs and had seen their young men dragged off to Tenochtitlán to be offered as sacrifices. Many of these conquered people supported the Spaniards, hoping that the newcomers would help them get revenge on the Aztecs.

Cortés the Conqueror

When Montezuma learned that Cortés was enlisting support from his old enemies, he tried to talk Cortés out of coming to Tenochtitlán and even sent magicians to cast spells on the Spaniards. But Cortés and his men marched on, and Montezuma eventually bowed to the inevitable. He welcomed the Spanish and treated them as honored guests.

For a while all was peaceful in Tenochtitlán, but the Spaniards eventually grew nervous. They knew they were badly outnumbered. Their military situation was unsafe, even with their superior weapons. They took Montezuma hostage and demanded that he order the Aztecs to stop sacrificing to their gods. Montezuma refused. A few weeks later, fighting broke out. The Spanish, fearing that the Aztec priests were conspiring against them, attacked and killed hundreds of priests during a religious ceremony. The Aztecs responded by trying to wipe out the Spanish. Many men were killed on both sides, including Montezuma. Eventually, the Spaniards fled Tenochtitlán.

The Spaniards rebuilt their army by enlisting more of the Aztecs' old enemies. In 1521, Cortés and his allies surrounded the capital. With no supplies coming into Tenochtitlán, its people began starving. An outbreak of smallpox also swept through the city. This disease was carried by the conquistadors, who, because of their immunities, did not get sick. But the Aztecs had no immunities against European diseases, and the epidemic killed warriors, commoners, and nobles alike.

In May of 1521, Cortés organized the final bloody attack that ended the Aztec Empire and left Tenochtitlán in ruins. Spanish forces, armed with guns and cannons and reinforced by thousands of Indian allies, advanced along the causeways. The Aztecs fought bravely but were overwhelmed, not only by the attackers but also by the smallpox epidemic that had left thousands dying in the streets, or else too sick to fight. Tenochtitlán fell in August of 1521.

The End for the Incas

A few years later a similar series of events unfolded in South America. One day, a messenger dropped to the ground before the Sapa Inca.

"A house!" he exclaimed. "It drifts on the sea along the coast!" The report spoke of bearded ones with white skins. They were masters of lightning and thunder!

The Sapa Inca felt fear. There had been frightening omens. Violent earthquakes had split the ground. The sea had tossed gigantic waves ashore.

In this Diego Rivera mural, Cortés leads soldiers in the conquest of the Aztec Empire.

Not long after, the bearded ones disappeared in their "seahouse." But they left something behind—deadly infections the natives had never seen. Those along the northern coast became sick first. Later, travelers carried the diseases inland. The Incas, having no resistance to the European germs, fell ill and died by the thousands.

When the Sapa Inca died, two of his sons claimed the throne, and civil war broke out. This war between brothers was as bloody as any the Inca people had waged. When the battles were over, the son named Atahualpa (ah tah WAHL pah) had won. Atahualpa would not rest easy on his throne, however. Before long, another message arrived from the coast. The bearded ones had returned!

Francisco Pizarro

The bearded strangers were Spanish conquistadors led by Francisco Pizarro. Pizarro had heard rumors of an empire in South America that was wealthier than the Aztec Empire. In 1527, Pizarro led a group of about 160 men to find this empire. When Pizarro came across Inca temples decorated with gold and silver statues, he figured he had found what he was looking for.

The Spaniards marched toward Cuzco, traveling along the very roads that the Incas had built to unite their empire. Meanwhile, speedy Inca messengers notified Atahualpa that the Spaniards were coming, but the Sapa Inca did not take the Spaniards seriously. The omens from a few years earlier had been forgotten during the civil war. Also, since the Incas had no contact with the Aztecs, they had no way of knowing the fate of their neighbors to the north. Besides,

what could the mighty Sapa Inca, the all-powerful Son of the Sun, have to fear from a band of fewer than 200 men?

When the Spaniards approached Atahualpa's encampment near the town of Cajamarca (kah-huh MAHR kuh), a meeting was arranged. Atahualpa agreed to meet Pizarro in the town square. It was here that Pizarro set an ambush. His soldiers hid inside buildings surrounding the square. Though well armed, they waited nervously knowing that they were badly outnumbered.

"They approach!" Pizarro's lookout shouted. As Pizarro had requested, Atahualpa came as a friend. Atahualpa had left his warriors outside the city and was marching into Cajamarca with an escort of 6,000 unarmed nobles and attendants.

When the Sapa Inca reached the main square, a startling figure stepped from a doorway. A priest, dressed in a white robe and black hood, walked toward the splendid assembly. Spanish laws forbade Pizarro from attacking without warning. Before using force, he had to ask enemies to surrender and become Christians peacefully. Now, speaking through an interpreter, the priest urged Atahualpa to accept Christianity. The priest offered a Catholic prayer book to Atahualpa. The insulted ruler refused and knocked the book to the ground.

This was the moment the Spaniards were waiting for. Pizarro gave the signal for attack. The assault on the unarmed Incas was not a battle. It was a massacre! Cannons fired. Steel swords slashed. Spaniards on horses charged around, mowing down the unarmed Incas. Less than an hour later, Atahualpa was a prisoner and thousands of Incas lay dead.

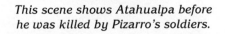

This scene shows Atahualpa before he was killed by Pizarro's soldiers.

A Deadly Bargain

Atahualpa offered to pay a ransom for his release. The Sapa Inca placed his hand high on the wall of his prison room. "I will fill the room to this height with gold," he told Pizarro. "This I give in exchange for my freedom."

The Sapa Inca's orders went out. His subjects stripped temples of their gold. They emptied storehouses and gathered up gold that would be worth tens of millions of dollars today. Once the Incas paid this fantastic ransom, Pizarro broke his promise. He charged Atahualpa with plotting against the Spaniards and had him executed.

The Sapa Inca's death was the beginning of the end for the Inca Empire. The Incas had been a mighty people, but they had been weakened by a lengthy civil war, ravaged by European diseases, and disoriented by the loss of their leader. They were in no condition to oppose the Spaniards. By June of 1534 Pizarro had conquered Cuzco and Quito; a few years later the Spanish conquest of the region was substantially complete.

In 20 years, the Spaniards had destroyed two mighty empires and set up a new empire of their own. The conquerors congratulated themselves for abolishing human sacrifice and bringing Christianity to the New World, but their greed for gold and lust for power also led to the destruction of two of the most intriguing civilizations in human history and the deaths of millions of people.

Glossary

alpaca a South American mammal valued for its long, woolly coat

causeway a raised road built over water to connect islands to a mainland

census a count of the number of people living in a certain area

city-state a city that is an independent political state with its own ruling government

conquistador the Spanish word for "conqueror"

equinox one of the two days in a year when there is an equal amount of daytime and nighttime

hieroglyph a picture or symbol representing an idea, an object, a syllable, or a sound

litter a chair attached to two beams and carried on the shoulders of several men

llama a South American mammal valued for its endurance and for its woolly coat and meat

terrace a flat piece of land carved out of the side of a mountain or hill

The Renaissance

Contents

A New Dawn

An Uncomfortable Visit In 1508, Desiderius Erasmus (des uh DAIR ee us ih RAZ mus), the greatest European scholar of his age, journeyed from Holland to Venice, Italy. There, he stayed in the home of the foremost printer in Italy—Aldus Manutius (AWL dus muh NOO shee us).

Erasmus found his lodgings most uncomfortable. The printer's house was drafty in winter and so full of fleas and bed bugs in summer that Erasmus could hardly sleep. As many as 30 scholars stayed in the printer's home at any one time. Manutius had little money to spend to make his guests comfortable. He provided the cook with moldy flour for baking and served up a meal of thin soup, hard cheese, and tough beef.

Why would Erasmus and other scholars travel long distances to Italy and endure uncomfortable living conditions? These scholars all shared an intense desire to learn more about the civilizations of ancient Greece and Rome. They were fascinated with works of classical literature, including the philosophical works of Plato (PLAYT oh), the poems of Virgil, and the orations of Cicero (SIHS ur oh). All around Italy these works were being rediscovered and studied.

At the printer's dinner table, the scholars talked about Plato and Cicero, exchanged ideas concerning ancient civilizations, described their projects and dreams, and commented on one another's work. What's more, they did all of these things in

Erasmus saw that the rediscovery of ancient Greek and Roman written works opened fresh areas of thought.

ancient Greek! If anyone slipped into another language, he was fined.

The scholars were dissatisfied with the world in which they had grown up. They felt that they had been born in an uncultured age in which people had forgotten about the great writers of Greece and Rome. They grumbled that the last several centuries had been centuries of famine, plague, warfare, ignorance, and superstition. Unfairly, some of them even dismissed the previous 1,000 years as the Dark Ages.

This dissatisfaction with the recent past made these men so excited about what was happening in Italy in their own day. In Italy the wisdom of the ancient Greeks and Romans was being rediscovered. Scholars known as humanists had been rummaging around in monasteries and cathedral libraries, digging up copies of ancient Greek and Roman books that had long been neglected. They were called "humanists" because of the subjects we call the humanities, including history, languages, and literature.

These manuscripts covered a wide range of topics. Some treated philosophy or history. Others had to do with literature, grammar, or

rhetoric. Still others had to do with art and architecture. The humanists studied the manuscripts they recovered with loving care. They compared and corrected them, translated and explained them. In the days before printing was invented, they made copies of their manuscripts by hand. After printing was invented, they began to give their precious manuscripts to a printer like Erasmus's host to publish.

When Erasmus contemplated the humanist movement of which he was a part, he felt he was witnessing the dawning of a brighter day. The other scholars around the dinner table were equally enthusiastic. They felt that they were participating in a rediscovery of the ancient civilizations of Greece and Rome, a rebirth of culture, literature, and the arts.

What All the Excitement Was About

What Erasmus and his fellow scholars were so excited about was the energetic period of change that we now call the Renaissance. *Renaissance* is the French word for "rebirth." When we speak of the Renaissance, we are referring to a period in history when a rediscovery of classical learning led to great achievements, not only in literature but also in philosophy, education, architecture, sculpture, and painting.

The Renaissance began in Italy about the middle of the fourteenth century, when scholars began uncovering and studying forgotten manuscripts in Greek and Latin. For the next 200 or so years (1350–1550), the center of creative and scholarly activity moved from one major Italian city-state to another, with Florence, Rome, and Venice all playing major roles. Later, in the sixteenth and seventeenth centuries, the spirit of the Renaissance spread to other places in Europe, including Germany, France, Spain, and England.

Although the Renaissance began with the rediscovery of old manuscripts, it didn't end there. The humanists dug up manuscripts on art, architecture, and literature, and these manuscripts led to increased interest in all these fields. Soon, people were digging up Greek and Roman statues and marveling at their beauty. Renaissance sculptors worked hard to capture the same beauty in their own creations. Painters were also inspired by Greek and Roman art; as the years went by, more and more of them modeled their works on Greek and Roman examples rather than on the more recent work of medieval artists. Architects studied ancient buildings and used them as models for new buildings. Renaissance poets tried to write poems as great (they thought) as the ancient poets had written. All these artists were using old art to create new art.

Once people saw what marvelous things human beings could create, they began to develop a new appreciation of humanity. Renaissance artists did not forget about God, but they started drawing more attention in their art to human beings. The paintings and sculptures they made had many different subjects. Some were about religion, and others portrayed historical events or tales from Greek and Roman literature and myths. They also made portraits. Since the Bible told them that people were created in the image of God, they believed that our creative powers are a gift from God and deserve special attention.

The Italian humanist Pico della Mirandola (PEE koh DAYL lah mee RAHN doh lah) captured this new feeling when he wrote his *Oration on the Dignity of Man.* In it, Pico argues that "there is nothing . . . more wonderful than man." According to Pico, man is "a miracle," for human beings are "constrained [held back] by no limits" and are able to become whatever they wish to become.

Important Renaissance Figures

Many years later the greatest writer of the English Renaissance, William Shakespeare, had one of his most famous dramatic characters hold forth on the same theme: "What a piece of work is a man!" exclaims Prince Hamlet. "How noble in reason! how infinite in faculty! in form and moving how express and admirable! in action how like an angel! in apprehension [understanding] how like a god! the beauty of the world! the paragon [greatest] of animals!" You don't need to understand every word that Hamlet says to feel the excitement in his voice and understand that, in these lines, he is thinking like a Renaissance humanist.

Shakespeare, Pico, and Erasmus are only three of many Renaissance figures who are still widely admired today. Others include the Italian artists Raphael (rah fah EL), Leonardo da Vinci (duh VIHN chee), and Michelangelo (mye kul AN juh loh); the Italian political writer Machiavelli (mak ee uh VEL ee); and the great Spanish novelist Cervantes (sur VAN teez). Indeed, perhaps no age in history has produced more eminent artists and writers than the Renaissance. In this unit you will learn about some of the most important of these artists and writers. But before we turn to individuals, let's look at some reasons why the Renaissance began where it did.

Italy the Innovator

As you read the opening paragraphs of this lesson, you may have been wondering why the Renaissance began in Italy and not in England or Germany. Scholars have argued about that question for years and have suggested some reasons why Italy led the way.

For one thing, Italy had been the center of the ancient Roman Empire. The ruins of that great empire surrounded the inhabitants of Italy: crumbling walls and toppled columns, arenas and temples overrun with weeds, once-splendid roads long ago fallen into disrepair. These reminders ensured that Ancient Rome was never entirely forgotten.

Business and commerce also helped pave the way for the Italian Renaissance. Italy is a boot-shaped peninsula, jutting out into the Mediterranean Sea. Trading ships sailed back and forth across the Mediterranean, from western Europe to the Middle East and from northern Africa to southern Europe. Because of its central location, Italy was in a good position to profit from this trade.

During the Renaissance there was no central government in Italy. Instead, the peninsula was divided into more than 250 city-states—most of them tiny, but some larger, like Florence, Venice, Milan, and Genoa. A city-state is like a small country. At its heart is a city that is the center of government and business, but it also includes the countryside with its farms and villages. Many of these city-states were located on the sea, or on rivers near the sea, and they used their advantageous locations to gain wealth by trading with

You can see how the ruins of the Forum, a public meeting place in Ancient Rome, influenced late Renaissance buildings such as the church in the background of this photograph.

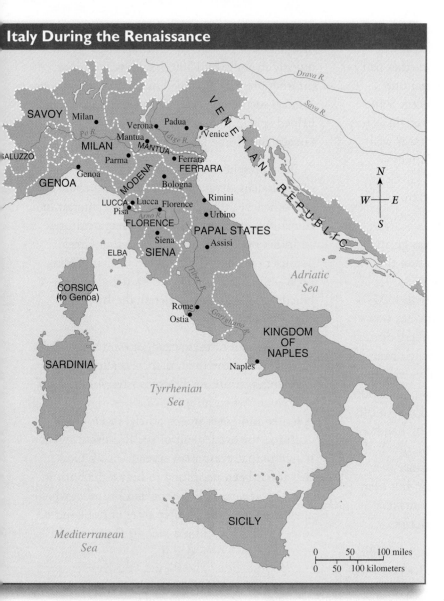

state. These ambitions led to a higher educational standard and a broader definition of what it meant to be educated. Merchants wanted their sons to know how to keep good business records. They also wanted them to know the law and to be skilled at negotiation and diplomacy so that they would know how to deal with their trading partners. Since these young men would be traveling around a lot, they also needed to learn history and geography. These merchants also wanted their sons to learn about religion and good morals. So some of them even wanted their sons to learn ancient Greek as well as Latin, so that they could read the best ancient books. This created jobs for humanists willing to work as tutors or schoolteachers, and helped spread their love of humanities through the city-states.

Italians came into contact with people from distant lands and of differing faiths. Some of these differences could be found close to home. While most Renaissance Italians were Christians, many city-states also included Jewish families. Business trips often sent Italian merchants to regions of northern Europe. Trade also brought them into contact with Muslims from the East and the South. Contact with Muslims was especially fruitful since, during the Middle Ages, Islamic scholars had preserved many Ancient Greek manuscripts.

> **vocabulary**
> **patron** a wealthy person who supports an artist

other lands. Competition among the city-states led to further improvements, as each city-state worked hard to attract the best traders.

As trade grew, a new merchant class sprang up in the more prosperous city-states. Many merchants grew wealthy, and some of them used their wealth to support humanistic scholarship and the arts. Wealthy merchants, as well as aristocrats and churchmen, who supported the arts were known as **patrons**. Without these patrons there probably would have been no Renaissance.

Members of the new merchant class were also eager to give their sons an education that would teach them how to be successful businessmen and good leaders who could help to run their city-

Islam also contributed to the Renaissance in a less direct way. As Islam expanded and the Muslim Turks began to take over lands that had previously been controlled by the Byzantine Empire, Byzantine scholars were displaced. Some of these scholars fled to Italy. They brought with them valuable Greek manuscripts, as well as something that was then a rarity in Italy— a thorough knowledge of the ancient Greek language in which the texts were written.

An Important Invention

Once the Renaissance began, it was greatly accelerated by an all-important invention that was made in Germany: the printing press. Around 1450, Johannes Gutenberg (yoh HAHN es GOOT en burg) developed an efficient way of printing with movable type. Gutenberg devised a system of movable letter stamps, which were inked and then pressed onto paper. This invention allowed numerous copies of the same publication to be produced quickly and cheaply. Prior to this invention, writings had to be copied by hand, a slow and expensive process. The humanists had been willing to copy manuscripts because they were so excited about their discoveries, but even the most energetic scholar could only make a handful of copies of any given manuscript.

Printing changed all that. It made it possible to share the knowledge the humanists had gathered by printing and distributing multiple copies. Use of movable type and the printing press spread quickly in Italy. By 1500, Italy boasted more printing presses than any other country in Europe. Printers such as the Manutius who Erasmus visited helped spread the important texts of ancient Greece and Rome far and wide.

The presence of ancient ruins, the prosperity of the Italian city-states, the rise of merchants and other wealthy patrons, increased interest in education, greater exposure to foreign cultures, an influx of Byzantine scholars toting Greek manuscripts, and the invention of the printing press—these are some of the factors that combined to initiate and accelerate the Italian Renaissance.

Because all of these changes were happening at about the same time, there was a feeling of excitement in the air. Erasmus gave voice to this excitement when he spoke of a new day dawning. A writer and government official in Florence captured the excitement of the Renaissance when he wrote that every man should "thank God that it has been permitted to him to be born in this new age, so full of hope and promise, which already rejoices in a greater array of nobly-gifted souls than the world has seen in the thousand years that have preceded it."

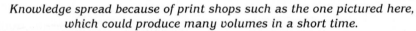

Knowledge spread because of print shops such as the one pictured here, which could produce many volumes in a short time.

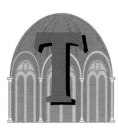

he Artist Elevated When we visit an art museum, we are not surprised to notice that an artist has signed his or her work by painting a name on the canvas or chiseling it into stone. Nor are we surprised that a museum might advertise an exhibit of artwork created by a particular artist.

We do not find it unusual that the architect's name is cut into the cornerstone of a building. When we hear a piece of music, we usually also expect to learn who composed it.

But it was not always that way. Before the Renaissance, painters did not generally sign their works, architects did not typically carve their names on the buildings they built, and musicians were rarely given credit for music they composed.

In the medieval period, artists did not have the status that they enjoy today. They were considered artisans or craftspersons. Painters and sculptors worked with their hands, like shoemakers or bakers or bricklayers, and they often worked for low wages, just as other craftspersons did. A medieval artist created precisely the work his employer paid him to produce, and he didn't even think of signing it.

The relatively low status of sculptors and painters was evident from the guilds, or trade associations, to which they belonged. Sculptors, for example, were members of the Guild of Masons, because, like **masons**, they worked with stone. Painters were members of the Guild of Doctors and Apothecaries because they depended on **apothecaries** (uh PATH uh ker eez) for many of their paints and supplies.

A Change of Status

During the Renaissance, however, the status of artists changed dramatically. The humanists discovered that the ancient Greeks and Romans had great respect for artists and architects; and when beautiful Greek and Roman statues were put on display, people began to see why. People began to feel that if artists could create such beautiful objects, then an artist must be something much greater than a baker or a bricklayer.

The humanists also unearthed manuscripts that described forgotten artistic techniques and showed artists how to use mathematical principles to give form and structure to their works. Artists mastered these techniques and principles, imitated the ancient works that had been recovered, and created impressive works of their own.

Gradually, a change began to take place. Painters and sculptors began to think of themselves as artists rather than just artisans, as creators rather than just craftspersons. They began taking credit for their creations by signing them. The best artists also began to charge handsome fees, particularly in the late fifteenth and early sixteenth centuries. A few great artists even felt free to change or ignore their patrons' directions. This did not always create good will between the patron and the artist. But it says something about the rising confidence and status of artists. If they lost the patronage of one leading family, they could hope for work from another.

Some painters and sculptors even took to inserting likenesses of themselves in their works. Lorenzo Ghiberti (loh REN tsoh gee BER tee) a successful bronze sculptor in Florence in the

> **vocabulary**
> **mason** a person who builds or works with brick or stone
> **apothecary** a druggist or pharmacist

first half of the fifteenth century, included a self-portrait in one of the magnificent doors he created for the famous Baptistery of the cathedral in Florence. Sandro Botticelli (SAHN droh baht uh CHEL ee), a fifteenth-century painter from Florence, painted himself in one of his paintings of the *Adoration of the Magi.* In the painting Botticelli stands to one side, looking straight out at the viewer.

Artists were not alone in exhibiting themselves through artwork. Prominent men commissioned portraits and busts of themselves. Important families engaged artists to create works that would memorialize family members. In the Renaissance many people began to display a heightened awareness of themselves as unique individuals.

The Renaissance was, in many ways, a self-conscious age. Erasmus believed humankind was undergoing a fundamental change. Renaissance artists and their patrons were interested in themselves, their social standing, and their own special personalities. Their medieval counterparts would have been astounded by this focus on the individual self.

Portrait Painting

This heightened awareness of one's self as a unique individual went hand in hand with an increased emphasis on realism in art. Medieval painters had paid relatively little attention to realistic detail; the figures in their pictures were identifiable as human beings, but they generally didn't look like anyone in particular. They were symbols. Renaissance artists, with their new interest in the individual, began to strive for increased realism. They wanted their portraits to capture the exact appearance of a particular person in a particular situation. They wanted the figures in their portraits to have distinct facial expressions revealing emotions that viewers could understand. People in these paintings must seem to live and breathe, just like people in real life. To arouse the viewers' emotions, the picture must be dramatic.

Botticelli's Adoration of the Magi *shows wise men visiting the baby Jesus (center), but it also includes a self-portrait of the artist (lower right).*

The Natural World

Renaissance painters also began to pay more attention to the natural world. Most medieval art was made for churches and other religious settings. Both painters and their patrons liked to fill the spaces around the figures in their paintings with gold leaf, to show their love and respect for the figures and stories in these paintings. They wanted just enough detail so that anyone who saw the work of art would know easily what it was about. By the time the Renaissance reached its full bloom, people wanted paintings that looked lively and more like the world around them. They also wanted paintings that showed off the skill and creativity of the artist.

The painter and architect Brunelleschi (broo nel LES kee), who worked in Florence and Rome in the early fifteenth century, made one of the most important advances on the road to more realistic depiction of life. Brunelleschi was inspired by an essay on architecture written by an ancient Roman writer named Vitruvius (vih TROO vee us). Vitruvius described how buildings and other objects painted on a flat surface could be made to "advance and recede" so the painting would look more realistic and almost three dimensional. Brunelleschi applied what he read to a drawing he made of the public square in front of the cathedral of Florence. In doing so, he rediscovered the technique of **perspective.**

Brunelleschi taught the principles of perspective to a young Florentine painter named Masaccio (mah SAHT choh). Masaccio, and after him many other Renaissance painters, mastered perspective and used it to produce magnificent, realistic art. Renaissance painters were now able to place realistic figures in realistic backgrounds; indeed, they began to create spaces so realistic that viewers felt they could step through the painting into the world depicted.

Brunelleschi's rediscovery of perspective was a good example of how Renaissance artists managed to go forward by looking backward. Brunelleschi learned what he could from the ancient writers and then used what he had learned to improve his own art. By devoting himself to realism and teaching others how to use the principles of perspective, he helped foster a new appreciation for art and paved the way for a great flowering of the arts in Florence.

Notice the difference between the flat feeling of this medieval painting of the Adoration and the use of perspective in Botticelli's work.

49

The Cradle of the Renaissance

he City on the Arno To experience all the wonders of the Renaissance, one only had to visit the city of Florence in the 1400s. Its economy, artists, architects, writers, and philosophers all helped make Florence a model of Renaissance culture.

Florence was well situated to become a center of trade and commerce. Like other important Italian cities of that age, Florence enjoyed important geographic advantages. It had been founded in Roman times on flatland alongside the River Arno. To the west, the river gave it access to the sea. The city was accessible in other directions through a variety of mountain passes.

By the time of the Renaissance, Florence had grown large, rich, and, in comparison with other Italian city-states, politically stable. Like other cities, Florence was by no means free from violence. Nor was it free from the filth caused by inadequate sewage systems. In contrast to many other cities, however, its commercial success and its form of government allowed the city to overcome these handicaps and enabled some of its richer citizens to make lasting contributions to Western civilization.

Near the height of its influence in 1472, the city of Florence boasted a powerful merchant class that was the envy of rival city-states. One Florentine silk merchant self-importantly declared, "A Florentine who is not a merchant, who has not traveled through the world, seeing foreign nations and peoples and then returned to Florence with some wealth, is a man who enjoys no esteem whatsoever."

Florence became best known in history for its painters, sculptors, architects, and scholars. But these artistic successes depended on the city's commercial successes, since it was the wealthy Florentine merchants who served as patrons and made the flowering of the arts possible.

Florence became an intellectual center as well. The leading men in Florence turned to the study of ancient Roman authors. These classical writers told a story of great political, commercial, and military accomplishments that appealed to the rising merchant class. An appreciation of classical civilization developed in Florence. This helped create an atmosphere in which bold political and artistic ideas could grow and flourish.

Wool and Banking

Florence's wealth during the Renaissance was heavily dependent on two industries: wool and banking. It is estimated that at the wool industry's peak, about one-third of Florentines worked in the wool business. The names of the city's streets testify to wool's importance. There were, for example, the Street of Shearers, the Street of Cauldrons (giant pots in which wool was cleaned and treated), and the Road of Dyers. Each of them was dedicated to a process required to turn raw wool into the cloth that Florentine merchants sold throughout the world.

The leading Florentine merchants involved in the wool business were members of the Wool Guild and the Calimala Guild. Members of the Calimala trade association controlled the importing, dyeing, and finishing of cloth. This guild was the most important and powerful of the greater guilds of Florence. Many cloth merchants also were members of the Guild of Bankers and Moneychangers. Quite often it was these influential families who ran the government of Florence.

The structure of the government of Florence was complex. Inspired by the example of Greece and Rome, Florence considered itself a **republic**.

In those times, that meant that power was in the hands of a ruling class of citizens rather than a single monarch. About 800 leading families in Florence were responsible for electing the city's government officials. The citizens were governed by a council composed of rich and educated men who represented the people.

A Powerful Family

Banking made a few merchants as rich and as powerful as the nobility for the first time in history. Imitating the nobility, these bankers and merchants became patrons of the arts.

No Florentine family was more rich and powerful than the Medici (MED uh chee) family. The Medici were wool merchants who rose to prominence largely on the basis of their banking business. By 1417 the family had bank branches in several important cities in Italy as well as in other key European cities. Perhaps most important, the Medici were the moneylenders to the pope, the leader of Christians in Europe. They enjoyed a most profitable relationship with the papal office responsible for collecting and spending church revenues.

In 1429, Cosimo de' Medici assumed leadership of the Medici family, upon the death of his father. Like his father, Cosimo possessed a genius for

banking. In time, the government of Florence came to depend on the Medici banking operation for the generous loans it made.

Cosimo soon became the leading citizen of the republic. He rarely held government office himself, but he was able to ensure that his friends often held office. Through them he maintained effective control of the government.

The education Cosimo received during his youth had nourished in him a deep respect for the ancient civilizations of Greece and Rome. From his youth, Cosimo paid agents to search for manuscripts abroad. He employed a staff of about 45 men to copy for his library any manuscripts he was unable to purchase.

> **vocabulary**
> **republic** a system of government in which voters elect officials to run the government and make laws

Later in life he would demonstrate his respect for the civilizations of Greece and Rome by spending large sums of his family's money on classical art and architecture. He funded many architects, sculptors, and painters, including the architect Brunelleschi, who, as we have seen, rediscovered the technique of perspective. Among Brunelleschi's most important works was the dome of the Santa Maria del Fiore (SAN tuh mah REE uh del FYOH ree) cathedral in Florence, often called the Duomo (DWOH moh).

Building of the cathedral was begun in 1294, and many great artists and sculptors worked on the church before it was completed in 1436.

You can appreciate why it took more than 100 years to build the great cathedral in Florence.

In 1415, Brunelleschi was given responsibility for designing and building the dome for the church. The sculptor planned to build a large stone dome. But daringly, Brunelleschi built the dome without interior supports to hold up the heavy stone and bricks. Brunelleschi obviously understood enough about structural design to recognize that the dome would be stable without using supports. Brunelleschi became known as the first genius of the Renaissance. His dome was considered the greatest engineering feat of the time.

Upon Cosimo de' Medici's death in 1464, his son Piero assumed leadership of the famous family. Piero lived only five years more. He was succeeded by his son Lorenzo, who became known as Lorenzo the Magnificent.

Lorenzo the Magnificent

Lorenzo de' Medici strove to make Florence a center of festivals, pageants, and processions. He commissioned artists to create works for himself and for the public spectacles he organized. But he was most influential in encouraging other prominent men to hire the city's artists.

During nine years of relative peace and prosperity, Lorenzo de' Medici was able to exert political influence, as his grandfather had. But in 1478 he was the victim of a plot hatched by a rival family in Florence. The plan was apparently backed by Pope Sixtus IV. Lorenzo survived an assassination attempt and a subsequent war with the pope's forces. When he returned to Florence in 1480, he determined that nothing like that would happen to him again. So he surrounded

The Medici were the richest family in Italy. Under Cosimo, shown here, they became a powerful political force.

himself with armed guards and took control of the government—becoming, in effect, the sole ruler.

For the next 12 years, Lorenzo concentrated on making Florence Italy's capital of art and learning. He brought the most famous teachers of Italy to the city-state. He spent large sums on art and books. He founded a school to provide boys with training, not only in art but also in the humanities. The sculptor, architect, and painter Michelangelo spent four years in Lorenzo's school.

Michelangelo became a member of the Medici household and showed his patron the results of his work each day.

Unfortunately, Lorenzo did not have the same interest in the Medici's banking business or the same business skills as his grandfather. As a result, the bank's fortunes declined, and so did the fortunes of the city of Florence. Trade with the East decreased. The city's cloth merchants found themselves unable to compete with cloth merchants in Flanders, in present-day Belgium. Florence's role as a center of art and learning did not end, but other cities were better able to compete with it.

Lorenzo died in 1492. He was succeeded by his son Piero, who was forced into exile two years later. The Medicis returned to power in Florence in 1512. But it was not only as rulers of Florence that the family continued to influence the course of the Renaissance. Lorenzo had arranged for his son Giovanni (joh VAHN ee) to be named a cardinal in the church. Giovanni would eventually become Pope Leo X. And it was in Rome that Leo X was able to promote the splendor of Renaissance art and learning.

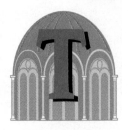

The **Splendor of the Popes** Popes occupied a unique and powerful place in Renaissance Italy, indeed in the world. They considered themselves the successors of St. Peter, one of the 12 apostles of Jesus and the first leader of the Christian Church.

It was a pope's responsibility to lead the Christian Church, to shepherd the believers whom Jesus had referred to as "my flock." The popes managed the largest organization in Europe—the Roman Catholic Church.

The popes were rulers of a large part of Italy called the Papal States. The territories they ruled had been given to them over the course of many centuries. By the time of the Renaissance, the popes ruled the largest kingdom in Italy except for the Kingdom of Naples. They governed these territories from the Vatican, the center of the Papal States, located in Rome. They believed the territories gave them political independence.

Pope Nicholas V is the pope who is usually credited with bringing Renaissance thinking to Rome. Nicholas was a dedicated humanist. He made teachers, historians, and thinkers welcome in Rome. He rebuilt and repaired many of the city's buildings and bridges and hired artists to increase their magnificence. In that way he made Rome more hospitable to tourists and pilgrims, who helped fill the treasuries of the church and of Roman merchants.

Among Pope Nicholas's successors, some eagerly accepted humanism and others rejected it. Pope Sixtus IV improved Rome's roads and buildings, added more than a thousand books to the Vatican library, built the Sistine Chapel in the Vatican, and brought the best artists to Rome to add to its beauty.

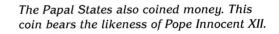

The Papal States also coined money. This coin bears the likeness of Pope Innocent XII.

Pope Julius II, like his uncle Sixtus IV, was much involved in worldly matters. He was a brilliant administrator and an effective military leader. Julius II managed to reassert authority over the Papal States, which had been weakened under the reign of a predecessor.

Also like his uncle, Julius II expanded the Vatican library. To celebrate the church's glory and its teachings, he invited important artists to come to Rome to apply their skills to existing church properties and to create and beautify new ones. He hired the young painter Raphael to paint **frescoes** on the walls of the papal apartments. Julius II also hired Michelangelo, first to design his tomb and then to paint the ceiling of the Sistine Chapel.

The artists that Julius II brought to Rome were influenced by their exposure to antiquity in this ancient capital of the Roman Empire. It inspired them to create works whose beauty and nobility are still recognized today.

St. Peter's Basilica

For 1,200 years a church had stood on the site where it was believed that St. Peter had been buried. In 1506, under Pope Julius II, workers began building a magnificent new **basilica** to replace the original church.

> **vocabulary**
> **fresco** a painting made on fresh, moist plaster with color pigments dissolved in water
> **basilica** a Christian church building, often in the shape of a cross

The Square in front of St. Peter's was built to hold the huge crowds that came, and still come, for important papal ceremonies.

St. Peter's Basilica was not completed for 120 years. Great artists, such as Michelangelo and Raphael, applied their skills to this massive design and construction project. The Church and Renaissance artists worked together to create one of the most remarkable and beautiful buildings in the world. This project also confirmed the importance of the Church.

Julius was succeeded by Lorenzo de' Medici's son Giovanni, who took the name Leo X. Leo X was elected pope in 1513, the year after his family was restored to power in Florence. As pope, he showed both a love of art and a love of luxury. Like his father, Leo encouraged and sponsored festivals, pageants, and processions, starting with his own magnificent coronation ceremonies. He hired the best artists, including both Michelangelo and Raphael, and welcomed scholars and poets to the Vatican.

Leo's efforts to increase the splendor of Rome were expensive, especially the continuing construction of St. Peter's Basilica. To pay the immense costs, Leo X raised taxes and borrowed huge sums. Like the popes before him, he approved the sale of positions of authority in the Church. And, in 1514, he extended throughout much of Europe a campaign that Julius II had limited to Italy: the sale of the so-called St. Peter's indulgences. Leo X promised that contributors to the building fund would receive special spiritual benefits and that the punishment that God would impose for their previous misdeeds would be lifted. This practice would help trigger what was later called the *Protestant Reformation*, which resulted in divisions in the Christian Church that remain unhealed. (You will learn more about the Reformation after you finish reading about the Renaissance.)

Although Leo's goal was noble, the way he went about reaching his goal was not so noble. This mixture of honorable purpose and questionable ways of achieving the purpose came to characterize much of Renaissance Rome.

Last of the Renaissance Popes

Clement VII, the nephew of Lorenzo de' Medici and a cousin of Pope Leo X, became pope in 1523. Clement shared his family's love of the arts. But Clement proved unable to make wise decisions in the alliances he made to ensure the independence of the Papal States. Enemies attacked Rome in 1527. They looted churches and monasteries and destroyed many manuscripts in the Vatican library. They damaged some of the artwork the popes had commissioned, including one of Raphael's frescoes in the papal apartments.

Clement made peace with his enemies and was returned to power in 1528. But Rome never returned to its position as the center of the Renaissance. Its intellectual and artistic leaders had been scattered. Never again would such an impressive attempt be made to join Christianity with the values and ideals of classical antiquity.

Glittering City "You should visit Venice if you want other cities to seem like poorhouses," a prominent resident once told a friend. Built on 117 small islands, Venice, in northern Italy, was the western world's foremost commercial city in 1500.

Venice's islands, located in the middle of a **lagoon,** were divided by more than 150 canals and connected by more than 400 bridges. Many of its buildings rested on pillars driven into the mud. Venice was safe from an attack. Enemy ships found it impossible to move in the shallow waters. Venice also had a strong navy which was the foundation of its considerable wealth.

The people of Venice, called Venetians (vuh NEE shunz), were proud of their splendid city. Visitors also shared their admiration. A French diplomat visiting Venice painted a glowing picture of this unusual city. "The houses are very large and lofty and built of stone," he reported. "Within they have, most of them . . . rich marble chimney pieces, bedsteads of gold color, their portals [doors] of the same, and most gloriously furnished. In short, it is the most triumphant city that I have ever seen."

How did Venice gain its prosperity? Like Florence, Venice built its wealth primarily on trade. Over two centuries, the Venetians fashioned an extensive trading empire. They were not trying to gain territory over which to rule. Rather, the goal was to ensure that they could carry on their trading activities without interference.

> **vocabulary**
> **lagoon** a shallow body of water, especially one separated from a larger body of water by a sandbar or reef

Venice became the great maritime power of the Renaissance.

Venice wanted safe access by sea to ports in Syria and Egypt and along the coast of the Black Sea. There, Venetian merchants could purchase the herbs, spices, and dyes that originated in the Far East and the cottons, silks, and silver goods of the Middle East. There, too, they could offer in trade the many products of Venice's own industries, such as glass, textiles, and jewelry.

Therefore, during the thirteenth and fourteenth centuries, Venice established ports and island strongholds along the Adriatic Sea, leading to the Mediterranean Sea. They were defended by a formidable navy, whose flat-bottomed **galleys** were built in Venice. This shipbuilding enterprise employed about 2,000 workers and probably was the largest industry of its time.

Venice also wanted free access to its trading partners north of the Alps. So, during the fifteenth century, Venice conquered mainland territories to its north and west, including Padua (PAJ oo uh) and Verona (vuh ROH nuh) in present-day Italy. These conquests assured safe overland passage for goods that Venetian merchants wanted to sell in Germany and elsewhere in northern Europe.

> **vocabulary**
>
> **galley** a large, flat-bottomed ship propelled by sails and oars and used in the Mediterranean for trade and war

Late in the fifteenth century and early in the sixteenth, Venice suffered some military setbacks, however. First, Turkish forces seized many of Venice's eastern territories. The Turks forced Venice to pay a yearly fee for trading in Turkish ports. Then, an alliance of Italian, German, French, and Spanish forces, headed by Pope Julius II, recaptured some of the mainland Italian territories Venice had conquered. (See the map of the Italian city-states.) Within a few years, Venice won back part of these possessions, though at great financial and human cost.

Its efficient navy gave Venice the military force it needed to defend a substantial empire. Its distinctive form of government gave it the stability it needed to establish and maintain this empire.

Republican Government

Venice, like Florence, was not a monarchy but a republic whose government was controlled by the city-state's leading families. The head of the government was called the doge (dohj), which comes from a Latin word meaning "leader." The doge was chosen for life by members of the Greater Council. This council also selected from its members those who would serve in other governmental bodies, including a senate and a committee for public safety. Although the doge was Venice's chief of state, real power lay in the hands of the council and the other governmental bodies whose members it selected.

As in most other republics up to that time, not all Venetians could participate in government. At the end of the thirteenth century, the Greater Council passed a law that said only male descendants of men who had sat in the council before 1297 were allowed to be members. The name of everyone eligible was written down in what became known as the *Book of Gold*. Only about 200 families were named in the book. They became hereditary rulers of Venice.

In the late fifteenth and early sixteenth centuries, the wealth its merchant traders amassed allowed Venice to compete with Florence and Rome for leadership of the Renaissance.

Aside from its wealth, Venice relied on an additional resource—displaced scholars. In 1453 many persecuted scholars fled Constantinople, the capital of the Byzantine Empire, after it was conquered by Muslim Turks. They began to make their way into Europe. A notable number of them moved to Venice. They brought not only their knowledge but also their precious manuscripts from Ancient Greece.

As in Florence and Rome, architects, scholars, and artists patronized by wealthy Venetians made lasting contributions to Western civilization. Some of Venice's most remarkable buildings, such as the Basilica of St. Mark and the Palace of the Doges, had already been constructed by the time of the Renaissance. But Renaissance architects left their mark in the new buildings they designed and the styles they created during this period.

Printing Advances

Venice made an especially notable contribution to classical learning by encouraging the development of the new craft of printing. By 1500 this city-state alone had more than 200 printing presses. Because many printers were scholars, they devoted themselves to searching out and publishing classical manuscripts, particularly those of Ancient Greece.

The printer whom Erasmus visited in Venice, Aldus Manutius, was so dedicated to his craft that he placed a notice over the door of his office: "Whoever you are, you are earnestly requested by Aldus to state your business briefly and to take your departure promptly. For this is a place of work." Aldus Manutius later died exhausted and poor, but he had succeeded in enriching his own age and ages to come by using this new means to preserve an ancient heritage.

Venice's Greatest Artist

Of all the arts for which Renaissance Venice became known, painting was the foremost. No Venetian painter was more respected for his artistry than Tiziano Vecelli (tee SYAH noh vay CHEL lee), known in history as Titian (TIHSH un). Born about 1488, he was brought to Venice at age nine or ten to study with some of the city's most important painters. When his long career came to an end in 1576, he had surpassed them all.

This portrait of Isabella d'Este, a prominent woman of the Renaissance, shows how Titian was able to make the viewer aware of the luxury of her dress, furs, and jewels.

Titian was noted for his appeal to the emotions and senses rather than to the mind. His use of color and his pioneering use of oil paints gave his works a rich and luxurious feel. Among Titian's most famous paintings is *The Assumption of the Virgin*, a powerful, exciting work showing the Virgin Mary being taken to heaven.

Although most Venetians admired Titian's work, not everyone agreed. Michelangelo, for example, admired Titian's "coloring and style." But he noted, "It was a pity good design was not taught in Venice."

Also famous is Titian's series of portraits of the Holy Roman Emperor Charles V, who became his patron, as well as portraits of Francis I of France and Philip II of Spain. So much did Emperor Charles V admire Titian that, it is reported, he once picked up the artist's paintbrush when Titian dropped it on the floor—something unheard of for an emperor to do for a mere commoner!

Decline of Venice

Even during its golden age of art and learning, Venice was already losing ground as the foremost trading power of the world. The Muslim Turks had successfully challenged Venetian dominance in the Mediterranean. New sea routes to the Far East discovered by Portuguese explorers would turn trade away from the Mediterranean and the Middle East to the Atlantic Ocean and beyond. Venice would remain an independent state until the end of the eighteenth century. But it would never again exercise the central role in world trade and commerce that it held in the glory days of the Renaissance.

Imagining Things That Are to Be A young man named Leonardo da Vinci applied for a job with the ruling duke of Milan (mih LAN). To convince the duke of his worth, Leonardo sent a lengthy description of the services he could offer. Today, we would call the description his résumé.

"I have plans for bridges, very light and strong and suitable for carrying very easily," he wrote. "When a place is besieged I know how to cut off water from the trenches and how to construct . . . scaling ladders and other instruments." He went on to describe his plans for destroying fortresses, constructing various "engines" for attack and defense, and making cannons and armored cars.

If we knew nothing else about him but his description of what he could do, we might think him an engineer or a soldier. In fact, he was also one of the foremost artists of the age, indeed of any age.

Like many great Renaissance artists, Leonardo was a jack-of-all-trades. He was a sculptor, a painter, a designer, and a scientist. Most of all, he was a visionary.

Leonardo was born in 1452 near the village of Vinci, about 60 miles from Florence. When he was about 15, his father took him to a famous artist in Florence. He persuaded the artist to make his son an **apprentice**.

Apprentices observed the master at work and did whatever menial tasks he gave them. Gradually, they began to learn how to work at the various branches of painting, designing, and sculpting under the master.

Apprentices' work was demanding. They rarely had days off. They spent long hours copying drawings so they would become familiar with the master's style. In fact, although a painting bore the master's name, it was quite possible that an apprentice actually had completed the work.

Leonardo spent less time as an apprentice than most boys. And, as time would demonstrate, he was spectacularly talented. A story is told that once Leonardo was assigned to paint an angel in one of his master's commissioned paintings. When the master saw what Leonardo

> **vocabulary**
> **apprentice** in the Middle Ages and the Renaissance, someone who agreed to live with and work for another for a specified period, in return for instruction in a trade or craft

Leonardo da Vinci drew this self portrait when he was an old man.

had done, he found it so beautiful he knew that he could never equal it. The master then gave up painting to concentrate on sculpture. The story may be a legend, but it serves to emphasize what later became apparent to the world: Leonardo da Vinci was an artist of rare ability.

About five years after he began his apprenticeship, Leonardo established his own workshop in Florence. Leonardo completed some remarkable work during this time. But he also began a habit of starting works that he would not complete.

The Master of All Trades

Leonardo was about 30 years old when he sent his résumé to the duke of Milan. He had heard that the duke was looking for a military engineer, a painter, an architect, and a sculptor. Leonardo offered himself as all four in one person. The duke would not be disappointed.

During his 17-year stay in Milan, Leonardo completed some of his greatest work. After he arrived in Milan, the duke asked him to paint on the wall of a monastery dining room a picture of the Last Supper. This represented the final meal Jesus shared with his twelve apostles. The artist labored for three years on the project. It was said that the **prior** complained that the artist was taking too much time to complete the work.

When the duke asked Leonardo why it was taking so long, the artist explained that he was having trouble painting the faces of Jesus and of the apostle Judas, who would betray Jesus. He could not imagine how to paint a face so beautiful that it was worthy of Jesus, nor could he imagine how to paint the features of a man as horrible as Judas. He cunningly suggested to the duke that he might use

vocabulary
prior the person, or officer, in charge of a priory, or monastery

the face of the prior as a model for Judas. Word must have gotten back to the prior because, from that time on, Leonardo was able to work at his painting without any complaints from the prior.

When Leonardo completed *The Last Supper*, it was recognized as a masterpiece. The painting remains in its original place today, but it has suffered greatly over the years from dampness, neglect, and natural deterioration. Nonetheless, many people feel it is the greatest painting that the Renaissance produced up to that point.

These pages from Leonardo's notebooks show how keen his mind was and how varied his interests were.

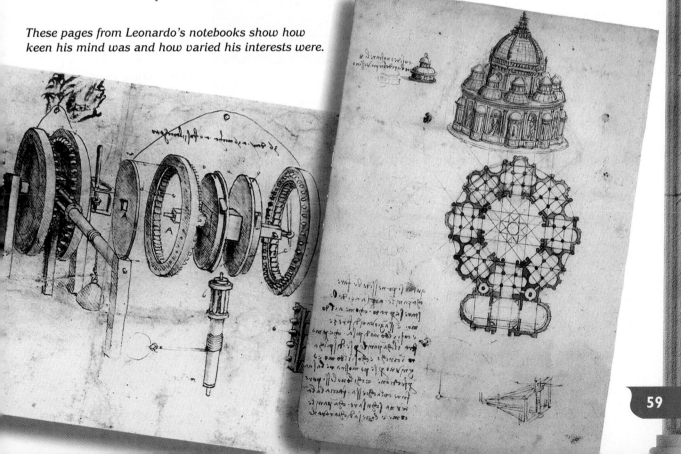

True to his résumé, Leonardo applied himself in many fields. He designed a device that allowed a person to study the total eclipse of the sun without damaging the eye. He designed the first parachute. He designed a model city with two levels and a series of underground canals. An accomplished musician, he even invented musical instruments, such as mechanized drums and keyboards for wind instruments.

Leonardo spent countless hours observing nature, drawing and recording in many notebooks what he saw. He also studied mathematics because he believed it was the foundation of art. One of his famous drawings illustrates a formula that states that the span of a man's outstretched arms is equal to his height.

Beyond Milan

In 1499, France captured Milan. Leonardo moved first to the safety of Mantua (MAN choo wuh) and then to Venice, where he worked as a naval engineer. In 1500 he returned to Florence. Except for a year during which he worked for a powerful military leader, he remained in Florence until 1506.

Some people say that the Mona Lisa is so lifelike that her eyes seem to follow a viewer across a room.

During this period he completed his other most famous painting, and perhaps the most famous portrait in the world, the *Mona Lisa*. The painting portrays the wife of a prominent Florentine citizen. For centuries since, viewers have been attracted by the artist's use of light and shade, his attention to detail in the woman's clothing, and his use of an invented landscape as background. Viewers were fascinated by the woman's gaze and smile. What was she thinking? People today still ask that question as they file past the painting now displayed in the great Louvre (loov) museum in Paris.

Leonardo returned to Milan. He continued his artistic work there, but it became increasingly clear that science held his interest as well as art. When Leo X became pope, Leonardo moved to Rome, where Leo provided him with lodgings and pay. Later, at the invitation of King Francis I, Leonardo left Italy for France, to become the "painter, engineer, and architect of the King." There, he remained, until his death in 1519 at the age of 67.

Leonardo left behind relatively few finished works of art: only about a dozen paintings and not one complete sculpture. He did leave many detailed and highly accurate drawings of human anatomy and of various mechanical devices. And he left more than 5,000 pages from his notebooks.

Leonardo may not have been the best painter, sculptor, engineer, or thinker of his time. But no one then, and perhaps no one since, has so effectively combined the skills of each calling. No one was more able to imagine what could be. He was in many ways the embodiment of the Renaissance, a true **Renaissance man**, devoted to knowledge and beauty in all its forms and expressions. Like so much else, this idea was borrowed from the ancient Roman civilization. The Romans had held all-around competence, or ability, in high esteem. They would certainly have admired Leonardo da Vinci.

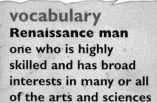

> **vocabulary**
> **Renaissance man**
> one who is highly skilled and has broad interests in many or all of the arts and sciences

Staring at the Ceiling For four years the artist labored, often under trying conditions. Lying on his back on scaffolding he had erected, he slowly covered the ceiling's 5,000 square feet with scenes from the Old Testament. His patron was not pleased with the pace of his work.

In fact, one day the patron angrily whacked the artist with a cane and threatened to throw him off the scaffold if he did not speed up his work.

The artist had not even wanted to accept the commission, for he thought of himself as a sculptor, not a painter. But the money was very good, and his patron was not a man to be denied. He was the pope. So Michelangelo continued to labor on.

It took him four years to complete his work. But when he had finished, the demanding patron, Pope Julius II, had no grounds for displeasure. The artist, Michelangelo Buonarroti (bwoh nahr ROH tee), had created a work of unparalleled magnificence, the ceiling of the Sistine (SIS teen) Chapel in Rome.

Michelangelo was a master of many artistic abilities. He often protested that he was a sculptor, as if he could not be expected to succeed in any other artistic field. In fact, he also was a marvelous painter and an architect who changed the face of Rome.

Also like Leonardo, Michelangelo was born near Florence—23 years later—and apprenticed in an artist's workshop when he was a boy. In 1488, at the age of 13, Michelangelo entered the workshop of a well-known Florentine painter. He spent only one year there, learning how to mix paints, prepare backgrounds for paintings, create frescoes, and draw with precision. In the following year he accepted an invitation from Lorenzo de' Medici to join an academy Lorenzo had founded. There he studied the Medicis' rich collection of Greek and Roman statues and learned the techniques of sculpture. He associated with all the artists and humanist thinkers that Lorenzo had gathered around him.

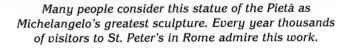

Many people consider this statue of the Pietà as Michelangelo's greatest sculpture. Every year thousands of visitors to St. Peter's in Rome admire this work.

To Rome

Four years after Lorenzo's death, Michelangelo moved to Rome. Like so many artists before him, he was fascinated by the ancient city's sculpture, architecture, and painting. He created his first major work in Rome, which made his reputation as a master sculptor. He was commissioned to create a large marble statue of Mary, the mother of Jesus, holding and mourning her dead son. A sculpture or painting of this scene is called a Pietà (pee ay TAH).

Michelangelo's extraordinarily lifelike Pietà was said to be the most beautiful work of marble in all of Rome. It remains in Rome today, and each year hundreds of thousands of visitors to St. Peter's Basilica continue to marvel at this magnificent sculpture.

The now-famous sculptor returned to Florence in 1501. There, he created a second masterwork from a colossal block of marble that had been discarded years earlier by another sculptor because it was flawed. It was an awe-inspiring statue of the young biblical hero David, who killed the giant Goliath. The statue almost seems alive. The artist's ability to overcome the imperfections of the marble to create this work marked him as the greatest sculptor of his age.

Four years later, Michelangelo was summoned back to Rome by Pope Julius II. Julius II wanted the artist to design and build a three-story tomb in which the pope would be buried. Thus began a peculiar love-hate relationship between the master artist and the demanding pope. The tomb was never completed as originally planned, because time and again Julius assigned new work for Michelangelo to do.

The Sistine Chapel

Many papal ceremonies were held in the Sistine Chapel. The pope gave Michelangelo the additional task of painting the ceiling. The artist designed the scaffolding, prepared the ceiling to be plastered—for this work was to be a fresco— and hired assistants to help him. In time he dismissed the assistants because he was dissatisfied with their work.

The Sistine Chapel is a huge space that took nearly four years to paint.

Michelangelo shut himself up in the huge room. He labored under extremely difficult conditions. When he climbed down at the end of a day's work, his back and neck ached, and his eyes were so used to focusing on a ceiling several feet away that he could not read a letter unless he held it at the same distance.

The finished work was a masterpiece. "There is no other work to compare with this for excellence, nor could there be," one artist wrote about Michelangelo's frescoes in the Sistine Chapel. The paintings depicted many scenes from the Old Testament, including the creation of Adam, the first man. The frescoes include more than 300 figures, some of them 18 feet high, and cover a space 118 feet long and 46 feet wide. The Sistine Chapel ceiling is Michelangelo's most famous work.

After Pope Julius died, Michelangelo stayed on in Rome under the new pope, Leo X. He had known this son of Lorenzo de' Medici in Florence. The artist continued work on the statues planned for Pope Julius's tomb. They included a monumental statue of Moses holding the tablets of the law, known as the Ten Commandments. The statue is found today in the Church of St. Peter in Chains, in Rome.

Return to Florence

In 1517, Michelangelo returned once again to Florence. The pope had asked him to design the facade, or front, of the Medici family church there. There were many problems with this project. Michelangelo not only had to train new workers to **quarry** the marble, but he also had to have a road built through the mountains to transport it. In time, the pope withdrew the commission. The artist had lost three years of work and was furious.

Nevertheless, when a new pope, Clement VII, was elected, Michelangelo agreed to stay in Florence and design the tombs of both Lorenzo de' Medici and his brother Giuliano (joo LYAH noh). He also agreed to design a library to be attached to the Medici church. His work was interrupted in 1527 when the troops of the Holy Roman emperor invaded Italy and sacked Rome. With Florence also in danger of attack, Michelangelo fled the city for Venice.

After order was restored, Michelangelo returned to Florence. He resumed his work on the library and tomb. Pope Clement asked him to return to the Sistine Chapel to paint the wall behind the altar. The pope died, however, as the artist was preparing to begin this work. The new pope, Paul III, named Michelangelo the chief painter, sculptor, and architect of the Vatican. He, too, asked the artist to paint the Sistine Chapel wall. As its theme the pope chose the Last Judgment, when all living and dead people would stand before God to be judged.

Last Judgment and Last Project

Michelangelo began the work, but it took him five years to complete it. He was 66 when he finished. The strain of the work took its toll on his health. Once, he fell off a scaffold, seriously injuring his leg.

The Last Judgment is a work of great power. The artist depicts Jesus both cursing the damned and welcoming the blessed. Its brown and orange colors, as well as the expressions and movements of Jesus and the other figures, give it a gloomy, even grim, feeling.

In 1546, Pope Paul III appointed Michelangelo, then 71 years old, chief architect for St. Peter's Basilica. His responsibilities included work on the exterior of the building as well as its dome, which became a model for domes throughout the western world.

The artist continued working almost until the day he died in 1564. When that day came, he remarked, "I regret that I am dying just as I am beginning to learn the alphabet of my profession."

Michelangelo was buried in Florence as he had wished. Michelangelo, who never married, left no children. His wife, he said, "was his art," and his children "the works I shall leave."

Daniele da Volterra, a sculptor who lived at the same time as Michelangelo, made this bronze bust of him.

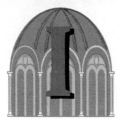

8 Two "How-to" Men

Instructors in Manners In the Renaissance, as today, much advice was available in print regarding how to live and act. Today, many books and magazine articles claim to teach readers how to succeed in various areas of life. Such books also were available in the Renaissance. A number of them were widely read.

Many books of this type concentrated on basic matters. They were quite specific about behavior that was or was not acceptable. One of the most popular of such books, *The Book of Manners*, was published in 1558. The author advises:

- Refrain as far as possible from making noises which grate upon the ear, such as grinding or sucking your teeth.

- It is not polite to scratch yourself when you are seated at table.

- We should . . . be careful not to gobble our food so greedily as to cause ourselves to get hiccups or commit some other unpleasantness.

- You should neither comb your hair nor wash your hands in the presence of others—except for washing the hands before going in to a meal—such things are done in the bedroom and not in public.

The purpose of many of these books was to instruct the newly rich about behavior that would help them enter the social class above them. But another type of book did more than

Raphael's portrait gives the impression that Castiglione would be an ideal courtier.

give instructions in how to behave politely in public. This sort of book had a broader purpose: It was meant to shape attitudes and to encourage a variety of achievements. It was meant to define the role of a gentleman.

The most famous and influential of these books was *The Courtier*, written by Baldassare Castiglione (bahl dahs SAH ray kahs tee LYOH nay). A courtier was an attendant in the court of a ruler. That is exactly what Castiglione was. He served as a soldier and **diplomat** in the court of the duke of Urbino (ur BEE noh).

By the time Castiglione joined the court at Urbino early in the sixteenth century, the hill town in central Italy had become known as a center of culture. The duke's court boasted one of the finest libraries of the time. A number of prominent artists, including the great painter Raphael, worked there. In fact, Raphael painted

vocabulary
diplomat one who represents a government in its relationships with other governments

a wonderful portrait of Castiglione, which now hangs in the Louvre museum in Paris.

How to Please Others

Castiglione's book was presented in the form of a series of conversations that supposedly took place at the court of Urbino. The conversations focused on what made men and women proper gentlemen and ladies.

The perfect courtier, according to the discussion, should be of noble birth, handsome, graceful, strong, and courageous. He should be skilled in war and in sports. Whatever he did, he should do it in such a way that it appeared "to be without effort."

The courtier, Castiglione and his companions decided, should have a high opinion of his own worth. He should not be afraid to advertise it to others but should do so in a way that did not appear boastful. So, he should ride near the front in processions to make sure he would be seen. He should try to accomplish his most daring feats where the ruler he served would notice him. He should not cheapen himself by mixing with people in social classes below him.

Machiavelli wrote a guide for rulers who wanted to create a lasting government.

The ideal courtier, according to Castiglione, also should be accomplished in learning. He should know Latin and Greek, be well read, and be able to write poetry and prose. He should appreciate painting, sculpture, music, and architecture, and be able to sing and dance gracefully.

Castiglione published his book in 1528. In a short time it was translated into French and English. It had a great influence for many years to come on standards of behavior and education, not only in Italy but also in France and England.

Today, it might seem as if the courtier the Italian diplomat described was all style and no substance. The ideal courtier of Renaissance Italy might strike us as someone more interested in making a good impression than in taking a stand. Castiglione argued that by developing the qualities he described, the ideal courtier would encourage his princely ruler to turn to him for advice. And by giving good advice, the courtier could exercise great influence in the way matters of government were decided.

How to Rule

Another important Renaissance writer argued strongly against this notion. In fact, he wrote, "It is an **infallible** rule that a prince who is not wise himself cannot be well-advised."

Niccolò Machiavelli (nee koh LOH mak ee uh VEL ee) lived and worked in and around Florence at the same time that Castiglione served in the court at Urbino. Like Castiglione, Machiavelli served as a diplomat, in his case for the government of Florence. From 1498 until 1512, Machiavelli held a number of positions in government. Each allowed him to observe how government worked or did not work. He was interested in how rulers gained and kept power.

Machiavelli was put in charge of the forces that were to defend Florence against armies headed by Pope Julius II. The

> **vocabulary**
> **infallible** incapable of error; certain

pope was angry that Florence had refused to help him expel French troops from Italy. He intended to put an end to the Florentine republic and restore the Medici family to rule.

Machiavelli's troops could not hold the line. The pope's forces took Florence, and the Medicis were returned to power. Machiavelli lost his government position, as well as his reputation. He went into exile on a small farm outside Florence. There, he spent most of his remaining years.

Advice for the Prince

The former diplomat long hoped for a return to government service. During his exile he wrote a small book of advice on how to govern, based on his own experience and study of history. If artists of the Renaissance drew their inspiration from the natural world, from the real shapes and forms they saw about them, Machiavelli did the same for politics. He looked at what happened in the actual world of power and government. He did not write about the ideal behavior of a Christian leader but of the actual behavior of present and past leaders. He called his most famous book *The Prince*, and many think of it as the first book of modern political science—the study of political institutions and how they work.

Machiavelli wrote the book hoping it would bring him to the attention of the Medicis. He wanted the Medicis to employ him once again in the city-state's government. That was not to be. In fact, the Medicis

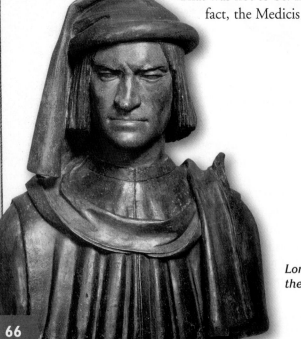

were suspicious of Machiavelli. They knew that he really wanted to see Florence ruled by a republican government, and not by them. Still, the book caused an enormous stir and had great influence.

The Prince was a total novelty. Because Machiavelli made no attempt to describe politics in a religious framework, he scandalized many. But he also described the workings of government very clearly, and rulers sat up and took notice.

Machiavelli agreed that, in general, it was praiseworthy for a prince "to keep his faith and to be an honest man." But he believed that a ruler might need to go back on his word in times of trouble or danger. Princes who acted boldly also won fame and glory, and that might be more valuable than keeping every promise. So he advised princes who wished to gain and maintain power "to learn how *not* to be good."

Like Castiglione, Machiavelli believed that appearances were important. A prince, he wrote, should be seen as "merciful, faithful, humane, sincere, religious." But he also wrote that when it served the ruler to be otherwise, he should "be able to change to the opposite qualities." Rulers, he insisted, sometimes had to use cunning, trickery, even cruelty, to get and keep power. "It is necessary for a prince who wishes to hold his own," Machiavelli wrote, "to know how to do wrong." Over the years many people have strongly disagreed with Machiavelli's judgments and directives. In fact, the term *Machiavellian* is still used to describe a person who is crafty and less than honest.

On the other hand, some scholars believe Machiavelli was simply being realistic. They say that his goal was to ensure the safety of the Florentine state. He believed any behavior that achieved this purpose was necessary, if not honorable. Machiavelli's defenders suggest that instead of writing a description of how an ideal Christian ruler should behave, he offered candid advice on ways efficient rulers should and did behave.

Lorenzo de' Medici looked like he could be the prince that Machiavelli described.

pread of Spirit and Ideas Both *The Courtier* and *The Prince*, we have seen, had influence well beyond the borders of Italian city-states. Both books were translated into other languages. Both found willing readers in countries throughout Europe.

Translation of the printed word was just one of many ways in which the ideas and values of the Renaissance in Italy were spread through the rest of Europe.

The spirit and notions of the Renaissance also were carried outside Italy by Italian artists who traveled to other countries. Leonardo, for example, spent his final years in France as painter, engineer, and architect to King Francis I. Other Italian artists of the Renaissance also worked outside Italy, sharing their skills and ideals.

Visitors to Renaissance Italy often carried home respect for Italy's ancient civilization and its artistic discoveries and methods. Some visitors, such as Erasmus, came for learning. They found inspiration in Italy and gladly shared it with citizens of their home countries. Others, such as the invading German and French armies, came to conquer and steal. In many cases they were influenced by the cultural riches they found. They too carried their discoveries back, along with their loot.

Several factors had made Italy the center of the Renaissance in the fourteenth and fifteenth centuries: the closeness of Roman ruins, the geography and prosperity of the independent city-states, the rise of merchants

and patrons, and the reform of education. So too several factors came together elsewhere in the sixteenth century to open other countries to new learning and new possibilities.

Northern and Western Europe

In the 1500s some countries to the north and west of Italy developed well-organized central governments. The center of trade shifted from

Europe During the Renaissance

The influence of Renaissance Italy spread to the nation states of northern and western Europe in the 1500s.

the Mediterranean to the Atlantic, bringing some of these countries new wealth. Royal courts in France, England, and Germany supported young artists. New wealth also allowed a thriving merchant class to become patrons of art and learning.

Most of all, in these countries, as in Italy, there arose scholars and artists of genius. Many of them began by imitating the Italians, but eventually they made their own unique contributions to Western culture.

The German-speaking countries of the Holy Roman Empire to the north of Italy were among the first to welcome Renaissance values and ideals. Men like Erasmus helped spread humanism in those countries. The German Renaissance soon became caught up in religious disputes between Catholics and Protestants that we call the Reformation. Nevertheless, it produced a number of important scholars and artists.

Dürer's self portrait shows a young man who is sure of his ability as an artist.

Perhaps the greatest German painter of this period was Albrecht Dürer (AHL brekt DU rur), born in 1471. His goldsmith father took him to his workshop to teach him the trade. But the father soon discovered that his son had a remarkable talent for drawing. He apprenticed him to a local artist, where young Dürer quickly mastered the technique of designing woodcuts. These were blocks of wood carved and inked and used for printing illustrations.

After he finished his apprenticeship, Dürer traveled to France. There he improved the engraving skills he had learned in his father's goldsmith shop. Engravings were images carved onto metal plates with a sharp tool. The plates were then inked for printing. Dürer was to do some of his finest work as an engraver and woodcutter.

Dürer traveled to Italy for the first time. He visited Venice and there discovered new artistic styles and new forms of expression that were quite different from anything he had experienced in his native country. While in Venice he copied the paintings of well-known artists to improve his technique. He also studied mathematics, read poetry, and carefully observed the landscapes and life that surrounded him.

After Dürer returned to Germany, he established his own workshop. He soon became enormously popular, both as a painter and as an engraver. Two of his most remarkable paintings were self-portraits. On the second of them he wrote the following message in Latin: "Albrecht Dürer from Nuremberg, painted this myself with incredible colors at the age of twenty-eight years." Dürer's inscription is an example of the new confidence that artists acquired during the Renaissance. By using the word *incredible*, Dürer seems to be marveling at his own achievement and boasting that he is a man with a special gift.

Dürer painted and drew many other portraits, including one of Erasmus. But he was especially interested in creating engravings and woodcuts. Among his best works of this type is a series of engravings based on the Book of the Apocalypse in the Christian New Testament.

The Renaissance in France

The Renaissance flourished in France in the middle of the sixteenth century. Invasions of Italy by French troops introduced French leaders to Renaissance culture. What they saw amazed them. Earlier you read about how King Francis I hired Leonardo da Vinci to come to Paris to be "painter, engineer, and architect of the King."

Francis and the kings who followed him began to purchase Italian Renaissance paintings and sculpture. They also succeeded in bringing other Italian Renaissance artists to France.

French monarchs also built a series of lavish **chateaux** (sha TOH), designed by Italian architects and decorated in Renaissance style.

The influence of the Italian Renaissance did not stop there. Life in the chateaux was modeled on life in Italian courts, as described by Castiglione in *The Courtier*.

The Renaissance in England

In England the Renaissance reached its height in the late sixteenth and early seventeenth centuries. In many European countries it was the sculptors, painters, and architects who made the greatest contributions to the Renaissance. In England it was the writers.

During this period a number of notable poets and playwrights wrote works that are still read, performed, and loved today. Among them was William Shakespeare, often called the greatest playwright of all time. Shakespeare was born in Stratford-upon Avon in 1564. Before he was 30, he had moved to London. There he established himself as both a playwright and a poet.

There is no record that Shakespeare ever visited Italy. But the influence of Italy and the Italian Renaissance is apparent in a great many of his plays. *The Merchant of Venice* is a drama about a merchant in Renaissance Venice, while *Othello* is a tragedy about a general in the same city. *Romeo and Juliet* takes place in Verona. Many of his plots were taken from famous Italian stories.

vocabulary
chateau a French castle, or large country house; *chateaux* is the plural form

Shakespeare also shared the Renaissance interest in classical Greece and Rome. He wrote several plays about Ancient Greece and four tragedies about Ancient Rome, including *Julius Caesar* and *Antony & Cleopatra*.

Even when he was not writing about Renaissance Italy or the classical world, Shakespeare wrote like a man of the Renaissance. We saw earlier how he made Prince Hamlet speak like a Renaissance humanist. Shakespeare was also just as interested in individual personality as any of the Italian painters; the only difference was that the Italians used paint and canvas to capture personality, whereas Shakespeare used pen and paper. Finally, one may say that Shakespeare was not only a man of the Renaissance but also a Renaissance man, for he wrote comedies, tragedies, histories, romances, and poems of all sorts. And he excelled at every kind of writing he attempted.

Many of Shakespeare's works were first performed at the Globe Theater (left). The first collected edition of his plays was printed in 1623 (right).

The Renaissance in Spain

The Renaissance also came to Spain relatively late. Spain's greatest Renaissance painter actually was a Greek, born on the isle of Crete and trained in Venice. His name was Domenikos Theotokopoulos (doh MEN ih kohs tha oh toh KOH poo lohs), but after he moved to Spain, in about 1577, he became known as El Greco, which is Spanish for "the Greek."

El Greco spent about 12 years in Venice. There, he learned to paint in the Italian Renaissance manner. He clearly was influenced by the paintings of Titian, as the rich colors of his own paintings bear witness.

From Venice, El Greco traveled to Rome, where his outspokenness did not win him many friends. El Greco learned a lot from artists in Rome, including Michelangelo. But he offended people by criticizing Michelangelo's paintings. When El Greco saw that he had worn out his welcome in Rome, he moved on to the Spanish city of Toledo (tuh LAID oh). El Greco spent the rest of his life in Spain. He received many commissions, often for paintings to adorn churches and chapels. Among his most famous works is a painting known as *The Burial of the Count of Orgaz*. The painting displays the long, slender figures that came to distinguish El Greco's work.

A Great Writer

Renaissance Spain also produced one of the greatest writers of that age, or any age. He was Miguel de Cervantes (mee GEL de sur VAN teez), and his best-known work is the novel *The History of Don Quixote de la Mancha* (dahn kee HOHT ay de la MAHN chah). The hero, Don Quixote, has a noble heart, but he does many foolish things as he tries to imitate the brave knights he has read about. Don Quixote insists that a simple peasant girl he loves is really a noble duchess. He jousts against windmills, thinking they are evil giants. Today, we use the word *quixotic* (kwihks AHT ihk) to describe someone who is impractical or who is striving for an unreachable ideal.

The phrase "tilting at windmills," describing a noble but impractical plan, comes from this scene from Don Quixote.

European Renaissance

As we have seen, the Renaissance began in Italy. It was in Italy that the following characteristics of the period first developed: an enthusiasm for the classical past as a source of inspiration, an interest in accurately portraying the natural world, a fascination with the individual, and an appreciation for artists and their work.

From the Italian city-states of Florence, Venice, and Rome, the spirit and ideals of the Renaissance spread to other countries. But far from simply imitating what had been done in Italy, artists and scholars in other countries developed their own individual styles. What had been done in Italy inspired them to enrich their own local and national traditions. Western civilization has reaped the rewards of their work.

Glossary

apothecary a druggist or pharmacist

apprentice in the Middle Ages and the Renaissance, someone who agreed to live with and work for another for a specified period, in return for instruction in a trade or craft

basilica a Christian church building, often in the shape of a cross

chateau a French castle, or large country house; *chateaux* is the plural form

diplomat one who represents a government in its relationships with other governments

fresco a painting made on fresh, moist plaster with color pigments dissolved in water

galley a large, flat-bottomed ship propelled by sails and oars and used in the Mediterranean for trade and war

infallible incapable of error; certain

lagoon a shallow body of water, especially one separated from a larger body of water by a sandbar or reef

mason a person who builds or works with brick or stone

patron a wealthy person who supports an artist

perspective a technique that allows artists to show objects as they appear at various distances from the viewer, with distant objects shown smaller and nearby objects larger

prior the person, or officer, in charge of a priory, or monastery

quarry to obtain stone from a pit or excavation by cutting, digging, or blasting it

Renaissance man one who is highly skilled and has broad interests in many or all of the arts and sciences

republic a system of government in which voters elect officials to run the government and make laws

rhetoric the art of using words effectively in speaking or writing

The Reformation

Contents

Changing Ideas in Europe The world is always changing. Borders shrink and expand; nations rise and fall; ideas are embraced and rejected. There has never been an age without change. But there are certain ages in which things change in especially significant or dramatic ways. In Europe the fifteenth and sixteenth centuries were one such age.

During the 1400s and 1500s, Europe experienced profound changes in three areas—communication, religion, and science. These changes ensured that life would never be the same.

Many people contributed to these changes, but seven in particular stand out. By studying their lives and work, we can learn about the changes they helped to trigger.

The seven were a diverse lot. Two were Germans. The rest were from Switzerland, France, Spain, Poland, and Italy. One of the Germans was a craftsperson and inventor. The other was a university professor of **theology**. The Swiss was a priest. The Frenchman was a scholar who had studied theology and earned a law degree. The Spaniard was a nobleman and warrior turned priest. The Pole was an astronomer, and the Italian was a mathematician, astronomer, and physicist.

> **vocabulary**
> **theology** the study of religion

With the exception of the Swiss and one of the Germans, there is no record that these men ever met each other. In fact, the German

This is an artist's idea of what Gutenberg may have looked like.

inventor died before the others were born, and the Italian scientist was born after the others had died. Nonetheless, all of them had a profound effect on the way we live and act today.

The German Inventor

Johannes Gutenberg created an invention that would change the way people communicate, and, ultimately, the way they think. Born in Mainz, Germany, around A.D. 1400, Gutenberg was trained as a metalworker and was associated with the goldsmith's guild. In the 1430s he moved to Strasbourg where he was engaged in such work as cutting gems, making mirrors, and teaching students these crafts. The few records we have of his stay in France tell us that even then he probably was at work on a new invention that would change the world.

By the late 1440s, Gutenberg had returned to Mainz. There he had entered into a partnership with two other men, one a businessman and the other a calligrapher, a person who professionally hand-copied books. From their workshop came a radical new process for duplicating written materials.

Up to that time, if written material was to be duplicated, it had to be copied by hand. The process was slow and expensive. Imagine how long it would take you to carefully copy by hand the small book you are reading. In Gutenberg's time it might require a professional copyist four or five months of steady work to copy a 200-page text. As a result only the clergy and the wealthy could afford books. The clergy could depend on **monks** in **monasteries** to do the copying required. And the wealthy nobles and merchants could afford to pay professional copyists to do the work. The common people were lucky if they knew how to read, much less to own a book.

There was another way to produce copies of a book, but it too was expensive and required painstaking work. Woodcarvers first drew outlines of pictures and words on single wood blocks. Next, they followed the pen-drawn outlines to carve out the letters and illustrations, which were raised up on the wood. Then, they applied ink to each block and pressed the block onto paper. Once carved, however, the words and pictures could not be changed. The impressions made on paper were generally uneven. And after repeated use, the wood wore down and produced printed copies of increasingly poor quality.

The Spread of Knowledge

What Gutenberg did revolutionized the way in which books and other written materials were produced and also revolutionized the way in which knowledge and opinions were communicated. Books and, therefore, knowledge would soon be available to many more people.

In medieval times monks in monasteries copied books by hand because there were no printing presses.

Gutenberg's solution to the problems posed by the need to duplicate books quickly and inexpensively was ingenious. It involved two separate developments, which he was the first to combine effectively.

First, Gutenberg succeeded in manufacturing separate letter stamps made out of durable metal. He began by carving a raised letter on an iron "punch," using a "counter-punch" to punch out the space inside the letter (see the illustration on next page). When only the outline of a raised letter remained, he hardened the punch and used it to make an impression into a copper bar called a matrix. Then he put the matrix into a mold and poured a melted lead **alloy** into it. The lead alloy piece took the shape of the letter punched into the matrix.

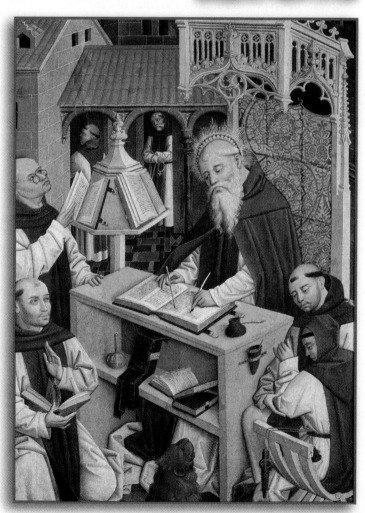

Gutenberg repeated this process several times, until he had a large collection of lead type for that letter. Then he went on to the next letter. He had to follow the same steps for each letter of the alphabet, including small letters and capitals, and for numerals and punctuation marks. And he did this for each size of type: small, medium, and large. All in all he created thousands of different pieces of type. These pieces were placed in an organizer with lots of little boxes, called a type case.

What Is Movable Type?

When the time came to print, the typesetter, or typographer, took the type pieces, letter by letter, from the type case. He arranged the letters, numbers, and punctuation marks of each line of text in correct order, with proper spacing, in a strip of wood called a composing stick. Because the metal pieces of type were reusable, and because they could be moved around in any arrangement required, they were called movable type.

Next, the typesetter locked the lines of type into a rectangular frame. Finally, he inked the type in the frame and pressed a sheet of paper against it. He could then make multiple prints of the same page. When printing was completed, he could break up the frame and return each piece of type to its proper place in the type case.

Although many think of Gutenberg as the original inventor of movable type, it was actually first created in China, sometime between A.D. 1040 and 1050 and had been developed even further in Korea 200 or 300 years later. However, Gutenberg probably was unaware of these developments. Gutenberg also had another advantage over his Asian predecessors. The Chinese and Korean printers were handicapped by the nature of their languages, in which each word has its own symbol. In order to print even a simple book, they needed to create thousands of different pieces of type. Gutenberg, on the other hand, was working with a relatively small collection of letters that could be combined into a massive number of words. This is probably one reason why movable type caught on in the West in a way it had not in the East.

The Printing Press

Gutenberg's second great development was his use of the wooden screw-and-lever press for printing. The German inventor took a press commonly used to make paper or wine and adjusted it to print words on paper. First, Gutenberg locked the type arranged for the text to be printed onto the press bed. Then, he applied an oil-based ink to the type by hand, using leather-covered pads. He fixed a piece of paper on top of the type and slid the type and

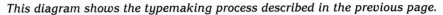

This diagram shows the typemaking process described in the previous page.

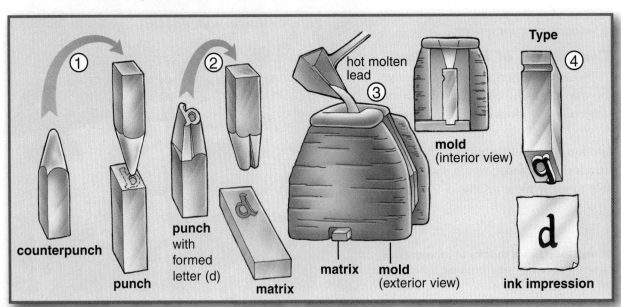

This illustration is an artist's interpretation of what Gutenberg's print shop looked like. The page shown here is from the Gutenberg Bible. The decorations were added by hand.

paper under the press's screw mechanism. He cranked a large lever, which lowered the screw so that its flat wooden surface pressed the paper against the type and created an ink impression.

Printing a single sheet in this fashion took Gutenberg and other early printers about two minutes, far less time than would have been required to copy a page of text by hand. The fact that Gutenberg could produce the same text again and again more than made up for the additional time it took the typesetter to arrange the pieces of type to be printed.

Among the most celebrated products of Gutenberg's press was a Bible he printed in about 1455. It has become so famous that it is called, simply, the Gutenberg Bible. The few copies that remain are worth millions of dollars each.

Within a period of less than 50 years, Gutenberg's techniques had spread throughout Europe. By 1500, printers' workshops were found in most major European cities. Printing changed the way information was collected, stored, and communicated. It dramatically increased the number of copies of the Bible and other books, and drastically reduced the number of hours required to produce them. A much larger number of people gained access to a greater variety of written material. Now it was possible for readers in various places to examine the same texts and images at the same time.

If you have studied the Renaissance, you may know that the work of printers such as Aldus Manutius in Venice helped spread the values of humanism in Renaissance Italy. In this book you will learn how the work of other printers helped spread religious and scientific ideas throughout Europe.

Bold Statements It was the eve of All Saints' Day, October 31, 1517. A short, sturdy figure walked with great purpose toward the Castle Church in the German town of Wittenberg. Under his arm he carried a placard, or notice, for display in a public place, on which he had written a series of bold statements.

When he arrived at the church door, the professor took the placard from under his arm. Then, he fastened it firmly on the door, so anyone who was interested could see what he had written. He did not know how people would respond to his statements, but he felt certain that he was right. Little did he know that his simple action would start a movement that would change the world in a major way. By posting his statements, the professor had taken the first decisive action in what would be known forever after as the Protestant Reformation.

This scholar was Martin Luther. He came along about 40 years after Johannes Gutenberg. Gutenberg's invention would be used to spread Luther's ideas.

The German Theologian

In 1483, on the eve of the feast of Saint Martin, a second son was born to Hans and Margaret Luther in Saxony, in present-day Germany. In honor of the saint, his parents named him Martin.

Martin's father was a miner who managed to save his money and purchase several mine shafts and two **foundries**. Hans Luther was ambitious for his son. Just as he had improved his station in life, he hoped his son would be able to improve his social position.

When Martin was still a young man, his father decided that Martin should study law. Martin obediently accepted his father's decision and began his legal studies. After only a few months, however, he abandoned his studies and, at the age of 21, entered a monastery.

By turning his back on the law, young Martin Luther angered his father. But Martin believed he was answering a call from heaven. He was an extraordinarily sensitive, sometimes moody young man. He was convinced that becoming a monk was the only way open to him to save his soul.

> **vocabulary**
> **foundry** an establishment where metal is melted and poured into molds

Martin was diligent in his pursuit of his duties as a monk, at times to excess. He fasted, prayed into the night, and confessed his sins repeatedly and in great detail. Finally, his confessor grew weary of his confessions. "Man," he exclaimed to the young monk, "God is not angry with you. You are angry with God. Don't you know that God commands you to hope?"

Although his superiors were sometimes annoyed at his enthusiastic devotion, they recognized his great intelligence. He was ordained a priest and, in 1508, he was sent to study and lecture at the new University of Wittenberg. Young Luther proved himself an able student and teacher.

A trip to Rome in 1510 disappointed him. The lavish palaces of the church's cardinals offended him. He was greatly upset by stories he heard about the pope, who seemed to be more like a worldly ruler rather than a spiritual leader. Martin found many of the people of Rome, including his fellow priests, little concerned, even irreverent, about their religion. While saying Mass one day, he was told by one priest to "Get a move on." In the time it took Luther to read one Mass with intense devotion, some of the priests in Rome would rattle off six or seven of them. Despite his disappointment, Luther's faith in the authority of the church was not shaken. That would come later.

When he returned to Wittenberg, Luther's superiors told him he was to become a doctor of theology and a preacher. Although he preferred to remain in the quiet of the monastery, in 1511 he began his studies. A year later he earned his degree.

A Teacher and Scholar

Professor Luther soon distinguished himself as a teacher. An older professor at the university predicted a famous future for him. "This monk will confuse all the doctors."

When Luther began his career as a teacher of theology, the Roman Catholic Church functioned both as a spiritual guide for millions of people and as a government. People depended on the Church to help them gain peace of mind and to learn what God wanted them to do, but it also ruled a large part of Italy called the Papal States. Its earthly ruler was the pope, and its princes (who elected the pope) were the cardinals. The pope maintained an army, waged war with other rulers, and made treaties. The Church had its own laws, its own courts, and its own financial agency, the *Curia*.

Martin Luther helped begin the Protestant revolution against the teachings of the Roman Catholic Church.

Sometimes the Church's political role interfered with performing its religious duties. And both its political and its spiritual activities cost money, which it raised in various ways. It demanded regular payments from kings and other rulers. It required anyone who held an important Church office to pay the pope a percentage of that office's income. It collected taxes. And it sold indulgences.

Disturbing Church Practices

When you studied the Renaissance, you may have learned about indulgences. The Church taught that indulgences were spiritual benefits that individuals could earn by saying certain prayers, doing certain types of **penance**, or giving money to the Church. People were told that, in return, God would not punish them in the afterlife for their misdeeds, or sins. But—and this was important—the indulgence would not work unless they also confessed their misdeeds to a priest and truly felt sorry for having done wrong.

> **vocabulary**
> **penance** an act, such as praying, done to repent for a sin or wrongdoing

Most often, indulgences were attached to giving for a specific purpose, such as to build churches or view the relics—the bones or clothing—of saints. Usually donors were promised a reduction in the number of years their soul would have to spend in **purgatory**.

Young Professor Luther's study of the Bible and of early Church teachers had convinced him that the Church misled people by offering them indulgences.

> **vocabulary**
> **purgatory** according to Catholicism, the place where, after death, souls are punished for a certain period of time for sins

He and the Church agreed that God would forgive sins only if people were truly sorry, but he thought that indulgence-selling gave people the false idea that they were expressing their sorrow simply by giving money. God's forgiveness, he

In 1517, Martin Luther attached a copy of his 95 Theses, or statements, to the door of the church in Wittenberg, Germany. These statements explained Luther's religious ideas.

believed, was not something that anyone could purchase. Salvation, to Luther, was a gift of God, and no one by his or her own efforts could achieve it. What was required was faith in Jesus Christ as savior. Faith alone, he said, brings salvation.

In April 1517, a traveling preacher set up shop outside Wittenberg, where Luther taught. He was a super-salesman. Disregarding Church law, and saying nothing about repenting for sins, he told customers that they could earn indulgences simply by contributing money for rebuilding St. Peter's Basilica, the pope's vast church in Rome. The indulgences he was offering, said the preacher, were so powerful that purchasers would not only be safe from purgatory but also could free their dead relatives from its fire. The preacher made his wild claims because he was under pressure to sell as many indulgences as he could. The money he raised would be shared with a local ruling family, which needed to pay the pope for having appointed one of its relatives as an archbishop.

Martin Luther was furious. In Latin he summarized on a placard his ideas about why the Church was wrong to sell indulgences. His placard listed 95 Theses, or statements, for debate. In October 1517, he nailed the placard to the door of Wittenberg's Castle Church, which was a kind of bulletin board for making university announcements. But if Luther's action was routine, what he had to say was very dramatic. He objected to the way in which the money was to be used. He denied that the pope had any power over the souls of the dead. And he charged that selling indulgences actually harmed people by making them think that all they had to do was offer money and their sins would be forgiven.

Luther was not the first to attack the practices and teachings of the Roman Catholic Church. For two centuries, various reformers had preached against what they saw as corruption in the Church. But none of these reformers had lasting success, nor did any of them have the printing press available to spread their ideas.

Spreading Luther's Ideas

Shortly after Luther nailed up his theses, they were translated into German, printed, and distributed throughout central Europe. It is not clear what role Luther played in this process, but he surely allowed it to happen.

Luther's opponents labeled him a **heretic** and called on Rome to condemn him. The pope at the time dismissed the incident as a quarrel among monks. But Luther did not stop with the 95 Theses. He began to publish leaflets and pamphlets in which he explained his opposition to indulgences and to other church practices. Soon he became a best-selling author.

Church authorities in Rome could no longer remain silent. Luther was called to a meeting with one of the pope's representatives. When he was told he must take back what he had written, he refused. When told that his teachings went against those of the pope, who was the highest authority in the church, Luther responded, "I deny that he is above Scripture."

During the next three years, Luther continued to publish writings that called for reform of the church and attacked some of its teachings. In his writings, Luther began to question the authority of the pope and to lay blame for abuses in the church on the papacy. He taught that only some of the church's religious rites, called sacraments, were based on the Bible and declared that those that were not should be done away with. He debated his views publicly with representatives of Rome, gaining support from a good portion of the German people.

Finally, the pope issued an official document, called a papal bull, in which he condemned Luther's writings and ordered them burned. He gave Luther 60 days to take back what he taught or be excommunicated, that is, cut off from membership in the church. Luther responded by writing a document of his own. In strong language he condemned the pope, calling him possessed by Satan.

Luther on Trial

Luther was ordered to appear before an assembly of religious leaders and princes, including the Holy Roman Emperor Charles V. He would be given a choice: admit his error or be declared an outlaw. The assembly, called a diet, was held in the city of Worms. The people in that city were overwhelmingly in favor of Luther.

At his trial, Luther was shown 20 of the books he had written and was asked if he would take back the heresies they contained. After being given a day to prepare his response, Luther returned to the assembly. There was no question about his decision. "My conscience," he said boldly, "is captive to the Word of God. I will not recant anything, for to go against conscience is neither right nor safe." In some accounts of the trial, Luther is said to have concluded by declaring, "Here I stand, I cannot do otherwise." Whether he actually said these words or not, they make clear what he thought and how he felt.

Martin Luther (standing, center) defended his ideas before a jury of German religious leaders, princes, and the Holy Roman Emperor Charles V.

A month later, Luther was declared an outlaw. He was forced to flee in disguise. He grew a beard and dressed as a knight. One of his supporters among the German princes arranged for him to hide in a castle fortress, where he remained for almost a year.

While in hiding, he translated the entire New Testament from the original Greek into German. In the meantime, the changes he had begun were taken up by people who agreed with him. Luther's ideas about faith and worship and the way the Church should be governed were put into practice in many areas of Germany and the neighboring countries.

When debate over the changes Luther had set in motion led to some violence in Wittenberg, Luther came out of hiding and restored order. With the support of some sympathetic princes, Luther was able to return to his work of preaching, teaching, and writing.

In 1526 the declaration that Luther was an outlaw was suspended. In 1529 an assembly of princes in the city of Speyer declared that what came to be called Lutheranism was to be tolerated in regions where it could not be suppressed without violence. In such lands the religious freedom of those who continued to follow the Roman Catholic Church was to be observed. But Lutherans who lived in strong Catholic regions were not allowed their religious freedom.

The followers of Luther and others who disagreed with Rome protested against the inequality of this arrangement. Their action is the origin of the term Protestant. The term now is used to designate members of churches that separated during this period of history from the Roman Catholic Church. The term also is applied to the reform movement that Luther began, the Protestant Reformation.

Martin Luther continued until his death in 1546 to preach and teach, and to write and publish. He spoke directly to the people in their own language, winning many of them over to a church not tied to Rome and not bound by many of the Roman Church's teachings. Today, followers of Martin Luther may be found in many countries throughout the world. The church they belong to is called the Lutheran Church.

Others before Martin Luther had raised or suggested many of the ideas that people found so convincing when Luther presented them. But earlier reformers did not have at their disposal the means of communication that Luther had. "Printing," Luther declared, "is God's latest and best work to spread the true religion throughout the world."

Luther successfully launched a revolution in religion by using the tools developed by Johannes Gutenberg that made communication easier, faster, and cheaper. Others would use those same tools to put their own stamps on that religious revolution.

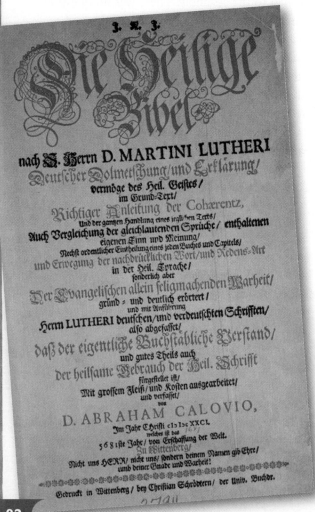

This is a page of the Bible Luther translated into German. This meant that ordinary German people could now read the Bible in their own language.

 **Second Wave of Religious Reformation** Southwest of Luther's Germany is Switzerland. This mountainous country's geography and forms of government encouraged independence among its citizens. The rugged Alps made it difficult for any would-be conquerors to overcome the Swiss. And the Swiss made sure of this by banding together for mutual defense.

In the early sixteenth century, Switzerland was divided into many smaller territories, called cantons. Each canton governed itself, but a number of cantons formed a **confederacy** to discourage common enemies and assure peace. The Swiss loved their freedom and were willing to fight to defend it.

It is not surprising that a second wave of religious reformation took place in Switzerland. In the early 1500s, most of the Swiss bishops claimed the privileges of feudal lords. Like the popes to whom they answered, they were more worldly leaders than spiritual leaders. They often showed greater interest in raising money than in saving souls. They often concentrated on satisfying their own desires rather than responding to their peoples' needs.

> **vocabulary**
> **confederacy** an alliance; a union of persons, groups, nations, or states

More Religious Reform

Abuses in the church rankled one Swiss citizen in particular. His name was Ulrich Zwingli, and he served as a priest in Zurich, then the leading city in the Swiss Confederation. In 1519, Zwingli undertook to reform his own congregation. He had become convinced that many practices in the church had no basis in the Bible. Like Luther, he opposed the practice of indulgences. He urged people not to purchase indulgence certificates. "Christ alone saves," he declared.

He also preached against other practices he said were not supported in the Scriptures. He dismissed the veneration of the saints. He ordered all statues and crucifixes removed from churches. He declared that Christians were not required to fast or go on **pilgrimages**. Since he could not find authority in Scripture for the use of music in worship services, he removed the organ from his church and banned the singing of hymns. Zwingli won many supporters in Zurich, both from members of his congregation and from some government officials.

Thanks to the assistance of a supportive Zurich printer, Zwingli's ideas were spread outside Zurich. Copies of his sermons and other writings reached Germany, where Zwingli's ideas began to compete with Martin Luther's.

> **vocabulary**
> **pilgrimage** a journey to a sacred place or shrine

Luther and Zwingli Meet

The two reformers did not always see eye-to-eye on all aspects of religious reforms. First, they conducted a pamphlet war. Then, in 1529 they met face-to-face to debate their differences. They agreed on many teachings. Both maintained, for example, that Scripture was infallible. But they differed strongly on other teachings. At the end of their meeting, Zwingli offered to shake hands with Luther. Luther flatly refused. "I will not let the devil teach me anything in my church," he later said.

Zwingli returned to Zurich, where he continued to write and preach and to exercise great influence over the city's government. His teachings provoked opposition from some cantons of Switzerland that still held to the Catholic faith. In 1531, five of

The Swiss reformer, Ulrich Zwingli (left) and the French reformer, John Calvin (right) both had major influences on the Protestant revolution against the teachings of the Roman Catholic Church.

these cantons mustered an army against Zurich. Zwingli, an ardent patriot, joined a smaller force of Zurich citizens against them. The reformer was killed in the battle. As he lay dying, he is reported to have said, "They may kill the body, but not the soul."

Despite Zwingli's death, the spirit of religious reform remained alive in Switzerland. Its focus, however, shifted to another Swiss city, Geneva. In Zurich, German was the common language, but in Geneva, located close to France, French was spoken by most inhabitants. It was a Frenchman who would bring the message of reform to Geneva and would assure that it spread to many other parts of Europe.

The French Scholar

John Calvin was born in 1509 in northern France. He studied theology and philosophy in Paris. There, he is said to have eaten and slept little but to have devoured books. It was expected that he would become a priest.

In the middle of his studies, his father sent him to another city, Orléans, to study law. Calvin completed his legal studies, but he never practiced law. While in Orléans, he became attracted to the study of ancient languages, cultures, and literature. He also began to read the writings of religious reformers and to associate with some of them.

Sometime around 1533, Calvin experienced what he called a "sudden conversion." Within a year he began to support Protestantism openly. In Catholic France, that was a dangerous position to take. So Calvin, fearing arrest, moved from France to Basel, Switzerland.

Calvinism

While in Basel, Calvin wrote a book titled *The Institutes of the Christian Religion*. He would rewrite and expand this book several times during his life. The *Institutes* defended the movement of religious reform and summarized Calvin's version of Christian teaching. It became probably the single most influential publication of the Protestant Reformation.

The first edition of the *Institutes* was published in Latin, but editions in French and other languages soon followed. Many of the beliefs the *Institutes* described were the same as those of the Church of Rome and of Martin Luther. But there were also significant differences. The God that Calvin described was a stern, forbidding God. Calvin emphasized God's supreme authority rather than his mercy, which Luther stressed. Catholic teaching held that believers could win salvation through good works. Luther believed that faith in a merciful God alone assured salvation. Calvin, however, proposed a "doctrine of the elect," by which only those who were chosen by God were saved. Calvin believed in predestination. According to Calvin, God had already decided which persons were among the "elect." Some were predestined to go to heaven; others were predestined to go to hell.

Calvin devoted a separate section of the *Institutes* to the relations between church and state. He maintained that the authority of civil rulers rested on divine authority. Lawful civil rulers, he said, acted as "lieutenants of God." But he made very clear that obedience to civil government should not lead believers away from obedience to God.

In 1536, Calvin set out for the German free city of Strasbourg, where he hoped to pursue a life of scholarly research and writing. But on his way, Calvin wrote, "God thrust me into the game."

Warring armies prevented direct passage to his destination, so he took a detour southward to Geneva. There, he was persuaded to stay and help turn the wealthy independent city into a center of religious reform.

A Calvinist Government

With the help of like-minded reformers, Calvin set about to establish a form of government in Geneva that would put his beliefs into practice. Not only did he instruct the people of Geneva in the teachings he proposed in the *Institutes*, but he also attempted to make belief in those teachings a test by which to determine citizenship in Geneva.

The statement of belief required citizens "to follow Scripture alone." It spelled out what the reformers said Scripture taught concerning God, law, salvation, prayer, the church, and many other topics related to religion and government.

Calvin also attempted to impose rules of behavior on Genevans. He placed restrictions on such activities as gambling, singing, dancing, and drinking.

The reformers wanted "persons of good life and repute" to watch over their fellow citizens' behavior and report any notable offenses. Those who continued to behave immoderately were to be subject to excommunication.

At first, Genevan officials could not accept the system Calvin tried to establish. They ordered him and his fellow reformers into exile. But three years later they called him back.

Only Calvin, they decided, could reverse what they saw as a collapse of moral behavior in Geneva. And they were worried that if he did not return, Catholicism would be restored in Geneva.

Calvin drew up a new set of rules for Geneva. The new laws where based on the Bible. It was to be interpreted by pastors and enforced by the civil government. A group of pastors and elders was to determine worship and oversee the behavior of every Genevan.

Although Calvin had no official role in this group, he dominated it by the sheer force of his personality and prestige.

Calvin also started an academy to train ministers. His students traveled throughout

A view of Geneva, Switzerland where the French reformer, John Calvin, fled after leaving his native country.

85

Europe and carried his influence well beyond Switzerland to France, the Netherlands, England, and Scotland.

In France and England, Calvinism had only limited success, but in the Netherlands and in Scotland Calvinism eventually became the dominant form of religion.

In Switzerland and the Netherlands, followers of Calvin called themselves the *Reformed Church*. In Scotland, they became known as *Presbyterians*. The name referred to the Church's form of government, in which elders, or presbyters, played important roles.

From the Netherlands and Scotland, Calvinism spread to other parts of the world, carried both by merchants and immigrants.

Henry VIII

In England, Henry VIII rebelled against the Roman Church for personal reasons. Henry's rebellion was not Calvinist or Lutheran. Henry was a Roman Catholic who had been declared "Defender of the Faith" by the pope for a thesis Henry had written against Luther. But Henry later rebelled against the leadership of the Church when the pope would not allow Henry to divorce his first wife. Henry wanted to divorce his wife because she had

not given him the son he wanted as an heir to the throne.

When the pope refused to do as the king wished, Henry divorced his first wife anyway, and married a young lady named Anne Boleyn. The Roman Church then excommunicated Henry, who proceeded to establish the Church of England, with himself as its head.

The new Church of England, or Anglican Church, broke all ties with Rome. Although Henry had broken with Rome, the new English Church was not as radically Protestant as the Calvinist churches.

There were some Englishmen who thought the English Church had not been sufficiently reformed and remained too much like the old Roman Catholic Church. These people, known as Puritans, were heavily influenced by Calvin's thinking. In the early 1600s many of these Puritans would sail to New England.

From Church to Churches

Protestant Reformers like Luther, Zwingli, Calvin, and Henry VIII changed the face of Europe in the sixteenth century. No longer would there be a single Christian Church. Instead there would be many churches professing belief in Jesus Christ.

The effects of those changes remain apparent today throughout the world.

King Henry VIII began the Protestant revolution in England.

Reform Within the Catholic Church Many members of the Catholic Church who did not join the Protestant reformers also disagreed with some of the Catholic Church's teachings and practices. They too were upset at the behavior of Church leaders who seemed more interested in the material world than in the spiritual good of their people.

But some of them decided to try to change the Church from within. They hoped they could change the course of the Church while holding to the Catholic faith.

Long before Martin Luther nailed his 95 Theses to the church door in Wittenberg, believers concerned about the failures of the Church had tried to reform it. In some places, such as Spain, reform leadership came from the top. Early in the sixteenth century, for example, the most powerful cardinal of the Spanish Church grew alarmed at the ignorance of many priests and the low standards of behavior in many monasteries. He devoted himself to the reform and education of priests and to ridding Spain's monasteries of corruption. He also founded the University of Alcalá, which became a great center of learning. In large part because of his work, Lutheranism and Calvinism never firmly took root in Spain.

Elsewhere, the reform movement came from the grassroots, as it did in Italy. New monastic groups devoted themselves to spreading religion and serving the poor and the sick. The Oratory of Divine Love was founded for that purpose in the same year that Luther posted his theses. The Franciscan Order of the Capuchins was organized 11 years later. The group's name came from the *capucini*, or hoods, the members wore. The Capuchins were devoted to teaching and preaching among the poor and to living simple, pious lives. The Ursulines, an order of women dedicated to teaching girls and caring for the sick and the poor, started up in 1535.

The Spanish Priest

One of the most effective of these Catholic reformers hardly started out in life as a champion of religious renewal. His name was Ignatius of Loyola, and he was born in 1491 to a noble family in northern Spain. In the fateful

In this painting, Pope Paul III (seated in large chair) gives his official blessing to a group of Franciscan Capuchins who were, and still are, devoted to helping the poor people of the world.

year 1517, when Luther posted his theses, Ignatius became a knight in service to an influential relative. Later in life he admitted that at that time he was interested mostly in military undertakings and in gaining fame for his success as a soldier.

In 1521 his life took another course. During a battle his leg was shattered by a cannonball, leaving him crippled. While he recovered from his wounds, he asked for books, hoping to read tales of knightly heroes and beautiful ladies. But the only two books available in the castle where he was recovering were a life of Jesus and a book on the lives of the saints. What he read moved him deeply. After much thought he decided to change his life and do penance for his misdeeds.

In 1522, Ignatius made a pilgrimage to a shrine dedicated to Mary, the mother of Jesus. There, he hung his sword and dagger near Mary's statue and took up the life of a beggar. For nearly a year he devoted himself to prayer and penance. He also wrote a little book, called *The Spiritual Exercises*, as a guide to self-reform. He would revise his book several times in his life, and it would be widely read and followed.

After a pilgrimage to Jerusalem, Ignatius undertook a long period of study. He was in his thirties, an age at which most men of his time had completed their training for their careers. He forced himself to sit with schoolboys and learn the basics of Latin and other subjects. His period of study lasted more than 12 years, first in Spain and then in Paris.

Following this time period, Ignatius gathered around him a small group of like-minded men who shared his strong beliefs and devotion to good works. Because of his convictions and his enthusiasm for sharing them, Ignatius often came under suspicion and was even arrested and accused of being a heretic. He was charged with heresy 10 times and was sometimes imprisoned, but each time he was found not guilty.

In 1537, Ignatius and most of his companions were ordained priests and began to minister to people. Two years later, in Rome, the companions decided to form a permanent group dedicated to serving the pope in whatever way he commanded. In 1540, Pope Paul III approved the new group. They were given the name the Society of Jesus, and Ignatius was elected their first head. In time the members of the society became known as Jesuits.

The Jesuits

For the next 15 years, Ignatius led the Jesuits to remarkable growth and vigorous activity. They devoted themselves to preaching, caring for the needy, educating the young, converting nonbelievers to faith in Jesus Christ, and fighting against heresy. The structure of their society resembled the structure of the military, perhaps because of the military experience Ignatius had had as a young man. Society members accepted rigorous discipline. They gave unquestioned obedience to their general, as the head of the order was called.

The scenes in this illustration from the life of Ignatius Loyola (shown with halo [circle] around his head) depict him visiting friends, preaching to the people, and healing a woman's injured arm.

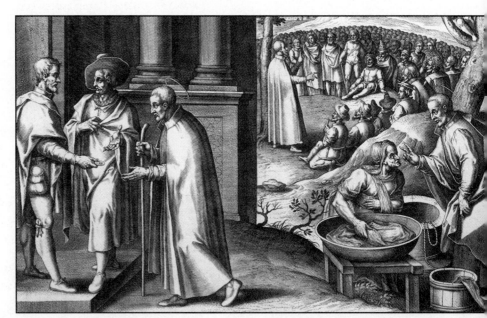

The Council of Trent met in 1545 to consider reforms for the Roman Catholic Church and reaffirm many of the Church's teachings.

The Jesuits became most well known for their work in education. Ignatius recognized the need for a highly educated force of members, so he established schools to train new members. In time the value of the Jesuits' training was widely recognized. Jesuits were asked to take over organizing and directing the work of many universities. By 1600, four of five Jesuits were teachers, and Jesuits were directing hundreds of schools and colleges. They approached their work with thorough organization and great zeal. Within 50 years they were the most important educators of Catholics in Europe.

Protestants came to look upon Ignatius as one of their principal opponents. So dedicated was he to the Catholic Church that he wrote, "We must always be ready to believe what seems to us white is black, if the hierarchical Church defines it so." He meant that Christians should accept without question what was taught officially by the Church.

Council of Trent

Although the Jesuits were highly influential in bringing about reform in the Church, they did not do so alone. In fact, the pope who approved their establishment, Pope Paul III, made important contributions of his own. He appointed a group of cardinals to investigate abuses in the Church.

Based on their recommendations, he began drastic reforms. He demanded that bishops actually live where they were supposed to serve. He set up the Roman Inquisition to investigate and root out heresy. Most important, he set up the Council of Trent, a meeting of Church leaders, which took place in northern Italy. The Council of Trent sought to examine and make clear the beliefs and practices of the Catholic Church.

The council began meeting in 1545 and did not conclude its work until 18 years and three popes later. The council was established in the hope of reuniting the various Christian groups that had developed, but the division among Christians had grown too great. Instead, the council vigorously reaffirmed many of the teachings Protestants had called into question.

Martin Luther and other reformers had declared that Scripture alone was the authority for Church teaching. The council said that Church tradition, that is, its time-honored practices and thinking, also provided such authority. And it claimed that the official church alone had the right to interpret Scripture.

Luther had taught that believers are saved by faith alone. The council agreed that faith is necessary for salvation. But it insisted that believers could also help assure their salvation by their good works and by their participation in the Church's sacraments.

Luther, Zwingli, Calvin, and other reformers had attacked the practice of indulgences. The council continued to teach that indulgences granted by the Church released believers from the punishment due for their sins. But the council also tried to correct some of the abuses associated with indulgences. And it warned against superstition in such matters as the worship of the saints and their relics.

Like the Protestant reformers, Catholic leaders of the Counter-Reformation made effective use of printing to achieve their aims. Printing presses made it possible for Ignatius of Loyola's *Spiritual Exercises* to reach a large audience, just as the presses had created large audiences for Luther's books and pamphlets and for Calvin's *Institutes*. Printing presses also allowed the Church to exercise greater control over some practices. Printed editions of the texts and directions to be used in worship services, for example, could now be made the same for everyone everywhere.

Forbidden Books

But some decisions made at Trent also aimed to hold in check the forces unleashed by Gutenberg's inventions. The council required authorization for new editions of the Bible in the languages of the people. It tried to discourage Bible-reading by laypersons. It established an Index of Forbidden Books. And it required writers of books on religious teaching to receive permission to publish their books.

In at least some ways, these efforts backfired. By forbidding certain publications, for example, the Church sometimes made them more attractive. The Index gave free publicity for the publications it listed. Copies of the Index were used by enterprising printers outside the control of the Church to determine which books to publish. The Index also assisted Protestants interested in attacking Roman Catholic teachings.

The dedicated work of men such as Ignatius of Loyola, who would become a saint, and members of various religious groups instilled a renewed sense of purpose in the Roman Catholic Church. The work of the Council of Trent succeeded in ridding the church of blatant abuses. It emphasized the importance of education, especially the training of its priests and teachers. It reaffirmed the Church's basic teachings and established a uniform set of rules and practices throughout the Church. In this way the Church survived the Protestant Reformation.

The Catholic Counter-Reformation came about as a response to the teachings of Protestant leaders such as Luther (first row center) and Calvin (rear row left), and others shown in this illustration.

C **hanging Scientific Ideas** While Catholics and Protestants engaged in religious disputes, scientific ideas were also changing. Gutenberg's combination of movable type and the printing press made it possible to spread new scientific ideas far and wide and with great speed.

Both Protestants and Catholics were initially skeptical about some of the new scientific ideas, but these discoveries would eventually revolutionize our understanding of the world in which we live.

The Polish Astronomer

In 1473, in what is now northern Poland, Nicholas Copernicus was born to a prominent merchant family. Young Nicholas received an excellent education. He studied first at the University of Kraków, where he became interested in mathematics and astronomy. Then he received further training at two universities in Italy, studying ancient Greek, philosophy, mathematics, medicine, and law.

By the time he came home to northern Poland, Copernicus had mastered almost all the learning of his day. From his uncle, a Roman Catholic bishop, Copernicus received a Church office that paid him an income for the rest of his life. Holding this office required him to become a priest, and he remained a loyal Catholic until his death.

Nicholas Copernicus was a Polish astronomer who taught that Earth and other planets in our solar system revolved around the sun.

The Church was very interested in astronomical problems in the 1500s because it realized that the calendar—designed by Julius Caesar and called the Julian calendar—was inaccurate. Christians were not correctly calculating the date of Easter. Scholars had to study the apparent movements of the sun and planets in order to determine more accurately the length of the year.

As he worked on this problem, Copernicus grew dissatisfied with the common understanding of the universe. Since ancient times, almost everyone had agreed that Earth stood still at the center of the universe.

In the second century A.D., the Greek astronomer Ptolemy had used complicated geometry to describe how the sun, moon, planets, and the stars circled Earth. Other experts said that these heavenly bodies moved on transparent spheres. But whatever the actual mechanism, Ptolemy and all the medieval astronomers who came after him believed that this system explained the clock-like regularity of the movements of the heavens in the course of every year.

However, Ptolemy's system was not totally accurate, and over 1,300 years his small errors had piled up until the calendar used in Copernicus's lifetime was off by about ten days! Copernicus began looking for a different way to figure out exactly how long a year was.

In ancient times, he learned, other Greeks had theorized that the sun stood at the center of the universe and that Earth, planets, and stars moved around it. Could these theories be used to recalculate at what speed the heavens appeared to rotate around Earth every year? But there were problems.

First, it seemed to violate common sense to suppose that Earth rotated around the sun—wouldn't we just spin off into space? Second, all the scientific wisdom that Europeans had inherited from ancient Greece said that Earth was solid, whereas the heavens were light and fiery—how could something as heavy as Earth be moving? Third, the Bible said that once God had made the sun stand still—wasn't it wrong to say that Earth moved and the sun didn't? Fourth, would Earth still be the center of God's creation if it turned out to be just one more planet circling the sun?

These objections didn't stop Copernicus. He concluded that Ptolemy was wrong, and he decided "to read again the works of all the philosophers" in order to find a better answer.

Copernicus would not have been able to undertake this study if it had not been for Johannes Gutenberg's inventions. Because of them, the Polish astronomer was able to examine a far wider variety of records and references than

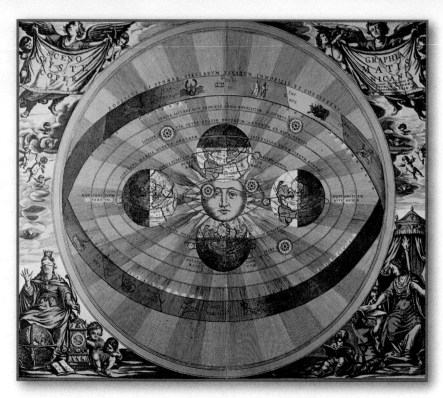

This seventeenth-century Dutch illustration is a drawing of the Copernican theory showing the sun in the center of the revolving planets.

any astronomer before him. He did not have to travel to distant libraries to read and copy hand-duplicated manuscripts. Instead, printed texts were available to him in Poland.

The Observations of Copernicus

As Copernicus studied the stars and reviewed what others had written about them, he became convinced that it was Earth that moved and that the sun remained stationary. Furthermore, he concluded that Earth moved in two ways: It turned on its own axis each day, and it revolved with the other planets around the sun each year. In his view, then, the sun, not Earth, was the center of its own system within a larger universe.

Although Copernicus came to these conclusions early in the sixteenth century, he would not publish them until many years later. In the meantime he gained renown as an astronomer. He even gained the favor of the pope, who approved the diagrams and calculations Copernicus used to explain his theories. In 1536, the Polish scientist was given permission to publish his findings.

An initial effort to have Copernicus's findings published in Germany failed, because of opposition from Martin Luther and other Protestant reformers. Luther had nothing good to say about Copernicus. "People gave ear to an upstart astrologer who strove to show that Earth revolves, not the heavens or the firmament, the sun and the moon," he said. "This fool wishes to reverse the entire science of astronomy; but sacred Scripture tells us that Joshua commanded the sun to stand still, and not the earth."

John Calvin, Luther's counterpart in Switzerland, was equally sarcastic in rejecting Copernicus. Calvin cited the opening verse of Psalm 93: "He has made the world firm, not to be moved." He went on to say, "Who will venture to place the authority of Copernicus above that of the Holy Spirit?"

Copernicus's book, *On the Revolution of the Heavenly Bodies*, finally was published in 1543. It is said that a copy of the book was brought to Copernicus on the day he died, May 24, 1543.

Copernicus's work provided a new starting point for the work of astronomers to follow him. Few made greater advances based on his work than the Italian scientist Galileo Galilei. And few suffered more for their efforts.

The Italian astronomer Galileo points to an object in the distance as one of his associates views the object through the telescope Galileo used to study the heavens.

The Italian Scientist

Galileo was born in Pisa, Italy, in 1564, just 21 years after Copernicus had died. He became fascinated with mathematics after a visit to the cathedral church in Pisa in 1583. There, he observed a lamp swinging back and forth at the end of a chain. He observed that no matter how far the lamp swung, each swing seemed to take the same amount of time.

The young man followed up his observation by carrying out a series of experiments with all sorts of pendulums. He discovered that his observation had been correct. Based on his discovery, he designed an adjustable pendulum that doctors could use to measure the pulses of their patients. Later, this discovery provided the basis for the development of the pendulum clock.

Until his observations of the lamp in the church, Galileo had received no formal instruction in mathematics. This event, along with a geometry lesson he overheard quite by chance, aroused his interest. He began to apply himself to the study of mathematics with great devotion. In time, he won appointments to important mathematics teaching positions, including a post at the University of Padua, where Copernicus had once studied. He showed himself well able to combine formidable mathematical skills with the observation, experimentation, and application skills he had demonstrated with pendulums.

Early in his career, Galileo showed great interest in determining the laws that govern the movement of physical objects in space. He disproved the notion, put forward by the ancient Greek philosopher Aristotle, that objects of different weights fall at different speeds. The story is often told that he arrived at his conclusion by observing what happened when he dropped two objects of unequal weight from the top of the now famous tower of Pisa. The story appears to be a legend, but it serves to emphasize how important experimentation and observation were to Galileo. In many ways he may be said to have founded the modern experimental method.

In 1609, Galileo learned of the recent invention of the telescope. In a short time he had built one of his own, which he began to use in astronomical observation. He had long been convinced that Copernicus's theory of a sun-centered universe in which the planets revolve around the sun was accurate. His use of the telescope confirmed his belief.

Galileo published the results of his telescopic observations in 1610, in a book titled *The Starry Messenger*. Opposition came quickly. Many Catholic and Protestant theologians felt threatened by his work. They believed it was contrary to Scripture. Catholic theologians persuaded the Church's Holy Office to take action against Galileo. The Holy Office was the agency of the Church responsible for rooting out heresy.

In 1616, Galileo was summoned before the Church's chief theologian. Galileo was informed that the Church had decided to condemn the ideas of Copernicus, upon which the Italian scientist had based his work. From now on, the writings of Copernicus would be placed on the Index of Forbidden Books. Galileo was told he could not teach that the work of Copernicus was true, but only theory. He agreed to do so, knowing full well that severe penalties, even torture, might follow if he did not.

For several years, Galileo worked quietly, continuing his studies but not publishing his results. In 1632 he broke his silence. He published the greatest of his astronomical writings, the *Dialogue on the Two Chief Systems of the World—Ptolemaic and Copernican*. It was a thorough defense of the Copernican system, written in Italian, not Latin, and intended for a wide audience. The reaction from the Catholic Church was swift. Although Galileo was now an old man, he was ordered to appear in Rome to be tried for heresy.

A council of high-ranking Roman Catholic Church officials put Galileo on trial for his teachings and condemned him for supporting the theory that Earth revolved around the sun. Galileo is the figure in black seated in the center of the painting.

The Church Condemns Galileo

On June 21, 1633, the *Dialogue* was condemned by the Church, and its author ordered to take back his support for the teachings of Copernicus. After being sentenced to imprisonment, the old scientist was forced to kneel and deny what he believed.

"I am . . . suspect[ed] of heresy," he was made to say, "that is, of having held and believed that the sun is the center of the world and immovable, and that the earth is not its center and moves." He continued, "I do abjure, curse, and detest [these] . . . errors and heresies." But, according to legend, when he had completed his confession, he stood up and stamped his foot . . . and, muttered to himself, "But it *does* move!"

Galileo spent the last eight years of his life under house arrest. He did not publish books on astronomy, but he did publish writing about motion and the structure of matter that provided a basis for modern physics.

In the years following his death in 1642, other scientists took up Galileo's work. In time the Copernican view of the universe prevailed among scientists and the educated public. It took the Church a little longer to recognize officially that it had done Copernicus and Galileo a great injustice. It took more than 200 years for the Church to grant permission to publish a book that presented the Copernican system as a physical fact.

Glossary

alloy two or more metals that have been melted and then fused together

confederacy an alliance; a union of persons, groups, nations, or states

foundry an establishment where metal is melted and poured into molds

heretic a person who teaches false ideas or opposes religious authority

monastery a house where a group of monks live and work

monk a man who is a member of a religious order

penance an act, such as praying, done to repent for a sin or wrongdoing

pilgrimage a journey to a sacred place or shrine

purgatory according to Catholicism, the place where, after death, souls are punished for a certain period of time

theology the study of religion

QUEEN ELIZABETH, BORN 1533. CROWNED 1559. DIED 1603. DAUGHTER OF KING HENRY VIII AND QUEEN A

England:
Golden Age to Glorious Revolution

Contents

GE GOWER

Elizabeth 1

ong Live the Queen According to legend, 25-year-old Elizabeth was sitting under an oak tree reading the Greek Bible on the morning of November 17, 1558. She was expecting important news. Maybe she had decided to read outside so that she could hear the hoofbeats of a horse as it galloped toward her house in the English countryside.

The horseman arrived shortly before noon that day. He must have bowed as he presented Elizabeth with the ring of Mary Tudor, Elizabeth's older half-sister. The ring was proof that Mary was dead. And if Mary was dead, Elizabeth was now queen of England.

Elizabeth is said to have closed her book and fallen to her knees. Speaking in Latin, she said, "Time has brought us to this place. This is the Lord's doing, and it is marvelous in our eyes."

A Dress of Gold and a Velvet Cape

Elizabeth certainly knew about time. She had been waiting to become queen for nearly 12 years, while first her sickly half-brother, Edward VI, and then her half-sister, Mary Tudor, sat on the throne. During these years, Elizabeth had had time to plan.

Within a week of Mary's death, she marched into London with a thousand men and women whom she had chosen as her advisers and servants.

From the beginning, Elizabeth understood that although heredity had put her on the throne, she needed the support of the English people to stay there. A march with a thousand people was a way to show her power.

The day that Elizabeth I was crowned, her **coronation** day, was a spectacular event. Ladies of the English court had sent to Belgium for silks and velvets to be made into gowns for the great day. Although years of religious conflict and war had left England deeply in debt,

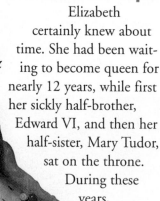

> **vocabulary**
> **coronation** the ceremony or act of crowning a ruler

Elizabeth I made sure her coronation would be unforgettable. She wore a dress of gold and a cape of crimson velvet lined with fur. On her head sat a gold crown.

These clothes were heavy and uncomfortable, but they looked like the clothes of a powerful monarch. That was exactly the impression Elizabeth I wanted to give to all who attended the coronation.

The coronation was a religious ceremony. Elizabeth I wanted to end the conflicts in England between Catholics and Protestants. At her coronation, she was crowned by a bishop, an official of the Catholic Church, but she insisted that the bishop read from an English Bible, the kind used

Queen Elizabeth I ruled England for almost a half century, raising her kingdom to a peak of glory.

by Protestants, rather than the Latin Bible used by Catholics.

A Dangerous Situation

From the time when Elizabeth was a little girl, her life had been in danger. England was a nation divided by religion. Elizabeth's father, King Henry VIII, had broken from the Roman Catholic Church in 1529 because the pope would not give him permission to divorce his first wife and marry Anne Boleyn, who later became Elizabeth's mother. Henry married Anne anyway and quickly established the Church of England, to be independent of the Roman Catholic Church. He proclaimed himself head of the Church of England. However, when Elizabeth was only two years old, her father had her mother executed.

After King Henry's death, English Catholics wanted a Catholic ruler again. Mary Tudor, Elizabeth's half-sister, was Catholic. In 1553 she became Queen Mary I and ruled for five years. Mary restored power to the Catholic Church in England and **persecuted** Protestants, many of whom were burned at the stake. Her brutal persecution of Protestants earned her the name "Bloody Mary."

Unlike Mary I, Elizabeth I was a Protestant, though she liked many of the Catholic rituals and customs. When she took the throne, however, there was a growing group of Protestants in England who wanted to do away with Catholic influences. Elizabeth faced the difficult task of keeping the peace between these two groups.

> **vocabulary**
> **persecute** to hurt or harass a group of people, in this case for their religion

Prisoners held in the infamous Tower of London included Elizabeth I and her mother, Anne Boleyn.

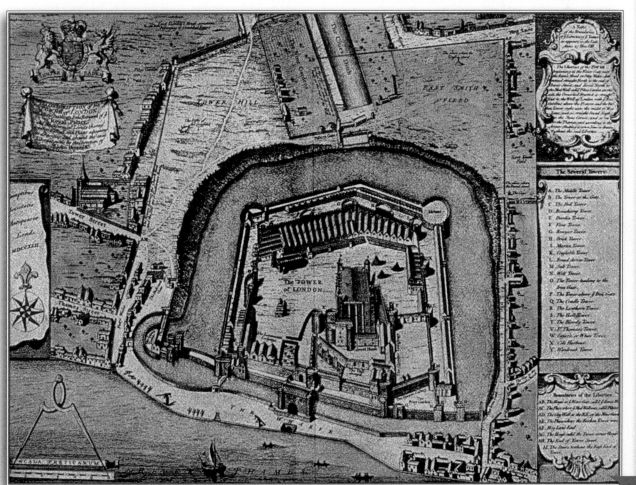

From an early age, Elizabeth had learned to pay attention to what was going on around her and to avoid putting in writing any thoughts or beliefs that her enemies might use against her. While Mary I was queen, Elizabeth had been arrested and imprisoned in the Tower of London. For two months, Elizabeth had lived in a cold, drafty cell, never knowing whether or when she might be executed. Queen Mary spared her life, but Elizabeth never forgot the horror of awaiting her own death sentence.

Even after she became queen, Elizabeth I had to be very careful. Another Mary, this one known as Mary Stuart or Mary Queen of Scots, plotted against Elizabeth. This Mary was the niece of Henry VIII. She believed that she herself, not Elizabeth, belonged on the throne of England, because the Catholic Church did not recognize Henry's marriage to Elizabeth's mother.

Elizabeth's advisers told her to have Mary Queen of Scots put to death. At first Elizabeth was reluctant to execute a relative who was a queen in her own right. Mary was held in custody for more than ten years, but when she was finally caught in a plot to have Elizabeth killed, she was brought to trial.

The verdict? Guilty. The punishment? Death.

Queen of Her People, Bride of Her Nation

In spite of this execution, Elizabeth I was known by many of her people as Good Queen Bess. Under Mary I, according to one writer, England had known "nothing but fining, beheading, hanging, quartering, and burning." Many in England breathed a sigh of relief when Mary I died. Elizabeth knew that one of the reasons Mary had spared her life in the Tower of London was that the English people loved Elizabeth. She believed that God had put her on earth to rule her subjects and to serve them. The day before she was crowned, Elizabeth said, "Be ye assured that I will be as good unto you as ever queen was to her people."

Throughout the first decades of her reign, Elizabeth's advisers and **Parliament** urged her to marry. They wanted her to have a child who could take the throne when she died. They also thought that a woman could not rule as well as a man. Many ambitious men asked for her hand in marriage, but Elizabeth I argued

> **vocabulary**
> **Parliament** the national legislative body of nobles and elected representatives in England

For 45 years Elizabeth's ornate signature appeared on England's legal documents.

To impress her subjects, Elizabeth wore lavish jewelry and expensive gowns when she went on her royal progresses.

that marriage would only distract her from her many duties as queen. She considered England to be her husband and her family. "Behold," she said, displaying her coronation ring before Parliament, "the pledge of this my wedlock and marriage with my kingdom. Every one of you, and as many as are Englishmen, are children and kinsmen to me."

The Queen's "Progresses"

Frequently in summer, Queen Elizabeth I and her court left London on journeys called "progresses." One reason was that she needed to escape from the hot, dirty, and smelly city. London was the largest city in Europe at that time. It had 90,000 people and no sewers, no running water, and no toilets. Because there was no refrigeration, food spoiled quickly. People didn't understand then that unclean conditions spread disease, but they did know that the city was unhealthy in the summer.

The number of people in Queen Elizabeth's court was enough to fill a large village. When her courtiers and their horses arrived at one of the queen's more than 60 castles or houses, they quickly ate all the available food. Although the queen's houses were grand, many were not big enough to fit her whole court. Some of the people who waited on her had to sleep in tents on the grounds. And with so many people in one place but without any plumbing, sewers, or an easy way to dispose of garbage, the area quickly became filthy and even unhealthy. People had to clear out so that the area could be cleaned up.

The trip from one residence to another was no small undertaking. Such a trip typically involved hundreds of carts and thousands of pack horses. When Queen Elizabeth I traveled, she was accompanied by her government officials, cooks, doctors, carpenters, people who sew and do laundry, and people to care for horses. The luggage in the caravan included the queen's clothes and jewels, documents, dishes, linens, equipment, tools, and her massive carved bed.

Even the best and most widely used roads in England were very poor by today's standards. They were made of dirt, which in wet weather became mud. In dry weather, deep ruts could tip a cart over or break its axle. The caravan of horses and carts could cover only 10 or 12 miles a day, roughly the distance that someone might cover on foot. It wasn't unusual for the journey from one castle to another to last a month. During this time, the queen and her advisers continued to conduct the business of the kingdom.

As Queen Elizabeth I traveled, she sometimes saved money by staying overnight in the houses of different nobles. It was very expensive for an **aristocrat** to feed the queen and her court, yet these nobles competed for the honor of hosting her. Their power and position depended on her favor. Some aristocrats even added extra rooms to their houses or added buildings to their estates in preparation for their queen's arrival!

Elizabeth's progresses were also exciting for the common people in her kingdom. She could see how they lived, the state of their towns and farms. And the commoners were allowed a chance to see their queen. People put on plays and pageants in her honor. Elizabeth listened patiently to their speeches and once stood in the rain to watch a presentation by schoolboys. The women of one town prepared a feast of 160 different dishes for her. To show her trust for her subjects, she ate the foods they had prepared without having a courtier taste them first to make sure they had not been poisoned.

At every opportunity, Queen Elizabeth I told her subjects that she loved them and expressed her appreciation for their loyalty. These progresses did a great deal to increase the people's affection for Elizabeth.

Gloriana

Elizabeth combined practices of both the Catholic Church and the Protestant Church when she reestablished the Church of England.

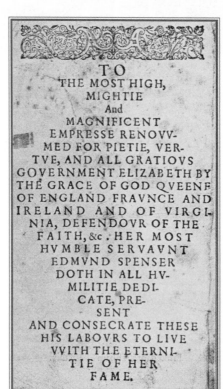

TO THE MOST HIGH, MIGHTIE And MAGNIFICENT EMPRESSE RENOVV-MED FOR PIETIE, VER-TVE, AND ALL GRATIOVS GOVERNMENT ELIZABETH BY THE GRACE OF GOD QVEENE OF ENGLAND FRAVNCE AND IRELAND AND OF VIRGI-NIA, DEFENDOVR OF THE FAITH,&c. HER MOST HVMBLE SERVAVNT EDMVND SPENSER DOTH IN ALL HV-MILITIE DEDI-CATE, PRE-SENT AND CONSECRATE THESE HIS LABOVRS TO LIVE VVITH THE ETERNI-TIE OF HER FAME.

The poet Edmund Spencer dedicated his poem The Faerie Queene *to Queen Elizabeth.*

Priests wore robes, as in the Catholic Church, but they were allowed to marry. Church services were held in English, as Protestants wished, but altars were adorned with crucifixes and candles in the style of Catholic cathedrals. Under Elizabeth I, neither Catholics nor Protestants were persecuted for their religion. People who disobeyed her wishes were another matter, however.

Perhaps because of the threats on her life, Elizabeth expected complete loyalty from everyone in her court. Her maids, who were women from noble families, had to get permission from her before they could marry. If one of them married in secret, Elizabeth might imprison the husband until she could be sure that he wasn't part of a plot against her.

Elizabeth demanded loyalty, and she received it. In a well-known poem of that time called "The Faerie Queene," Elizabeth I is portrayed as a goddess named Gloriana. The poem describes the ways in which Gloriana's knights try to outdo one another to please her.

William Shakespeare, the greatest playwright of the English language, wrote plays to entertain Elizabeth; composers wrote songs for her to enjoy. Francis Drake sailed around the world for her. She transformed England from a land weakened by conflict into a unified kingdom that could vie with mighty Spain and France for power.

Elizabeth I ruled for 45 years, from 1558 to 1603. By the time she died, the queen who was known by so many names—Good Queen Bess, the Virgin Queen, Gloriana—had given her own name to her era. It was a time of great literature and exploration, but it was not named for William Shakespeare or Sir Francis Drake. We remember it today as the Elizabethan Age.

Sir Francis Drake Depending on your point of view, Sir Francis Drake was either a hero or a pirate. To English people and to Queen Elizabeth I, he was a brave and skilled sea commander. To the Spanish, however, Drake was a pirate.

During the late 1500s, while Elizabeth I was on the throne, the Spanish were building a great empire. Spanish **galleons** carried gold, silver, precious stones, expensive dyes, and sugar across the ocean from colonies in the Americas. Sir Francis Drake and other English sailors attacked Spanish ships and grabbed some of these riches for themselves.

> **vocabulary**
> **galleon** a large Spanish sailing vessel, used as a warship or a trader

A Spanish nobleman whose ship was attacked by Drake described him this way:

He is called Francisco Drac, and is a man of about 35 years of age, low of stature [short] with a fair [light] beard, and is one of the greatest mariners that sail the seas, both as a navigator and as a commander. His vessel is a galleon of nearly 400 tons, and is a perfect sailor. She is manned with 100 men, all of an age for warfare. He treats them with affection, and they treat him with respect.

The Spanish nobleman added that Drake eats from "silver dishes with gold borders and gilded garlands. He carries all possible dainties and perfumed waters. He said that many of these had been given to him by the queen. . . . He dines and sups to the music of [violins]."

Elizabeth I touches a sword to Francis Drake aboard his ship, Golden Hind, *thereby making him a knight.*

English cannons blasted the ships of the Spanish Armada as they tried to escape.

Our Golden Knight

Francis Drake left home for the voyage of his life in 1577. A trip around the world! As he sailed down the west coast of Africa and then across the Atlantic Ocean and around the Americas, he took every opportunity to attack ships of Spain and Portugal and to seize their riches. By the time Drake returned to England three years later, the Spanish ambassador to London called him "the master-thief of the unknown world." The following year, however, Queen Elizabeth I dubbed him "our golden knight" and he became Sir Francis Drake.

To honor their queen and to cut into Spain's mastery of the seas, Englishmen like Drake explored the world in search of riches. Expeditions set out to establish trade routes across the Pacific Ocean. Walter Raleigh, another of Elizabeth's favorites, tried to start a colony in the Americas. The first Roanoke colony, on an island off the coast of North Carolina, didn't last. Most of the colonists returned home in a few months. A second group disappeared a short while later. Decades would pass before the English succeeded in establishing a permanent colony in North America.

The Invincible Armada

Whether or not the English colonies succeeded, however, they still annoyed the Spanish. Spain had claimed North America as its own. It had colonies in Mexico and in the areas of the United States now known as Florida, California, New Mexico, Texas, and Arizona. Nor did the Spanish like the way Drake and others attacked their ships and seized their treasure. There was more than that, however, to the tension between the two countries. Just before Queen Elizabeth I had Mary Queen of Scots executed, Mary had named the Spanish king Philip II as successor to the English throne. Remember, unlike Elizabeth, Mary and Philip were both Catholic. The pope later offered King Philip "a million in gold" if he would conquer England.

English and Spanish ships engaged in many battles over the years. After Sir Francis Drake led a surprise attack that destroyed ships in a Spanish harbor, Philip began plans to invade England and conquer it once and for all.

People heard rumors that Spain was building a fleet of warships called the armada (ahr MAH duh) for an attack on England. Day and night, coast guards peered across the ocean looking for the Spanish fleet. The English placed pans of flammable resin on little platforms on every hill of their largely flat island. If a lookout spotted an invading ship, he would light one of these beacons. As soon as the people guarding the beacons farther inland saw a coast beacon shining, they would light their beacons, signaling others farther inland. In this way, news of an invasion would spread quickly through England.

Finally, in July 1588, the Spanish fleet was spotted. Dubbed the Invincible Armada by the pope, because they could not be defeated, the Spanish ships were an impressive sight. The armada had 130 large ships that sailed in a tight formation. They were like floating fortresses, "with lofty turrets like castles." They advanced "very slowly, though with full sails, as if the winds were tired of carrying them, and the ocean groaning under the weight of them." These ships carried more than 30,000 people, as well as horses and weapons. The Spanish weren't planning a sea battle. They planned to invade England and capture it with a land battle.

The English fleet, on the other hand, carried only 1,500 men. Their ships were small, but they were nimble. The English sailors also knew all the currents of the waters in which they fought. They darted around the edges of the Spanish formation, picking at the outermost ships. "Their force is wonderful, great, and strong," said the admiral of the English fleet, "yet we pluck their feathers little by little."

The English set empty ships on fire and let the tide carry them toward the armada, forcing the Spanish ships to break out of their tight formation to avoid the flames. Still, Spain might have conquered England if it hadn't been for the weather. As the Spanish retreated, a powerful storm blew dozens of their ships onto the rocks of Ireland and Scotland. The ships that survived withdrew to Spain. Nearly half of the men in the Spanish armada had been killed.

A Date to Remember: 1588 Spanish Armada Defeated

Prayer and Thanksgiving

At that time, Spain was the greatest sea power in the world. Many of the English people were truly terrified that Spain would conquer England and make it a Catholic country once again. King Philip of Spain had counted on England's Catholics to rise against their queen and aid his invasion. Instead, the English Catholics stayed loyal to their own government. This gives us some idea of how much progress Queen Elizabeth I had made in healing the religious conflicts in her kingdom. Nonetheless, many people in England used the conflict with Spain as a reason to distrust Catholics.

In November 1588, Elizabeth declared a day of thanksgiving. Everyone was urged to go to church, just as Elizabeth herself did. She thanked God and asked her people to do the same. "At which," said one writer, "the people with a loud acclamation wished her a most long and happy life, to the confusion of her foes."

England's greatest foreign enemy had been defeated, opening the way for England to become a great sea power. Conflicts within the country still smoldered, however.

"And though you have had, and may have, many princes more mighty and wise sitting in this seat, yet you never had nor shall have, any that will be more careful and loving."

Elizabeth was known for her great speeches. Here is an excerpt from her famous farewell speech to Parliament in 1601.

After Elizabeth Queen Elizabeth I lived to be nearly 70 years old, which was a long life for someone in the 1500s—and for someone whom so many people had wanted to kill! It is said that as she lay dying, she whispered to the archbishop of Canterbury the name of her successor to the throne.

Whom do you think she named as the next ruler? She named her closest relative, James Stuart, who was son of her great enemy, Mary Queen of Scots.

Unlike his mother, however, James VI of Scotland was a Protestant. In England he would be called James I.

King James I

James I believed he ruled by **divine right of kings**. Like Elizabeth I, King James I wanted to keep the Protestants and Catholics at peace with each other. He held a conference in 1604, shortly after he was crowned, to try to bring the two groups together. The only thing they agreed on, however, was that England needed a new translation of the Bible. James ordered this, and the result was the King James Version of the Bible. It became one of the most widely read and quoted books in English.

In 1607 a group of English colonists settled in Virginia and named their colony Jamestown, after King James I.

A scholar at heart, King James I supervised the translation of the Bible. The King James Version is still used in the Church of England.

The Jamestown settlers endured many hardships, but they finally succeeded in establishing the first permanent English colony in North America.

Around this same time, a group of Protestants in England became unhappy with the Church of England and decided they wanted to worship in a simpler way that they felt was truer to the faith of the Bible. They were called Puritans because they wanted to "purify" the Church of England.

In 1620 a group of 103 Puritans who were unhappy in England decided to sail to North America to create a colony based on strict Puritan rules. They settled in Plymouth, Massachusetts, and we remember them today as the Pilgrims. Later, other English Puritans followed their example and settled in "New England," where they encouraged living in plain and simple ways and frowned on such pastimes as dancing, gambling, and wearing fancy clothes and jewelry.

When King James I died in 1625, his son, Charles I, took the throne.

> **vocabulary**
> **divine right of kings** the belief that kings and queens have a God-given right to rule, and that rebellion against them is a sin

Trouble All Around

Charles I was a weak, sickly child. He didn't walk until he was seven years old. Like his father, James I, and Queen Elizabeth I before him, he believed that he had been chosen by God to rule England. Unlike Elizabeth, however, Charles did not understand that he needed the support of his subjects to stay on the throne.

Charles I was devoted to the Church of England, but he decided to choose as his wife Henrietta Maria, the Catholic daughter of the king of France. As monarchs did back then, Charles married to form an alliance with another powerful country. The idea was that, if the king of England married a French princess, the two countries would be less likely to go to war against each other.

Charles I had his wife, Henrietta Maria, pawn the crown jewels of England for money that would finance a civil war.

The French Roman Catholic princess brought a large group of priests and other French Catholics to wait on her. When some members of the English government found this out, they were furious. Within a year, King Charles was forced to send a bishop, 29 priests, and 410 of the queen's attendants back to France.

The Church of England was headed by the king or queen of England, but it kept many of the rituals of the Catholic Church in its church services. As we have seen, some Protestants, such as the Puritans, did not like this.

By now the Puritans had become a more powerful group. In fact, many of the men in the English Parliament were Puritans or agreed with Puritan ideas. In Scotland, which was also part of Charles's kingdom, Protestants who wanted to remove Catholic influences from the Church of England were called Presbyterians.

Puritans and Presbyterians were suspicious both of Charles's Catholic wife and of his love of candles, statues, and other elaborate details in what they thought should be simple Protestant church services.

A Prayer Book and a Civil War

Worried about the growing power of the Puritans, King Charles ordered Presbyterians in Scotland to start using a prayer book based on the one used in the Church of England. One day an outraged Scotswoman threw a stool at a bishop who tried to read from the book, and riots broke out.

When Charles refused to take back his order, a Scottish army marched into England.

The English Parliament distrusted King Charles so much that it had not given him money for an army for many years. The army that he sent to fight the Scots in 1639 was unpaid and poorly equipped. The English soldiers ran away from the enemy. Charles asked members of Parliament again for money, but they responded by having two of his most important ministers, or officials, arrested. Charles then marched to Parliament with 300 soldiers, intending to arrest the ringleaders of the rebellion, but the men he was looking for escaped.

"I see the birds have flown," said Charles, and it was clear now that he had few, if any, supporters in Parliament. London was in an uproar, and King Charles realized that it wasn't safe for

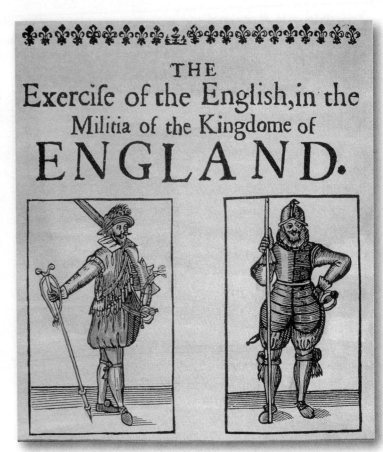

In the English Civil War, the Cavaliers, shown on the left, supported King Charles I. The Puritans, known as Roundheads, shown on the right, supported Parliament. The Roundheads had two advantages to winning the war: they had more money and they outnumbered the Cavaliers.

THE Exercife of the English, in the Militia of the Kingdome of ENGLAND.

A Cavalier   A Roundhead

him to stay in the capital city. In 1642 he escaped to northern England to raise an army with which to fight his own Parliament.

Roundheads and Cavaliers

Like most civil wars, this one was painful and confusing. Families were divided, with some members supporting the king and others supporting Parliament. Some were loyal to the king even though they thought he was at fault. One loyal nobleman, who was later killed in the war, said, "I will not do so base a thing as to forsake my king; and I choose rather to lose my life, which I am sure to do."

In general, nobles who had country estates supported the king. Many of the people who worked on these estates supported the king as well, either out of loyalty to their landowners or because they were afraid to take another position. The Royalists, those who supported the king, were also called Cavaliers. The word comes from the Spanish word *caballero*, which means "a man on horseback." Cavaliers were given that name by those who opposed them, who shouted "cavalier" at the well-dressed, aggressive young nobles who strutted about the streets of London. Today we might describe someone who seems arrogant and thoughtless as cavalier.

Most people who lived in London and other large towns supported Parliament. These people were known as Roundheads because they favored the short, simple haircuts of Puritans.

Soldiers on both sides lived in crowded, dirty conditions that allowed the spread of deadly diseases. These diseases sometimes spread to nearby towns and killed people who weren't even fighting in the war. Also, soldiers demanded taxes, food, and livestock from the villages through which they marched on their way to battle. All in all, the war brought suffering to everyone, even those who tried to stay out of it. By the end of the war, about one in five people in England had been killed by the war or the diseases it brought.

he End of the War The English civil war dragged on for four years. One reason it lasted so long was that neither side really knew what it was doing. In those days, England had no standing army—that is, no permanent troops ready to go to war at a moment's notice. Most of the men fighting on both sides were poorly trained.

The few professional soldiers in the country fought on the side of the king. Even the commanders had had very little experience on the battlefield. Yet there was one commander on Parliament's side who, though inexperienced like all the rest, seemed to have a talent for leadership. That man was Oliver Cromwell.

Young Oliver Cromwell

Oliver Cromwell was born four years before the death of Queen Elizabeth I. His family belonged to the class of people called the **gentry**. Members of the gentry were one step lower than nobles on the social ladder.

> **vocabulary**
> **gentry** people who own land and have high social standing but no titles of nobility

One of Cromwell's ancestors had been a high-ranking adviser to King Henry VIII, Queen Elizabeth I's father. When Henry broke away from the Catholic Church, he took land away from the monasteries in England and gave it to his friends. Cromwell's family had received a large grant of land.

Oliver Cromwell was a short man with a large nose. He knew he wasn't handsome, but he didn't care to be falsely flattered. Once, when he was having his portrait painted, he said, "Paint my picture truly like me . . . pimples, warts, and everything."

What Cromwell lacked in good looks, however, he made up in spirit. Throughout his life he was known for his restless energy. He wasn't much of a student. He preferred sports to studies, but he did like studying mathematics, and he enjoyed reading history books.

Although Cromwell was raised in a Puritan family, it wasn't until he was nearly 30 that he became deeply religious. After suffering from a series of mysterious illnesses, he had a religious experience and dedicated himself to serving God, which in Cromwell's view meant practicing self-discipline. He found ways to put his energy to use.

Oliver Cromwell was a better military general than political leader.

Cromwell in the Civil War

Cromwell was not happy under the rule of Charles I. He did not approve of Charles's sympathy for Catholics. Also, Cromwell was a member of Parliament, which was having its own troubles with the king.

When the English civil war began in 1642, Cromwell pulled together a troop of soldiers and led them in the fight against Charles I. As their captain, Cromwell demanded of his men the same qualities he demanded of himself: selfless dedication and strict discipline.

His troops won battle after battle, and Cromwell rose in rank. He began to build up Parliament's armies, trying to accept only religious men to serve as soldiers. He thought that a belief in God would give them a reason to fight. He did not allow swearing or drunkenness among his troops. He promoted officers according to their performance. Previously, a man's rank was often based on his wealth, not his skill as a leader. Cromwell said, "I had rather have a plain russet-coated captain that knows what he fights for, and loves what he knows, than that which you call a gentleman and is nothing else."

Parliament used many of Cromwell's ideas to create England's first national army, known as the New Model Army. Before this, different armies had been loyal to individual noblemen, not to the country as a whole. In 1646 the king's Royalist forces surrendered to the New Model Army. Parliament had won the war.

Once Parliament no longer had to fight the king, many disagreements broke out among different members of Parliament. Now what would Parliament do?

Treason!

Charles I believed that God meant him to rule England. The fact that the Cavaliers had lost to the Roundheads was not important to him. Charles tried to use the disagreements among the members of Parliament, the New Model Army, and the Scots to regain power for himself. He made a secret deal with the Scots, promising to share power with them if he could regain the throne. There soon began a second, shorter civil war, in which Cromwell once again defeated the king and his supporters.

Now Cromwell and other leaders of the army decided to put Charles I on trial for **treason**. This was such a shocking idea—that a king, chosen by God to rule a country, could betray it—that many members of Parliament, even those who had supported the civil war, objected. The army, however, was stronger than Parliament, and soldiers stood outside the courtroom, stopping members of Parliament who opposed the trial from entering.

> **vocabulary**
> **treason** the crime of betraying one's own country

The trial of Charles I lasted five days. At the end, Charles was condemned as "a Tyrant, Traitor, Murderer, and Public Enemy," to be "put to death by the severing of his Head from his body."

Cromwell led Parliament's army to victory in the English civil war. His troops, nicknamed Ironsides, *never lost a battle.*

This painting shows the beheading of King Charles I in front of his own palace. The crowd groaned as the executioner displayed the royal head.

The Ax Falls

On a cold day at the end of January 1649, Charles was executed. Thousands of people came to see the shocking sight of a king being executed by his own people. It must have seemed unbelievable to them that such a thing could happen.

Charles put on two shirts so that he wouldn't shiver and cause people to think that he was afraid to die. Even in the face of death, however, he did not change his views, declaring again that the common people should not have a share in government but should be ruled from above by their king, who was chosen by God. As the king was beheaded, one person who watched said, "There was such a groan by the thousands then present, as I never heard before, and desire I may never hear again."

Lord Protector

The army made Cromwell the head of the country. His title was Lord Protector. New laws were passed to reflect Puritan views. These laws called for a stricter observance of the Sabbath, dictating what people were or were not allowed to do on Sundays, and for harsher punishments for swearing, gambling, and drunkenness. These laws, however, were rarely enforced.

In his personal life, Cromwell was not as strict as he was in his public policies, nor was he as strict as many of his followers. He enjoyed sports, for example, and drank wine and beer in moderation. Cromwell pushed policies that were very cruel to the Irish Catholics, most of whose property he gave away to English landowners; yet in England, Catholics and smaller religious sects such as Quakers had more freedom than they had had under other rulers. Cromwell also allowed Jews more freedom to live and work in England than they had had for 400 years.

Cromwell was offered the crown by Parliament, but he refused it. If he had accepted it, the army probably would have turned against him. Cromwell was a king, however, in all but name. Throughout his five-year rule, he experimented with different forms of government, trying to find one that worked. He got rid of one Parliament and then, two years later, he created a new one, which he later dissolved. At one point, he appointed 11 major generals to manage different areas of England.

None of the methods that Cromwell tried worked very well, but today historians believe that his willingness to try different things helped to move England toward a more democratic system. For about two centuries after he died, however, he was remembered primarily as a king-killer and a dictator.

Merry Monarch and Brother

The Fugitive King Although the Parliamentarians, led by Oliver Cromwell, had executed King Charles I, they had not killed his son, Charles II. The people of Scotland were unhappy that the English had killed Charles I, who was their king, too. They proclaimed Charles II their new king.

In 1650, the year after his father was beheaded, Charles II led an army of Scots against Cromwell. As usual, Cromwell was victorious, and he claimed Scotland as part of England. Young Charles, little more than a teenager then, was suddenly on the run from Cromwell's army.

The Parliamentarians offered a large amount of money for the capture of "a tall young man two yards high, with hair deep brown to black." For six weeks, Charles hid in villages and forests until he could arrange for a ship to take him to France. In a short span of time, his life was transformed from that of the pampered son of a king to that of a fugitive hiding in the woods. Many people must have seen him and known who he was, yet no one turned him in.

Charles escaped to France and then, for the next eight years, he wandered around Europe. He had no money and few friends. Cromwell turned the governments of France and Holland against him.

The End of "Sword Rule"

People called the military government of Oliver Cromwell "sword rule." Remember, Cromwell had made the English army stronger than it had ever been. That had allowed the Parliamentarians to defeat the forces of Charles I and the Scots who fought for Charles II. Once the wars were over, however, the army was still strong. The army practically controlled the government, and the English people didn't like that.

When Cromwell died in 1658, his son took over, but he was not a strong leader. England seemed to be falling apart. Many in England felt the lack of a king and wanted to return to a government with a king and a Parliament. In 1660, one of Cromwell's generals convinced leaders in Parliament to invite Charles II back to England to be king.

English citizens restored the monarchy and welcomed Charles II back to England as their king.

The Merry Monarch

Charles II returned to England on May 29, 1660. It was a day of great excitement and rejoicing. People were tired of the strict Puritan laws and the high taxes collected by the army. One man who saw the procession of Charles into London described it as:

a triumph of above 20,000 on horse and foot, brandishing their swords and shouting with inexpressible joy; the ways strewed with flowers, the bells ringing, the streets hung with tapestry, fountains running wine. . . . I stood in the Strand [a major street in London], and beheld it, and blessed God.

Though tall, graceful, and witty, the Merry Monarch was not handsome. "Odd's fish, I am an ugly fellow!" he once moaned.

The return of a monarch to England was called the **Restoration**.

Their excitement over Charles's return and their hopes for a stable government led people to regard Charles as a hero for his years in hiding. Paintings and tapestries showed him hiding behind oak trees to escape from Cromwell's soldiers.

Inns and pubs called the Royal Oak sprang up all over England.

Charles, unlike his father, understood that he needed the support of Parliament and of his people to stay on the throne. He said that he had no wish "to go on his travels again." He supported Parliament as it reestablished the Church of England, which many people in England now saw as a good compromise between what most still viewed as the dangers of the Catholic Church and the strictness of the Puritans. Parliament also disbanded the army.

Charles was certainly no Puritan. He was known as the Merry Monarch because he loved the kind of pleasures that many Puritans had tried to outlaw during the rule of Cromwell. He liked to gamble and to go to horse races. He also enjoyed attending the theater. Under Charles II, women were allowed to appear on the stage as actors for the first time in England—before that, all parts for women had been played by men and boys.

Charles II was a charming and fun-loving man. The period of his reign is remembered as the time of Merry Olde England. But he had some unappealing qualities, too. He was rather lazy, and he didn't trust anyone. People believed that he would do or say anything just to stay on the throne, and

> **vocabulary**
> **Restoration** the historical period during which the monarchy was returned to England under Charles II

they were probably right. Yet his strong desire to keep everyone happy may have prevented great problems among different religious groups.

To escape the plague, many nobles fled from London to their country estates.

Parliament Has the Upper Hand

England had a king again, but there was no doubt about how the king had arrived. Parliament had invited the king back, and Parliament did not give up all its power when Charles arrived.

Charles would have been happy to allow religious tolerance in England. Many people believed that he was a Catholic at heart. In fact, he converted to the Catholic religion on his deathbed. During his reign, however, Charles knew that if he admitted that he was Catholic, he would lose his throne.

Charles would have liked to have let the English people practice any religion they wished. Parliament, however, was now suspicious of both Catholics and Puritans. Parliament restored the Church of England and made it stronger than ever. Puritans lost their jobs, and Puritan worship services were forbidden. People even stopped using the word *Puritan*. Instead, Puritans, Quakers, and other Protestants who did not belong to the Church of England were all called **Dissenters**. Some of them went to colonies in the New World to escape persecution.

Plague, Fire, and Trouble

Charles's laziness made many people anxious. In some ways, England seemed to be falling apart. The kingdom was running out of money. Rivalry over trade routes led to several small wars with Holland. When Dutch ships sailed into an English harbor, sank five English ships, and towed a battleship back to Holland, people ridiculed Charles for not paying enough attention to running his kingdom.

During Charles II's rule, two other setbacks occurred. They weren't Charles's fault, but they cast a shadow on his reign. One event was an outbreak of the **bubonic plague**. Officials recorded more than 68,000 deaths from the plague in London alone in 1665.

vocabulary
Dissenter any Protestant who refused to belong to the Church of England
bubonic plague a deadly disease spread by fleas on infected rats

The other unfortunate event happened the following year, when a baker's oven in a crowded section of London started a fire that burned out of control for four days. By the time the Fire of London was put out, some 13,000 houses had been destroyed, as well as many important churches. About 100,000 people were left homeless. A man who saw the fire from the other side of the Thames River wrote:

We saw . . . one entire arch of fire . . . about a mile long. It made me weep to see it. The churches, houses, and all on fire and flaming at once, and a horrid noise the flames made, and the cracking of houses at their ruin."

Most disturbing, however, was a problem all too familiar to the English monarchy. Charles II and his queen had no children. The next in line for the throne was Charles's brother James, and James was a Catholic.

James II

Remember that James and Charles II had had a French Catholic mother. Yet as the sons of Charles I (the king who was beheaded), both were raised in the Church of England. Their mother's beliefs, however, had influenced them. Charles II converted to Catholicism on his deathbed. James converted to Catholicism when he was about 35.

James's first marriage was to a Protestant Englishwoman. Their children were raised as Protestants in the Church of England. When his first wife died, however, James married a Catholic princess from Italy.

James took the throne in 1685 as James II. Although it had been more than a hundred years since a Catholic had ruled England, many English Protestants still feared that a Catholic ruler would burn Protestants at the stake and destroy Parliament. The English people were afraid of their Catholic ruler, James II.

Another reason that James II was unpopular was that, unlike his older brother Charles II, James was unfriendly and humorless. To make matters worse, he began to lose his mind a few years after he became king. He suspected people of plotting against him. He would say one thing one day and then another the next day.

When James's Catholic wife became pregnant, people became even more worried. If their unborn child was a boy, a long line of Catholic rulers might begin. Many powerful people in England decided that it was time to rid themselves of this king. To achieve this, seven important leaders in Parliament, known to later admirers as the Immortal Seven, decided to call in some help from the outside.

No one wanted to see England plunged into another period of war like the one it had suffered under Cromwell.

The Great Fire of London raged out of control until Charles II ordered all buildings in its path to be blown up.

William and Mary Before the birth of James II's son, the next in line for the throne had been James's older daughter, Mary. Mary was a Protestant, and she was married to William of Orange, a hero to Protestants in Europe.

William was a popular Dutch prince and the grandson of England's King Charles I. He was the major defender of Protestant Holland against the king of France. France had replaced Spain as the most powerful Catholic country in Europe.

In the fall of 1688, the Immortal Seven, the seven important leaders of Parliament, sent an invitation to William. They invited him to bring an army to England. They told him that they would support him. This was a very unusual thing to do. These seven leaders of Parliament were inviting a foreign ruler to invade their country!

William's Motives

William of Orange was only too happy to accept this invitation. He wanted England's military power on his side. William feared that France was going to invade Holland.

But William had two major problems. One was that England's Catholic king, James II, was an ally of France. The other problem was that if William sailed to England, France might take his absence from Holland as an opportunity to invade his country.

By pure chance, two events happened that changed history and allowed William to invade England. The first was that the king of France, King Louis XIV, decided to attack a Protestant region of what is now Germany instead of Holland. The second was that the wind shifted. Normally at that time of the year, the winds in the English Channel blew from west to east,

A Date to Remember:
1688
Glorious Revolution
Begins

making it difficult to sail from Holland to England. In 1688, however, a strong wind rose up that blew from the northeast. That was exactly the wind that William needed to invade England. This "Protestant wind," as it was called, allowed William to bring his ships quickly across the channel to England.

Once William landed on English soil, many landowners and members of Parliament joined his cause. The queen took her new baby and escaped to France. Because so many Protestant officers in James's army deserted to fight for William, the king panicked and followed his wife and child to France. William led his troops into London without fighting a single battle.

Everyone was quite surprised. When the Immortal Seven invited William to England, they were only hoping to scare James II. They wanted him to give up the Catholic religion and give more power to Parliament. They were not expecting that he would flee the country!

A King and a Queen

Now there was real confusion. William was not in line to take the English throne. His wife, Mary, was the daughter of King James II. Yet William was not willing to rule simply as the companion of the queen. "No man could think more of a woman than he did of the Princess," one writer said, "but he could not think of holding anything by apron strings." If William could not rule as king, he would "go back to Holland and meddle no more in [England's] affairs."

Many English leaders thought it was impossible that Mary, the heir to the throne by birth, should be passed over by a more distant relative. They could think of only one solution. In February 1689, Parliament decided that James II had abandoned the throne when he left England for France. Therefore, Parliament declared that the throne was vacant. The crown was offered to William *and* Mary. William would be King William III and Mary would be Queen Mary II. The king and queen would rule together as equals.

An Unusual Coronation

Like many monarchs before them, William and Mary had a grand coronation. Never before, however, had two people received crowns at once. And what crowns they received! It is said that the two gold crowns were decorated with 2,725 diamonds, 71 rubies, 59 sapphires, 40 emeralds, and 1,591 large pearls. The crowns were so heavy that both William and Mary looked tired from

William (at right) and Mary (center) became the king and queen of England at the request of Parliament.

the effort of wearing them before the coronation ceremony was over.

There was another way in which the coronation was unusual. Previous rulers had promised to uphold the laws of their ancestors when they were crowned. William and Mary, however, promised to uphold the laws of Parliament. They also agreed to uphold the Protestant religion.

The transfer of power from James II to William and Mary became known as the Glorious Revolution or the Bloodless Revolution. It was an important step toward **democracy**. Instead of accepting the idea that the choice of a ruler should be based on birth alone, leaders of Parliament had chosen a ruler based on what they thought was best for the country. The rulers themselves agreed to uphold the laws made by Parliament, not the laws made by previous

kings and queens. And the English got rid of a ruler they didn't like without executing him.

The Bill of Rights

It wasn't enough just to choose a new king and queen, however. In 1689, Parliament passed one of the most important acts in the history of England: the Bill of Rights.

The Bill of Rights is one of the foundations of the English government. It puts limits on the power of the monarch and gives important powers to Parliament. Since 1689, Parliament has met every year.

The part of the United States Constitution that we call the Bill of Rights was written about a hundred years after the English Bill of Rights. The American Bill of Rights is very different from the English Bill of Rights, however. The American Bill of Rights lists and protects the rights of individual citizens. The English Bill of Rights states some basic rights of Parliament, which originally consisted mostly of wealthy landowners, in relation to the king or queen of England. Once these basic rights were established through the Glorious Revolution, however, Parliament continued to claim more rights. The English Bill of Rights was an important step in limiting the power of kings and queens and in creating a more democratic government in England.

Important Points of the
English Bill of Rights

- **A ruler is not allowed to set aside laws made by Parliament.**

- **Parliament must meet frequently.**

- **The ruler of England must be a Protestant and cannot marry a Catholic.**

- **The ruler cannot maintain a standing army in times of peace.**

- **A ruler cannot collect taxes without the consent of Parliament.**

- **A ruler cannot interfere with the election of members to Parliament.**

- **All subjects have the right to petition the king.**

- **A ruler cannot interfere in freedom of speech and debate in Parliament.**

- **Protestants can bear arms to defend themselves.**

- **People should not have to pay excessive bail or fines, nor should they be given cruel and unusual punishments.**

William and Mary accepted the Bill of Rights, which made it clear that Parliament ruled England.

aristocrat a member of the upper, or noble, class

bubonic plague a deadly disease spread by the fleas on infected rats

coronation the ceremony or act of crowning a ruler

democracy a system of government in which power is vested in the people

Dissenter any Protestant who refused to belong to the Church of England

divine right of kings the belief that kings and queens have a God-given right to rule, and that rebellion against them is a sin

galleon a large Spanish sailing vessel, used as a warship or a trader

gentry people who own land and have high social standing but no titles of nobility

Parliament the national legislative body of nobles and elected representatives in England

persecute to hurt or harass a group of people, in this case for their religion

Restoration the historical period during which the monarchy was returned to England under Charles II

treason the crime of betraying one's own country

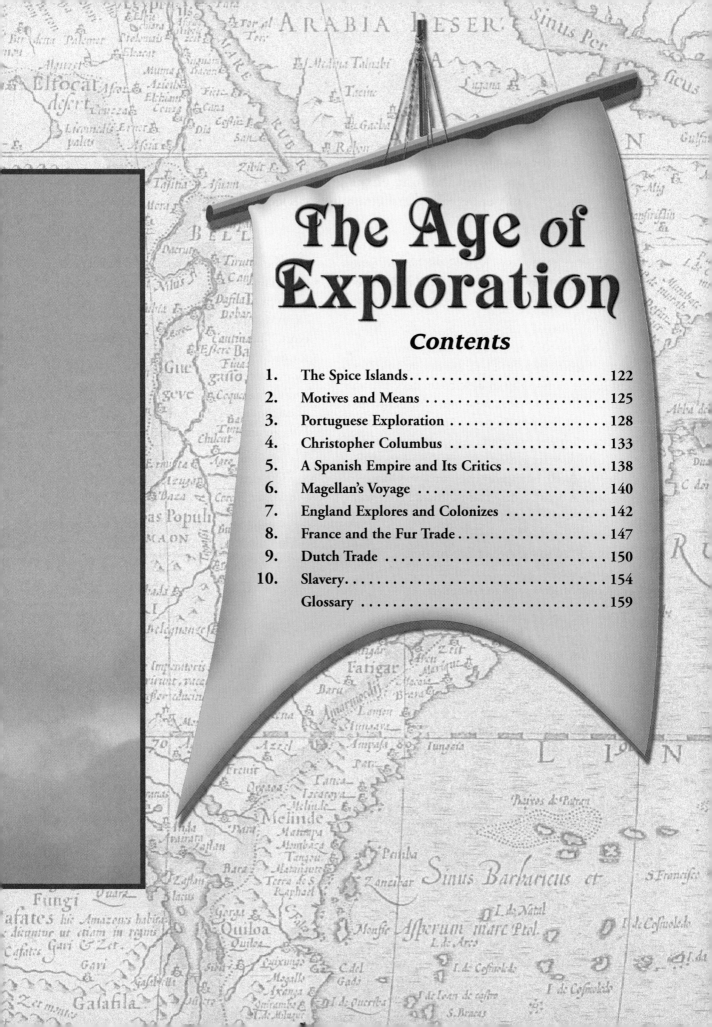

The Age of Exploration

Contents

The Spice of Life History can be changed by many things—a battle, an election, an earthquake, even a rainstorm. But would you ever have imagined that one of the greatest changes in history took place because of peppercorns and cinnamon sticks?

Hard as it may be to believe, the United States exists today because people who lived in Europe during the Middle Ages were crazy for spices in their food.

If you go to a supermarket today, you see all sorts of spices for sale. There are dozens of different kinds, all lined up in little containers. But in the Middle Ages, spices were much harder to obtain. Spices like pepper, cinnamon, ginger, cloves, and nutmeg were grown in Asia, and Europeans had trouble getting them. When they were available, they were outrageously expensive. Once Europeans decided they had to find a better way to get these spices from Asia, the whole history of the world changed. The desire for spices led to the Age of Exploration, and the Age of Exploration led to the European discovery of the Americas.

The Spice Islands

Different spices come from different places, but many of the most desirable spices, including pepper, nutmeg, and cloves, come from the islands of present-day Indonesia. As you can see from the map, Indonesia is an **archipelago** of islands stretching from the Malay Peninsula in Southeast Asia to Australia. This archipelago, known as the Malay Archipelago, contains more than 13,000 islands. Some, like Sumatra and Java, are large. Others are smaller, like the Molucca islands, located south of the Philippines. Of all the spice-bearing islands, the Moluccas are probably the most famous. Indeed, they were known as the *Spice Islands* for many years.

The islands of the Malay Archipelago occupy a special position. They mark the boundary between two sections of Earth's crust. The ridge formed there has many volcanoes and a great deal of earthquake activity. It is part of the Ring of Fire, an arc of volcanoes around the rim of the Pacific Ocean.

> **vocabulary**
> **archipelago** a chain of islands

The equator runs right through the middle of the Malay Archipelago, so temperatures on the

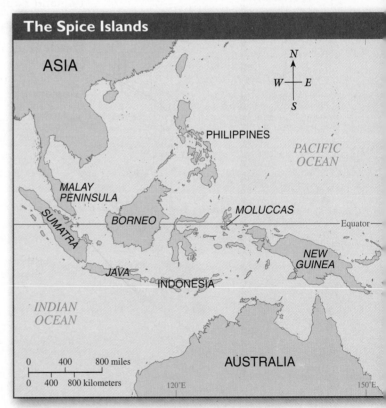

The Spice Islands

Today, the Spice Islands are part of the nation of Indonesia.

islands are warm. Daytime temperatures are between 70° and 90°F year-round. Rainfall can range from as much as 320 inches a year on the forested mountain slopes of some islands to fewer than 20 inches on the **rain shadow** side. Generally, however, the islands receive an average of 80 inches of rainfall a year. Heat, heavy rainfall, and rich soil provide farmers on the islands with just what they need to produce exceptional spice crops.

An Arab Secret

You might be wondering why, if the Europeans were so desperate for spices, they didn't just sail over to the Spice Islands and buy some. It wasn't that simple. For one thing, the Europeans did not yet know that it was possible to sail around the southern tip of Africa. And even if they had been able to sail around Africa, they would not

> **vocabulary**
> **rain shadow** an area that gets less rain because it is on the protected side of a mountain

have known where to go. For many years the location of the Spice Islands was a closely guarded secret.

During the Middle Ages, the spice trade was controlled by the Arabs. Arab traders had cornered the market not only on nutmeg and cloves from the Spice Islands, but also on ginger from China and cinnamon from India. For hundreds of years, from around 1100 until 1400, the Arabs managed to keep the location of the Spice Islands a secret. They even made up stories about how dangerous it was to sail to these islands. If you talked to an Arab trader, he might tell you that the spice crops were guarded by fantastic monsters and hideous flesh-eating birds. Stories like these were designed to help the Arabs preserve their **monopoly.**

Here's how the spice trade worked: Arab traders sailed east to trading centers in India, Ceylon (now Sri Lanka), and the Spice Islands. After loading up their ships with spices and other valuable goods, they sailed west again. A typical

Arab merchants sailed over the Indian Ocean in ships like the one shown in this thirteenth century picture.

route took them around the Arabian peninsula, into the Red Sea, and north to Egypt. In Egyptian trade centers such as Cairo and Alexandria, the Arabs sold the spices to merchants from Venice in Italy. The Arabs made huge profits from this exchange.

The Venetians did well too. They had made an agreement with the Arabs to distribute spices throughout Europe. Any Europeans wanting to purchase spices had to deal with Venice. Once they paid the Arab traders, the Venetian merchants could set whatever prices they pleased and charge fees and taxes on top of that. This agreement made Venice a very wealthy and powerful city. It also made the Venetians very unpopular.

> **vocabulary**
> **monopoly** complete control of selling a product or service

Europeans could get along without the spices and other luxuries pouring in from the East. However, they had come to enjoy the exotic things that were available in the Venetian marketplace. They soon began to resent the high cost of doing business with Venetian spice merchants. The Venetian merchants themselves resented paying such high prices to the Arab traders. They dreamed of dealing directly with merchants in the Spice Islands themselves.

The Travels of Marco Polo

Maffeo and Niccolò Polo were brothers who lived in Venice in the second half of the thirteenth century. The two were great traders and travelers, and when the overland trade routes that had existed in Roman times opened up again they set out to find the legendary markets of the East. At the time, the Mongols controlled much of Asia and part of Europe. The Mongols made the roads safe for travelers, and many adventurers were anxious to seek their fortunes. Some went to trade for silk, gems, porcelain, and tea. Others hoped to find sources of the world's most exotic spices.

When the Polo brothers started out on their second journey east, in 1271, they decided to take Niccolò's young son, Marco, with them. The expedition ended up taking them 24 years to complete. The three spent time in the service of the Mongol ruler Kubilai Khan and traveled throughout Asia by land and by sea.

Marco's father and uncle served as military advisers to the Great Khan. Kubilai Khan took a liking to Marco. He sent Marco to distant parts of his kingdom on diplomatic missions. Wherever he went, he observed, asked questions, and remembered what he had seen.

Marco Polo returned to Venice. Soon after his return he was captured during a war with a neighboring city. Polo was sent to jail. His cellmate was a writer from the city of Pisa. During his days in prison Polo talked about his travels, and the writer wrote down what Marco said. Together, the two cellmates produced a book that helped change the world. *The Travels of Marco Polo* was read by people all over Europe, first in handwritten copies and later in printed editions. Polo was the first European to write about China, Thailand, the Malay Archipelago, and other Asian lands. His book inspired European mapmakers to put some new places on their maps. Almost two hundred years after it was written, it also inspired an Italian sea captain named Christopher Columbus.

For centuries, the Spice Islands drew explorers, adventurers, and dreamers like a magnet. On their way to finding the Spice Islands, these explorers found lands, oceans, and peoples that they never knew existed. It is no exaggeration to say that the desire to reach the Spice Islands led to the exploration of the entire planet.

The Catalan Atlas, published in 1375, presented the known world—complete with "portraits" of famous travelers such as the Polo family.

The Value of Spices By the mid-1400s, Europeans had several motives for exploration. For one thing, they wanted to gain access to the spice-growing areas described by Marco Polo.

Because of the Arab and Venetian monopoly, spices were valuable throughout Europe. In some places, spices were so valuable that peppercorns were used in place of coins. Payments were counted out peppercorn by peppercorn. Spices by the pound were used to pay fees, tariffs, taxes, rents, and ransoms.

Europeans were enthusiastic about spices because the food they had to eat was not very tasty. Remember that the Europeans did not have any of the fruits and vegetables native to North and South America. Potatoes, tomatoes, corn, bananas, chocolate, peanuts, strawberries, blueberries, and pineapples were all unheard of. Europeans did not have sugar until the late Middle Ages. They also had no coffee or tea.

> **The Silk Road: For many centuries this was an overland trade route of nearly 4,000 miles that crossed mountains and deserts between Asia and the Arab and European cities near the Mediterranean Sea.**

Europeans typically slaughtered livestock in the fall. They used salt to cure the meat for long-term storage. After a few months, much of this meat was not very appetizing. A pinch of pepper, cloves, or ginger could make bad-tasting or even spoiled meat much easier to eat.

Europeans developed a taste for the bark, buds, nuts, seeds, and roots of plants grown on tiny islands in a faraway sea. But getting spices wasn't easy. The Arabs and Venetians charged high prices, and in the fifteenth century the Turks shut down the Silk Road, which had previously been used to transport spices from the East.

The Europeans needed a sea route to Asia. Nobody was sure that such a route existed, but everybody hoped one would be discovered. The great kings of Europe began looking for brave explorers, shipbuilders, mapmakers, and others who could help them discover a sea route to Asia.

Christianity and Curiosity

Europeans had other reasons to set sail for distant lands. For one thing, they felt that it was their duty to spread Christianity. People who believed in their own gods and worshiped in their own ways were thought to have no religion. They simply needed to be told about Christianity and shown the correct way to think. Although some explorers were willing to spread Christianity by peaceful means, others were willing to use force to conquer the people they could not convert peacefully.

In the Middle Ages, generations of European knights and soldiers went on Crusades to the Middle East to capture the Holy Land from Muslims. The Europeans were convinced that they had a more advanced civilization than the Muslim **infidels.** But when they got to the Middle East, they saw that Islamic civilization was

> **vocabulary**
> **infidel** someone who does not believe in what is considered the true religion

very advanced. The experience of the Crusades planted the seeds of curiosity in Europe. During the later Middle Ages and the Renaissance, people became more curious about what lay out there beyond their borders.

New Ships

The Arabs had been sailing to and fro across the Indian Ocean for centuries and had built up a great deal of knowledge about **navigation** and shipbuilding. The Europeans were used to taking short hops from port to port around the Mediterranean. They navigated mostly by sailing near the coastline and watching for known landmarks. In order to set sail in uncharted waters, they needed a different type of ship and a way to keep track of travel across miles of open sea.

In the early 1400s, northern and southern Europeans were building different kinds of ships. Ships built in the Mediterranean shipyards of southern Europe typically had large triangular sails, called *lateen sails*. These sails provided easy handling in the winds that blew along the Mediterranean coast.

Northern ships had square sails, which were more effective on the open ocean. They also had **hulls** built with thick, overlapping planks. These hulls were built to withstand the rougher waters of the Baltic Sea and the Atlantic Ocean.

Both of these ship designs had advantages, but neither was ideal for long voyages on uncharted waters. Then, in the 1400s, Portuguese shipbuilders combined features from these two different kinds of ships to build a ship that was well suited for long ocean voyages. These new, more seaworthy vessels were called *caravels* (KAR uh velz). The caravels had the sturdiness of the northern ships and the maneuverability of the southern ships. Their masts were rigged with lateen sails so that the ships were easy to handle, but the caravels also had square sails to take advantage of strong winds that would send the ships across the open ocean. The ships had hulls sturdy enough to sail on rough seas, and they were large enough to carry men, supplies, and trade goods. They were also able to carry cannons. In these new ships, Europeans were ready to take command of the sea.

> **vocabulary**
> **navigation** traveling by ship from one place to another
> **hull** the sides and bottom of a boat

The caravel was developed for sailing on long voyages under various conditions.

Finding Their Way

Once sailors traveled out of sight of land, they had to find ways to keep track of where they were and where they were heading. Sailors relied on the sky to help them find their way, using the sun during the day and stars at night.

During the day, sailors could plot their direction in relation to the sun's apparent movement across the sky from east to west. For example, the sun setting on the right side of the ship would mean that the ship was heading south. The sun setting on the left would mean that the ship was heading north.

At night, pilots relied on the North Star to help them stay on course. Instruments such as the astrolabe and the sextant were used to find latitude by measuring the angle made by an imaginary line from the North Star to the horizon. You can imagine, however, that taking exact measurements on a bobbing ship was difficult.

Speed was measured by a log attached to a rope. The rope had knots tied along it at regular spaces. The sailor kept count as the knots slipped through his hands. The number of knots that were let out during a certain amount of time was used to calculate the speed. This is why ship speed is still measured in *knots* today!

The magnetic compass had been in use in other parts of the world for centuries. The Europeans also relied on it to determine direction. However, many captains and navigators did not really understand how or why it worked the way it did. The movement of the needle frightened some sailors. Because of this, ships were built with a special housing for the compass. It was called the *binnacle*. Inside the binnacle, the compass was handy for reading, but it remained hidden from the crew. The captain did not want his sailors to think that he was using magic to navigate!

Imagine sailing across an ocean, especially an unknown ocean, just using instruments like the hourglass and sextant shown here.

Time was kept on board ship using a sand hourglass. If you were the ship's cabin boy, it was your job to turn the glass every half hour during your watch. The time calculated was checked against sunrise and sunset to make up for the sand running too fast or too slowly.

Navigation methods also took into account observations made by the crew. Information about the clouds, birds, waves, and anything floating in the water was also used to track a ship's position on the sea.

The Europeans had a motive: They wanted a share in the treasures of the East. They had a mission: They wanted to get rich and to spread the word of their faith to every part of the world. They had means: navigation skills, the caravel, and courage would help them achieve their goals.

Pioneers of the Sea The most powerful European nations in the 1400s were Spain, France, England, and some of the city-states in Italy—such as Venice. But none of these countries led the search for a sea route to the East. Portugal was a small, poor country, but the Portuguese were sea-going pioneers.

Portuguese leadership in exploration was largely due to one person. Prince Henry, often called the Navigator, had a strong desire to explore the oceans. Although Henry never went on any expeditions himself, he supported the design of the ships. He encouraged mapmakers, craftsworkers, and instrument makers to share information. All of this information and equipment was made available to the explorers of his day. Most important, he helped to convince his father, King John I, to pay for expensive expeditions in the name of Portugal. Like other Europeans, the Portuguese had a strong desire to set up trade routes, spread Christianity, and gain knowledge.

Prince Henry sent explorers down the west coast of Africa on dozens of expeditions. The brave Portuguese seafarers faced many challenges. Prior to this, no European had sailed very far from Europe. Sailors told hair-raising stories about sea monsters and steaming cauldrons of waves that boiled up in the ocean. It was hard to convince crews to go southward. They did not think it was safe, and they were terrified of the unknown territory. Reaching Cape Bojador (BOH juh dor) off the western Sahara on the Atlantic coast was a great achievement.

Over the years, Prince Henry's navigators pushed farther south down the African coast. They brought back gold, ivory, spices, and slaves. The first African slaves arrived in Portugal in 1441 to work as servants and laborers. Africans were also taken along on expeditions to serve as interpreters and help set up trade agreements in new ports. Portuguese traders set up trading posts and challenged the **Moors** for leadership in West Africa.

> **vocabulary**
> **Moor** a North African follower of Islam

This modern statue of Prince Henry was erected in his honor in Lisbon, the capital of Portugal. Prince Henry is shown holding a ship.

Bartolomeu Dias

As the Portuguese slowly made their way down the west coast of Africa, each expedition expanded the horizon and added information to the maps, and each expedition helped to get rid of the sailors' superstitions.

The exploring continued. In 1487, Bartolomeu Dias (bar tuh luh MAY uh DEE ahsh) set sail with a fleet of three ships. The fleet traveled far beyond the point where anyone had sailed before, stopping at various ports along the coast. The stops were marked with stone pillars supplied by the king to show that the Portuguese had been there.

Then, stormy seas forced the fleet offshore. For a few days, the fleet sailed away from the sight of land. When the seas calmed, the ships turned back to make a landfall. They looked for the land that had been to the east of them as they journeyed southward. They could not find it. It was only when the ships turned north that land finally was sighted. But, surprisingly, the land was on the left side of the ship. This could mean only one thing: The fleet was traveling north up the east coast of Africa. They had sailed around the southern tip of Africa without knowing it!

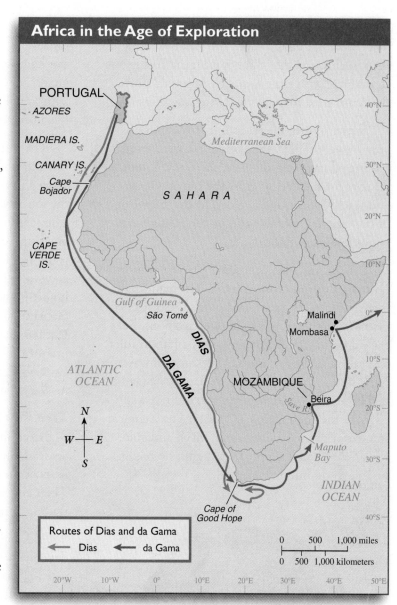

Africa in the Age of Exploration

Most of what Europeans of this time knew about Africa was restricted to the coasts of the continent.

Dias was excited by this discovery but also concerned about being so far from Portugal. He turned his fleet around. As the fleet rounded the southern tip of Africa and headed north for home, Dias spotted what he called *Cabo Tormentoso* (Cape of Storms), which we now call the Cape of Good Hope. He had shown that it was possible to sail around Africa and had found the route to the Indian Ocean.

Vasco da Gama

When it came to exploration, the Portuguese were always pushing forward. They used the experience and knowledge gained on one expedition as the starting point for the next. Once Dias rounded the Cape of Good Hope, it was only a matter of time before that route was extended.

In 1497, a fleet of four ships left Lisbon led by Vasco da Gama (VAH skoh duh GAH muh). The fleet came around the Cape of Good Hope and headed northeast along the east coast of Africa. Stops were made at the main centers of trade along the way, including Mombasa, Mozambique, and Malindi.

In Mombasa and in Mozambique, the Portuguese ran into trouble with Arab traders. These merchants had controlled the trade centers along the coast of East Africa for hundreds of years. They were not happy about the idea of sharing their wealth, and they did not want the Portuguese to interfere with their business. At several ports, the Arabs tried to seize the Portuguese ships.

Farther north, the reception at Malindi was very friendly. There, the Portuguese were given a ship's pilot to help them on their way. It took 23 days for the fleet to cross the Indian Ocean and reach Calicut, India, aided by the knowledge of the experienced pilot and by the strong west winds known as trade winds.

Calicut was a major trading city and seaport on the southwest coast of India. The main trade items were spices, gems, and pearls. Vasco da Gama was anxious to set up trade relations, but the Zamorin (zah MOR ihn), as the Hindu ruler was called, had other ideas. The Zamorin was not impressed with the ordinary items that da Gama had brought to exchange. He also did not want to make the Arab merchants angry. The Zamorin wanted bright red fabric, coral, silver, and gold. If da Gama could supply these items, he might be able to do business.

The Portuguese fleet was anchored at Calicut for several months. When it came time to leave, the Zamorin tried to seize all of the Portuguese goods. Vasco da Gama and his crew departed in a hurry, taking with them all of their goods and five hostages, too.

The return trip across the Indian Ocean took three terrible months. Many of the men died of **scurvy** during the journey. They set fire to one ship because it did not have a crew to sail it home. Vasco da Gama finally reached Lisbon in 1499. In spite of the terrible losses on his trip, Da Gama's return was cause for celebration, and he was called a hero by the king.

vocabulary
scurvy a disease caused by a lack of vitamin C, which is found in fresh fruits and vegetables

The Portuguese in East Africa

After Vasco da Gama's exploration of the east coast of Africa and visit to India, the Portuguese launched a number of follow-up expeditions. Their aim was to seize control of the flourishing trading cities on the eastern coast of Africa.

Although the African economy in general depended on farming and raising livestock, trade was well established by the time the Portuguese arrived. Demand was high for copper, iron ore, gold, ivory, salt, tools, and pottery produced in the African interior. These goods were traded between inland and coastal trade centers. From the African trade centers, goods were transported north to Egyptian and Mediterranean trade centers or east to trade centers in India. So were slaves.

Historians sometimes call the East African coast the Swahili (swah HEE lee) Coast, because the African language Swahili was spoken by many of the people in this area. The people who lived along the Swahili Coast were

Vasco da Gama was another of the daring Portuguese sea captains who sailed into unknown waters.

Portuguese colonists clung to a few settlements on the east coast of Africa.

a mixture of Africans, Arabs, and Persians. The dominant religion was Islam.

The Portuguese set up trading posts along the Swahili Coast in places like Beira and Maputo Bay, both in modern-day Mozambique. Beira was an especially valuable trade center. Gold that was mined inland was shipped down the Save River to Beira. From there it was shipped home to Portugal.

Once the Portuguese took control of Beira, they were anxious to learn more about the inland sources of its riches. For decades, the Portuguese tried to gain control of the rich resources of the interior of Africa. They sent missionaries to gain the confidence of the native peoples and convert them to Christianity. They also sent soldiers to try to take territories by force. The Portuguese made some progress, but Swahili traders and local people resisted, and Portugal was never able to gain full control of the African interior. In general, Portuguese expansion was limited to a few small colonies and a handful of plantations run by private landowners using slave labor.

Although the Portuguese were disappointed by their failure to establish strong colonies in the African interior, they were pleased with what they accomplished along the coast. They managed to break the long-standing Arab monopoly. They set up a network of trading posts, not only along the Swahili Coast but also in India, the East Indies, and the Spice Islands. Little by little, the Portuguese emerged as the dominant force in East Africa.

Pedro Alvares Cabral and Brazil

A fleet of 13 ships set sail from Portugal for India under the command of Pedro Alvares Cabral (kuh BRAHL). He was supposed to follow the route of Vasco da Gama. His goal was to make contact with trade centers in the East and to see what else he could find. Before leaving Lisbon, Cabral met with Vasco da Gama. Da Gama shared maps and told Cabral about his experiences sailing to India.

Cabral sailed out of Lisbon harbor and turned south. He followed the coast of Africa until he had passed the Cape Verde Islands (off present-day Senegal). Da Gama had told Cabral to be careful not to get stuck in the Gulf of

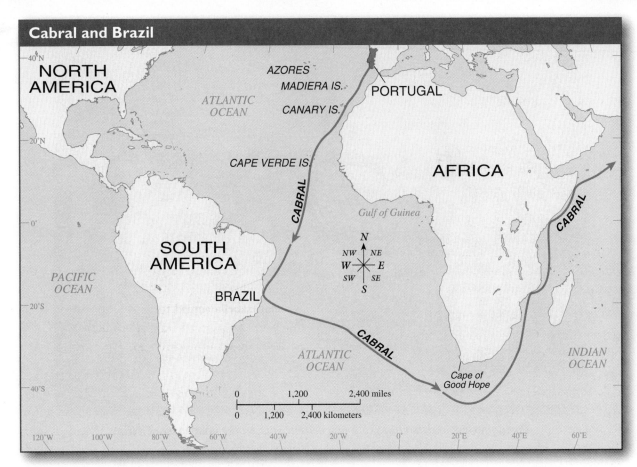

NORTH AMERICA

ATLANTIC OCEAN

AZORES
MADIERA IS.
CANARY IS.

PORTUGAL

CAPE VERDE IS.

AFRICA

Gulf of Guinea

CABRAL

SOUTH AMERICA

PACIFIC OCEAN

BRAZIL

N
NW NE
W——E
SW SE
S

CABRAL

ATLANTIC OCEAN

CABRAL

Cape of Good Hope

INDIAN OCEAN

0   1,200   2,400 miles
0   1,200   2,400 kilometers

The distance between the east coast of Brazil and the west coast of Africa is not great.

Guinea. The ocean there could be as calm as a pond, with no wind to carry ships on their way. Cabral was told to head southwest and sail out into the Atlantic Ocean instead. Cabral did so, and in April 1500, he sighted land. The expedition had reached the coast of Brazil.

We tend to think of the western and eastern hemispheres as being very far apart. But if you look at a map, you can see that Brazil juts out into the Atlantic Ocean toward the western coast of Africa, so that they are really not so far apart. All it took was a southwestward swing by Cabral and some strong winds, and the Portuguese explorer had found a new world for Portugal, which he claimed in the name of the king.

Cabral sent a ship home to tell the king of his find, naming it *Vera Cruz* (VAIR uh KROOZ), the Island of the True Cross. He made contact with the people living in the area and stayed for 10 days before setting out to complete his expedition. Four ships were lost as the fleet came to the Cape of Good Hope. Among the men

who drowned was Bartolomeu Dias, the explorer who had been the first European to spot the cape 12 years before.

Cabral continued on with what was left of his fleet, trading at a number of ports in the Indian Ocean and loading his ships with precious spices. He started back to Portugal. On the return journey more ships were lost. Only four ships sailed back into Lisbon harbor.

For a time, Cabral's claim to the lands across the Atlantic was followed up with great enthusiasm. However, even though the Island of the True Cross was bigger than anyone had thought it would be, it did not seem to be bursting with tradable resources. Red dye made from the bark of the brazilwood tree was in demand in the courts of Europe, but for years this bark was the only resource that interested Europeans. The Portuguese were busy gaining power in the rich ports of Africa, India, the East Indies, and the Spice Islands. They did not want to bother with this new territory—at least not for a while.

Sailing West to the East Indies On August 3, 1492, three ships left Palos, Spain, and headed for the Canary Islands, off the African coast. In those days European ships often sailed to the Canary Islands, either to trade or to rest before continuing south along the coast of Africa.

However, after a few days in the Canary Islands, these three ships did something very unusual. They sailed due west.

The admiral in command of the ships was an Italian named Christopher Columbus. Columbus had read Marco Polo's account of the East Indies and was eager to find the sources of the spices Polo had described. However, Columbus believed that there was a better way to get to the Indies than by sailing all the way around Africa, as Dias had done just a few years earlier. He believed the best way to reach the East was to sail west. Columbus knew that the world was round (which most educated people of his day also knew), but he also believed that the world was a good deal smaller than it actually is. Therefore he thought that the East Indies could not be very far west of the Canary Islands.

Columbus had spent seven years trying to convince the rulers of Europe to sponsor a westward expedition to the Indies. He was turned down by the king of Portugal and put off by the king of France. At first, the rulers of Spain declined as well. However, in 1492, King Ferdinand and Queen Isabella agreed to pay for an expedition. They instructed Columbus to claim any new lands he discovered for Spain.

So in September, the three ships, the *Niña,* the *Pinta,* and the *Santa María,* left the Canaries and headed west into unknown waters. According to Fernando Columbus, the son of the explorer, many sailors "sighed and wept for fear they would not see [land] again for a long time." Columbus "comforted them with great promises of land and riches." Columbus also came up with a strategy to keep his sailors from getting too worried. On the first day of the voyage, he decided to understate how far they had actually traveled. He told his crew that they had covered only 15 **leagues,** even though they had really gone 18. This way he kept a secret reckoning.

Columbus kept this up for weeks. If the ships traveled 25 leagues, he would write down 20. If they covered 39, he would record 30. It was a clever strategy. But by early October the sailors had begun to get worried, in spite of the inaccurate distances Columbus was giving them. They had been sailing west for a month, without any sign

> **vocabulary**
> **league** an old measurement of distance equal to approximately 3 miles

Columbus searched for many years for support of his plan to find a new route to Asia.

of land, and many of the men feared they had now gone so far west that they would not be able to find their way back to Europe. Some of the more superstitious sailors weren't too sure about the world being round. Maybe the ships might sail off Earth's edge.

The sailors began to talk among themselves. Why did Columbus insist on sailing west? Hadn't Dias found the true way to the Indies by sailing around Africa? How much longer would the food supplies hold out? Did they even have enough food and fresh water for the trip back to Spain?

Eventually, the sailors threatened a **mutiny**. They warned that if Columbus did not turn back, they would throw him overboard and tell the authorities in Spain that he had fallen in by accident one night while looking at the stars.

Columbus avoided a mutiny by promising to turn slightly to the south. He also promised that,

if the ships did not find land within the next few days, they would turn back.

This was a risky promise to make, but it paid off. Just a few days later, sailors began to see encouraging signs.

They spotted birds that were known to live on land, and they found a bush floating in the ocean, with a few berries still clinging to the branches.

Finally, in the early morning hours of October 12, 1492, an excited shout rippled across the water. *"Tierra! Tierra!"* called the Spanish lookout on the *Pinta*. "Land! Land!"

The men came running up on deck, and there, on the horizon, was a dark outline, barely visible against the night sky. It was indeed land.

The captains and crews of the three ships led by Columbus faced a hazardous voyage into unknown waters.

The First Encounter

When the sun rose on that day, Columbus took a landing party ashore to meet the inhabitants of what he thought surely was Asia. In fact, he was in the Bahamas, a group of islands just east of Florida. Columbus decided to name the island San Salvador (Holy Savior). He personally carried the **royal standard** ashore to claim the land for Spain.

The natives of the island were "as naked as when their mothers bore them." The lush green land did not look much like the Asia described by Marco Polo, and there were no silks or spices to be seen. Columbus nevertheless was convinced that he had landed on an island in the East Indies. He called the native people *Indians*. The name stuck, even after later explorers proved that what Columbus had found was not the East Indies but the outskirts of two new continents located between Europe and Asia.

In fact, the inhabitants of the island were members of the Taino (TYE noh) tribe. They

were peaceful people who fished in the waters around their island and lived in large thatched huts. The Tainos came down to the shore to look at Columbus and his men. They had never seen white men or sailing ships before, and they were not sure what to think.

Columbus had brought along a translator who spoke Hebrew and Arabic. He felt sure the Indians would understand one of these two eastern languages, but, to his frustration, they did not. The Spanish and the Indians were forced to communicate by sign language.

In a letter, Columbus described this historic first encounter between Europeans and Americans.

As I saw that they were very friendly to us and perceived that they could be much more easily converted to our holy faith by gentle means than by force, I presented them with some red caps, and strings of glass beads to put round their necks, and many other trifles of small value, which gave them great pleasure. . . . This made them so much our friends that is was a marvel to see. Afterwards they came swimming to the boats, bringing parrots, balls of cotton thread, javelins (spears), and many other things which they exchanged for articles we gave them. . . . (In short,) they took all and gave what they had with good will.

Columbus was impressed by the intelligence of the Tainos. He noted that "they very quickly learn such words are as spoken to them." He also remarked, "I am of the opinion that they would very readily become good Christians." And yet Columbus clearly did not think of these native peoples as his equals. In the same letter, he remarked that the Tainos "would be good

servants." And two days later, he wrote that these island people were so meek that "I could conquer the whole of them with fifty men and govern them as I please." For the moment, Columbus merely took a half dozen Tainos on board to show them back in Europe.

In order to locate what he believed would be China, Columbus soon sailed on, landing on what are now the islands of Cuba and Hispaniola. Today the island of Hispaniola is divided between the countries of Haiti and the Dominican Republic.

By January 1493, supplies were getting low, and he set sail for Spain. Columbus traveled until he reached the latitude of 40°N, which put him on a line with Spain. Then he turned the ships east for their return home.

Columbus, sure that he had landed somewhere in Asia, easily mistook the chief of Cuban natives as a descendant of the "great khan" whom Marco Polo had described.

The Triumphant Return

When Columbus reached the court of King Ferdinand and Queen Isabella, he told them everything he had seen in the lands that he had claimed for their country. He presented the monarchs with the Tainos he brought back with him. He also gave Queen Isabella a present of colorful parrots. Columbus described his meetings with an Indian chieftain, whom he called the "great khan," and his visit to Cuba, which he thought was Japan. He described the contacts he had made.

King Ferdinand and Queen Isabella rewarded Columbus by giving him gifts of money and grants of land. They also gave him the title Admiral of the Ocean Sea. Columbus was gratified by these rewards.

News of the success of Columbus's voyage quickly spread through Europe. However, not everyone was convinced that Columbus had found a westward route to Asia. Among the biggest doubters were the Portuguese. They thought that Columbus had simply explored part of the African coast or an unknown group of islands in the Atlantic. The Spanish themselves did not really know what to think. At last they decided that Columbus had found some faraway place, and whatever that place was, they wanted it for themselves.

The Treaty of Tordesillas

Now that both Spain and Portugal were involved in exploration, there was a possibility that the two countries would get in each other's way. The pope tried but failed to settle the dispute. Then diplomats from the two countries sat down and worked out an agreement, drawing an imaginary line from the North Pole to the South Pole 370 leagues (1,185 miles) west of the Cape Verde Islands. The Treaty of Tordesillas (tor day SEEL yus), signed in 1494, said that all land to the west of this line could be claimed by Spain. All land to the east could be claimed by Portugal. Neither country was to occupy any territory already in the hands of a Christian ruler. However, non-Christian lands were fair game.

Today we know that the Treaty of Tordesillas was a good deal for Spain and a not-so-good deal for Portugal. Almost all of North and South America lay to the west of the treaty line, on the Spanish side; only Brazil was on the Portuguese side. This would mean that, over the next hundred years or so, millions of people in North and South America would learn to speak Spanish, while only the Brazilians learned Portuguese.

However, in 1494, when the treaty was signed, nobody was quite sure what had been divided, or who had the rights to what. At the time Cabral had not yet discovered Brazil (that would happen in 1500), and no one knew exactly what Columbus had discovered in 1492. Queen Isabella of Spain sent a letter to Columbus, urging him to determine where the treaty line was and which lands lay on the Spanish side.

The Later Voyages of Columbus

Columbus made three more voyages to the Americas during the next few years, but none of these was as successful as his first. He mapped most of the islands of the Caribbean Sea and established the permanent colony of Santo Domingo on Hispaniola on his second voyage. He left his brothers Bartholomew and Diego in charge while he went exploring. He searched the Caribbean Sea for gold but did not turn up enough to make the trip a financial success.

The third voyage (1498–1500) was even worse. While Columbus explored the north coast of South America, Bartholomew and Diego angered both the native peoples and the Spanish settlers of Hispaniola. The Columbus brothers forced the natives to work in gold mines, and they favored some Spanish settlers over others. Eventually complaints reached the Spanish court. Columbus lost his position as governor of the colony, and his brothers were sent back to Spain.

The fourth voyage (1502–1504) was the worst of all. Columbus and his men were shipwrecked on the island of Jamaica for a year. By the time Columbus returned from this voyage, his health was broken and his reputation had been almost completely destroyed.

As new explorers came along, people forgot about the man who had made the first discoveries. When Columbus died in 1506, his death went almost completely unnoticed. However, in 1542 his bones were sent back to Hispaniola. They were buried in the Cathedral of Santo Domingo.

The Final Blow

As if a damaged reputation were not enough, the continents Columbus had discovered were soon named not for him, but for another explorer, Amerigo Vespucci (ves POO chee) who explored the coast of South America for Portugal in 1501. Vespucci wrote letters about his voyage which were published. He said "I have found a continent more densely populated [then our known world]. We may rightly call this continent the New World." A German mapmaker was so impressed he labeled the new continent *America* on the map he was working on.

A Spanish Empire and Its Critics

fter Columbus The Spanish continued to expand their holding in the Americas after Columbus died. And the stronger the Spanish became, the worse the situation became for the Indians. Many of the Spaniards were ruthless colonists.

Indians died by the hundreds in the gold mines the Columbus brothers had started, and thousands more died from European diseases against which they had no immunities. The effects were devastating. Within 20 years of the arrival of the Spaniards, the native population of Hispaniola went from one million people down to only 30,000.

Cattle ranches and sugar plantations were introduced when the gold mines stopped bringing in the profits that the Spanish crown demanded. But with deadly diseases killing off the native population, there were not enough laborers to get the work done. By the sixteenth century, slaves were being imported from Africa to fill the need for labor.

The Conquistadors

In the 40-year period from 1495 to 1535, Spanish conquistadores (kon KEES tuh dorz) conquered much of South and Central America. The conquistadores were soldiers who came to this new world in search of adventure and wealth. You have learned about Hernán Cortés, the conquistador who conquered the mighty Aztec empire in modern-day

Balboa took possession of the Pacific Ocean in the name of Spain.

Mexico. You also learned about Francisco Pizarro, who conquered the Inca civilization in Peru.

Pizarro actually spent many years working for another famous conquistador, Vasco Núñez de Balboa (VAH skoh NOO nyath de bal BOH uh). Balboa and Pizarro explored isthmus of Panama together. During their explorations, some Indians told them about a great sea to the west. In 1513, Balboa organized an expedition to find this sea. He chose 190 of his toughest men, including Pizarro, and enlisted about 100 Indians to carry equipment and supplies. The party crossed swamps by stripping off their clothing and carrying it on their heads as they splashed along. They fought off snakes, crocodiles, and mosquitoes, hacked their way through thick jungles, and climbed over mountains. They attacked a number of Indian tribes but befriended several others.

Balboa and his men were rewarded for their struggles. They stood atop a mountain and peered out at the Pacific Ocean, which Balboa called the South Sea. Balboa marched down to the ocean and tasted the salt water, just to be sure. Then he claimed all lands washed by this sea in the name of Spain "both now and [for] all time, as long as the world endures."

Unfortunately, Balboa got tangled up in a political rivalry with the governor of Panama. The governor ordered Balboa arrested. The man who came to arrest him was his old friend and fellow explorer, Francisco Pizarro. Balboa was stunned. Balboa was taken into custody, given an unfair trial, and beheaded.

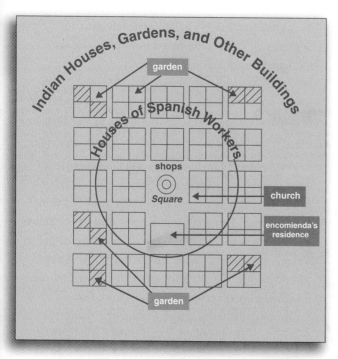

The encomienda system worked well for the Spanish settlers, but not for the Indians whose land they took.

Encomiendas

Of course, conquest was only the first step to building a new civilization. The Spanish also needed to encourage Spanish settlers to move to their newly conquered lands. They set up land and labor arrangements called *encomiendas* (en koh MYEN dus). A settler was given a large plot of land and a group of workers from the native population. The number of workers depended on the importance of the colonist.

In theory, this system was supposed to help establish new communities. The aim was to convert the native people to Christianity, build a strong economy, and make a profit for the Spanish crown. The encomienda system did make a lot of money for Spain and the Spanish settlers, but it did not succeed in building strong communities, and it led to the enslavement of the Indians.

Bartolomé de Las Casas

Many Spaniards got rich by conquering or enslaving the Indians, but others spoke out against such cruelty. One of those men was Bartolomé de Las Casas (bahr toh loh MAY de lahs KAH sahs).

Las Casas came from an exploring family. His father and his uncle had sailed with Christopher Columbus. In 1502, Las Casas sailed for the New World himself. He settled in Hispaniola, where he became a priest and where he was granted a large encomienda, complete with Indian workers. Eventually, though, Las Casas decided that the encomienda system was wrong because it enslaved the Indians. He began preaching sermons against slavery.

Las Casas returned to Spain to try to win the support of the king. He also wrote a long book telling people in Spain what was happening in the Americas. Las Casas's *The Devastation of the Indies: A Brief Account* helped convince the king. In the book, Las Casas wrote, "The reason why the Christians have killed and destroyed such an infinite number of souls is that they have been moved by their wish for gold and their desire to enrich themselves in a very short time."

The king did change the laws regarding the treatment of the Indians. But it was hard to enforce these laws thousands of miles away from Spain, and so Indians continued to suffer. Las Casas went on to write a history of the Spanish conquest of the Americas that is the source for much of what we know of conquered peoples such as the Aztecs in Mexico and Incas in Peru. Today Bartolomé de Las Casas is widely admired for being the first European to condemn mistreatment of the Indians.

erdinand Magellan The conquistadores conquered new lands for Spain, and sea captains continued to explore the oceans. One of the most famous of these captains was Ferdinand Magellan.

Magellan was born in Portugal during the great age of Portuguese exploration. As a boy, he served as a page in the Portuguese court and dreamed of a life at sea. Magellan was 13 when Columbus sailed back to Spain with tales of his westward travels. Columbus was an inspiration to Magellan, who went to sea.

Magellan was a hot-tempered fellow, and he was usually in one kind of trouble or another. His first expeditions took him to trading centers in the East, first as a crew member and later as a fleet commander in the Portuguese navy. But Magellan's hot temper eventually cost him the support of the Portuguese crown. The king refused to send him on any more expeditions.

Magellan's friends talked him into turning to Spain for support. In 1517, John of Lisbon, who was a famous navigator, had just returned from a Portuguese expedition to explore the coastline of Brazil. At about 35°S, even with the Cape of Good Hope at the southern tip of Africa, John said he had found a **strait.** He had information that might lead to the discovery of a route through the middle of the continent. John of Lisbon fired up Magellan's imagination. When another friend helped him get command of the Spanish expedition to explore this strait, Magellan jumped at the chance, turning his back on his homeland forever.

> **vocabulary**
> **strait** a narrow waterway connecting two bodies of water

Five ships carrying 277 men left port in September 1519. The boats began leaking immediately, and a mutiny occurred only a week into the three-month journey that took the fleet to the coast of Brazil. But Magellan asserted his command. In January 1520, the ships reached the waters that John of Lisbon had described.

However, Magellan was soon disappointed. The crew sent to explore the strait came back to say that it was a dead end. The strait led not through the continent and into the Pacific Ocean but into a bay. Magellan called a meeting of his officers to discuss their next move. Some wanted to sail back to Africa and on to the Spice Islands, following known routes. Some wanted to go back up the coast for the winter. Magellan made the decision to keep sailing south.

High winds and rough seas slowed the fleet, and the ships took a beating. In March, heavy snow finally stopped progress altogether. Magellan led his angry crew into a harbor on the coast of what is now Argentina. It was there, in early April, that Magellan faced his second mutiny. Once again, he was able to regain control of the men.

Finding the Strait

After losing one ship in rough seas, Magellan resumed the journey in October. Near the southern tip of South America, a storm blew the four remaining ships into a narrow strait. This strait turned out to be the strait Magellan had been seeking all along. Unfortunately, it was not easy to navigate. Tall cliffs loomed up on both sides, and violent tides threatened to smash the ships against the rocks.

Many of Magellan's men felt that discovering the strait was good enough; they were afraid to sail on through the strait, and they urged Magellan to turn back. But Magellan refused. The crew of one ship mutinied, and it turned back, but the other three pressed on. It took more than a month for the fleet to pass through the straits that would eventually be called the Straits of Magellan.

Finally, they emerged into a vast and pleasantly calm ocean. Magellan and his crew knelt down and recited a prayer of thanksgiving. Magellan then turned to his crew and announced, "Gentlemen, we are now steering into waters where no ship has sailed before. May we always find them as pacific [peaceful] as they are this morning. In this hope I shall name this sea the Pacific Ocean."

The fleet turned north and continued on its journey. The ships followed the west coast of South America until they could pick up the currents that would carry them west, across the ocean. Magellan, not knowing the size of the Pacific Ocean, figured that crossing the Pacific Ocean to Asia would take a few days. It took almost four months. The ships made landfall at some of the Pacific islands. But the ocean was so vast that supplies ran out quickly.

Finally, on March 16, Magellan and his crew spotted the easternmost island in the Philippine archipelago. The men who had survived the ordeal were able to gather their strength.

It was now a year and a half since they had left Spain, and the men were anxious to head for the Spice Islands and make their way home. But Magellan wanted to explore the Philippine Islands. This decision proved to be Magellan's final command to his weary men. Magellan got involved in a battle with some village chieftains and was killed in the fighting.

The crew sailed homeward under the command of Juan Sebastián del Cano. They finally reached Spain in September 1522, nearly three years after they had begun the journey. Only one ship of the original five remained, and only 18 of the original 277 men. But this ship and these men had done something not known to have been done by anyone before. They had **circumnavigated** the globe. Amazingly, the one ship carried home enough exotic spices to pay for the entire expedition.

> **vocabulary**
> **circumnavigate**
> to travel completely around something (as the earth), especially by water

Natives of a Pacific island, paddling out to meet Magellan and his men, had not seen ships like these before.

ohn Cabot In 1490, Giovanni Caboto (joh VAH nee kah BOH toh) moved his family from Venice to Spain. Caboto was caught up in the spirit of exploration. Years of experience as a Venetian spice trader had made him an expert seaman.

King Henry VII backed John Cabot's plans for a voyage to claim some of the riches of the East for England.

Caboto was ready to form an expedition to test his idea that there might be a northwesterly route to the Spice Islands. Unfortunately, the monarchs of both Portugal and Spain had other plans.

The Portuguese had established their own route to the East around the Cape of Good Hope at the southern tip of Africa. When Christopher Columbus returned from his voyage, the Spanish believed that they had found another route. No one wanted to hear Caboto's proposal for still another route.

Caboto moved on with his family. They settled in the port city of Bristol, England, where

Giovanni Caboto changed his name to John Cabot. The English monarch, Henry VII, and the merchants at the port were happy to give the explorer their support. They hoped he would bring them great wealth.

Under an English flag, John Cabot set sail in 1497 with only one ship and a crew of 18. The ship crossed the North Atlantic. After five weeks of travel, the crew spotted what they called "new found land." You may have learned about this area when you studied the Vikings and the colony they called Vinland. Cabot believed that he had found an island off the coast of Asia. He returned to England to report his find.

The sailors did not have any spices or silks to show for their journey, but they were able to describe scooping codfish out of the water in baskets. The voyage was judged a success, and another trip was planned for the following year.

Cabot again set sail, this time with a fleet of five ships. One of his ships returned to Bristol after a storm. Cabot and the other four ships were never seen again. To this day, nobody knows what happened to them.

The Northwest Passage

John Cabot was one of the first explorers to seek the Northwest Passage to the Indies. But he was not the last. Cabot's son Sebastian followed in his father's footsteps, as did many other explorers. For many years, all of these explorers were frustrated in their attempts. Those who went south found a continuous band of land blocking their way—the eastern coast of North America. Explorers who went farther north were literally stopped cold: ice in the water prevented their passage. Besides that, the farther north explorers went, the fewer goods they could find to bring back home. Northern explorers generally had almost nothing to show for their efforts.

Even though the explorers failed to find a shortcut to the Indies, the many attempts to find the Northwest Passage did have some positive results. Explorers looking for the passage made maps of the east coast of North America and thus set the stage for the colonization of the continents.

Sir Francis Drake

Once the Age of Exploration was underway and the seas were crowded with European ships carrying valuable materials, adventurous men could make lots of money as pirates. Indeed, one of the greatest English explorers made his name as a pirate, robbing Spanish and Portuguese ships and presenting the booty to Queen Elizabeth. His name was Francis Drake. Drake may have started as a pirate, but he turned into one of the greatest sea captains ever.

During his early years on the ocean, Drake's ship was attacked and robbed by a Spanish ship. Drake never forgot these attacks and spent much

of his adult life getting revenge on the Spaniards. As Drake crisscrossed the Atlantic, he took every opportunity to loot Spanish trade ships loaded with spices and silver. He also led raids on Spanish ports in the Americas.

In 1577, Drake convinced a group of people to invest in one of his voyages. He took a fleet of five ships with 164 crewmen on what at first seemed to be nothing more than one of his usual raiding parties. Instead, Drake followed Magellan's example by embarking on a journey around the world. Drake's surprised crew should have had a clue when Drake plundered a Portuguese ship and took not only several sacks of silver but also an experienced Portuguese pilot. This hostage guided Drake's fleet on its journey across the Atlantic.

Crossing from the Atlantic Ocean to the Pacific Ocean, through the Straits of Magellan, Drake observed the southerly area called by Magellan Tierra del Fuego (meaning "land of fire," for the campfires burning in native villages along the shore). He noted that this area was an archipelago rather than a part of the continent. This observation would lead future navigators to the open sea around Cape Horn at the southern tip of South America.

By the time the expedition passed through the Straits of Magellan and reached the west coast of South America, Drake was down to only 58 men on one ship, the *Golden Hind*. As the *Golden Hind* moved up the coast of what are now Chile and Peru, Drake captured ships and raided ports.

The world had never seen a sailor with the courage and daring of Francis Drake. In Peru, Drake sailed into a harbor crowded with Spanish ships and proceeded to rob each ship of its treasure. He learned that a ship loaded with gold and silver had just left port a few days earlier. The ship also had many powerful guns. That didn't stop Francis Drake.

Drake set sail, racing up the coast after the heavy and slow-moving Spanish treasure ship. When he saw it, he hung water barrels off the back of his ship to make *Golden Hind* look like a merchant ship. When he got close, he cut loose

Francis Drake circumnavigated the earth and terrorized Spanish settlements in the Americas at the same time. This is a reproduction of his ship, the **Golden Hind.**

the barrels and pulled up next to the Spanish ship. Drake's trained sailors jumped aboard the Spanish ship and cut down the Spanish crew, throwing many of them overboard. Then they looted the ship of its treasure and set it on fire.

Sailing farther north, Drake noted geographical features of the west coast, including San Francisco Bay, mapping his progress northward to what is now the Canadian border. Some historians think that he may have been searching for the opening to the Northwest Passage in the bays and rivers on North America's west coast. Along the way, Drake claimed California for Queen Elizabeth. He called the area New Albion, which was the ancient name for Britain.

After exploring the west coast of North America, the *Golden Hind* crossed the huge expanse of the Pacific, traveling southwest thousands of miles, helped along by charts stolen from a Spanish pilot. Drake explored the Spice Islands and filled the ship with spices and other valuable cargo before heading back to England.

Drake and his crew completed their round-the-world voyage loaded down with gold, silver, and spices. The treasure he presented to Queen Elizabeth paid off a large amount of the country's debt, and there was still enough profit left over to repay the investors nearly 50 times for their original investment. Queen Elizabeth rewarded Drake with a knighthood for his achievement.

The Spanish Armada

Spain was very angry about the actions of Francis Drake. Drake might be a hero in England, but to the Spanish he was nothing but a pirate. The Spanish ambassador called him "the master-thief of the unknown world." The Spaniards demanded that Queen Elizabeth return the stolen treasure and have Drake hanged. When the queen refused, Spain declared war.

Spain considered itself the strongest naval power in the world. It put together an armada, a fleet, of big ships loaded with heavy cannons and soldiers. The armada set sail in 1588 to invade England.

Drake and other English sea captains used imaginative battle tactics to defeat the Spanish. The English knew that they could not fight the huge Spanish fleet as a unit. So they set small ships on fire and sent them into the Spanish battle formations. The Spanish, afraid that the ships were loaded with gunpowder, broke formation. Then the English in their smaller, more mobile ships ganged up on the lumbering Spanish battleships, sinking many. As Spanish ships retreated, a storm sank still more ships. In the end, only about half of the more than 130 ships that set sail in the mighty armada returned safely to Spain.

England had won a great victory. The defeat of the Spanish Armada also marked a change in the balance of sea power from Spain to England. The 1500s had belonged to Spain. In the 1600s and 1700s it would be English ships that ruled the seas.

Building Colonies

In the 1500s, Spain had conquered Mexico and Central and South America. The Spanish extracted a great fortune in gold and silver from their American colonies. Indeed, the main purpose of many Spanish colonies was to find gold and silver and send these precious metals back to Spain. Even the encomiendas you learned about were set up for the benefit of a few wealthy Spaniards.

England took a different approach to building colonies. The area that England claimed, the Atlantic coast of North America, did not have

easily obtained riches like gold and silver. These lands needed permanent settlements where people would farm, fish, cut timber, and harvest the other resources of the region.

Building colonies took a lot of money. The English kings and queens did not want to spend the money. Instead, they gave grants of land to well-to-do people or businesses called **joint-stock companies** to build the colonies.

In the sixteenth century, Spain was a great maritime nation with an armada of many ships like this one.

The first English colony was founded by Sir Walter Raleigh in 1585. Raleigh shipped a group of men to Roanoke Island, off the coast of modern-day North Carolina. Unfortunately, Raleigh's colonists grew discouraged by the hard work and lack of women. After only a few months, they hitched a ride home with Sir Francis Drake.

In 1587, Raleigh sent a second group to the island. This time, he sent women and children along with the men. He hoped that a community of families would stay put.

The colony got off to a good start. A baby girl, Virginia Dare, was the first English child born in the land that would become the United States. But in 1590, a supply ship reached the colony and found that everyone had disappeared without a trace,

> **vocabulary**
> **joint-stock company** a company that raises money by selling shares, or interest in the company, in the form of stock

145

perhaps wiped out by a hostile Indian tribe. All that was left was one word carved on a tree. The colony that Raleigh founded is now known as the "Lost Colony."

In 1607, a joint-stock company called the London Company started a colony at Jamestown, Virginia. Jamestown was the first permanent English settlement in North America. The colony struggled for its first years. But Indians taught the colonists how to grow tobacco, a crop that was native to North America and unknown in Europe. Tobacco was a big success and quickly turned into a cash crop for the colonists.

Massachusetts was settled by English colonists searching for religious freedom. In 1620, the Pilgrims settled at Plymouth. Ten years later, the Puritans formed the Massachusetts Bay Company and settled in Boston.

During the 1600s, the English settled most of the Atlantic coast. They also built colonies on islands in the West Indies in the Caribbean Sea.

English colonies survived and prospered. By 1700, well-established English colonies stretched from the fisheries of Newfoundland to the sugar plantations of the Caribbean. These colonies were built on strong trade connections. They became home to people who were looking for wealth, religious freedom, and unlimited opportunities for themselves and their children.

Pursuing the Spice Trade

While England was successfully building colonies in North America, it had not forgotten about the rest of the world. It was also active in competing for a part of the spice trade in Asia.

The East India Company decided that traveling all the way to the Spice Islands from England was too dangerous and too expensive. Instead, the company directors chose India for their base of operations. Before long, the East India Company had settlements in the Indian cities of Surat, Madras, Bombay, and Calcutta and was granted the authority to raise an army. It was only a matter of time before the English expanded their holdings in India and started permanent trading posts there.

This is an English engraving of the establishment of the Roanoke colony in 1585. Sir Walter Raleigh's plan for a successful colony failed.

rance Joins In In the early 1500s, Spain was finding gold and silver in Mexico and Peru. Portugal ruled the spice trade in the Indian Ocean. England had sent John Cabot to look for the Northwest Passage. The king of France, Francis I, was not about to be left behind.

Cartographers were important participants in the voyages of early explorers. This map shows Jacques Cartier's explorations of New France.

In 1524, the king hired an Italian explorer named Giovanni da Verrazano (joh VAH nee da ver rah ZAH noh) to explore North America and look for a passage to the East. Sailing with Verrazano was his brother, a **cartographer.** This was a new world that had

> **vocabulary**
> **cartographer** a mapmaker

not been mapped. One of the goals of the trip was to bring back accurate maps of the Atlantic coast.

Verrazano was the first European to sail up the Atlantic coast of the present-day United States. He sailed from North Carolina up to Newfoundland. He sailed into New York Bay and noted what a fine deepwater harbor it was. Today the entrance to New York Harbor is spanned by the Verrazano-Narrows Bridge, named in his honor.

Verrazano was the first European to have contact with the Indians who lived around New York, and he gave a very favorable report of them.

> These people are the most beautiful and have the most civil customs we have seen on this voyage. They are taller then we are. They are of a bronze color and some tend to whiteness, others to a tawny color. The face is clear-cut, the hair is long and black, and they take great care to decorate it.

When Verrazano explored New York Harbor, many friendly Indians rowed out to greet him. But not all of the tribes in the new world were as happy to see the explorer. Several years later, on his third voyage to the Americas, Verrazano went ashore on a West Indian island inhabited by a tribe of cannibals. He was captured, killed, and eaten.

Jacques Cartier

The French king was sorry about Verrazano's fate. But he was determined to keep searching for the Northwest Passage. In 1534, he asked Jacques Cartier (zhak kar tee AY), a French ship captain, to explore the coast of North America.

Cartier sailed to Newfoundland, where he found English and Spanish fishing fleets. John Cabot may have failed to discover the Northwest Passage, but he did notice the Grand Banks off the coast of the island of Newfoundland. The Grand Banks was one of the richest fishing grounds in the world.

Cartier continued exploring the coast of Labrador and the Gulf of St. Lawrence. The French captain was an excellent sailor, but on this voyage he made a bad mistake. He thought the Gulf of St. Lawrence was just a bay and not the outlet for a mighty river so he did not explore further. Cartier claimed all the land he saw for the king of France.

Cartier returned to France. In the next year he returned to North America, this time sailing up the St. Lawrence. As he sailed up the mighty river, Cartier admired the land that he saw. He wrote in his logbook:

> Along both shores we saw the most excellent and beautiful land that can be seen, smooth as a pond, covered with the finest trees in the world, and along the river were so many vines laden with grapes that they seemed to have been planted by human hands.

Cartier made friends with some of the Indians. He visited an Indian village on an island in the St. Lawrence. He climbed a hill and named it Mount Royal. This site eventually became part of the Canadian city of Montreal.

During the winter, Cartier's men became sick with scurvy. Many of them died. Cartier gave up hope of ever returning to France. The snow was four feet deep. There seemed to be nothing to do but wait to die.

The friendship between Cartier and the Indians saved him and his men. The Indians taught the French how to brew a drink made from evergreen trees. (Today we know that such a brew is rich in vitamin C.) It cured the French explorers of their scurvy, and in the spring they were able to return to France.

Cartier returned on a third voyage to what is today Canada. The king wanted a colony in North America. But no settlers could be persuaded to go. So the king sent prisoners.

The colony was doomed from the start. The prisoners were happy to get out of jail but not eager to work. Supply ships were late in arriving. Cartier gave up and returned to France.

In the next 60 years, France was racked by political troubles and wars. Little attention was paid to the land Cartier claimed for France.

Champlain and New France

During the 1500s French ships came to the Grand Banks to fish. Some of the ships started trading with the Indians. The Indians were eager to have tools, hatchets, and other metal goods.

The French wanted to trade for furs, particularly beaver skins, which were in great demand in Europe for making men's hats.

The growth of the fur trade got France interested again in building colonies in the land they called New France. The key figure in the settlement of New France was an explorer named Samuel de Champlain.

In 1603, Champlain sailed to New France for the first time. He explored the coast of Maine and Nova Scotia. The first settlement Champlain founded was in Nova Scotia. In 1608, Champlain moved the settlement to the site of Quebec City, on the banks of the St. Lawrence River. At a point where the river narrows, Champlain built a town on the heights with a view of the river.

New France grew in a very different way from the English colonies. At first very few settlers came to New France. The winters were long and hard. Farming was difficult because the **growing season** was so short.

People attracted to New France were rugged adventurers who liked to travel up the rivers in canoes to trade with the Indians. For a while that suited the French government just fine. The colony made a profit, and there weren't a lot of demanding colonists to deal with.

Colonists in New France also dealt with the Indians differently from the way the English in the colonies to the south treated them. English colonists needed land, so they sometimes fought wars with the Indians to push them off their

La Salle, surrounded by crew members, priests, and Native Americans, claims the land along the Mississippi River for France.

land. In New France, fur traders generally made friends with the Indians. The French made alliances with some Indian nations and helped them in their wars with their rivals.

The fur trade resulted in further exploration. Brave fur traders canoed and **portaged** farther and farther into the North American wilderness. In 1673, an expedition led by Jacques Marquette (mahr KET) and Louis Jolliet (joh lee ay) became the first European expedition to reach the Mississippi River.

In 1682, a French explorer with the imposing name of René-Robert Cavelier, Sieur de La Salle (reh NAY roh BAYR kah vel YAY syer duh lah SAL) sailed down the Mississippi River to the Gulf of Mexico. La Salle claimed all the land drained by the Mississippi for the king of France.

By 1700, New France was a sizable empire with one big problem: There were hardly any settlers. There were about 10,000 Europeans in the entire area. Although the fur trade was profitable, it was going to be hard for France to defend its empire when a rival appeared. And the rival was right next door. England and France had been rivals in Europe, and they would soon became rivals in North America as well.

> **vocabulary**
> **growing season** the days available to plant and harvest crops
> **portage** to carry a canoe and supplies overland from one waterway to another

ontrol of the Spice Trade For many years, the Portuguese had control of the spice trade from the Cape of Good Hope to the most distant shores of the Indian Ocean. They had settlements up and down the African coast and a main trade center at Goa, on the west coast of India.

In the meantime, Spain was busy mining the gold that had been discovered in the Americas. Spain did not care very much about the spice trade except to make sure that others did not benefit from it too much.

The death of King Henry of Portugal in 1580 changed the history of the spice trade. The death of a king could create political unrest when it was unclear who should succeed him. That's what happened in Portugal. Henry had no adult son. There were seven different people who presented themselves as having the right to be the next king of Portugal. One of them was King Philip II of Spain. Philip was related to Henry on his mother's side. After some confusion, Portugal became part of Spain.

At first there was little effect on the spice trade. The Spanish navy was the most powerful in the world, and it was there to protect Portuguese ships sailing to Asia. Only now a good part of the profits went to the king of Spain.

In 1588, the defeat of the Spanish Armada tipped the balance of sea power in the world. The defeat crippled Spain as a sea power. As Spanish power declined, the Dutch, who were at war with Spain, saw an opportunity to take control of the spice trade.

The Dutch were excellent sailors and merchants, and they were able to make a strong showing in the spice trade. A Dutch seaman named Jan van Linschoten (yahn vahn LIHN skoh tun) played

The animals and vegetation of the Spice Islands continued to inspire the imagination of artists and storytellers.

an important role. Linschoten spent his seafaring life looking for a northeastern route to the Spice Islands, a route that did not exist.

When he quit exploring, Linschoten worked in India. He kept long and detailed notes about the Eastern traders he worked with, and the information he gathered was a great help to the Dutch as they entered the spice trade.

The Dutch set up their main trade center on the island of Java in present-day Indonesia. They named the community Batavia. (Today it is called Jakarta and is the capital city of Indonesia.) It was far away from the Portuguese on the African coast but close to the nutmeg, mace, and cloves in the Molucca islands.

In the early 1600s Dutch merchants formed a joint-stock company called the Dutch East India Company. The company received a **charter** from the government giving it a monopoly on all trade stretching east from the Cape of Good Hope in Africa to the Straits of Magellan in South America.

The Dutch took charge of the spice trade at its source. However, the Netherlands is a very small country without many resources of its own. As a result, the Dutch did not have many goods to trade from their home ports. Instead, they traveled throughout the East gathering up goods to trade. Dutch ships called at ports all over Africa, India, and other Asian countries. They voyaged into the Persian Gulf and all the way to Japan. They got silver from one place and cloth or tea from another. The trades were set up so that, in the end, spices ended up in the hands of the Dutch for transport to Europe.

The Dutch worked hard to control every part of the spice trade. They carefully controlled the amount of spices available in Europe. If there was too much cinnamon available, they burned it rather than allow the price to fall. They also soaked their nutmeg in lime juice. The flavor stayed the same, but the juice killed the germ of the nut so no one could use the nut as a seed to plant more nutmeg.

Since the trading center at Java was so far away from the Netherlands, the Dutch company got permission from the monarch to set up a government of its own. The leaders of the Dutch East India Company had their own army, minted their own money, and created their own laws to keep everyone in line.

A Stopover Colony

Traveling back to the Netherlands took a very long time. The Dutch needed a rest stop along the way, so they set up a colony at Cape Town, on the southern tip of Africa. The Dutch actually found Cape Town by accident. A Dutch ship damaged by a storm managed to limp into Cape Town's Table Bay before sinking. The surviving sailors found that Table Bay had everything needed for a supply station, including a good harbor and a fair climate. The Dutch built Cape Town, and the colony soon become a major settlement.

> **vocabulary**
> **charter** a document issued by an authority giving a group certain rights

Over the years, many Dutch explorers set out across the Pacific to find new trade centers. Sailing from southeast Java, Dirk Hartog found Australia. In 1643, Abel Tasman discovered the island he named Tasmania, off Australia's southeastern coast. By sailing around Australia, Tasman showed that it was a huge island unconnected to any other land.

The Dutch did not follow up these explorations. As a small country, the Netherlands did not have thousands of people willing to move to new colonies in distant places. Many were hardworking businesspeople. If a region did not have goods that could help them keep control of the spice trade, they had little interest in the region. For 200 years, through the 1600s and 1700s, the Dutch profited from the spice trade in Asia.

Henry Hudson and New Netherland

An English explorer named Henry Hudson got a job in 1609 with the Dutch East India Company. As you have learned, countries involved in the spice trade were eager to find a quicker way to reach Asia from northern Europe. Maybe Hudson would be the lucky explorer to find the Northwest Passage that everyone was seeking.

Hudson took a small crew on a small ship called the *Half Moon.* He sailed north, following the coast of Norway. The farther north the *Half Moon* traveled, the colder and icier it got. The crew began to grumble. Conditions on the ship soon went from bad to worse. Hudson had planned to find a passage that would take him right over the pole and down to the Malay Archipelago. Instead, he changed his mind and headed west.

Hudson charted the *Half Moon's* course down the Atlantic coast of North America to find the Northwest Passage. At the mouth of what is now the Hudson River, he claimed land for the Netherlands.

For the first few days that the *Half Moon* sailed up the Hudson River, Hudson must have felt great excitement. The river was wide and deep, with steep sides and a strong current. Surely this was the passage—the way through

Mutinous crew members force Henry Hudson off his ship to face certain death in the cold and barren area.

the continent. Hudson sailed up the river to the site of present-day Albany, New York. But as the river grew more shallow, it became clear that it was not the way to the Pacific Ocean. Hudson returned to Europe.

The next year, Hudson returned to North America, this time on an English ship, the *Discovery.* Hudson was sure that to find the Northwest Passage he would have to sail north. He discovered the huge inland sea in Canada now called Hudson Bay. Hudson thought he had managed to sail to the Pacific Ocean.

Hudson's excitement did not last long. It soon became clear that he and his men were in an inland sea. Winter came quickly, and the ship got stuck in the ice. As food ran low, the crew got angry and mutinied. Hudson, his son, and some loyal sailors were put over the side in a small boat. They were never heard from again. Sailors on the *Discovery* made it back to England. They were never punished for the mutiny.

New Netherland

Dutch merchants were eager to make money from the land claimed by Hudson. A joint-stock company called the New Netherland Company was formed by a group of Dutch merchants in 1614.

The company's first activity was fur trading. A trading post was built at Fort Orange (today,

Albany, New York) far up the river explored by Hudson. The fur trading went well and merchants prospered. But the company was unsuccessful in getting colonists to come to this new land. The population of the Netherlands was still small. Most people were reluctant to leave their settled homeland to live in a distant wilderness.

Eventually a new company called the Dutch West India Company took over. In 1626, Peter Minuit (MIHN yoo iht), the head of the Dutch West India Company, came to the island of Manhattan, today the heart of New York City. In one of the most famous business deals in history, Minuit bought the island of Manhattan from the Indians for beads and trinkets worth about $24. (Today a tiny building lot in Manhattan sells for many millions of dollars.) On the southern tip of Manhattan, the Dutch built a town they called New Amsterdam. The town grew slowly and the Dutch government didn't think the North American colony was worth the high cost of defending it.

In 1664 an English warship sailed into New York Harbor and took over the colony. The English changed the name of New Amsterdam to New York in honor of the duke of York. The Dutch attempt to colonize North America was over.

The early settlement of New Amsterdam consisted of a fort and several small buildings, including a windmill.

t' Fort nieuw Amsterdam op de Manhatans

Long Tradition There had been slaves for many years prior to the Age of Exploration. For centuries people throughout the world had enslaved those they had conquered. So Europeans did not invent slavery. But they did use their power and wealth to spread it on such a vast scale that it changed the lives of millions of people.

Slavery had been part of African life long before Europeans arrived. For centuries, Africans had been marched across the Sahara to Arab slave markets in the Middle East, or shipped across the Indian Ocean from East Africa. Besides supplying victims for this cruel traffic, many African cultures also practiced slavery. But among at least some African peoples, slaves had certain rights. For example, in the Ashanti kingdom of West Africa, slaves could own property and marry, and they got their freedom after working for a set amount of time. Most important, Ashanti slaves did not pass their status on to their children. This was still slavery, but of a slightly more humane form than what would be spread by Europeans.

The African slave trade was opened up in 1415 when the Portuguese seized the city of Ceuta (seh YOO tuh) on the North African coast. Slaves became one of the trade goods that were transported back to Europe as the Portuguese pushed their way down the west coast and up the east coast of Africa. During the next hundred years, nearly 200,000 Africans were taken as slaves to parts of Europe and to islands in the Atlantic.

In the 1400s, Portuguese and Spanish explorers discovered several groups of islands in the Atlantic Ocean. Colonists soon descended on these islands. Portugal built colonies on Madeira (muh DEER uh), São Tomé (sou tuh MEH), and the Azores (AY zorz). Spain colonized the Canary Islands.

Spanish and Portuguese colonists realized that the land and climate in these islands would be good for growing sugar, and the demand for sugar in Europe was tremendous. But growing sugar was not like the farming that Europeans were used to. Sugar was a cash crop. In order for it to be profitable, huge fields of sugarcane had to be planted and harvested. This required lots of workers. For Spanish and Portuguese plantation owners, slavery was the answer to their need for labor. As sugar plantations sprang up, the slave trade took off.

Slavery in the Americas

When Columbus discovered the islands of the Caribbean sea, the Spanish quickly colonized the region. Spanish colonies were set up to help get the wealth of the Americas back to Spain. In Mexico and Peru, the Spanish gathered vast amounts of gold and silver. They used Indians to work in the mines.

The West Indies were not rich in mineral wealth. But the land and climate were well suited for growing sugar and other crops. Experts from the Canary Islands came to Hispaniola and other islands to help set up sugar plantations. But these plantations also needed a labor force. At first, plantation owners thought they would use local Indians to work the plantations. But disease and war had killed many of the Indians in the islands.

As had been the case in the Azores and the Canary Islands, slaves from Africa provided the perfect answer for plantation owners. The Spanish were not the only Europeans who thought of this solution. Portuguese colonists found that sugar was well suited to the coastal regions of Brazil. They imported slave laborers to raise sugarcane there. In the 1600s, England colonized several islands in the West Indies, including Jamaica and St. Kitts. British planters, too, turned to African slaves to work on their sugar plantations. Sugar

The great profit that came from the sugar plantations was the result of slave labor.

made the planters rich. But the sugar growers created another business that could make someone rich—the slave trade.

The Slave Trade

The Portuguese were the first Europeans in the Atlantic slave trade. Their explorations of the African coast had opened up new sources for slaves. Later, when Portugal's power collapsed and the Dutch took over the spice trade, they took over much of the Atlantic slave trade as well.

In 1619, a Dutch ship sailed into the mouth of the James River in the English colony of Virginia and dropped anchor. On board were Dutch pirates who had been attacking other ships on the high seas. They had taken a shipload of Africans from a Spanish vessel heading for the Caribbean. Now they were traveling north and needed supplies. The Dutch sailors traded the Africans for food. This was the first arrival of Africans in the English North American colonies.

One of the trade centers the Dutch had taken from the Portuguese was Elmina on the west coast of Africa (in present-day Ghana). For years, Elmina had been a Portuguese trade center where ivory and gold were exchanged. As the slave trade increased, Elmina became one of the forts where Africans were imprisoned before being transported to Europe or to the Americas. Before long, Elmina was the center of the Dutch slave trade.

By 1655, the Dutch were transporting 2,500 slaves a year across the Atlantic. When England seized control of New Netherland, there were 500 Dutch-speaking Africans in the colony.

The slave trade was one side of a trading triangle. The first segment of the triangle carried goods from Europe to Africa. Ships carried items such as iron, guns, gunpowder, knives, cloth, and beads. The second segment transported slaves from Africa to the Caribbean islands and later to the English colonies in North America. The third segment of the triangle made a return trip to

Europe. These ships carried tobacco, sugar, and rice from the plantations of the Americas.

Middle Passage

Africans typically passed through several stages in their journey into slavery. First, they were captured, sometimes by European slavers but usually during wars among the African tribes. Next they were marched to a seaport like Elmina. There they were packed into ships for the journey across the Atlantic. Those who survived the journey were sold at a slave market in a seaport in the Americas and transported to plantations.

The trip across the Atlantic Ocean was known as the Middle Passage. It was a terrible, dehumanizing experience. Slave ships usually carried between 150 and 600 Africans. Slaves were treated like cargo, not people. They were chained on platforms. Each person had a space about 6 feet long and 16 inches wide. Because they were chained in place, they could not even turn over. How did they get up to go to the bathroom? They didn't.

As the ships passed through tropical latitudes, temperatures in the **hold** would rise to over 100 degrees. Slaves were fed a little rice and water, twice a day. On some ships, they were led up on deck once a day for exercise. Some ship captains then had the hold cleaned out. But not all of them did.

The trip across the ocean took between two and four months depending on the weather and the destination. It is no surprise that illness and death were common occurrences. Disease spread easily with no way to dispose of human waste, no sanitation whatsoever, and the close quarters. Historians estimate that about 15 percent of slaves did not survive the journey. The Atlantic slave trade lasted nearly 300 years, and in that time, European slave traders made approximately 54,000 voyages across the Atlantic.

The Growth of Slavery in the Colonies

In the colonies of North America, the demand for slaves came later in the slave trade. The Pilgrims and Puritans had settled in the colonies in the Northeast, where the soil was not very good, and the winters were cold. These conditions were not ideal for growing cash crops, so there was no need for a large labor force to carry out the business of the colony. Slavery on a small scale did exist in these northern colonies, though.

In the South, the situation was different. Plantation owners who lived in the southern colonies grew tobacco to export to Europe. They needed many workers to run these plantations. At first, plantation owners thought the Native Americans would make up the workforce.

However, these people were accustomed to moving in small groups over a wide area. So it was hard to bring many of them together. Many Indians also became ill and died from the diseases that the Europeans carried.

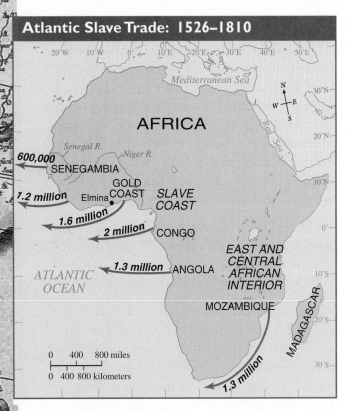

Atlantic Slave Trade: 1526–1810

This map shows the number of Africans forced into slavery in the Americas.

To find a supply of workers, plantation owners began paying for British **indentured servants** to come to the colonies. In return, the servants agreed to work for a certain number of years. A steady supply of workers could be brought from the home country, but it didn't work out very well.

It was hard to keep the workers alive. The hot weather, high humidity, and swampy water were perfect conditions for breeding disease. Even those indentured servants who were able to get used to the new climate did not live very long. The work was very hard, and the conditions were very bad. Many of the servants did not survive long enough to fulfill their contracts. It was necessary to keep paying for servants to cross the ocean.

Despite these problems, when the plantations first got started, the owners were glad to pay for indentured servants instead of slaves. In fact, the first Africans brought over to work were indentured servants. At the end of a certain amount of time, they were granted their freedom.

In time, the use of indentured servants began to seem less attractive to the plantation owners. Little by little, the plantations moved away from the coast, where disease had been a big problem. Servants were living longer. They ate better and could avoid drinking bad water. You would think that having healthy, strong servants would be an improvement for the owners. But healthy servants started living long enough to fulfill their contracts. The plantation owners started having to pay out more in "freedom dues."

Freedom dues were what you received once you had put in your time as a servant. According to the contract, an indentured servant was given food, clothing, money, and some livestock. Those who were given land could finish their contracts and start farming right next door.

Before long, purchasing slaves from Africa was more profitable and efficient for the plantation owner. Slavery spread in the 1700s. Millions of acres were planted with tobacco. Planters also introduced a new cash crop, rice, which needed lots of labor to plant and harvest. In the late 1700s and early 1800s, cotton became a third cash crop grown in the American south. And cotton cultivation relied on slave labor.

Plantation Life

The life of a slave was very hard. Slaves were sold at a market where owners bid against each other. Slaveholders bought the slaves they thought would work best for them. That meant that frequently families were broken up, children separated from parents, husbands from wives.

On the plantation, slaves had no freedom. They had to do what their masters told them to do and could not travel anywhere without permission. They could not testify in court, so an owner could mistreat a slave and get away with it. Many colonies also had laws that made it illegal to teach slaves to read or write. White slaveholders did not want slaves getting any ideas about freedom.

Slaves worked from dawn to nightfall, with an hour off midday in the heat. The work was hard. They worked in the cotton and tobacco fields. They chopped wood, built fences, cleared roads, and dug wells. Slaves were watched by a person called an *overseer.* Any slave who did not work hard could be whipped.

Not all Africans in the colonies lived as slaves. Some managed to win their freedom. There were a few slaveholders who gave their slaves freedom. Free Africans in northern colonies made their living as farmers and craftsworkers. After the American Revolution, slavery was abolished in the northern states.

Slaves frequently tried to run away. Some were successful in reaching northern states or Canada, where slavery was outlawed. But slavery spread in the American South, where it survived until the end of the Civil War.

Summing Up the Age of Exploration

The Age of Exploration brought tremendous changes to the world. The United States and Canada had their first beginnings in this era, and they might not exist if the explorers discussed in this unit had stayed home. For this we must be grateful. It is also hard not to admire the courage of men like Columbus and Magellan who risked their lives to sail on uncharted waters.

However, to have a full and well-balanced understanding of the Age of Exploration, we should also recognize that this age, like most ages, was better for some people than others.

For many Europeans it was a great time to be alive. A few made fortunes. Many found new lives, abundant land, and religious freedom in a new world.

For other people the Age of Exploration was a time of hardship and often death. The native peoples of the Americas were devastated by contact with Europeans. Many died in battle, and millions more perished from disease. And, for millions of Africans, contact with Europeans meant a lifetime of slavery. The image of the ship braving the rough waters of the Atlantic becomes much less inspiring when we remember that many of these ships carried human cargo in inhuman conditions. An understanding of the age must take into account both the heroism of the explorers and the tragedies that resulted from exploration.

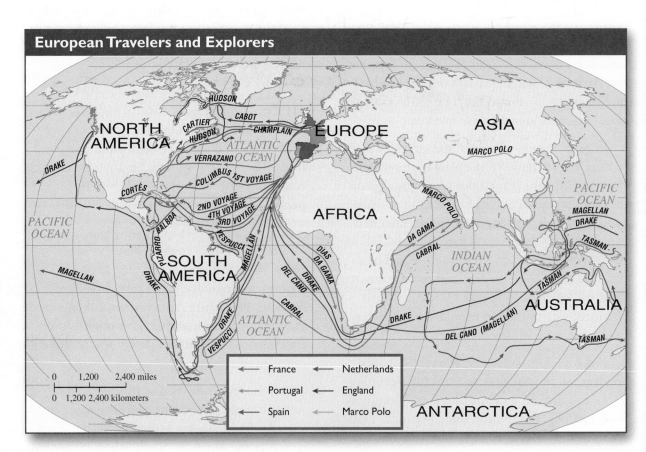

European Travelers and Explorers

We might not be living where and how we are today if it had not been for the courage, curiosity, and greed of the explorers.

Glossary

archipelago a chain of islands

cartographer a mapmaker

charter a document issued by an authority giving a group certain rights

circumnavigate to travel completely around something (as the earth), especially by water

growing season the days available to plant and harvest crops

hold the interior of a ship below the decks

hull the sides and bottom of a boat

indentured servant a person who owes an employer a certain amount of work for a certain amount of time

infidel someone who does not believe in what is considered the true religion

joint-stock company a company that raises money by selling shares, or interest in the company, in the form of stock

league an old measurement of distance equal to approximately 3 miles

monopoly complete control of selling a product or service

Moor a North African follower of Islam

mutiny a rebellion against a leader such as a ship's captain

navigation traveling by ship from one place to another

portage to carry a canoe and supplies overland from one waterway to another

rain shadow an area that gets less rain because it is on the protected side of a mountain

royal standard a monarch's flag

scurvy a disease caused by a lack of vitamin C, which is found in fresh fruits and vegetables

strait a narrow waterway connecting two bodies of water

Early Russia

Contents

eet the Giant Imagine a giant standing with his left foot in one world and his right foot in another. The people of each world have their own languages, customs, and religions. The giant takes a little from one world and a little from the other world, and tries to get along with both.

That giant is the huge country of Russia, standing with one foot in Europe and the other in Asia. Russia is a big country. In fact, it is the biggest in the world—nearly twice the size of the United States.

Russia is so wide that it stretches from eastern Europe across northern Asia to the Pacific Ocean. It spans not only two continents, but also 11 time zones. That means that someone living in western Russia is waking up just as someone living in eastern Russia is eating dinner.

As you learn about early Russia, you will read stories of high adventure, wars, weak and strong rulers, and the growth of a mighty country from its humble beginnings in the early 800s to a great empire in the eighteenth century.

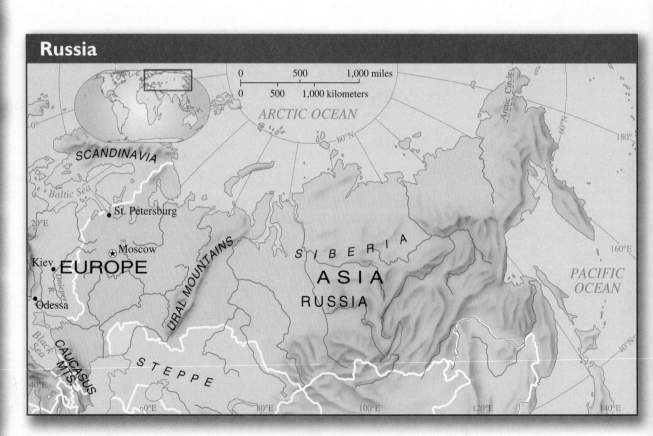

Russia is a giant country that stretches across two continents—Europe and Asia.

The Roots of Russia

Russia was not always as large as it is today. What we now call Russia first began as a series of small villages along the rivers in the western part of modern-day Russia. In the early years of the country's history, various groups of people spread throughout this area. Sometimes these people came to trade and sometimes they came to conquer. But always they brought new ideas and customs. Among the earliest groups of people in Russia were the Slavs.

The Slavs originally came from the area of modern-day eastern Poland, the western Ukraine, and the Czech (chek) Republic. For the most part, these people were farmers. Some became merchants who traded with people in other countries. The Slavs spread throughout central Europe and Russia.

By A.D. 800, or the early Middle Ages, the Slavs had built a number of towns along the rivers in southern Russia. The Slavs used the rivers as trading routes. They developed contacts with many different groups of people and sometimes went to war with them.

The Vikings

As the Slavs were settling into the lands now called Russia, they collided with the Vikings, who were moving south from Scandinavia, the lands we now know as Sweden, Norway, and Denmark. The Vikings, also called Norsemen, were great warriors and traders.

As they pressed south, the Vikings were seeking trading partners. They wanted to trade their products from Scandinavia for products they did not make at home. Some of the long river routes the Vikings followed into central Europe took their war and trading ships through the lands of the Slavs beginning in the 800s. The Slavs called the Vikings "Rus (roos)," which was their term for "Swedes."

The Vikings liked the lands they found on their voyages throughout central Europe and along the Dnieper (DNE pur) River in what is now Ukraine, once a part of Russia. Some of them decided to make their homes among the Slavs already living there.

The Vikings were more powerful than the Slavs. They forced the Slavs to trade with them, whether the Slavs wanted to or not. The Vikings often threatened to destroy the Slavs if the Slavs did not give the Vikings certain amounts of goods or money every year. This payment made by the Slavs to the more powerful Vikings was called **tribute.**

Over the years, however, the Slavic and Viking peoples blended together. They began to adopt each other's customs, blending into the first people we call Russians today.

> **vocabulary**
> **tribute** money or goods that weaker people are forced to pay to stronger people

The Coming of Christianity

Another powerful influence on early Russia was the Christian religion that the Russians soon adopted as their own. At the time of the Viking and Slav settlements, most Russians worshiped a variety of gods. As the Russians came into contact with other countries, they learned about religions such as Islam, Judaism, and Christianity that taught there is only one God.

Russian holy paintings are called icons. This is an icon of St. Nicholas.

Christianity worked its way into Russia from the Byzantine (BIHZ un teen) Empire, which was to the south of Russia. In the 800s the Byzantine Empire was one of the most powerful empires in the world. Its capital was Constantinople. Greek missionaries from Constantinople brought Christianity to the Russian city of Kiev (KEE ev) around 900. The Byzantine form of Christianity was known as Orthodox, or Greek Orthodox, Christianity.

These missionaries taught some of the early Russians about Christianity. One of these Russians was a princess named Olga living in Kiev. Princess Olga was married to Igor I, the ruler of Kiev. After Igor was killed in 945, Olga took control of the government because her son was too young to rule. She was probably the first woman ruler in Russia.

A few years after she came to power, Olga traveled to Constantinople. While there, she met the Byzantine emperor, who supposedly was so struck by her beauty and wisdom that he asked her to marry him. She turned down the emperor's offer of marriage, but asked him to teach her about his religion.

The emperor wanted to please Princess Olga, so he asked the patriarch (PAY tree ahrk), or leader, of the Orthodox Christian Church in Constantinople, to teach her about Christianity. According to legend, Olga learned about Christianity "like a sponge absorbing water."

Olga then returned to Kiev and introduced the Orthodox Christian religion to her people. Most Russians, however, stayed true to their old gods—the gods of nature, the winds, the fields, and the family. Even Olga's son resisted her attempts to Christianize Kiev.

Years passed, and wooden statues of many different gods still stood in Kiev. Now, Prince Vladimir, grandson of Princess Olga, ruled the city. Vladimir wanted Kiev to be a great power and was interested in the religions of other great powers. He listened to traveling merchants who came to Kiev and spoke of religious beliefs in the Byzantine Empire and in western Europe. Instead of many gods, the merchants spoke of a single almighty God.

Prince Vladimir asked his nobles what they thought about other religions. They told him that if he wanted to learn more, he should send "ten good and true men" to visit other lands and observe how people in those lands worshiped. Prince Vladimir did as the nobles suggested. When the ten advisers returned, they reported that the Orthodox Christian religion with its ornate churches and ceremonial chanting, was the best religion they had seen.

In 988, Vladimir became an Orthodox Christian, like his grandmother Princess Olga. He destroyed all the statues and pictures of the old gods and goddesses and ordered all the people in Kiev to be baptized as Christians.

Prince Vladimir of Kiev made Christianity the official religion of that city.

The Mongols "Give us trade," demanded the Vikings from the north. "Try our religion," urged missionaries from the south. Now a new voice was heard throughout Russia. "Pay us taxes," ordered the Mongols of the east.

The Mongols spread fear and destruction throughout Russia in the 1200s.

Because of its geography, Russia is a relatively easy country to invade from both east and west. It has suffered major invasions throughout its history. A little more than 700 years ago, Russia endured one of the greatest and most important invasions in its history when the Mongols of central Asia invaded from the east.

The invasion route into Russia from the east is especially easy. A grassland known as the steppe (step) stretches some 5,000 miles from eastern Europe into central Asia.

Most of the steppe is a low, level grassland. The steppe has cold winters and hot, dry summers, much like the Great Plains of North America. Hard-riding tribes from central Asia have used the steppe as an invasion route into Russia and eastern Europe for thousands of years.

Russia does have one important mountain range, the Urals, but the Urals are not very high mountains. Over the centuries, erosion has worn them down to not much more than forested hills.

Mapmakers often use the Urals as a dividing line between Europe and Asia. Many geographers consider Russia west of the Urals as part of Europe and Russia east of the Urals as part of Asia. To be sure, the Urals make a better boundary than barrier. While the Alps in Europe have been high enough to block the movement of traders and warriors, the Urals have never been much of an obstacle. In the thirteenth century, the Urals did little to stop the fierce Mongol invaders who galloped in from the Asian steppe.

A Ferocious Conqueror

During the thirteenth century, the Mongols were one of the most powerful peoples in the world. They originated in central Asia and spread out in all directions. They conquered China and most of western Asia, as well as Russia. They created the largest empire ever known.

The Mongols were bloodthirsty warriors who swept across Russia on horses specially trained to withstand the snow and cold. The Mongols were vicious in war. They would thunder into an area and destroy anyone or anything in their way. They left behind them a trail of dead bodies, charred villages, and ruined farm- lands. People were terrified of the Mongols, and a warning of their coming sent people running for a hiding place, but there were few places to hide.

This is one of the earliest known paintings of Moscow.

The Mongol attack on Russia was especially destructive and deadly. In 1238 the Mongols charged into Russia and burned 14 cities in a single month. Two years later they attacked and burned Kiev, killing most of the people and destroying houses and buildings. Kiev had been the most important city in Russia, but it would never again be as powerful as it had been before the Mongol invasion.

The Mongol armies did not remain long in Russia. After they left, a group of people called the Tartars ruled Russia. The Tartars were a blend of Mongol and Turkic tribes. They gave some power to the local Russian princes, who acted as tax collectors for the Tartars.

The Beginnings of Moscow

Kiev had been losing power even before the Mongol invasions. Civil wars and raids by various nomadic tribes weakened the once-powerful city, and fewer merchants came to trade there. As a result, the Russians in and around Kiev began to move to the northeast, where they built new farms, churches, and towns.

Moscow, one of these new settlements, rose from a small town to a key city. Located on strategic land and water trade routes, Moscow grew to become the most impor- tant center of a Russian state called Muscovy.

One contin- uing problem kept most of the Russian princes from growing even more powerful than they were. This was the problem of land ownership. When a Russian prince died, his sons split up his lands among themselves, so as each prince died, the areas they ruled became smaller.

In Muscovy power was not equally divided among the ruler's sons. The oldest son received the largest share of land. Thus, Muscovy remained large while other city-states shrunk.

Muscovy had some very strong rulers during the early part of the fourteenth century. Among them was Grand Prince Ivan I, who remained on good terms with the Tartars, mostly because he was a very efficient tax collector for them. He was known for his tight control over financial matters and made himself very wealthy. He was so good at his job that he was nicknamed "Ivan the Moneybag."

Strong Ruler The next strong ruler of Muscovy was Ivan III, who became known as Ivan the Great. Ivan became Grand Prince of Muscovy in 1462 and ruled until 1502. He came into power at a time when all the Russian princes were still competing among themselves and struggling against the Tartars.

No prince wanted power more dearly than Ivan III. He dedicated his entire life to making Muscovy the strongest state in Russia and to ridding his country of Tartar rule. No wonder he became known as Ivan the Great.

Ivan grew up in a period of almost continuous warfare. Often, this warfare took place among members of the same family. When Ivan was only a boy, some of his own relatives rebelled against his father. They kidnapped his father, blinded him, and held him prisoner while they tried to govern Muscovy themselves.

With the help of some friends, young Ivan escaped capture, but not for long. One of the men who had helped him escape later betrayed him and told the rebels where the young prince was hiding. The rebels found Ivan and carried him off. Ivan became a prisoner, like his father.

The struggle for control of Muscovy went on. Soon the supporters of Ivan and his father triumphed over the rebels. Ivan and his father were released, and they took power again.

As the years went by, Ivan became a strong military leader. He led an army against his father's enemies and finally defeated them. He also fought against the Tartars. By the time he was 22, Ivan had had plenty of experience. He had already married, and he was ready to take on the duties of Grand Prince of Muscovy. After his father died, young Ivan ruled alone.

Ivan III copied the Tartar and Byzantine traditions of ruling with absolute power, a power no one could challenge.

Winning Back Russia

As Ivan III gained power in Muscovy, there was conflict among the Tartar leaders in Russia. In 1480, a group of Russian princes led by Ivan III and his son forced the Tartars to retreat without much of a fight. Russia was at last free from foreign rule. Ivan took power into his own hands. Under his reign, and that of his son, the territories of Muscovy tripled in size and began to form a larger and more unified nation.

As Ivan gained lands, he clamped down more tightly on all those he ruled. It became his mission to limit the power of the **boyars,** or landowning nobles. Ivan issued new, stricter laws. He punished anyone suspected of plotting against him with prison or death. A few unfortunate boyars who spoke against Ivan had their tongues cut out.

vocabulary
boyar a powerful Russian landowner
czar title of a Russian emperor

"Like God, the Highest"

Ivan III copied the Tartar and Byzantine traditions of ruling with absolute power, a power no one could challenge. Like the Byzantine emperors of the past, Ivan used the double-headed eagle as his symbol. In addition to his title of grand prince, he called himself **czar** or *tsar,* the Russian word for "Caesar."

In the 1400s, when Ivan became Grand Prince of Muscovy, great intellectual, artistic, and scientific progress was taking place in western Europe. Historians call this period of history "The Renaissance." These great changes began in Italy and soon spread throughout western Europe. But Russia was backward and the Renaissance had only a small impact on the country. Russia was mostly cut off from the progress in the arts and sciences taking place in western Europe.

There was one high-ranking person in Moscow who had first-hand knowledge of the changes taking place in western Europe. That person was Ivan's second wife, Sophia, who had been raised in Italy and had been given a Renaissance education. But Sophia didn't seem to change Ivan much.

"The czar," Ivan was fond of saying, "is in nature like all men, but in authority, he is like God, the highest."

Ivan dressed as if he were, indeed, a god. He often appeared in robes woven from gold threads and lined with ermine fur. What a contrast this was to the tattered clothing and leaky boots of Russian workers and **serfs.**

The serfs were the millions of poor people in Russia who suffered under the harsh rule of the Russian princes and boyars. Most of the serfs were poor farmers. They farmed the land, did the hard work, and lived in miserable conditions.

When one landowner sold his farm to another, the serfs went with the sale. Some landowners also sold serfs singly, just like slaves. Serfs were not allowed to move from place to place without the consent of the landowner. Over the years, life for the serfs did not improve. For the most part, it got much worse.

Building His Reputation

Ivan III made up imaginary ancestors who just happened to be Roman emperors. He created legends about himself that showed him as glorious and strong.

To complete his image of greatness, Ivan started huge new building projects in the city of Moscow. Most large Russian cities had **kremlins.**

The kremlins were built as walled fortresses to protect Russian cities. The rulers of a city usually lived inside the kremlins.

The czars lived in the Moscow Kremlin, which had been badly damaged by fire and needed repair. Ivan the Great soon set about building many fine and grand structures inside the walls of the Moscow Kremlin, including several very elaborate cathedrals, as well as government buildings and palaces. The newly rebuilt Moscow Kremlin stood as a grand symbol of Ivan's growing might and power.

If Ivan the Great seemed power-hungry and harsh, he might be considered mild-mannered and kind compared with his grandson, Ivan IV.

> **vocabulary**
> **serf** a farmer who did not own the land that he was required to work on
> **kremlin** a fortress built to protect a Russian city

Ivan the Great married his second wife, Sophia, in a grand imperial ceremony.

earful Times A storm shook Moscow on August 25, 1530, and as the thunder rolled, Ivan IV was born. A priest had warned Ivan's father that he would have a wicked son. "Your states will be prey to terror and tears; rivers of blood will flow," the priest had said. And he was right.

The boy who was to become Ivan IV was a troubled, angry child. Unfortunately for the Russian people, he became their czar. He soon launched a reign of terror that fulfilled the prophecy about him. He became known in history as Ivan the Terrible.

When Ivan was three, his father died. Ivan became the Grand Prince of Muscovy, but he was only a child, and real ruling power rested in the hands of his mother and the boyars who supported her.

Ivan's mother ruled for the next five years, receiving advice from relatives and boyars. Suddenly, one day she doubled over with pain. Within hours she was dead. Some people believed that Ivan's mother had been poisoned.

Ivan was alone in the world. He was only eight years old, still far too young to rule Muscovy. A power struggle broke out among the boyars for control over young Ivan. Which one of them, the boyars wondered, would rule the kingdom until Ivan grew up?

As a young boy, Ivan probably felt afraid and uncertain. He spent his childhood being told he was a ruler, but for the most part, he was ignored. The Grand Prince of Muscovy lived in Moscow's Kremlin, where life was filled with violence as the nobles fought for power.

Ivan saw people unfairly arrested, exiled, and even beheaded. He grew to distrust everyone around him. In his mind, a shadow in his bedroom became a jealous boyar with a dagger. In his mind, people whispering in the palace courtyard were traitors plotting his end.

A Czar Is Crowned

Ivan wanted to be crowned Czar of Russia. His grandfather, Ivan III, had claimed the title, but no Russian monarch had ever been crowned czar.

"Grand Prince" or "czar?" It made little difference to the boyars. They agreed to his wishes. In Moscow on January 16, 1547, Ivan was crowned Holy Czar, Monarch of all the Russians.

Czar Ivan IV was now ready to marry. According to tradition, boyars paraded their daughters before him. The moment Ivan saw Anastasia (an uh STA seeya) Romanovna (roh MA nov nah), he offered her a jeweled handkerchief. He had found the woman he wanted to marry.

Ivan IV is also known as Ivan the Terrible.

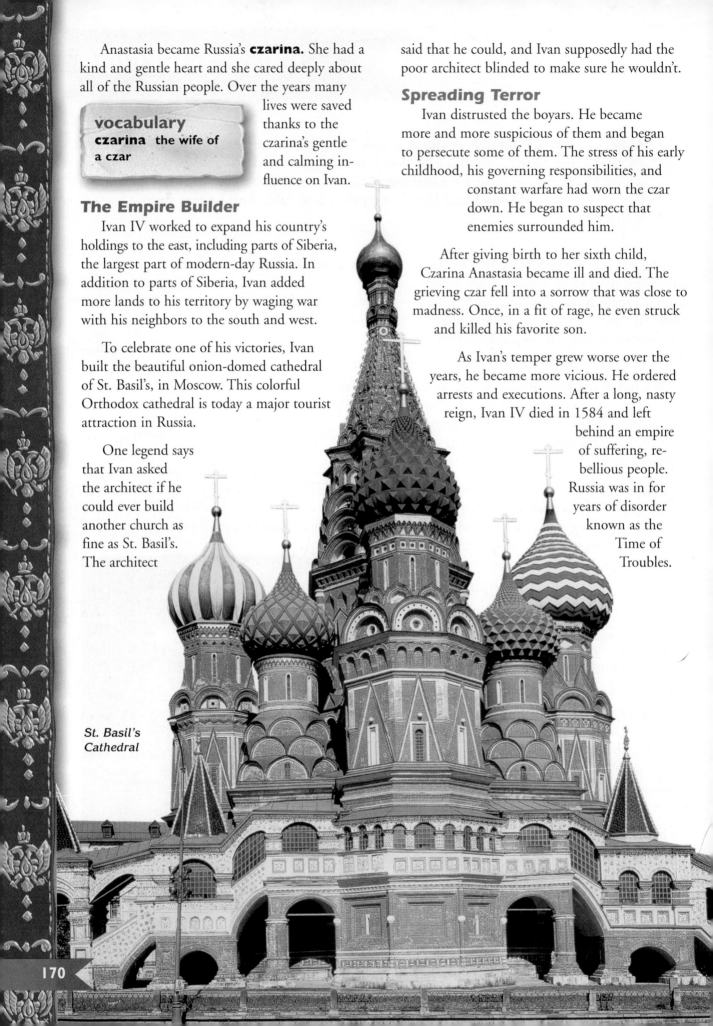

Anastasia became Russia's **czarina.** She had a kind and gentle heart and she cared deeply about all of the Russian people. Over the years many lives were saved thanks to the czarina's gentle and calming influence on Ivan.

The Empire Builder

Ivan IV worked to expand his country's holdings to the east, including parts of Siberia, the largest part of modern-day Russia. In addition to parts of Siberia, Ivan added more lands to his territory by waging war with his neighbors to the south and west.

To celebrate one of his victories, Ivan built the beautiful onion-domed cathedral of St. Basil's, in Moscow. This colorful Orthodox cathedral is today a major tourist attraction in Russia.

One legend says that Ivan asked the architect if he could ever build another church as fine as St. Basil's. The architect said that he could, and Ivan supposedly had the poor architect blinded to make sure he wouldn't.

Spreading Terror

Ivan distrusted the boyars. He became more and more suspicious of them and began to persecute some of them. The stress of his early childhood, his governing responsibilities, and constant warfare had worn the czar down. He began to suspect that enemies surrounded him.

After giving birth to her sixth child, Czarina Anastasia became ill and died. The grieving czar fell into a sorrow that was close to madness. Once, in a fit of rage, he even struck and killed his favorite son.

As Ivan's temper grew worse over the years, he became more vicious. He ordered arrests and executions. After a long, nasty reign, Ivan IV died in 1584 and left behind an empire of suffering, rebellious people. Russia was in for years of disorder known as the Time of Troubles.

St. Basil's Cathedral

New Dynasty In 1613 Mikhail (mih kuh EEL) Romanov (roh muh NAWF) was crowned czar. He was related to Czarina Anastasia Romanovna. A young man from a noble family, Mikhail brought some order back to Russia. The Romanov family would rule for more than 300 years.

Czar Mikhail was eventually succeeded by two of his grandsons: Ivan and Peter, who were half-brothers. Ivan was older but mentally slow. Peter, who was born in 1672, had a quick mind and was very intelligent. The boys received crowns together and sat upon a special double throne. Because both were young, their older sister Sophia served as ruler.

Young Peter

As a teenager, Peter explored Moscow's German Quarter, the section of town where Moscow's Germans and other foreigners lived. Its residents wore western European clothes and ate western European food. Their western ways fascinated Peter.

The crown of Mikhail Romanov

By age 23, Peter was a man who towered over his subjects in every way. In his boots, he stood nearly 7 feet tall, which would be considered big even by today's standards. Back in 1695 he was such an unusually tall man that people sometimes called him "Peter the Giant."

After his sister was overthrown and his half-brother died, Peter reigned alone. Czar Peter lived by one main belief: Whatever he wanted, he should get. Most of all he wanted to make Russia a modern European nation.

The Traveling Czar

In 1697, Peter began a lengthy tour of western Europe. He was the first Russian czar to travel outside of Russia. He planned to travel in disguise, but it was difficult to hide a nearly 7-foot czar. Peter brought home chests filled with weapons and scientific tools. He even brought home a stuffed crocodile. He also returned to Russia with a group of European engineers, soldiers, and scientists who would teach their skills to his countrymen. Two barbers were among Peter's group of Europeans. The czar had decided that his noblemen should get rid of their old-fashioned long Russian-style beards.

"Shave off your beards . . . or else," Peter ordered, and his order became the law of the land. Any upper-class Russian who wanted to wear a beard had to pay a beard tax that allowed him to keep his whiskers.

Under Peter the Great's orders, Russian noblemen had to have their beards cut off or pay a beard tax.

Peter used his power as czar to push through his new ideas. He replaced the old Russian calendar with the newer European calendar, which numbered the years from the birth of Jesus. He had engineers design canals to link Russian rivers, and he had instructors teach Russians mathematics and navigation.

Yet in some ways, Peter clung to the past and widened the gap between Russia and western Europe. Serfdom had died out in western Europe. In Russia, it spread. As the country of Russia grew, more and more serfs spent their entire lives working the land and paying taxes to the land-owners. Others toiled building roads and canals. Unlike some of the poor farmers in western Europe who were enjoying new freedoms, Russia's serfs remained very much in the past.

Seeking a Warm-Water Port

While Peter made many changes in Russia, he could do nothing to alter its geography. Russia's first seaports were on the Baltic Sea and the Arctic Ocean. If you look at the map of Russia, you'll find that these large bodies of water are located along the northern coast of the country. In winter they are choked with ice.

As a result, early Russia was a country bordered by oceans that froze in the winter. For centuries Russian rulers had fought bloody wars to gain a **warm-water port** where they could trade year-round. They especially wanted a port on the Black Sea, but their efforts had been unsuccessful. Peter the Great also tried to gain a warm-water port for Russian trade, but Peter also failed.

Window on the West

Czar Peter found Moscow a gloomy place. He decided to build the city of St. Petersburg and make it his capital. French and Italian architects planned buildings that looked like some of the grand structures in the major cities of western Europe—cities like Paris, Vienna, and London.

Peter chose a swampy site near the Baltic Sea for his new city. When serfs were forced to drain the marshes, thousands fell ill and died. People began to call St. Petersburg the "city built on bones."

Many of the nobles did not want to leave Moscow, but Peter ordered them to build costly homes in St. Petersburg. He was sure this new city, which he called his "Window on the West," would establish Russia as a European power.

A Great Title

In his last years as czar, Peter signed a treaty with Sweden that protected the lands around St. Petersburg. To celebrate, Peter decided to call himself "Peter the Great, Emperor of Russia."

By the time he was 52 years old, illness had drained Peter's energy. One winter's day he waded into the icy sea to rescue some fishermen. He saved the men, but it took all his strength. On January 28, 1725, Czar Peter died.

The Winter Palace in St. Petersburg was built in the style of western architecture of the time.

 **German Princess** Following the death of Peter the Great in 1725, a series of weak rulers governed Russia for 37 years. Toward the end of this period, a dynamic young woman from Germany became a part of Russian history.

Picture a situation like this: In a small principality in Germany, the ruler asked his 15-year-old daughter, "What do you think, Sophia? How would you like to marry a Russian grand duke?"

Young Sophia considered the offer. After all, this particular grand duke, Peter III, was in line to become Russia's czar. It would be a good match for an ambitious German princess. This Peter was rumored to be a bit of a fool, and far from handsome. "Still," thought Sophia, "as grand duchess, I might sooner or later rise to power myself."

The princess traveled to Russia to meet the 16-year-old grand duke. Peter, who had spent much of his life in Germany, was willing to marry the girl chosen for him. Before the wedding in 1744, Sophia converted to the Russian Orthodox religion. She also took a new name, Catherine.

As grand duchess, Catherine learned Russian and made many new friends. She was, however, less pleased with her husband. Peter seemed young for his age and uninterested in his bride. It is said that he still played with toy soldiers every night before bed.

You can see the symbol of the Russian Empire, the double-headed eagle, in this portrait of Catherine the Great.

Catherine Takes the Crown

As expected, Peter inherited the throne of Russia. Czar Peter III made few friends and plenty of enemies. Some of his royal orders were just plain silly. One of his laws allowed nobles to hunt in the streets of St. Petersburg. Finally, he went too far. He threatened to plunge Russia into war. His enemies sprang into action. They planned to replace Peter with his capable wife.

Catherine agreed to the overthrow of her husband, and Peter was soon arrested. A few days after Peter's arrest, Catherine received a note saying her husband was ill. It came as no great surprise when Catherine learned that the ailing Peter had died. Although most historians believe Catherine had no hand in a murder, Peter's death did open her path to the throne.

At age 33, Catherine became an empress—a crowned ruler with absolute power. Like Peter the Great, Catherine admired western Europe. She read many books by French writers that filled her mind with new ideas. She asked her nobles to speak French and to adopt French styles.

Catherine, following in Peter the Great's footsteps, also demanded action. She put officials to work improving roads and rebuilding towns and cities. She offered free education for some Russian boys and girls. However, free education was not offered to the children of Russia's serfs. Since the serfs made up the vast majority of the population, most boys and girls in Russia did not receive an education.

The Serfs

Although she was intelligent and forward-thinking, Catherine, like Peter the Great, continued to support serfdom. Actually, Catherine did study the notion of freeing Russia's serfs but decided against it. She feared that the end of serfdom would weaken her country. It would surely displease the nobles. In fact, as Catherine's empire added lands, the number of serfs increased. She "donated" hundreds of thousands of serfs to various noblemen as rewards for their loyalty and service. Life became even harder for the serfs as their landlords insisted that they work longer hours.

At this time in the history of Russia, serfs were not much different from slaves. They had little or no control over their own lives and almost no chance of improving their situation. When a noble put a farm up for sale, he might advertise how many serfs went with the farm and what the condition of the serfs was.

Other countries were struggling with the idea of slavery in the eighteenth century. Just as southern plantation owners in the American colonies could not at this time bring themselves to free their slaves, so Catherine the Great could not see a way for Russia to free its serfs.

A Stronger Russia

Catherine shared Peter the Great's goal of gaining a warm-water port. After a war against the Turks, Catherine achieved that goal. She conquered the northern shore of the Black Sea and built a warm-water port, called Odessa. The treaty of peace with the Turks gave Russian ships on the Black Sea free passage through the narrow strip of Turkish-controlled water between the Black Sea and the Mediterranean. At last, Russian ships could sail and trade when northern seas were frozen.

In 1796, Catherine died of a stroke at the age of 67. Even the last years of her life had been active ones. She set up a fur-trading colony in Alaska and continued to take care of her government.

Fifty-two years had passed since the young German princess dreamed of power and glory. In some ways she did not do much to help her people. Most of her subjects, the serfs, were little more than slaves. Yet in other ways she brought Russia into the future by building roads and schools, and by securing the warm-water port Russian czars had been seeking for centuries.

For more than three centuries, Russia's serfs (left) were almost like slaves under the control of Russian nobles (right).

boyar a powerful Russian landowner

czar title of a Russian emperor

czarina the wife of a czar

kremlin a fortress built to protect a Russian city

serf a farmer who did not own the land that he was required to work on

tribute money or goods that weaker people are forced to pay to stronger people

warm-water port a port with waters that are not frozen during the winter; ships can use a warm-water port all year long

Feudal JAPAN

Contents

The Rise of an Empire

apan, Now and Then Japan is an island nation in the Pacific Ocean, located east of the Korean Peninsula and China. To people in these lands, the sun seems to rise first over Japan, and the Japanese therefore call their country Nippon, which means "the origin of the sun."

There are four major islands and thousands of small ones in the Japanese **archipelago** (ar kuh PEH luh goh). The largest island is Honshu (HAHN shoo), the home of the capital city of Tokyo (TOH kee oh), Kyoto (kee YOH toh), and other great cities. To the south lie the major islands of Shikoku (shih KOH koo) and Kyushu (kee YOO shoo), and to the north is Hokkaido (hah KYE doh).

Today these islands make up one of the most economically advanced nations in the world. Japanese companies ship automobiles and electronic goods all over the world, and thousands of travelers fly in and out of the busy Tokyo airport every day. But Japan was not always so open to foreigners. For several centuries, Japan distrusted outsiders and lived in self-imposed **isolation**. Although at various times in their history the Japanese were deeply influenced by their near neighbors—the Koreans and the Chinese—they shut their doors almost completely to Europeans and Americans between the 1600s and the mid-1800s.

History and Legends

Throughout much of their early history, the Japanese lived in social groups of families and friends called clans. Each clan had its own chief. It also worshiped one god or goddess as its ancestor—its link to heaven.

About A.D. 400, the Yamato (yah MAH toh) clan, which lived on the central island of Honshu, became the strongest of the clans. The Yamatos identified themselves as descendants of the goddess Amaterasu (ah mah ter AH soo) and declared their right to rule Japan.

vocabulary
archipelago a group of many large and small islands
isolation the state of living apart from other people

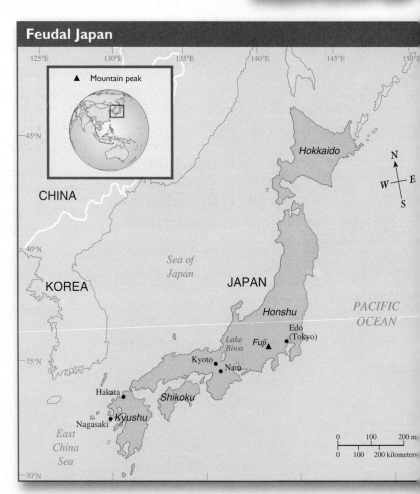

Feudal Japan

Because it is an island nation, Japan found it easier to cut off contact with westerners for several centuries.

The Legend of Amaterasu

The Yamatos backed their claim to the throne with this mystical legend: A god and goddess were strolling on the rainbow bridge that led from the sky to the dark sea below. They dipped a jeweled spear into the ocean and shook it into the sky. Drops of sea spray became the first island of Japan. The goddess then gave birth to the rest of the islands.

The godly pair created children to help rule the islands. One was Amaterasu, goddess of the sun, who lived in the sky. As time passed, Amaterasu bore many gods and goddesses. Among her first children was one man. He became Japan's first emperor.

In 645, based on his family's power and the legend of Amaterasu, the head of the Yamato clan became emperor of Japan. He called himself the son of heaven and chose the rising sun as the symbol of his empire. For centuries, the Japanese honored their emperors as living gods. Today's emperor still traces his roots to the Yamato clan.

Borrowing From Neighbors

During this early period of Japanese history, the Japanese borrowed heavily from Korea and China. Scholars believe that the Koreans taught the Japanese to read and write. It appears that the early Japanese had no written language. When Koreans began visiting the islands, they brought their written language, which itself was based on Chinese writing. The Japanese used features of Korean and Chinese writing to create a writing system of their own. Korean craftsmen also taught the Japanese to make tools and ornaments of bronze and iron.

However, the Korean import that had the greatest impact on Japan was a new religion. The Japanese had long practiced a nature religion known as Shinto. Around 550, the Koreans introduced a Chinese form of Buddhism.

One day a Korean boat dropped anchor on the Japanese shore. Korean sailors moved a large box down the gangplank. A gong sounded. Priests chanted as a gold and copper statue of Buddha was lifted from the box and displayed to the people.

日本

This is the word Japan written in Japanese characters.

The new religion spread slowly, but eventually it took root in Japan. The ceremonial gongs, priestly robes, and candlelit altars of Buddhism attracted many Japanese. The new religion also increased Japan's fascination with mainland culture and especially with all things Chinese.

In the 600s, a powerful Yamato prince became fascinated with China. He realized that much of what the Japanese had learned from the Koreans was actually coming from China. Instead of learning about Chinese ideas indirectly, through the Koreans, the emperor decided to go directly to the source. He sent young Japanese nobles to China to study its culture.

After this expedition, Chinese ways became examples to follow. The Japanese built their first capital city at Nara, laid out like the capital of China. Japanese nobles began dressing in Chinese fashions. The Japanese studied Chinese geography, medicine, and astronomy. They imitated Chinese patterns of government and adopted the Chinese calendar. They imported the custom of tea drinking and established elaborate tea ceremonies. They even learned to breed silkworms and weave silk.

Japanese Culture

All of these imported ideas helped Japan grow stronger. Eventually the country no longer felt the need to rely so heavily on its mainland neighbors. The Japanese changed some Chinese ways to suit Japanese needs and styles. For instance, instead of choosing government officials based on tests of ability, as the Chinese had done, the Japanese decided to fill government positions with the sons of Japanese nobles, thus ensuring aristocratic control of the government. There were cultural changes as well. Japanese artists added color to the traditional black ink of Chinese paintings. They wrote their own poems and sculpted in bronze. Wealthy landowners supported artists and encouraged a Japanese style. All of these changes led to the development of a distinctively Japanese culture.

2 Religion in Japan

Native and Imported Religions Two of the religions that have helped shape the Japanese people are Shinto and Buddhism. Shinto is the native religion. Buddhism, on the other hand, is the faith that Korean missionaries brought from China.

Shinto: Spirits in Nature

Shinto, Japan's oldest religion, is based on nature. Japan is a land of pine forests, oceans, and green rice fields. It is the place where snowcapped Fuji, the country's tallest mountain peak, rises high into the clouds. From the earliest times, Japan's people have celebrated their country's beauty in poetry and art. This love of nature also lies at the heart of Shinto.

Followers of Shinto believe that each part of nature contains a spirit. These spirits are known as kami (KAH mee). Believers in Shinto worship mountains, rivers, rocks, and trees. They believe that heavenly bodies have life: The sun is the golden goddess Amaterasu, and the moon is her silvery brother Tsukiyomi (soo kee YOH mee).

The Shinto religion is based on ceremonies rather than rules. No one person is named as its founder, and the ancient beliefs have no sacred book or "bible." The faith did not even have a name until the Chinese labeled it Shinto, which means "way of the gods." The name was first used in the sixth century A.D. to distinguish the native Japanese religion from Buddhism.

Shinto does not dwell on the fierce aspects of nature, such as the earthquakes, **typhoons**, and volcanoes that often threaten Japan. Rather than emphasize the brutal side of nature, Shinto celebrates everything that is wonderful, beautiful, or

A torii is the traditional gateway to a Shinto shrine. This shrine is dedicated to the god of learning.

remarkable. One of the kami might be found in an oddly twisted tree, an unusual insect, or a wise old man. Have you ever felt a sense of awe when viewing a full white moon or a scarlet maple leaf? Someone who follows Shinto would say such feelings are inspired by kami.

Shinto followers worship their gods at simple wooden shrines. These holy places are usually surrounded by sacred trees and have flowing water nearby. Rituals begin with washing ceremonies. You may have heard the saying

vocabulary
typhoon a severe tropical storm or hurricane that occurs in the Pacific Ocean

"cleanliness is next to godliness." According to Shinto, one must be clean in the presence of spirits.

Millions of Japanese practice Shinto today. They worship in their homes, at small roadside shrines, and at larger temples and gardens. They recite prayers and offer gifts of cakes, flowers, and money to the kami.

Buddhism: The Open Mind

Imagine yourself standing before a Buddhist master. He poses a question and tells you that by answering you will better understand the ways of the Buddhist. The master says: "You have climbed to the top of a ten-foot pole. How can you climb the rest of the way?"

How would you answer the question? Do you think that no one can climb higher than the top? If so, the Buddhist master would probably suggest that you **meditate** and open your mind to all possibilities.

This bronze statue of the Great Buddha dates back to 1252.

To understand the master's advice, it will help to learn a little about the founder of Buddhism, Siddhartha Gautama (sih-DAR tuh GOW tuh muh). In the 500s B.C., this young prince from India asked searching questions about life. Eventually he became known as the Buddha, or the "Enlightened One."

> **vocabulary**
> **meditate** to think in a quiet, serious way

It was under a giant fig tree, after a long period of meditation, that Gautama became "enlightened." Believing that he had gained knowledge of the true path in life, he spent the rest of his life teaching others what he had learned.

The followers of the Buddha carried his teachings from India to other parts of the world, including China, Korea, and Japan.

The Four Truths and the Eightfold Path

What were those thoughts about life that the Buddha had under the fig tree? In his first sermon, the Buddha spoke of Four Noble Truths. These messages are the heart of Buddhism.

The Four Noble Truths of Buddhism

1. All life, from birth to death, is filled with suffering.

2. This suffering is caused by a craving for worldly things.

3. Suffering will stop when one learns to overcome desire.

4. We can learn to overcome desire by following the eightfold path.

You probably noticed that the fourth Truth refers to an "eightfold path" that a person should follow. According to the Buddha, there are eight things one must do to achieve enlightenment—an absence of desire or suffering.

A dharma wheel is the symbol for this eight-fold path. By getting rid of greed, anger, and fear, people could gain happiness and serenity. The Buddha called this complete peace *nirvana*.

As Buddhism took root in Japan after A.D. 500, different groups tried to understand exactly what the Buddha had meant. Some believed that the ideal of Buddhism was to follow the Buddha's path, achieve nirvana, and become a Buddha oneself. Other groups believed that the ideal was to put off entering nirvana, stay in touch with the world, and help others follow the right path.

Zen Buddhism followed the second school of thought. Zen masters put off entering nirvana in order to teach their students the way to peace. Zen taught that people could find happiness not only through meditation but also through doing orderly tasks such as daily work, the ritual tea ceremony, and even martial arts. Zen Buddhism stressed discipline and meditation.

Do you remember the question about climbing above the top of the pole? It was a Zen master who encouraged students to do that. What he meant was that Buddhists should allow their *minds* to climb higher than the top of the pole, even if their *bodies* could go no farther. Zen Buddhist teachers encourage their students to meditate and go beyond the limits of normal thought, to open their minds to all possibilities. For a Buddhist, "climbing above the pole" means giving the mind freedom to rise above the things of this world and attain true understanding.

Shinto and Buddhism

When Buddhism first arrived in Japan, some Japanese saw the new religion as a threat to Shinto. In time, however, most people began to look at things differently. They came to see Buddhism not as a replacement for Shinto, or as a rival religion, but as a supplement, or complement. Many followers of Shinto began to embrace Buddhism without giving up their older ideas. Both Shinto and Buddhism live on in modern Japan, and it is not unusual to find Japanese men and women who honor the kami at Shinto shrines but also cultivate the mental discipline of Zen Buddhism.

Each spoke on this Buddhist dharma wheel stands for one of the eight "right" things a Buddhist must do to achieve nirvana.

Rise of Feudal Japan You may have learned about feudalism when you studied the European Middle Ages. Feudalism is a system of government in which land is exchanged for loyalty and services. Under feudalism, people were born with a permanent position in society.

By A.D. 800, the descendants of the Yamato clan were firmly established as the rulers of Japan. They built a splendid palace at the present-day city of Kyoto, where emperors would continue to live for more than 1,000 years. Safe inside the palace walls, these rulers of Japan strolled in gardens where golden sunbeams sparkled on lotus pools. They dressed in silks and drank ceremonial tea.

Outside the palace walls, however, life was very different. As the rich got richer, the poor got poorer. Ordinary people eventually grew tired of paying high taxes to support the fancy lifestyle of the court. Some began to refuse to pay their taxes. Others moved away from the emperor's court and placed themselves under the protection of wealthy landowners. These **defections** decreased the emperor's tax income and increased the power of the landowners.

If the emperors had understood what was happening, they might have taken steps to prevent these defections. However, they lived their lives behind the high palace walls, isolated from the everyday world. What's more, many of them believed that, as "sons of heaven," it was beneath them to pay much attention to politics or everyday affairs.

So the defections continued. More and more

peasants sought protection from landowners, and the landowners began to exert more and more influence over political affairs. Landowners also began to build up private armies of warriors known as **samurai** (SAH-muh rye). Soon the landlords became warlords, and eventually the warlords began to struggle with one another.

> **vocabulary**
> **defection** the abandonment of one's country, leader, or group
> **samurai** a Japanese warrior; also several of these warriors

Yoritomo and the Rise of Shoguns

After many years of conflict, a warlord named Yoritomo came out on top. Yoritomo's march to power began when a rival warlord executed many of his family members, including his parents. Yoritomo swore he would get revenge.

Yoritomo and his brother established an army, with Yoritomo's brother as general. At first only 300 samurai marched behind them, but eventually there were more than 20,000. The army won battle after battle, and Yoritomo gained military control of the country.

Yoritomo now held power, but he was worried. His followers had sworn

This painting shows a samurai on horseback. The samurai were fierce warriors.

loyalty to him, but they had also followed his brother into battle. Yoritomo saw his brother as a threat and sent soldiers after him. Eventually, Yoritomo's brother was forced to commit suicide.

In 1192, the emperor declared that Yoritomo was the supreme military commander, or **shogun** (SHOH gun). Yoritomo continued to honor the emperor, but the real power had shifted from the emperor to the shogun. The emperor was now nothing more than a **figurehead**, an honored symbol of the empire. The shogun had all the military power, and he soon began making all the political decisions as well. This was the beginning of the feudal period in Japanese history.

Japanese Feudalism

During the European Middle Ages, a king granted land to a lord who, in return, swore loyalty to the king and agreed to fight in the king's army. Then the lord made similar land grants to his own vassals, who agreed to serve him. Thus, society was made up of a network, with the king on top and the merchants at the bottom.

In Japan, the system was similar but the names were different. The top man under the emperor was the shogun. Below him were high-ranking nobles known as daimyo (DYE myoh). Then came the samurai warriors. As in Europe, ordinary people—peasants, artisans, and merchants—were on the bottom rungs of the ladder.

Because the Japanese empire was so big, the shoguns put the daimyo in charge of large pieces of land. In return, the daimyo pledged their loyalty to the shogun and promised him the support of their armies. The daimyo then built strong forces of samurai warriors.

The samurai pledged loyalty and service, but not to the central government. Instead they were loyal to their local lords, the daimyo. Indeed, the word *samurai* means "those who

serve." The samurai swore to serve and protect their lords—or die trying.

The long period of shogun rule, which lasted from the late 1100s to the late 1800s, was also the great age of the samurai. In many ways, these samurai warriors were like the medieval knights of Europe. They were professional fighters who served their lords, and they lived in accordance with a demanding code of behavior.

The Story of a Samurai

In order to get an idea of how the samurai lived, let's look at the life of an imaginary young samurai named Katsu. Katsu was born to be a samurai. He was the son of a samurai, and his sons would be samurai too. As soon as Katsu could talk, his father began teaching him what it meant to be a samurai. He told him about Bushido (BOO shih doh), or the way of the warrior. This code of values guided every samurai's life.

"Honor, bravery, and loyalty, my son," instructed Katsu's father. "These come before all else. This is the code by which you shall live

Japan's Feudal Society

Emperor

Shogun

Daimyo

Samurai

Peasant   Merchant   Artisan

your life." On his fifth birthday, the boy received his first sword—now he was a samurai.

Indeed, this was something to be proud of. Only about 5 percent of the people in all the empire were samurai. Other than the shogun or a daimyo, only a samurai could wear a sword.

Katsu's family lived in a large house near the families of other samurai. His father served the daimyo, who inhabited a strong central castle. Around the daimyo and samurai lived artisans, merchants, and peasants. The daimyo, the samurai, and the ordinary people dwelled in three separate worlds, and a person living in one of them would never dream of living in any other.

Katsu's father had faced death on the battlefield many times. But it was peacetime now. The ruling shogun was firmly in power, and there was no threat of civil war. Katsu's father served the daimyo by overseeing his many peasant villages.

A samurai took all tasks seriously. To fall short in his duties would bring disgrace on him and his whole family. Disgrace was a serious matter. A samurai who failed to serve honorably and loyally was expected to commit seppuku (seh POO-koo)—to take his own life.

Katsu had a lot to learn. He learned to read and write, and he became an expert in fencing, wrestling, horseback riding, and archery.

Studying the ways of Zen Buddhism, he learned to calm his mind and racing heart and to consider all possibilities before taking action. Somehow, Katsu and other warriors balanced the Zen traditions of

Hundreds of tiny scales make up this samurai's armor. This design gave the warrior flexibility, as well as protection.

serenity and kindness toward all creatures with samurai fierceness.

Most important, Katsu learned to face hardship and death without fear. To harden himself to suffering, he walked barefoot in the winter's snow. He went without food for days and worked in the blistering summer sun until he was faint.

Samurai handbooks taught Katsu what was expected of him. He read instructions like the following from the *Handbook for Samurai:*

Every morning make up your mind how to die. Every evening freshen your mind in the thought of death. . . . Thus your mind will be prepared.

For you there should be no thought but of service to the one master who has a claim on your grateful heart.

Between ages 13 and 15, a samurai officially became an adult. He took part in a special coming-of-age ceremony and received a suit of armor. He began tying his hair back in a topknot. From now on, a samurai carried two swords. The first, a long sword, was his battle weapon; it was meant to kill others. If Katsu ever failed to serve his daimyo loyally, if he ever faced disgrace or dishonor, he would use his second sword, a short sword, to end his own life.

As Katsu grew to manhood, he came to recognize the serious role he'd been born into. As a samurai, he was more than a well-trained soldier. He was a protector of all that was right and honorable. He was always ready to defend his lord and protect the feudal way of life.

he Townspeople The daimyo lived in a castle, surrounded by a "castle town." High-ranking samurai lived closest to the daimyo; farther out were the dwellings of lesser samurai, and then those of artisans, merchants, and priests. Scattered through the nearby countryside were peasant villages. What was daily life like for ordinary people?

Townspeople wore clothes made of coarse linen and cotton rather than the bright silks of the upper classes. Their daimyo did not allow them to build big houses or to use gold or silver for decoration. Their children did not go to school, as young samurai did. Instead, they went to work.

The artisans ranked higher on the social ladder than the merchants. The upper classes felt that the merchants were the lowest type of people because they produced nothing by themselves; they only bought and sold what other people made. Members of the upper classes also looked down on merchants because they spent their time handling money. This was something noblemen shunned. Ideally, a samurai never handled money himself; he had servants to perform such tasks.

Even the artisans had to follow strict rules. A baker might take great pride in his profession; probably he was descended from a long line of bakers. Nevertheless, the baker would never go to where the samurai lived without an invitation. If he had to deliver a cake to a samurai house, he would do so modestly and quietly, and he would be sure to remove his wooden clogs before stepping into the samurai's house.

The Peasants

On the edge of town were temples, shrines, and burial grounds. Next came the farmlands, a checkerboard of rice paddies interrupted here and there by tiny villages.

The seasons directed a peasant's life. There was the planting time when men, women, and children pushed rice seedlings into the knee-deep mud. There were long days of harvest when they hurried to bring in crops before the heavy rains.

The peasants did backbreaking labor, but their work was highly valued. After all, their rice was the source of the daimyo's wealth.

Arts and Entertainment

There was one activity that brought pleasure to the townspeople but was considered too common for the samurai. Several times each year, the traveling players of the Kabuki (kuh BOO kee) theater came to town.

Performance day had to be sunny, because the theater had no roof. Performers in colorful costumes exaggerated their movements and wore heavy makeup. Filling the stage, they sang, danced, and acted out stories of love, war, and heroism.

Sometimes the spectators joined the actors on the stage. It was a noisy, lively affair. Tea and food vendors squeezed through the audience. The snacks they sold were in great demand—a performance could last up to 18 hours.

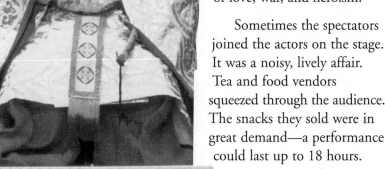

Even today, a Kabuki player appears in colorful costume and distinct makeup.

An earlier form of drama, the Noh theater, was seen as more fitting for the upper classes. In contrast to Kabuki, a Noh play had little action. Two actors wearing carved masks performed on a bare wooden stage. Meanwhile, a chorus of men chanted about ideals such as unselfishness and honor. The only scenery was a single screen painted with a pine tree. This served as a reminder that Noh plays were originally performed at Shinto shrines, often in front of sacred trees.

This is a Noh mask of a young monk.

Some high-ranking daimyo, or lords, had Noh stages built at their own castles. In several ways, the actors were a lot like the samurai themselves. The all-male Noh casts were very physically fit. The actors were well trained and highly disciplined. Before each show they spent time in a special "mirror room" where they meditated and focused their minds on their performance.

The Flow of Life in Three Lines

By now, you probably picture feudal Japan as a warrior's world, and in many ways it was. But there was one samurai who became famous by using his pen rather than his sword. Taking the name of Basho, this young samurai became a master of a poetry form called **haiku** (HYE koo). In just three written lines, Basho could create a picture, reflect a feeling, or capture the meaning of life. For centuries, other haiku artists took inspiration from him.

vocabulary
haiku a form of Japanese poetry having 17 syllables in three lines

The Japanese nobility had enjoyed poetry since the early days of the empire. Because haiku was short and simple, everyone could understand and appreciate it.

Basho was the pen name used by Matsuo Munefusa (shown standing), a 17th-century samurai who wrote haikus.

Haiku spoke of nature—a part of everyone's experience. It would become one of the world's most popular poetry forms. Sometimes funny and sometimes sad, haiku captures the flow of everyday life. As you end this reading, let yourself imagine what this poet of Japan saw and felt more than 300 years ago:

Young leaves coming out,—
Ah, that I could wipe away
The drops from your eyes!

—Basho

The Mongols A peaceful, prosperous life for the townspeople and peasants depended on how well the local daimyo and samurai could defend their territory. But there were also times when Japan had to defend itself against outside invaders.

One of the most powerful military forces the world has ever seen were the great Mongol armies of the twelfth and thirteenth centuries. The Mongols created an empire that stretched from China to Eastern Europe. The Mongol ruler Kublai Khan, grandson of the great conqueror Genghis Khan, set his sights on Japan in the late 1200s.

In 1268, Kublai Khan sent a letter to Japan's capital. He threatened to attack if the Japanese did not agree to pay him money to keep peace. Both the emperor and the shogun ignored the threats.

Kublai Khan launched an invasion from Korea. The first attack came in 1274 when a fleet of 900 ships arrived on the shores of the empire's southernmost island, Kyushu.

On the first day of the battle, the Mongol invaders were victorious, and they returned to their ships that night. It was a deadly mistake. A storm blew in, splintering the invaders' vessels and killing one third of their troops. The invasion failed.

A much larger attack came in 1281. This time, two separate armies joined in the assault on Hakata Bay. About 40,000 Mongol, Korean, and northern Chinese troops met up with another 100,000 troops from southern China. Some 4,400 Mongol warships arrived on the shores of Kyushu. Kublai Khan meant business.

Before the invaders could launch their attack, another storm blew in. This time it packed the fury of a full-scale typhoon, destroying most of the attacking ships and nearly half of the Mongol forces. Once again the remaining Mongol invaders went home in defeat.

The Japanese did not believe that these storms were accidents or coincidences. They believed that each of the two storms was an example of kamikaze (kah mih KAH zee) or "divine wind." The gods, wanting to protect Japan, had sent these "divine winds" to defeat the Mongol invasions.

The Europeans Arrive

Almost 300 years later, a different kind of threat reached Japan. In September 1543, an unusual ship appeared off the shore of one of Japan's smaller islands. It carried newcomers who

came to trade. They brought one item unlike anything the Japanese had ever seen. According to one account, it caused an explosion like lightning and a report like thunder.

The remarkable object was a musket, and the strangers who brought it sailed from Portugal. The Portuguese had already explored the coasts of Africa and Asia, as well as many of the islands of the Pacific. Now they had come to Japan, bringing the musket—a firearm that would change Japanese warfare forever.

Unlike China and Korea, Japan at first welcomed the Western traders. After the Portuguese vessels, Spanish, Dutch, and English trade ships also arrived. Japan's daimyo were intrigued by the Western ideas. They were also eager to obtain firearms. Over the centuries, the daimyo had spent many years fighting among themselves, struggling to determine who would be the shogun. The musket soon became an important weapon in these struggles. After the arrival of the Europeans, no daimyo could hope to become shogun unless he was backed by an army of musketeers.

Along with the Western traders came missionaries. A Catholic group, the Jesuits, hoped to set up permanent missions in Japan. On the west coast of Kyushu, a local warlord offered the Jesuits harborside land in the little fishing village of Nagasaki (nah guh SAH kee). This village would, in time, become the chief city on Kyushu.

For 25 years, the westerners—both traders and missionaries—enjoyed a welcome in Japan. The technology and ideas they introduced would greatly influence the course of Japanese history.

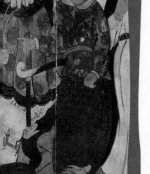

This painted screen shows Japanese women playing musical instruments for travelers from Portugal.

A Closed World

In 1603, the Tokugawa (toh koo GAH wuh) family of shoguns gained control of Japan and ruled from the city of Edo, which is now Tokyo. Earlier shoguns had welcomed Western trade and ideas. Now, the Tokugawas yanked away the welcome mat, banning all foreign missionaries from Japan. Many Japanese had grown tired of the Christian missionaries' intolerant attitudes toward Buddhism, which had emerged as the country's official religion. The ruling shogun ordered that no Japanese would be permitted to practice Christianity. He even used torture and execution to persuade people to abandon the religion.

Still, the missionaries and priests kept coming, along with foreign trade ships. The Japanese worried that these visitors would be followed by foreign armies determined to turn Japan into a colony. From 1600 to 1868, shoguns barred nearly all westerners' ships from Japan's harbors. Only the Dutch were allowed to visit, and they were confined to one port near Nagasaki.

The shoguns prevented their own people from traveling abroad. It was against the law to build a big, seagoing ship. The surrounding seas helped the shoguns isolate their people, although Japan continued to trade with its Asian neighbors.

In 1636, the shogun issued an **exclusion** order. Here are two of its articles. Notice the strict penalties for breaking the rules.

> No Japanese may go abroad secretly. If anyone tries to do this, he will be killed. The ship and owner will be placed under arrest.

> No offspring of Southern Barbarians [Europeans] will be allowed to remain. Anyone violating this order will be killed and all his relatives punished. . . .

Under the Tokugawa shoguns, Japan became known in Europe as a **hermit** country. The nickname would stick, and Japan would remain a closed world for more than 200 years.

> **vocabulary**
> **exclusion** the act of refusing to let in
> **hermit** one who lives alone, apart from others

Opening Doors

At the end of the eighteenth century, Japan was still maintaining its "exclusion" policy, banning trade with all westerners except the Dutch. However, three nations—Russia, Britain, and the United States—began to knock loudly on the doors of the hermit country.

In the early 1700s, Russia's energetic ruler Peter the Great asked that Russian ships be allowed to stop at Japanese ports for supplies. Peter died before setting up trade relations with Japan, but in the late 1700s Catherine the Great renewed his efforts. Czarina Catherine tried to force the shogun to open his ports, but the Russian strong-arm methods backfired, and Japan closed its doors more tightly. The shogun ordered that any foreign vessel that came close to his shores be destroyed.

Meanwhile, Britain had forced trade agreements with China. The shogun's fears increased. He worried that Japan, too, would be forced to welcome foreign ships.

He was right to worry. In July 1853, four black-hulled American vessels steamed into Tokyo Bay. A stern-faced United States naval officer, Commodore Matthew Perry, came before the shogun. Perry presented a letter from the president of the United States. It demanded that Japan open its ports to trade.

Perry soon made a second visit—this time bringing four extra warships. The American show of force did the trick. The shogun and his advisers knew that they could not stand up against the United States Navy. They signed a trade treaty with the United States.

This first treaty turned out to be only the beginning. After agreeing to trade with the United States, how could the shogun refuse other nations? Britain, France, and Russia soon demanded and won trade rights too. Suddenly Japan was bustling with foreign traders.

The End of Shogun Rule

After several years of foreign trade, some Japanese grew unhappy with the situation. They felt that the foreigners had been given special privileges, and they blamed the shogun for allowing this to happen. Japanese from every social class complained about their lives under the shogun. Merchants, although making plenty of money, remained near the bottom of the social ladder. Peasants paid heavy taxes. Samurai, much less important than before because of the growing importance of commerce, were discontented. Daimyo grumbled about being forced to maintain expensive houses in the capital.

Commodore Matthew Perry (shown holding his hat) arrived in Tokyo Bay in 1853. His visit helped to open trade relations between Japan and the United States.

Eventually a rebellion against the shogun broke out. Where did the rebels look for the solution to their problems? They looked to the emperor. Remember, although shoguns ruled the land, an emperor still served as a royal figurehead. "Honor the emperor!" became the rebels' cry.

In 1867, the shogun stepped down and in 1868, a new government was formed. The emperor was restored to the role of official head of state. Shinto was once again declared the state religion, reminding people that their emperor ruled as a descendant of the sun goddess Amaterasu.

This was not, however, a return to the old days when the emperor ran the affairs of state. A new government conducted business in the name of the emperor.

The end of shogun rule marked the end of Japan's feudal age. The new government announced that rank in Japanese society was now to be determined by an individual's mastery of Western science and practical affairs. The old system of inherited rank—samurai, peasants, artisans, and merchants—was abolished, and Japanese of all ranks were equal under the law. Samurai could buy and sell goods; artisans, merchants, and peasants could serve in Japan's new modern army.

The Japanese adopted a new attitude about the world they shared. Remember when the shoguns closed Japan's doors to westerners and did not allow its people to leave their home shores? In contrast, the new government pledged that "knowledge shall be sought throughout the world."

The Japanese began to visit the United States and Europe. They studied Western science, shook off their longtime dislike for trade and commerce, and built a mighty naval fleet. The Land of the Rising Sun was preparing to take a powerful place in world affairs.

Glossary

archipelago a group of many large and small islands

defection the abandonment of one's country, leader, or group

exclusion the act of refusing to let in

figurehead a person who rules in name only

haiku a form of Japanese poetry having 17 syllables in three lines

hermit one who lives alone, apart from others

isolation the state of living apart from other people

meditate to think in a quiet, serious way

samurai a Japanese warrior; also several of these warriors

shogun title meaning "great general" given to the strongest military leader in Japan

typhoon a severe tropical storm or hurricane that occurs in the Pacific Ocean

WESTWARD EXPANSION BEFORE THE CIVIL WAR

Contents

Getting Around in Early America   "National Airways, Cindy speaking. . . . Yes, we fly from Boston to New York every hour. Monday? We can put you on the 8:00 A.M. flight, and you'll arrive in New York about an hour later. . . . Fine, you are confirmed on flight number 6305."

And just as easily as that, you have arranged a trip that will take you more than 200 miles in hardly an hour.

Things were not so simple for Sarah Kemble Knight, a Boston school teacher, when she made that same trip in the year 1704. Mrs. Knight traveled on horseback, riding on "roads" that were really just paths through woods and across meadows.

With no road signs it was easy for first-time travelers like Mrs. Knight to get lost. Fortunately, mail riders—young horsemen who carried the mail between towns in their saddlebags—also traveled these roads. Part of their job was to guide travelers along the way.

These mail riders had schedules to keep, though, and it was up to the travelers to keep up with them. So each night, when the mail rider stopped at a roadside inn, Mrs. Knight stopped also. There she could count on poor food and a bad night's sleep—until 3:00 in the morning, that is, when the mail rider set out again!

The distance between Boston and New York was about 200 miles. Riding over rocky and sometimes muddy paths and crossing rivers and streams on ferryboats, Mrs. Knight covered that distance in seven days and six nights.

Mrs. Knight's trip reminds us that in that early part of our history, traveling was no easy matter. In fact, for all of her discomforts, Mrs. Knight made the journey more swiftly than did most others of her day, for she had the use of a horse. For the vast majority of people, the most common way of getting from one place to another, no matter how close or far, was to walk.

Americans Move West

With travel so difficult you would expect most people to stay close to home. Most did, never going more than a few miles from their farm or village. But thousands of other restless Americans were on the move. What drove these people on, despite all the hardships of travel? Some were in search of adventure. Some sought new, rich land for farming. Still others simply wanted a place where they could start over. And so they moved on west, into the American wilderness. They came to be known as pioneers.

It was hunters and trappers who led the way into the wilderness, and the most famous of them all was Daniel Boone. Born and raised close to the edge of Pennsylvania's wilderness area, Daniel was already a skilled rifleman by the time he was 12. Daniel loved to spend time with the Native Americans who lived nearby, and it was they who taught him how to hunt and trap forest animals.

When Daniel was 16, his family moved to North Carolina, along the eastern side of the Appalachian Mountains. At that time only a handful of settlers lived in this wilderness land, but for Daniel that was a handful too many. He was one of those people who felt crowded if they could see the smoke from a neighbor's cabin.

Soon Daniel was spending several months each year in the woods, with only his rifle for company. He hunted for his food and slept under the stars. He earned money by selling the furs of the animals he killed.

Daniel eventually grew up, got married, had a family, and started a farm. But the wilderness had

Many pioneers were like Daniel Boone—always moving on.

a hold on Daniel Boone's imagination and would not let go. Every autumn after harvesting the crops, he headed back to the forest, living there alone until returning in the spring in time to plant the next year's crop.

The Wilderness Trail

The western frontier marked the end of the settled area and the beginning of an almost unknown wilderness. By the 1760s, the frontier had reached the Appalachian Mountains. But there it stopped. The mountains stood as a great barrier to the west.

For years Daniel Boone had been hearing other hunters and traders tell of a rich land on the other side of the Appalachians. There was, they said, an old Indian trail called the Warriors' Path that led there. But though Boone searched for this trail several times, he failed to find it.

Finally, in 1769, Boone and a group of five companions found what they were looking for. The Warriors' Path led them into a gap, or narrow pass, between the mountains. Arriving at the other end of the pass, Boone and his friends found themselves on the western side of the Appalachians. There, for the first time, they gazed down upon the beautiful green meadows of Kentucky. The mountain pass through which they had crossed came to be called Cumberland Gap.

Boone was to cross through Cumberland Gap many times over the next several years. In 1775 he was hired to turn the Warriors' Path into a trail wide enough for settlers traveling with wagons and animals. Boone and a crew of 40 men chopped down trees and cleared away the underbrush to widen the trail. In just a few months, the new road, now called the Wilderness Trail, was ready for use.

The first settlers to follow the Wilderness Trail into Kentucky were some of Boone's relatives and friends. They started a settlement called Boonesboro. They were quickly followed by hundreds, then thousands of other pioneers searching for new, rich land south of the Ohio River.

While thousands poured across the Wilderness Trail into Kentucky and neighboring Tennessee, thousands more came by way of the Ohio River. They floated downstream on their **flatboats** until they reached the land they desired. By 1792, Kentucky had enough people to become a state. Tennessee became a state just four years later.

During those same years, pioneers also moved into the land known as the Northwest Territory, which was north of the Ohio River. Most of them settled along that river or near the streams that emptied into it. The Ohio River, and the Mississippi River too, became the water highways for westerners to get their farm products to market.

> **vocabulary**
> **flatboat** a boat with a flat bottom and square ends, used to transport heavy loads in shallow water

Unknown Territory The United States gained the vast area of land between the Mississippi River and the Rocky Mountains known as the Louisiana Territory. Strange as it may seem, when the United States made this purchase from France, we knew very little about what we were getting. Neither did anyone else.

Was the land good for farming? What kinds of plants grew there, and what kinds of animals lived there? What about the Indians who lived there—were they peaceful or warlike? How high were the Rocky Mountains? Was there a way to cross them? Better still, might the land possibly contain a way to reach the Pacific Ocean entirely by water—the long-dreamed-of Northwest Passage?

President Thomas Jefferson decided to send an expedition to find the answers to these and a hundred questions like them. To lead it, he chose 29-year-old Meriwether Lewis. Lewis was then serving as President Jefferson's private secretary. This man, however, was no ordinary secretary. He had served as an army captain on the frontier,

and he was also an experienced explorer. To lead the expedition with him, Lewis asked a friend from his army days, William Clark. Both men were filled with the spirit of adventure. A good thing, too, for there would be plenty of that—and danger, also—in the times ahead of them.

But first, the two leaders had to prepare for the long journey ahead. They hired strong men to make the trip with them. They bought large amounts of clothing, tools, and medical supplies. They also bought plenty of ammunition, for even though they were bringing along several tons of food, they would have to hunt for most of what they would eat.

Knowing they would be meeting and dealing with many groups of Native Americans, they also

"Lewis and Clark at Three Forks" by Edgar S. Paxon, Courtesy: Montana Historical Society.

The Lewis and Clark expedition was the first of many to explore the land that came with the Louisiana Purchase. Lewis, Clark, and Sacagawea are shown in the center. The other people are York, Clark's servant, and two frontiersmen.

put together a shopping list of goods to trade and to give as gifts, including 2,800 fish hooks, 4,600 needles, large quantities of colored beads, silk ribbons, and mirrors.

Finally the Lewis and Clark expedition was ready. On a clear morning in May 1804, the explorers—23 soldiers, several experienced frontiersmen, and three interpreters who spoke various Indian languages—climbed into their boats on the Missouri River near the town of St. Louis. They were joined by two canoes carrying 15 more men, who would travel with them part of the way. Together the men began to paddle the boats upstream.

Lewis, Clark, and their men were about to leave civilization behind. There would be no more letters, no more supplies, no help if it were needed. They knew that for the next two years and maybe more, they would be on their own. The great adventure had now begun.

Several months later the group reached what is now North Dakota, where they stopped to spend the winter in a Mandan Indian village. There they used their time well, repairing their equipment, making six new canoes, and learning all they could from the Mandans about the land and the Indian tribes that lay ahead.

Sacagawea

Realizing they would need more people who understood Indian languages, Lewis and Clark

Lewis and Clark needed guides like Sacagawea on their journey.

added two new people to their company. One was a French Canadian trapper named Charbonneau (shar bah NOH), who had lived among the Indians for many years. The other was his pregnant 16-year-old wife, Sacagawea (sak uh juh WEE uh).

Sacagawea had had more than her share of troubles in her young life. Born a member of the Shoshone people, she had been kidnapped by rival Hidatsa Indians when she was only 11. Five years later the Hidatsa sold her to several Mandan warriors. She became the wife of Charbonneau when he won her in a bet with the Mandans.

With the arrival of spring, the Lewis and Clark expedition set out once more, paddling up the Missouri River in their new canoes. The exploring party was now smaller, for this was as far as those extra 15 men from St. Louis went. But the expedition had also added a passenger by then. It was Sacagawea's infant boy.

In summer, 1805, they reached the source, or starting point, of the Missouri River, in present-day Montana. They were entering the country of the Shoshones—Sacagawea's people.

Fortunately for the explorers, the land here was familiar to Sacagawea. When they came to a fork in the trail, she was able to lead the group along the right path toward their destination.

One day, Lewis and several of his men met a war party of 60 Shoshones. The Indians could easily have wiped out the entire expedition then and there, but they did not. Instead, they accepted the explorers as friends.

Several days later it was arranged that Sacagawea would meet with the Shoshone leader. When she did, she could hardly believe her eyes. The chief of the group was her very own brother! There was a joyful reunion filled with tears and laughter. Later, with Sacagawea doing the translating, Lewis was able to trade goods for the horses that were needed to move on across the Rocky Mountains.

Shortly after, the Lewis and Clark party stood at the Continental Divide. This is the line high in the Rockies from which all the rivers flow to the east on one side and to the west on the other. It was an exciting moment for the group, but dangerous rocky trails lay ahead as they began their climb down the western slopes.

In October the men lowered their canoes into the waters of the Snake River. They paddled down the Snake into the Columbia River, until, in November 1805, they sighted the Pacific Ocean. Lewis wrote in his journal: "An Indian called me . . . and gave me . . . a piece of fresh salmon roasted . . . this was the first salmon I had seen and perfectly convinced me that we were on the waters of the Pacific Ocean."

Missouri Historical Society

William Clark drew this picture of a Columbia River salmon for his journal.

Imagine the thrill this group of explorers felt at the moment they first spotted the ocean! William Clark wrote in his journal entry for November 7, 1805, "Ocean in view! O! the joy . . . ," but no words could possibly have captured that moment.

The Return Trip

After a mild winter on the Pacific coast, it was time to start back. Sacagawea, her husband, and their infant son left the group when it reached the Mandan village from which they had started. The rest of the explorers returned to St. Louis in September 1806.

From there, Meriwether Lewis continued on to Washington to report to President Jefferson about this newest territory of the United States. All in all, the Lewis and Clark expedition traveled a total of over 7,000 miles in just under two and one-half years. For the first time, people had crossed the North American continent from one side to the other.

Zebulon Pike

Lewis and Clark were the most famous of American explorers of the West, but they were not the only ones. Another was a United States Army officer named Zebulon Pike. In 1806, the very year that Lewis and Clark returned from their great journey, Lieutenant Pike set out toward the west from Missouri. Meeting the Arkansas River far upstream, he followed it toward its source in the Rocky Mountains. There he sighted the mountain named for him today, Pikes Peak, in present-day Colorado.

F **allen Timbers** Some settlers moving west liked to say they were moving on to "empty land." They really knew better. Far from empty, much of this land was inhabited by Native Americans who had lived there for hundreds of years. And with every new push westward by the pioneers, the resentment of the Native American inhabitants grew.

From time to time organized warfare would flare up. Indians fired arrows at settlers on their flatboats on the Ohio River. They attacked groups of pioneers traveling on the Wilderness Trail. For their part, settlers and United States Army troops attacked and killed Indians.

More usually, though, there were simply isolated killings by both sides in the silence of the forest. Hate was answered with hate, and blood with blood. Indian tribes in the Ohio Territory managed to win several victories against the United States Army. However, in 1794 they were defeated at the Battle of Fallen Timbers, near what is today the city of Toledo. The Indians were forced to give up nearly all of Ohio and move farther west. As the Indians left the Ohio

Territory, settlers poured in. Soon there were enough there for Ohio to become a state.

When the settlers and the army weren't driving out Indians by force, they were gaining Indian land by purchase and by trickery. Soon after the Ohio Territory was won, settlers began to push into the Indiana Territory, right next door. The governor of the Indiana Territory was William Henry Harrison, a man who would later become President of the United States.

Governor Harrison did not try to drive the Indians out by force. Instead, he pressured and tricked several of their chiefs into signing agreements to give up huge amounts of their lands in exchange for small amounts of money—sometimes as little as a half penny an acre!

Their defeat at the Battle of Fallen Timbers cost the Native Americans their Ohio homelands.

Tecumseh

As one piece of Indian land after another was handed over to white settlers, a Shawnee Indian chief named Tecumseh watched with rising anger. Tecumseh had been fighting against white settlers since boyhood, when his father was killed in cold blood by a band of white hunters. He had seen the remains of Shawnee villages after army troops had destroyed them. He had tasted the bitterness of being forced to leave the tribe's lands in Ohio after the defeat at Fallen Timbers.

Now, in Indiana Territory, he was determined that the loss of Indian land must stop. "These lands are ours," he declared. "No one has a right to remove us because we are the first owners. The Great Spirit above has appointed this place for us, on which to light our fires, and here we will remain."

Once, after learning of another Indian sale of land, Tecumseh exploded: "Sell a country! Why not sell the air, the clouds and the great sea, as well as the earth? Did not the Great Spirit make them all for the use of his children?"

But Tecumseh knew it would take more than words to hold off the tide of white settlement. There was only one way for Indians to do that, he believed, and that was to unite.

Tecumseh spent several years traveling up and down the frontier, urging the

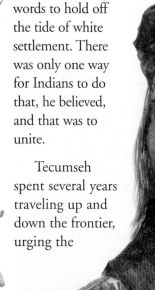

Indian nations to join together. A number of them did.

Meanwhile, Governor Harrison watched Tecumseh's successes with growing concern. In 1811, while Tecumseh was in the south urging more chiefs to join him, Harrison sent 900 American soldiers to the site of a Shawnee village on the Tippecanoe River. The soldiers camped near the Native American settlement. While Tecumseh was gone, his brother Tenskwatawa ordered the Shawnee to attack the Americans. Tenskwatawa told the Shawnee that the white men's bullets could not hurt them. It was a fatal mistake. The Shawnee's attack touched off the battle of Tippecanoe. Harrison's forces defeated the Shawnee and burned their village to the ground. Returning home, Tecumseh found his home in ruins. Worse still, the defeat at Tippecanoe weakened Tecumseh's efforts to get other Indian nations to unite with his Shawnee.

Revenge

Tecumseh vowed revenge. For the next year, Indians in the Northwest Territories attacked other settlers. When the United States went to war against Great Britain in 1812, Tecumseh joined with British forces and led several Indian tribes into battle against the Americans. His bitterness against the Americans knew no limit. "We gave them forest-clad mountains and valleys full of game," Tecumseh told the British general, "and in return what did they give our warriors and our women? Rum and trinkets and a grave."

In 1813, however, Tecumseh was killed. When he died, his dream of stopping the white advance through a union of all Indian tribes died with him.

Tecumseh almost succeeded in uniting Indian nations against white settlement.

Getting Around As America's population grew and spread, one thing became clear: The United States would need to improve its transportation system. Roads like the ones Mrs. Knight traveled on back in 1704—dirt paths really, dusty in summer, muddy in winter, with tree stumps sticking up here and there—would not do for a growing nation.

By 1800, improvements had, in fact, been made on many of the roads that connected the growing cities and towns of the East. They had been widened and were able to handle wagon traffic as well as horses. It was now possible to travel between the main towns by stagecoach.

The stagecoach got its name from the fact that it made its journey "in stages": every 15 or 20 miles, the driver of the coach stopped at a station to change the team of horses for the next stage of the journey.

Cut logs laid across roads were supposed to make stagecoach travel easier and safer, but the roads remained dangerous.

Although stagecoach travel was an improvement over travel on horseback, it was still hardly a comfortable experience. You began your trip at 2:00 or 3:00 in the morning. Sitting on hard wooden seats in a coach without springs, you felt every bump and hole in the unpaved roads. Male passengers learned not to dress in fancy clothes because when the wheels of the coach got stuck in a mudhole the men were expected to help lift the coach out.

When the sun went down and your stagecoach stopped at an inn, you found things hadn't changed much since Sarah Kemble Knight's day.

You still got a poor meal and a terrible night's sleep. Often travelers slept four in a bed, with males in one bedroom and females in another.

Turnpikes

Another improvement was the development of roads called turnpikes. Just before 1800 a number of people figured that if they could build good roads, they could charge people for using them. Every ten miles or so, the road's owners would collect a toll, or fee. They did this by placing a pike, or pole, across the road, blocking passage until the traveler paid the toll. That is how the turnpike got its name: when the toll was paid, the pike would be turned, allowing the traveler to pass.

Some of these turnpikes were actually paved with stone or gravel. Most, though, were just improved versions of the old dirt road—a little smoother, a little wider, with the tree stumps in them a little lower—but the newer roads were just as dusty or muddy, depending on the season, as the older roads. And most of them ran between the cities of the East, where there were lots of users to pay the tolls. No turnpike ran very far west.

None of these improvements, then, answered the growing needs of people who were moving west. There were few roads wide enough for wagons. Pioneers, therefore, still traveled mainly on foot, leading a horse or mule that carried their supplies.

Steamboats

Improved roads were a big help, but they were still a very slow and expensive way for westerners to ship their farm products to the markets of the world. Rivers provided a better way to do that. Most of the streams west of the Appalachian Mountains emptied into the Ohio River, and the Ohio in turn emptied into the great Mississippi River. That is why so many settlers chose to farm the land along these waterways. They could load their goods on flatboats and float them downstream all the way to the port of New Orleans, and from there they could be sent by ship anywhere in the world.

But flatboats could not return upstream against the current without great human effort. Most farmers therefore, after selling their crops in New Orleans, would break up their boats and sell them for lumber. They then returned north by horseback or on foot.

Was there some way that would allow river travel to go upstream as well? An American inventor named Robert Fulton believed he knew how. He built a boat, placed two large **paddle wheels** on its sides, and installed a steam engine. His idea was that power from the steam engine would turn the paddle wheels, which would work like oars and push the boat through the water.

Fulton named his boat the *Clermont*. Others who saw this odd-looking boat laughed and called it a different name: *Fulton's Folly*. But Robert Fulton had the last laugh. In August 1807, the *Clermont* steamed up the Hudson River, against the current, from New York City to Albany—150 miles in only 32 hours. Fulton's steamboat made the trip in far less time than a horse-drawn wagon could, and it carried a much larger cargo. It did not take long for steamboats to make their appearance on the Ohio and Mississippi rivers, carrying passengers and goods down and especially up these water highways.

> **vocabulary**
> **paddle wheel** a wheel with paddles around it, used to push a boat through the water

Steamboats like the **Clermont** *changed river travel by allowing people and goods to travel upstream.*

Connecting Waterways As important as the steamboat was, it could not answer all the transportation needs of the growing nation. Steamboats could only travel where the rivers ran. In the area then being settled, between the Appalachian Mountains and the Mississippi River, the rivers run mainly north and south.

Anyone wishing to send goods east or west still had to send them over roads, and as you have read, most roads were poor and wagon travel was slow and expensive. An even bigger problem was getting across the Appalachian Mountains. As you see on the map titled "The United States Grows," other than the Cumberland Gap, there are just a few low places that cut through these mountains.

One such place is in the northern part of New York State. Rather than build a road there, however, Governor De Witt Clinton of New York had another idea. Why not build a canal—a waterway that would connect Lake Erie with the Hudson River? This would allow farmers near

the Great Lakes to ship their corn, wheat, and hogs all the way over to Albany on a canal, and from Albany down the Hudson River to New York City and the world.

Governor Clinton's proposal was breathtaking. True, several canals had already been built in the United States. However, the longest was only 27 miles. The Erie Canal—that is what it would be called—would be 363 miles long, the longest ever built in the United States! Keep in mind that this was before the days of chain saws, steam shovels, and bulldozers. Every tree along the route would have to be cut down by hand, and all the dirt would have to be dug by thousands of workers, one shovelful at a time.

Goods could be shipped more easily and cheaper by canal than by wagons over poor roads.

New York Governor De Witt Clinton proved that the Erie Canal could be built.

Many people felt that it was an impossible task. Even Thomas Jefferson, who was always interested in new ideas, said this particular idea was "little short of madness." In spite of such opinions, work on the Erie Canal began in 1817. Eight years later the job was finished. To celebrate the event, a fleet of boats, pulled by mules walking on a path alongside the canal, set out from Buffalo at the western end of the canal on October 26, 1825. On the first boat was Governor Clinton, with two red, white, and blue barrels filled with water from Lake Erie. Arriving in New York harbor eight days later, the governor dramatized the great accomplishment by dumping the barrels of fresh water from the Great Lakes into the salt water of the Atlantic Ocean.

The Erie Canal was an instant success. And no wonder: goods that previously had cost $1 to ship overland from Buffalo to New York City could now be sent for less than a dime—and in half the time. As a result of the growing trade, Buffalo grew from a small town into a large city; and New York became the largest city in the young nation.

Other states rushed to copy the success of New York State with east-west canals of their own. Even though none was as successful as the Erie, these canals also encouraged settlement in the West.

Railroads

Not long after the success of the canal systems, there appeared a still greater improvement in transportation—the railroad. The world's first railroad had been built in England in 1825. Three years later the first one in the United States was built in Baltimore, Maryland. The whole railroad was just 13 miles long. A team of horses pulled the wooden coaches along the tracks, which were made of wood with a strip of iron on top.

In 1830 a young mechanic named Peter Cooper designed and built a steam engine to pull a train. This locomotive, as Cooper called it, was able to reach a speed of 18 miles an hour—many times faster than a wagon or a canal boat.

However, a person needed a taste for adventure to ride on one of those early railroads. The passenger cars that rode on the rails were basically stagecoaches. You could choose to sit inside the coach or on the seats outside on top. Either way, you could expect to be showered with the sparks and cinders that belched from the locomotive's smokestack. One passenger riding inside during the 1830s counted 13 large holes burned in her dress on a trip of just a few miles. Of course, if you were riding on top, it was worse. To add to your discomfort, smoke from the locomotive blew in your face the entire journey. The coaches often jumped off the tracks, and the steam engines had a nasty habit of blowing up. If the locomotive broke down, the male passengers had to get out and push the train to the next town.

In the 1840s, railroad companies started to use passenger cars shaped like long boxes, with seats on each side and an aisle down the middle. That was a bit better for the passengers, but not much. In the winter, the companies put a stove at each end of the long car for warmth. However, if you were sitting near the hot stoves, you roasted, but if you were anywhere near the middle of the car, you still froze. At some stops, young boys climbed on board with hot bricks to sell for warming your feet.

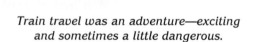

Train travel was an adventure—exciting and sometimes a little dangerous.

Despite all these discomforts, traveling by railroad quickly became popular. In the 1830s and 1840s, hundreds of railroad companies sprang up. Nearly all of them were small companies, with tracks only 40 or 50 miles long. At that time, each company decided for itself how far apart to set its tracks.

One might set them five feet apart, another two inches wider, a third two inches narrower. That meant that each company's locomotives and cars could only roll on its own tracks.

Think of what this meant if you were traveling a long distance. Every 40 or 50 miles, when the train reached the end of one company's line, you had to get off and walk a few blocks to the next company's railroad line, with its wider or narrower tracks. If you were traveling from Albany to Buffalo in New York State, a distance of about 320 miles by train, you rode on seven different trains—and probably missed connections on several of those changes. The whole trip took a day and a half.

Still, a day and a half was a lot faster than you could get there by canal boat, which traveled only as fast as a mule could tow it—about four miles an hour. Also, water cannot flow uphill, so a canal required fairly level ground. But you could build a railroad almost anywhere. Further, water in the northern canals would freeze over in winter, whereas the railroad could be used year-round. Thus, farmers could ship their products to market faster, from almost anywhere, and at any time of the year. By the 1840s, railroads had become the most important form of transportation in the country.

Native Americans React With each new improvement in transportation, white Americans applauded. Those who wanted to move farther west could do so, knowing they would be able to grow farm products and get them to market in the East cheaply and quickly.

To Native Americans, however, each new road, steamboat, canal, and railroad brought closer the day when they would be pushed off their land.

Northern Tribes

You've already read how Indians who lived north of the Ohio River lost their lands to the United States government and advancing white settlers. By 1830 most of Indians had been forced to move west of the Mississippi River.

Still, nearly 100 tribes remained on land in the East that white settlers wanted. Congress helped them get it by passing the Indian Removal Act in 1830. This law said that the Indians must move west of the Mississippi River to an "Indian Territory" set aside for them in the present-day state of Oklahoma. So, helpless and bewildered, the native people were forced to leave their beloved land, their home of countless years. A few tribes resisted, but it was a losing struggle.

In 1832 the Sauk and the Fox Indians fought against the United States Army in Illinois, but in the end they were defeated and forced to move. By then nearly all the Indians who had lived north of the Ohio River had been driven to the other side of the Mississippi.

Five Civilized Tribes

Knowing that fighting against the United States Army was a losing battle, five Native American tribes that lived in the southeastern United States decided on a different strategy. These five tribes—the Choctaws, Creeks, Cherokees, Chickasaws, and Seminoles—believed that their best chance to keep their land was to adopt the ways of white Americans. They learned to farm like the white settlers, growing the same crops. They dressed like them, and they built homes like theirs. Many of them became Christians.

The Cherokees even developed a written language. This was the work of a Cherokee named Sequoyah. Sequoyah created a written symbol for each of the 86 syllables in the Cherokee's spoken language—it was "like catching a wild animal and taming it," he explained. Once these 86 symbols were learned, any Cherokee could become a reader and a writer.

Soon Cherokees were building schools for their children. They started a weekly newspaper. They formed a government like that of the United States, and they wrote a constitution based on the United

Thanks to Sequoyah and his alphabet, the Cherokees were soon printing newspapers and books in their own language.

States Constitution. White Americans came to call the Cherokees and the four other tribes of the southeast the Five Civilized Tribes—"civilized" in the mind of the white settlers because these tribes had adopted so many of their ways. In the end, none of the efforts of these tribes did them any good. White settlers wanted their land, and that was all that mattered to the newcomers. When gold was discovered on the land of the Cherokees in 1828, their doom was certain.

It made no difference that the Cherokees had made a treaty with the United States government in 1791 that stated this was their land. Even though some white Americans, including the Supreme Court of the United States, agreed that the treaty should be honored, President Andrew Jackson did not. He sent the army to help remove the Cherokees, just as it had been removing other tribes of the Five Civilized Tribes all through the 1830s.

The scenes of the Native Americans being forced to leave their homes and lands were heartbreaking even to some of the army soldiers. One of them later wrote, "I saw the helpless Cherokees arrested and dragged from their homes, and driven by bayonet into the **stockades.** And in the chill of a drizzling rain on an October morning I saw them loaded like cattle or sheep into wagons and started toward the west."

Osceola was a great Seminole leader who was finally defeated by trickery.

The journey to Indian Territory took several months. Most of the Indians walked the whole way. They suffered from disease, hunger, and bitter cold. Although about 15,000 started out, only 11,000 arrived in Indian Territory alive. Indians called this journey *Nuna-da-ut-sun'y,* which meant "The Trail Where They Cried" or "The Trail of Tears."

Osceola and the Seminoles

Of the Five Civilized Tribes, the Seminoles held out against the United States Army the longest. Seminoles had originally lived in the southern part of present-day Georgia. When the British colonists in Georgia tried to make them slaves, they had fled south to Florida. This was in the mid-1700s, when Florida was owned by Spain. The Seminoles began life in Florida as hunters and gatherers, but like the other Civilized Tribes, they soon settled down to a life of farming.

In 1821, the United States gained Florida from Spain. That was bad news for the Seminoles. Within a few years the government was trying to remove them and send them to Indian Territory.

> **vocabulary**
> **stockade** an enclosure or pen in which prisoners are kept

One of the Seminole chiefs who fought against removal was Osceola (ahs ee OH luh). As a boy, Osceola and his mother had moved from present-day Alabama to Florida. He was determined not to be forced to move again. Osceola said he would fight the white invaders of Seminole land "till the last drop of Seminole blood has moistened the dust of my hunting ground."

Osceola and his warriors defeated troops from the United States Army in several battles. The army commander invited Osceola to meet to discuss peace, but it was a trick. When Osceola arrived, he was taken prisoner. Although he was not kept in a prison cell, he was not allowed to leave the army fort. In a few months, Osceola's health became poor, and he died.

The Seminoles fought on bravely, but they were finally defeated and sent to Indian Territory in the West. Only 500 Seminoles remained, hiding in the swamps and **Everglades** of Florida. They were often joined there by black runaway slaves.

A Land-hungry Nation

When it came to the endless desire of Americans for land, most Europeans just shook their heads. And no wonder. Consider this: by the 1770s, settlement in the American colonies had spread from the Atlantic coast to the Appalachian Mountains. That was already an area four to five times as large as Great Britain, and for only one-third as many people.

You might think, Europeans said, that this would be enough land to satisfy even those land-hungry Americans. It wasn't.

In 1783—about ten years later—the United States won its independence from Great Britain and gained all the land between the Appalachian Mountains and the Mississippi River. This doubled the size of the new nation, which was now more than twice as big as Great Britain and France put together.

You might think, Europeans said, that certainly this would be enough land to satisfy even those land-hungry Americans. It wasn't.

In 1803—just 20 years later—President Jefferson bought the Louisiana Territory from France, doubling America's size once again and pushing its western boundary all the way to the Rocky Mountains. The new nation had grown almost as large as the whole continent of Europe, except for Russia.

Surely now, Europeans said, that was enough land to satisfy even those land-hungry Americans. It wasn't.

By the 1820s and 1830s, many Americans were eyeing other parts of the North American continent. One was the huge area from Texas to California, between today's Mexican border and the present-day states of Colorado and Utah. Another was the area north of California, between the Rocky Mountains and the Pacific Ocean, known as Oregon Country.

Manifest Destiny

Why did so many Americans think it was important for their country to keep expanding? One reason was that in an age when nine in ten Americans made their living by farming, you could never have too much good land. With America's population just about doubling every 25 years, some said the United States needed to have more and more land for future generations.

But there was more to it than that. Americans believed that they had created a special nation—something new on the face of the earth. In the United States, citizens chose their own government, and the government respected and protected the rights of the citizens. In a world filled with tyrants who used force to crush their own people, this was a truly remarkable achievement. By expanding their country's boundaries, Americans said, they would be "extending the area of freedom" and bringing the blessings of liberty to the people who would live there. In addition, Americans were a people of great energy and

Believing in the idea of Manifest Destiny, pioneers kept moving westward.

ambition. Many believed it was only right and natural that their nation should expand. They took it for granted that this would happen sooner or later. In fact, they said, it was America's *Manifest Destiny* to expand to the Pacific Ocean. By that, they meant that it was obvious to all ("manifest") that America's march to the Pacific Ocean was a certainty in the future ("destiny"). Many believed that God himself intended that the United States should extend from one ocean to the other.

Manifest Destiny was an exciting idea, but it was not without its problems. For one thing, when white Americans spoke of spreading "the blessings of liberty," they did not always intend to spread those blessings to African Americans and Native Americans.

Manifest Destiny also angered countries that controlled land along the U.S. border. Mexico and Great Britain claimed most of the land that the United States wanted for itself. They did not think that America's march to the Pacific was bound to happen. In fact, they were determined to prevent it.

Mexican Independence The first of these lands to become part of the United States was Texas. In the early 1800s, Mexicans rebelled against Spain, which had ruled them for nearly 300 years. Mexico won its independence in 1821 and took over all the Spanish lands in North America, including Texas.

At that time few Mexicans actually lived in Texas. The new government of Mexico wanted to build up the area, but it was unable to persuade many Mexicans to move there. When an American named Stephen Austin offered to start a colony of American settlers in Texas in exchange for land, the Mexican government gladly accepted.

In the early 1820s, Austin brought 300 settlers from the United States into Texas. Later he brought several hundred more. Austin wrote that the land was "as good in every respect as a man could wish for, land all first rate. . . ." The Mexican government soon made the same deal with a number of other Americans, and they too started colonies in Texas.

It wasn't long before the Mexican government realized it had made a big mistake. Before getting their land, the settlers had made a number of promises: They had promised to adopt the Catholic religion of Mexico and to become loyal Mexican citizens. They also promised to free any slaves they had brought to Texas. They hadn't kept any of these promises. Even worse, they were ignoring the laws of Mexico and demanding more self-government. Some even talked about becoming independent from Mexico.

So, in 1830, the Mexican government announced it would welcome no more American settlers. It was too late. There were already more than 16,000 Americans in Texas—far more than the 5,000 Spanish-speaking Mexicans. And since it was easy to cross the border into Texas, still more American settlers came every year, regardless of what Mexico said.

Remember the Alamo
In the early 1830s the Mexican government announced that it would tighten its rule over Texas. Texans became angry. In a number of settlements, fighting broke out between Texans and Mexican soldiers. At a meeting, Texas leaders decided to form an army. To lead it, they chose a one-time United States Army officer and former governor of Tennessee, Sam Houston.

The Texans lost the Battle of the Alamo but gained a symbol to fight for, as well as an inspirational slogan, "Remember the Alamo!"

To Mexico's new ruler, General Antonio López de Santa Anna, that was the last straw. Early in 1836, General Santa Anna led an army of 4,000 soldiers toward the settlement of San Antonio, where he intended to crush his rebellious subjects.

San Antonio was being defended by a small group of Texans under the command of 27-year-old William Travis. Travis and his men could have safely retreated from San Antonio and lived to fight another day. Instead, they decided to take shelter behind the thick walls of an abandoned Spanish mission known as the Alamo. There, said Travis, they would make their stand. It was a decision that would cost them their lives.

On February 23, 1836, Santa Anna gave the order to begin the attack on the Alamo. Day after day Mexican cannons pounded the Alamo. The Texans returned the fire. After 12 days, however, the Texans' ammunition was nearly gone, and the men were exhausted. At 4:00 in the morning of March 6, Mexican troops stormed the walls of the Alamo. Twice they were beaten back. Finally, however, the Mexican soldiers poured over and through the walls.

The newly independent Texans designed a flag for their republic.

In the fighting that followed, all of the defenders of the Alamo were killed, including such famous pioneers as Davy Crockett of Tennessee and Jim Bowie, who invented the bowie hunting knife. Only the lives of seven women, children, and servants were spared. But the battle had cost the Mexican army 1,500 men and had given Texans their rallying cry: "Remember the Alamo!"

Texas Gains Its Independence

By the time the Alamo fell, Texans had already declared their independence from Mexico and formed their own country, the Republic of Texas. Their new flag had a single broad stripe of white and another of red, running side to side. In the midst of a broad stripe of blue, running up

and down, they placed a single white star. As a result the new Republic of Texas came to be called the Lone Star Republic.

Of course, just declaring independence was one thing; actually winning it was another. To succeed, the Texans would first have to defeat the Mexican army. And in 1836 it did not seem likely that they could. Mexico was a country of many millions. Texas had hardly 35,000 people. How could it hope to assemble an army large enough to fight off the Mexicans?

In fact, for six weeks after the Alamo, General Sam Houston and his Texans retreated again and again before the larger Mexican army. Santa Anna was confident he would catch up with them and defeat them.

What Santa Anna did not realize was that during those weeks that Houston was avoiding battle, he was building up and training his small army. He knew that he must be patient and choose the right place and the right time to fight if he was to have a chance to win.

Finally that time came. On April 21, 1836, the Mexican army was camped less than a mile away, near the bank of the San Jacinto [san juh SIHN toh] River. In those days, battles nearly always began in the morning and ended at nightfall. It was now 3:30 in the afternoon. Believing there would be no fighting until the next day, the Mexican commander, General Santa Anna, allowed his men to put down their guns and rest.

This was Sam Houston's chance. His army numbered only 783 men, less than half the size of the Mexican force near the river. But Houston knew that his great ally would be surprise. At 4:00 P.M. he lifted his sword—the silent signal for his army to move forward. The Texans moved out of the woods that had sheltered them and advanced quickly and silently through a meadow of tall grass.

About 200 yards from the Mexican camp, they were spotted by Mexican guards. The Mexicans fired. Two Texas cannons quickly answered the fire. With General Houston shouting the warning, "Keep low, men! Hold your fire!" the Texans moved forward quickly.

Twenty yards from the edge of the Mexican camp, Houston gave the order: "Kneel! Shoot low! Fire!" The Texans halted and opened fire. Then Houston, riding high on horseback, waved his hat—the signal to advance. The Texans rushed forward, guns firing and knives drawn, shouting, "Remember the Alamo! Remember the Alamo!"

The Battle of San Jacinto was over in less than 20 minutes. Half the Mexican army had been killed, and the rest had been captured. The Texans' losses were nine killed and 23 wounded, including General Sam Houston, who took a bullet in the ankle.

At the end of the battle, the Texans captured Santa Anna. They threatened to put him to death unless he signed an agreement promising to withdraw all Mexican troops from Texas and to accept Texan independence. Santa Anna signed and was released.

Texas Becomes a State

With the fighting over, Texans elected Sam Houston to be the first president of their new country. Actually, Houston and most other Texans really wanted Texas to become a state in the United States. However, Texas allowed slavery, and many people in the United States were opposed to bringing another slave state into the Union.

Texas had to wait nine years before the Congress of the United States agreed that it could become a state. But in 1845, Texas joined the Union as the twenty-eighth state.

General Santa Anna agreed to give Texas its independence after he lost the Battle of San Jacinto.

General Sam Houston led the Texans to independence as first president of the Republic of Texas.

Oregon Country As with Texas, many Americans felt that gaining the Oregon Country was part of their nation's Manifest Destiny. The Oregon Country was a large area between the Rocky Mountains and the Pacific Ocean. Its northern and southern borders were Alaska and California.

Getting the Oregon Country, however, turned out to be far more difficult than gaining Texas had been. It almost led to a war with Great Britain, and in the end, the United States got only half of what it wanted.

It was the fur of its animals, not the richness of its soil, that led Americans to become interested in Oregon. Beaver and sea otter furs, used in making hats and fine coats in the East and in Europe, were bringing high prices by 1800. Always on the lookout for profitable trade, New England merchants sent sailing ships around Cape Horn and up to Oregon to trade with Native Americans.

This was a long and dangerous journey of thousands of miles. Cape Horn, at the southernmost tip of South America, is known for its wild storms and rough water. However, many merchants were willing to risk its perils to trade for furs with Oregon's Native Americans.

The British also set up a fur-trading company in Oregon. And soon, with little regard for the Indians whose homes and hunting grounds they were invading, both Britain and the United States claimed the Oregon Country as their own. But since few Americans or British actually lived there, the two countries agreed to put off the matter of ownership for a later time.

Mountain Men

While British ships continued to make the long and difficult journey to Oregon, America's fur traders soon found a way to carry on the fur trade over land. In the Rocky Mountains there

Stories about the yearly meeting of Mountain Men and fur traders stirred the imagination of many Americans.

lived a number of hardy adventurers and fur trappers known as Mountain Men. Big, lean, bearded men who dressed in buckskin, these Mountain Men wanted nothing more than to be as far away from civilization as possible. They lived alone, sleeping under the stars in good weather and in caves or lean-to huts in bad.

Once a year these trappers would leave the mountains to meet a wagon train sent by fur traders from St. Louis at some agreed-upon halfway point. There they traded furs for coffee, sugar, gunpowder, bullets, whiskey, and blankets.

These Mountain Men became important in the story of Oregon. Although most couldn't read or write, they knew everything there was to know about the Rocky Mountains. It was Mountain Man Jed Smith who discovered South Pass, the best route through the Rocky Mountains for people headed for Oregon.

Some of these strong, tough Mountain Men were African Americans. They loved the free and adventurous life. One of these was Jim Beckwourth. Beckwourth was born in Virginia, probably into a slave family, but he grew up in St. Louis as a free man. For 11 years he lived with the Crow Indians who called him Morning Star. Later in his life he became an army scout and found a pass through the Sierra Nevada Mountains to California. Today this pass is called Beckwourth Pass.

Yet another Mountain Man, Jim Bridger, saved the life of many a traveler heading west by providing supplies and information at his station known as Fort Bridger. Bridger's first wife was the daughter of a chief of the Flathead tribe. They had two children before she died. His second wife was a Ute. She died in childbirth. It is said that Jim Bridger raised his motherless baby on buffalo milk.

Travelers did not begin heading for Oregon Country until the 1830s, when some missionaries went there to convert Native Americans to Christianity. The missionaries did not succeed in converting many Indians, but their reports about the beauty, mild climate, and rich farmland of Oregon encouraged some easterners to emigrate there.

On the Oregon Trail

Soon a small trickle of farm families began heading for Oregon. The first really large group of 1,000 did not leave until 1843, but that one was quickly followed by more. These settlers traveled in wagon trains that sometimes were a mile or more long. A team of mules or oxen pulled each wagon in the slow-moving columns. Cows, **pack animals,** and even sheep moved alongside or behind the wagons.

In the early spring the families would gather in Independence, Missouri, and make final preparations for the half-year-long, 2,000-mile trip. A month or so later, when enough grass had grown along the trail for their animals to feed on, they said their good-byes and set out on the Oregon Trail.

> **vocabulary**
> **pack animal** an animal, such as a donkey, used for carrying supplies

For most of the men, women, and children who went, the trip to Oregon was the great adventure of their lives. The first part of the trail followed the shallow Platte River across the Great Plains, where the grassland stretched as far as the eye could see.

Days on the trail began at 4:00 in the morning, with breakfast and morning chores: milk the cows, load the tents and bedding into the wagons, hitch up the oxen. Then it was off again for another 15 or 20 miles before nightfall. Does that seem like a lot of walking for one day? Every day? It probably is for us. But people then were used to walking everywhere, and 15 to 20 miles a day would not have been unusual for persons on a long journey.

You might think that everyone rode inside the covered wagons, but only mothers, small children, and the sick or injured were allowed to. The rest of the wagon was filled to the top with the family's belongings—everything they could take to start a new life when they arrived at their destination. Most of the men rode on horseback, guarding the wagon trains and sometimes riding off to hunt for food for that night's dinner. Older children walked, keeping the cattle moving along with the wagons.

At nightfall the wagons pulled into a circle, with the animals inside to keep them from wandering off. There could be dinner, perhaps a game of tag for the children, some singing around the campfire, and then an early bedtime to be ready for the next day.

That's when things were going well. Often, they did not. Wagon wheels and axles broke; animals died; rainstorms turned the trail into mud. But the wagon train had to keep moving no matter what, for it would have to get across the mountains before the snows arrived.

From the edge of the Great Plains, the trail wound upward toward South Pass. After a short stop at Fort Bridger, the wagon train pushed on, across the pass to the rugged western slopes of the mountains. Here was the hardest part of the trip, when families sometimes had to throw away furniture and other heavy goods brought from home in order to lighten the load in their wagons. Sadly, sometimes precious possessions, such

as a treasured clock, had to be left along the trail. Then the trail improved once again as it followed the Snake River and the Columbia River. And finally, the green meadows of a broad and beautiful valley opened before them—the sight which made it all worthwhile.

Oregon Country Is Divided

With Americans now pouring into the Oregon Country, the United States insisted that Great Britain should give up its claim to the area. Oregon—all of it, right up to the southern boundary of Alaska at 54° 40′ north latitude—must belong to America. Many Americans demanded, "Fifty-four forty or fight!"

The British, however, insisted that Oregon was theirs. For a time it looked like the two countries might go to war. But in 1846 they compromised. They agreed to divide the Oregon Country at 49° north latitude. The southern part, which included the present-day states of Oregon, Washington, Idaho, and parts of Montana, went to the United States. The northern part, which is presently part of western Canada, went to Great Britain.

Travel on the Oregon Trail was not easy.

Another War While the United States was able to avoid a war with Great Britain, another war was fast approaching. Near noon on March 11, 1846, members of the United States Congress took their seats to hear a special message from the President of the United States. Most of them knew, of course, that relations with Mexico had gone from bad to worse.

They also knew that President James Polk had been spoiling for a fight with Mexico for some time. Was there something else, something new, that the President was about to report to them?

Shortly after noon the President's written message arrived, and the clerk began to read it aloud to the hushed Congress. Less than two days earlier, wrote the President, he had received a message from General Zachary Taylor, commander of American troops at the Texas border. The general had reported that Mexican troops had crossed the Rio Grande and attacked his troops. Sixteen American soldiers had been killed or wounded.

"Mexico," continued the President, "has passed the boundary of the United States, has invaded our territory and shed American blood upon American soil." This was an act of war, and the President was now asking Congress to declare war on Mexico. Two days later, May 13, 1846, Congress did just that, and the United States and Mexico were at war.

Why had relations between Mexico and the United States grown so bad? Why had war broken out between these two neighbors? Was President Polk correct when he said that American blood had been shed upon American soil?

A Boundary Dispute

You'll remember that after the Battle of San Jacinto, Texas soldiers captured the Mexican ruler, General Santa Anna, and that to gain his release, he promised to recognize Texas's independence. Even before Santa Anna returned to Mexico City, however, his government took back his word. Mexico said it would not honor "an agreement carried out under the threat of death."

People were eager to get news about the war with Mexico.

Nevertheless, during the next nine years, Mexico did nothing to take back Texas. After that, Texas became part of the United States.

Mexico burned with resentment over the loss of Texas. In addition, Mexico and the United States disagreed about the boundary between Mexico and Texas. Mexico said the southern border of Texas was the Nueces (noo AY says) River. That is where it had been for a hundred years, back in the days when Spain controlled all the land, and that is where it should be now. The United States said the border was the Rio Grande. That river was 150 miles farther south and would give Texas still more Mexican territory.

President Polk Looks to California

President Polk had his eye on something else besides the land between those two Texas rivers. That something was California. Back in the late 1700s and early 1800s when the Spanish still ruled much of the American continents, they established missions up and down the coast of California. These missions became small trading centers. Spanish settlers from Mexico also arrived in California, bringing their cattle with them and starting ranches.

When Mexico won its independence from Spain, all the rest of Spanish-owned land in North America, including California, was turned over to Mexico, too. With large gifts of California land given to them by the Mexican government, some important Mexican families took up ranching there.

Early in the 1800s a number of Americans also started to arrive in California. Sailors aboard American merchant ships that came to trade with the California ranchers found the climate so pleasant that they decided to stay on. After Mountain Man Jim Beckwourth discovered the pass through the Sierra Nevada Mountains, traders and fur trappers started to travel to California, and some of them stayed, too.

Still, as late as the 1840s, there were hardly 1,000 Americans living there. There were ten times that many *Californios,* or Spanish-speaking people from Spain and Mexico. And there were 250 times as many Native Americans. However, none of that troubled those Americans who

insisted it was America's Manifest Destiny to have control of California one day soon.

It certainly didn't trouble President Polk. President Polk didn't know a great deal about California—no Americans at the time really did—but he did know that it had many fine harbors. These harbors could be excellent jumping-off points for trade with China and all of Asia. He also feared that Great Britain had its eye on California and might take it first. He was determined that that must not happen.

President Polk also wanted New Mexico, the territory located between California and the western part of the United States. About 60,000 Spaniards and Mexicans lived there, while almost no Americans did. However, Americans had long traded at the territory's only town, Santa Fe. Each spring a long line of them made the journey there from Independence, Missouri, along the Santa Fe Trail. Armed men rode alongside the line of wagons and pack mules to protect them from unfriendly Indians. In Santa Fe they traded their goods for silver, furs, and other products of the frontier.

The United States Declares War on Mexico

In 1846, President Polk offered to buy California and New Mexico from Mexico. The Mexican government, however, refused to sell. All right, Polk decided, if he could not get California one way, he would get it another. That way was war.

The early Mexican settlers of California kept many of their Spanish customs.

217

The President ordered the American commander in Texas, General Zachary Taylor, to move troops across the Nueces River and to station them on the bank of the Rio Grande. This put American troops onto the very land the Mexicans claimed was theirs. President Polk expected the Mexican army to oppose this move. Sooner or later a fight would break out, and the President would have his excuse for war.

Actually, Polk intended to ask Congress to declare war whether fighting broke out or not. But the very evening he was preparing to write his message to Congress, word arrived from Texas with the news he had hoped for. Now, to all his other reasons for war, the President could add that Mexico had "shed American blood upon American soil"—even though it was not really American soil at all.

Some Americans Oppose the War

Not all Americans were pleased that their country had gone to war. Some felt that President Polk had not been completely truthful when he said that American blood had been shed on "American soil." Didn't the fighting take place in the very area that *both* countries claimed? Since that disagreement hadn't been settled, how could the President say it was "American soil"? And why had he sent troops into that area? Wasn't that certain to cause the Mexicans to resist? Or was that what the President wanted anyway?

One of the people who felt that way was a tall young man from Illinois serving his first term in Congress. His name was Abraham Lincoln. Lincoln challenged the President to point to the exact "spot" on "American soil" where American blood had been shed. Another member of Congress said that the war was "unholy."

In Concord, Massachusetts, a writer named Henry David Thoreau decided to protest the war by refusing to pay his taxes. He was put in jail overnight, but then his aunt paid the tax for him. While in jail, Thoreau was supposedly visited by his friend Ralph Waldo Emerson, a famous minister and author who was also opposed to the war with Mexico. "Henry!" exclaimed his friend. "Why are you here?"

"Waldo," replied Henry Thoreau, "Why are you *not* here?" Thoreau meant that when people believe their government is doing evil, as a matter of conscience they should refuse to participate in that evil. They should refuse peacefully, but they should refuse. If that means they must go to jail, then so be it. This kind of behavior based on one's conscience is called civil disobedience. Thoreau later wrote an essay with that title, explaining his beliefs.

General Zachary Taylor, the hero of the Mexican War, was elected President of the United States in 1848.

The Bear Flag Republic

People like Abraham Lincoln and Thoreau were in the minority, however. The war was popular with most Americans. Tens of thousands of young men volunteered for the army.

In September 1846 the United States armies quickly struck against the Mexicans. An American army led by General Taylor marched into northern Mexico. There, in a battle that lasted three days, Taylor captured the town of Monterey in spite of a courageous defense by the trapped Mexicans. Soon after, he defeated a Mexican army at the Battle of Buena Vista.

A second, smaller army marched into New Mexico and captured the capital city of Santa Fe. From there the army marched on to California. When it arrived, it found that a handful of Americans living in northern California had already overthrown Mexican rule. Because they raised a white flag with a cutout of a brown grizzly bear sewn on it, their uprising came to be called the Bear Flag Revolt. They also set up their own government, which they called the Bear Flag Republic. Shortly after, ships of the American navy landed at Monterey, California. Raising the American flag, the naval commander proclaimed that California was now part of the United States.

The United States Grows Larger

There was still more fighting ahead in California, but less than eight months after the war began, both New Mexico and California were in the hands of the United States.

The war did not end, however, until the American navy carried an American army to the shores of Mexico itself. There the army defeated the Mexicans in several battles and, six months later, entered the Mexican capital, Mexico City, in triumph.

In the peace treaty that ended the war in 1848, Mexico gave up just about all of the present-day Southwest. California, the land that became the states of Nevada and Utah, most of what became the state of Arizona, and large parts of present-day Wyoming, New Mexico, and Colorado all became part of the United States. In return, the United States agreed to pay Mexico just $15 million.

Five years later the United States bought one more piece of land from Mexico. This strip of land forms the southern parts of today's Arizona and New Mexico. It is known as the Gadsden Purchase.

By 1853 the United States had spread from ocean to ocean and from Canada to Mexico.

The United States Grows

Reasons to Move West Most pioneers in America who moved west went in search of new land. However, two large groups that helped settle the Far West went for different reasons. And it is hard to imagine two more different groups. One moved west to escape religious persecution. The other was drawn to the West by greed for gold.

The Mormons

Mormons were members of the Church of Jesus Christ of Latter-Day Saints. The church had been started in western New York in 1830, and most of its early members probably would have been content to remain right there if their neighbors had left them alone.

But many of those neighbors disliked the religious teachings of the new church and forced the Mormons to leave. That began a long trek for the Mormons that for a time must have seemed to them a journey without end. First they moved to Ohio, then to Missouri, and then to Illinois. In each place they met with persecution and even violence. Partly the residents disliked the newcomers' religious beliefs; partly they didn't like the Mormons efforts to convert others to their beliefs. And partly they didn't like the fact that Mormons were often sympathetic to nearby Indian tribes.

When the Mormons moved to Illinois in the early 1840s, they felt they had finally found a home where they could prosper and grow. It didn't last. In 1844 a mob killed Joseph Smith, the founder of the Mormon religion and the leader of the Mormon community. More persecution followed, and by 1846 angry mobs had chased out the last of the Mormons.

Led by their new leader, Brigham Young, they headed westward in 1846 in search of a place that would be far from everyone else, where they would be left alone to follow their religious beliefs. From Iowa the group headed south until it picked up the Oregon Trail. They followed this trail until they reached South Pass. Then they turned south again.

In July 1847, Young and his exploring group of about 150 Mormons reached the top of a range of mountains near the Great Salt Lake, in the present-day state of Utah. The area around

Persecuted for their religious beliefs, the Mormons kept moving westward to find a peaceful place to settle.

the lake was very dry, and most people would not have chosen it as a place to farm. But Young knew that the soil was rich and that if the Mormons irrigated it and worked hard, they could succeed there.

In addition, the land at that time was not part of the United States. It belonged to Mexico. This meant the Mormons would not be subject to the laws of the United States. They would be left alone to make their own rules and to live as they wished. Looking down at the valley below, Young announced to his followers, "This is the place." Any man who wanted to settle there, said Young, would receive as much land as his family needed practically free.

Within a few months, more than 500 wagons and 1,500 of Young's followers arrived to make a new life for themselves. Working under the direction of church leaders, the Mormons prospered. Knowing that the salty water from Salt Lake was not suitable for farming, the leaders ordered that **irrigation canals** be dug between mountain streams and the desert plain. Before long, Mormon farmers were producing fine crops of wheat, vegetables, and other foods. Mormons also sold supplies to pioneers who were heading west to settle in California.

Before long the Mormon population reached 15,000. Most of the Mormon settlers lived in the City of the Saints, which later was called Salt Lake City. Others moved into the valleys of what would eventually become the states of Utah and Idaho.

Gold in California

Imagine what it must have been like to be James Marshall. John Sutter has hired you to build a sawmill for him on his land near the city of Sacramento in California. You get your crew started on the job and leave. Now it's a cold morning in January 1848, and you have gone back to Sutter's land to see how the construction is going. The sawmill is located next to a stream, of course. It's the running water from that stream that will provide the power to run the sawmill. You are standing next to the shallow stream when you look down and notice something shiny in the stream bottom.

Miners searched through gravel and mud for gold.

That's odd, you think, I never noticed that before. You bend down and pick it up. It's a piece of yellow metal, about the size of a tiny stone. You look down again and there's another. You pick up that one, too. Now your eyes begin to widen as you realize what you are holding. These little stones—they're gold! Pure gold!

You race over to Sutter's house to tell him the news. You and he agree—we have to keep this discovery a secret. If we don't, half the world will soon be here grabbing the gold for themselves.

> **vocabulary**
> **irrigation canal** a ditch through which water is brought to crops

Now, perhaps if you really had been James Marshall, you would have kept that secret. Perhaps John Sutter would have, too. And soon enough you'd both be rich.

But it didn't happen that way. Which one of them talked, we don't know. Maybe other people just guessed from something that Sutter and Marshall had said or done. In no time at all, the secret was out. "Gold has been found at Sutter's mill!" The news quickly spread through California. In the growing port city of San Francisco, people left their jobs, their ships, and their families as they rushed off to Sutter's land.

The news went far beyond California. Within months it had reached the entire United States and even Europe. From everywhere, people hurried to California to get their share of the wealth.

And Jim Marshall and John Sutter? They managed to get a little of it for themselves, but not much. Neither of them died a wealthy man.

California was far, far away from where most people lived. Those traveling from the East could choose from among three routes, two by sea and one by land. One was to sail around Cape Horn and then north to San Francisco. From America's East coast, that trip took between six and eight months. On the second route, they could sail south only as far as Panama, then cross the steaming, mosquito-filled jungle by mule to the Pacific side, and then go by ship again north to California. A third way was to go overland by wagon, following the route that pioneers took west, then breaking off and heading south to California.

Not one of these routes was fast. Not one was comfortable. Yet so great was the lure of easy riches that more than 80,000 people journeyed to California in the year 1849 alone to seek their fortune. They became known as the forty-niners.

Most forty-niners went to find gold, but some went to make a living selling miners things they needed or wanted. Merchants became rich by buying picks and shovels back East, shipping them to California, and selling them for 10 or 20 times what they had cost. A woman from Boston baked pies to sell miners. She made $11,000 in one year—which was a huge amount of money in those days. And a German immigrant named Levi Strauss made work pants for miners. These "Levis" caught on, and Strauss made a small fortune.

As for the miners, the earliest to arrive quickly scooped up most of the gold that lay in the beds of shallow streams and on or near the surface of the earth. After that, it took a lot of digging and even more luck to find the precious yellow metal. A few miners did strike it rich. Most of them, though, barely found enough gold to make a living. In time, many of them gave up mining and raised crops or livestock instead. There would be other gold rushes in the American West, but by 1860 the great gold rush of California was just about over.

An imaginative artist pictured different ways to get to California, some real, and some imaginary.

Everglades large swampy grassland located in southern Florida

flatboat a boat with a flat bottom and square ends, used to transport heavy loads in shallow water

irrigation canal a ditch through which water is brought to crops

pack animal an animal, such as a donkey, used for carrying supplies

paddle wheel a wheel with paddles around it, used to push a boat through the water

stockade an enclosure or pen in which prisoners are kept

THE CIVIL WAR

Contents

1 Slavery

A Remarkable Anniversary The date was July 3, 1826. As the fiftieth anniversary of the Declaration of Independence approached, a great drama was playing itself out in the homes of two of the men most responsible for that document. At Monticello in Virginia, Thomas Jefferson, now age 83, slipped in and out of consciousness as he lay on his deathbed.

And in Quincy, Massachusetts, John Adams, now age 90, also neared the end. Would these two great patriots and former Presidents make it to see this fiftieth Independence Day? Americans everywhere hoped and prayed that they would.

As midnight arrived, Thomas Jefferson stirred in his bed and whispered to a young relative, "This is the Fourth?" The young man nodded yes, and Jefferson sighed contentedly. He said no more, and by noon he was gone.

At that very moment in Quincy, Massachusetts, as the roar of a cannon was signaling the start of that town's celebration, John Adams struggled to utter what proved to be his last sentence. His granddaughter, bending close to the old man, was able to hear his final whispered words, "Thomas—Jefferson—still—surv—." Before the sun had set, he too was gone.

In their lifetimes, Thomas Jefferson and John Adams had seen their beloved United States grow from a struggling group of new states into a strong, confident nation. During those fifty years following the Declaration of Independence, the United States had gained vast new lands and developed into a democracy that was a model for the world.

In one important way, however, America had not changed and was not a model at all. Almost from the beginning, even during colonial times, slavery had been part of American life. When the 13 colonies became the first 13 states, nearly one in every five Americans was an African American and nearly all African Americans were slaves. By far, most of these slaves lived in the South. But there were slaves in the Northern states, too. At the time of the American Revolution, for example, one in every ten New Yorkers was a slave. Slaves in the North worked mainly as house servants for rich families. Now, 50 years later, Southerners wanted to see slavery spread to the new western territories as well.

For a short time after the Declaration of

Even though he was a slaveholder, Thomas Jefferson felt it was wrong for one person to own another.

Independence was written, there seemed a chance that slavery might die out. Partly that was because of the words that lie at the very heart of the Declaration:

> We hold these truths to be self-evident; that all men are created equal, that they are endowed by their Creator with certain unalienable rights, that among these are life, liberty, and the pursuit of happiness.

Slavery, of course, was the opposite of liberty. How could people accept slavery and still live up to the words of the Declaration of Independence? A growing number of Americans, both Northerners and Southerners, believed that they could not. As John Adams wrote to his wife, Abigail, slaves "have as good a right to freedom as we have." Before long, five Northern states took steps to end slavery. No Southern state went that far, but a few made it easier for slave owners to free their slaves, if they wished to.

A number of slave owners who believed that slavery was wrong did just that. They included George Washington, who owned many slaves at Mount Vernon, his home in Virginia. Like Washington, these slave owners declared that when they died, their slaves were to be set free. As a result, by the early 1800s there were about 150,000 free African Americans, most of them living in the Southern states.

But not everyone who believed slavery was wrong automatically favored equal rights for the freed African Americans. Almost none of them did. Ending slavery was one thing. Allowing African Americans to have the full rights of citizens, like voting, holding office, serving on juries, living where they wanted to live, working in whatever jobs they were suited for—well, that was something else altogether. Prejudice against African Americans, even those who had been free for several generations, was strong.

The Cotton Gin

There had never been very many slave owners who willingly freed their slaves, and by about 1810 there were almost none. The main reason for the change in attitude is that slaves had become much more valuable. A new invention called the cotton gin now made it highly profitable to use slave labor to grow cotton. Here is why the invention of the cotton gin was so important. Southerners had started growing cotton back in the mid-1700s, but it was not an important crop at first. That's because the kind of cotton that grows best in the American South is filled with sticky green seeds, and those seeds have to be removed before the cotton can be used. At that time it took a single person a whole day to clean the seeds from just one pound of cotton. This increased the cost of southern cotton a great deal. So most makers of cotton goods looked to other parts of the world for their supply of raw cotton.

In 1793, Eli Whitney changed all that. That year, Whitney, a young New Englander who liked to tinker with machines and solve problems, paid a visit to

The Declaration of Independence stated that liberty was a right that all people had. John Adams thought that this applied to enslaved people too.

The cotton gin made cotton a profitable crop in the Southern states and territories.

a Georgia plantation. The owner of the plantation showed Whitney some freshly picked cotton, complete with green seeds. She suggested that he might like to try to invent something that would remove the seeds more easily.

Whitney did—in just ten days! The invention was a system of combs and brushes on rollers, small enough to fit into a small box and powered by turning a handle by hand. Later, Eli built a larger machine that cleaned up to 50 pounds of cotton a day. Whitney called his machine a cotton engine, or cotton gin for short.

Eli Whitney's invention made it possible for Southerners to sell their cotton cheaply. Factories in the North and especially in Great Britain now were ready to buy all the cotton they could grow. Soon, planters were starting large plantations on the rich lands of the Mississippi and Alabama territories. Cotton quickly became the South's largest crop. By 1820 the South was growing 100 times as much cotton as it had raised before Eli Whitney built his cotton gin.

To grow this cotton, the plantation owners needed more laborers to plow, plant, cultivate, and harvest. As a result, slaves were in greater demand than ever. The price of buying a slave doubled. Far from freeing their slaves, Southern planters now sought to buy more slaves.

Does this mean that if the cotton gin had not been invented, most Southern slave owners would have freed their slaves? Probably not. Even without cotton, slavery was important to the Southern economy. Without slaves, the South would have to find a new source of cheap labor.

Also, slavery was important to the owner's comfortable way of life. Not many would have been willing to give that up. Even most of the Southern planters who thought slavery was wrong could not bring themselves to free their slaves. Included among these men was Thomas Jefferson, author of the Declaration of Independence, who owned slaves until the day he died.

Slavery in the South What was life like for slaves in the American South? Much depended on where they worked and who owned them. Slaves on small farms usually worked in the fields alongside their owner. They did many other tasks also, for on a small farm everyone turned a hand at doing a little bit of everything.

On large plantations, though, slaves usually did only one task. A small number worked and lived in the Great House with the master's family. These house servants cooked, cleaned, and did other housework. They also helped raise the children in the master's family. Some other slaves became skilled carpenters, blacksmiths, brick makers, and barrel makers. By far, however, most slaves on a large plantation worked in the fields.

Whether they lived on a small farm or a great plantation, slaves worked from dawn until dusk. Hard work, however, is not what made slavery such a terrible wrong. After all, many people who were not slaves also worked hard.

No, what made slavery wrong is that slaves were not free. They did not have, in the words of the Declaration of Independence, the right to

"life, liberty, and the pursuit of happiness." Another person owned them and was their master.

An owner could treat his slaves like pieces of property. He could buy them; he could sell them. He could sell some members of a slave family and not others, or sell husbands and wives and children to different buyers. In fact, three in every ten slave families were broken up by such sales.

Slaves could be whipped for not working hard enough or fast enough, or for not showing proper respect to members of their owner's family, or for any of a dozen small reasons—sometimes for no reason at all. Not all owners were this cruel, but some certainly were.

In addition, slaves could not leave the plantation without their owner's permission. Only the kindest and most unusual of owners allowed their

Children as well as adults worked in the fields picking cotton.

slaves to learn to read and write. In many states it was illegal to teach slaves to read and write.

Slave owners told themselves, and anyone else who would listen, that their slaves were really happy in slavery. They said their slaves were happy to have masters to take care of them. And probably some of these slave owners actually believed that. After all, it's a lot more comfortable to believe that people are grateful to you than to believe that they hate being held against their will.

Slave Resistance

Of course, if the slaves were really happy being slaves, then they would not have fought against the slavery system. But they did. A few slaves organized uprisings, or rebellions. One such person was Nat Turner. Turner was owned by a plantation owner in Virginia. His master's family thought of him as a religious, peaceful man—until one day

in 1831. On that day, Nat Turner led a group of slaves in an uprising. Over the next three days, he and his followers killed 60 men, women, and children. In the end, all the slaves who took part in Turner's Rebellion were caught, tried, and hanged.

Not many slaves rebelled as Nat Turner did, for they knew they had almost no chance to succeed. Many more simply ran away at one time or another, even though they knew their chances of successfully escaping were not much better. Runaway slaves from Mississippi or Louisiana, for example, would have to cross hundreds of miles of slave states before finally reaching a Northern state where there was no slavery. Chances were that slave catchers, anxious to collect rewards, would hunt them down long before they could reach freedom and return them to their plantations, where they would receive harsh punishment.

Most slaves resisted slavery in other ways. Sometimes they would simply work very slowly. They would pretend to be ill or let themselves become ill on purpose. They also would "accidentally" break tools or set fire to the buildings where the tools were kept. Masters might suspect that these things had been done on purpose, but they never knew for sure.

Of course, slaves did not dare to speak openly of their misery and their longing for freedom. Instead, they spoke through their songs, called spirituals. If the masters really thought their slaves were happy to be held in bondage, they could not have been listening very carefully to these spirituals.

Most spirituals told of the weariness of the slaves and of their hope for a better world to come. You can tell their message by just looking at the first lines. Here are a few: *O brothers, don't get weary; Nobody knows the trouble I've seen;* and *Sometimes I feel like a motherless child.* Those are not the words of happy people grateful to have masters to take care of them.

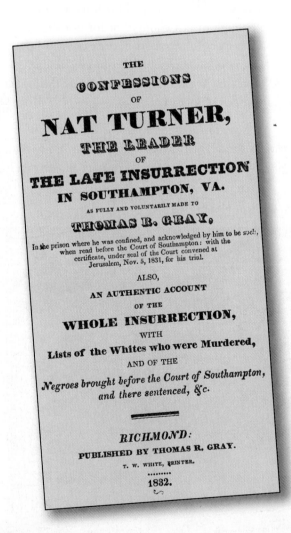

THE

CONFESSIONS

OF

NAT TURNER,

THE LEADER

OF

THE LATE INSURRECTION

IN SOUTHAMPTON, VA.

AS FULLY AND VOLUNTARILY MADE TO

THOMAS R. GRAY,

In the prison where he was confined, and acknowledged by him to be such, when read before the Court of Southampton; with the certificate, under seal of the Court convened at Jerusalem, Nov. 5, 1831, for his trial.

ALSO,

AN AUTHENTIC ACCOUNT

OF THE

WHOLE INSURRECTION,

WITH

Lists of the Whites who were Murdered,

AND OF THE

Negroes brought before the Court of Southampton, and there sentenced, &c.

RICHMOND:
PUBLISHED BY THOMAS R. GRAY.
T. W. WHITE, PRINTER.
1832.

Revolts like that led by Nat Turner in Virginia made many slave owners fearful.

In some spirituals, slaves expressed their longing to be free. Doing that openly was dangerous, so they used code words, like *deliverance,* to stand for freedom from slavery. This is one such spiritual:

Didn't my Lord deliver Daniel,

deliver Daniel, deliver Daniel?

Didn't my Lord deliver Daniel?

Then why not every man?

He delivered Daniel from the lion's den,

Jonah from the belly of the whale,

And the Hebrew children from the fiery

furnace,

Then why not deliver every man?

Some spirituals used words from the Bible story of Moses leading the people of Israel out of slavery in Egypt to the Promised Land, called Canaan (KAY nun). So when the slaves sang *Oh Canaan, sweet Canaan, I am bound for the land of Canaan,* they really meant the North, where there was no slavery. Another spiritual, called "Go Down, Moses," begins, *When Israel was in Egypt land, Let my people go.* Only a person who didn't *want* to get the message could miss the meaning of those spirituals.

Working in the fields from sunup to sundown was not the whole life of slaves, however. After work they returned to

Joel Chandler Harris, a newspaperman, collected some slave stories about the adventures of the clever Brer [brother] Rabbit.

their cabins in the slave quarter, which was the section of the plantation where they lived. Here, slave families could be by themselves.

In the slave quarter, slaves created their own community. They told and retold stories and folk tales handed down from the earliest slaves. In many of these stories, a weak character outwits a strong one—for example, a clever rabbit might trick a hungry fox. Can you see why such stories would be popular among the slaves? The slaves also kept alive African music and dancing. Some continued to hold on to the religious beliefs and practices of their ancestors in Africa.

Even those who became Christians, as most did, often mixed some African religious beliefs and customs in with their new beliefs. And as they blended their old cultures with the culture of their new world, they created something new and different—the beginnings of an African American culture.

BRER RABBIT

The · awful · fate · of · Mr. · Wolf

The Spread of Slavery By the early 1800s, Southern slaveholders were demanding that slavery be allowed to spread into America's western lands. Most Northerners were opposed to this idea. In the end, this disagreement between North and South would become one of the major issues that led to a great civil war.

Before then, however, the two sections tried to settle their disagreement through **compromise.** To understand this issue, you'll need to know something about the difference between states and territories in our history. Today the United States of America has 50 states. Each has its own state constitution, and each makes many of its own laws.

In the beginning, though, you'll remember that there were only 13 states. The 37 others were formed over time from the huge chunks of land that the United States gained, most of it from Great Britain, France, and Mexico.

Early in our history, Congress wisely decided to set up a three-step process for turning those lands into states. In the first step, Congress created a territory, or sometimes several territories. In this first step, Congress made the laws for the territory. The second step came when the population of a territory reached 5,000 adult males. Then the people were allowed to elect their own representatives and make many of their own laws. When a territory's population reached 60,000, it could ask Congress to admit it into the Union, with its own state constitution. That was the third and final step—the step that allowed the territory to become a state.

In those days each state decided for itself whether to allow slavery within its borders. Southern states allowed slavery. Most Northern states did not. But a territory—that was a different matter. During a territory's first step toward statehood, it was Congress that made all the rules, including whether to allow slavery or not.

Suppose Congress voted *not* to allow slavery in a territory. Would anyone who owned slaves or who wanted to own slaves choose to live there? Certainly not. So when the population became large enough for the territory to start making its own laws, almost no one living there would be in favor of slavery, and the new legislature would pass laws against it. Later still, when the territory was ready to become a state, it would write a state constitution that would prohibit slavery. Of course, the opposite would happen if Congress permitted slavery when the territory was formed.

> **vocabulary**
> **compromise** a settlement of differences between two or more sides reached by each side giving up some of what it wanted

Slave or Free?

So however you felt about the spread of slavery into the western lands, that first law Congress passed for any territories would be important to you. That is what led to a big argument in 1820 between North and South. The argument concerned slavery in the huge area the United States had bought from France, known as the Louisiana Purchase. When Congress began to form new territories in this region, it did not make laws about slavery, one way or the other. Southern slaveholders felt free to move there with their slaves. The first of these new territories to become a state was Louisiana, which entered the Union in 1812 as a slave state. Seven years later a second territory was ready for statehood. This was the Missouri Territory, which also asked to come into the Union as a slave state.

At that time there were 11 slave states and 11 free states in the Union. The Northern free states were against more slave states coming into the Union. They said this would give the South too much power in Congress. Nonsense, replied the South. Without any more slave states, it was the North that would have too much power in Congress.

Each side was determined not to give in. One New York newspaper editor wrote that the Missouri question "involves not only the future character of our nation, but the future weight and influence of the free states. If now lost—it is lost forever."

The Missouri Compromise

For more than a year, Congress angrily debated the question. Finally, a compromise was reached in 1820. It happened that Maine, in northern New England, was also ready for statehood. Therefore, Congress admitted Maine and Missouri together, one as a free state and the other as a slave state. That kept the balance between slave and free states. At the same time, Congress drew a line starting at Missouri's southern border, which was at 36°30′ north latitude, straight across the rest of the Louisiana Purchase. Slavery, said Congress, would be prohibited in territories above that line and permitted in territories below it. This came to be known as the Missouri Compromise.

For the time being, the Missouri Compromise quieted the anger over the spread of slavery. By making a law that dealt with slavery in all the remaining western lands owned by the United States, Congress thought it was settling the slavery question once and for all.

Time would show how wrong Congress was.

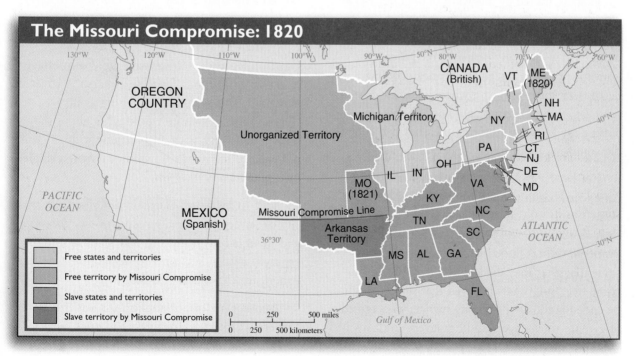

The Missouri Compromise attempted to settle the question of the spread of slavery.

Terrible Wrong Today, most people would agree that slavery is a terrible wrong. The idea that one person can actually own another, can buy and sell someone like a piece of property—no one in America and few people anywhere else in the world would say that that is right.

It's hard for us to understand that not everyone has always felt that way. But the sad fact is that slavery has existed in many times and places—in ancient Greece and ancient Rome, in Africa, in parts of Europe during the Middle Ages, and elsewhere. It's been only in the last 250 years, really, that a growing number of people have come to believe about slavery as we do today. And even when many people finally began to believe that slavery was wrong, few were ready to do anything to get rid of it.

Earlier you saw how a number of Southern slaveholders, moved by the words of the Declaration of Independence, freed their slaves. By the early 1800s, however, few slave owners did that anymore. And while many people in the North didn't want to see slavery spread any farther, very few raised their voices against it where it already existed. That is why Congress could believe that, in passing the Missouri Compromise, they had ended the argument about slavery once and for all.

But by the 1820s a small number of Americans began to speak out against slavery. Some simply tried to persuade owners to treat their slaves more like human beings than like property. Others hoped to get more owners to agree that after they died, their slaves would become free. Still others believed that slavery might be ended gradually by paying owners who agreed to give up their slaves. Ending slavery in this way would take many, many years.

Abolitionists

There was another small group, however, that wanted to abolish slavery, to end it right away—end it everywhere it existed and end it completely.

These people came to be called **abolitionists.** One of their leaders was William Lloyd Garrison.

Garrison was a deeply religious man who believed that slavery was a great sin in the eyes of God. He saw slaveholders as sinful people, along with everyone else who was not ready to work to end slavery immediately. In 1831, Garrison started a newspaper called *The Liberator* to carry his message to other Americans.

> **vocabulary**
> **abolitionist** a person opposed to slavery and in favor of ending it right away

In the very first issue of *The Liberator,* Garrison let readers know what kind of message to expect from him. "*I will be* as harsh as truth," he wrote, "and as uncompromising as justice." Garrison meant that he would write about the cruelty of slavery, without prettying it up. "I will not excuse," he wrote. "I will not retreat a single inch—*and I will be heard.*"

True to his word, Garrison described the cruelty of slavery in issue after issue of *The Liberator,* and he urged his readers to take steps to end slavery right away. Garrison also helped organize the American Anti-Slavery Society in 1833.

Another important abolitionist leader was Frederick Douglass. Douglass had once been a slave himself, but he had escaped to the North. He became friends with Garrison and soon began giving talks on what it was like to be a slave. In one speech he recalled the slave trade in Baltimore, where he had lived before escaping to freedom. "In the deep, still darkness of midnight," said Douglass, "I have been often aroused by the dead, heavy footsteps, and the piteous cries of the chained gangs that passed our door . . . on the way to the slave-markets, where the victims are to be sold like horses, sheep, and swine. . . . My soul sickens at the sight."

What powerful words! How Douglass's listeners must have been moved by them! Douglass also wrote a book in which he told the story of his life and his escape from slavery. Later he started an antislavery newspaper of his own in his home city of Rochester, New York.

At first, abolitionists were a small group. In the whole country only a few thousand people bought Garrison's newspaper, and most of them were free blacks who hardly needed to be told that slavery was bad. Not many people bought Frederick Douglass's book, either.

Not surprisingly, Garrison's attacks on slavery and the Southern way of life angered Southerners. But they angered many in the North, too. Most Northerners were not yet ready to hear Garrison's abolitionist message. To them, Garrison, Douglass, and the other abolitionists were just a bunch of troublemakers. Several times, angry mobs broke up public meetings at which abolitionists were speaking. They attacked abolitionist speakers and sometimes beat them. Once a mob dragged Garrison through the streets of Boston, where he had gone to give an abolitionist speech.

In time, however, the number of people who agreed with the abolitionists grew. More and more Northerners came to agree that slavery was an evil and that somehow, some way, it must be ended.

The Underground Railroad

Some people were already striking a blow against slavery. These were the members of the Underground Railroad. The Underground Railroad was not a real railroad at all. It was a network of people who helped runaway slaves escape to free states in the North or to Canada. These people offered their homes, cellars, barns, and places of work to hide runaways. At each such "station" on the railroad, the runaway slaves, or "passengers," rested and received instructions for getting to the next station. The people who hid the slaves and guided them were known as "conductors."

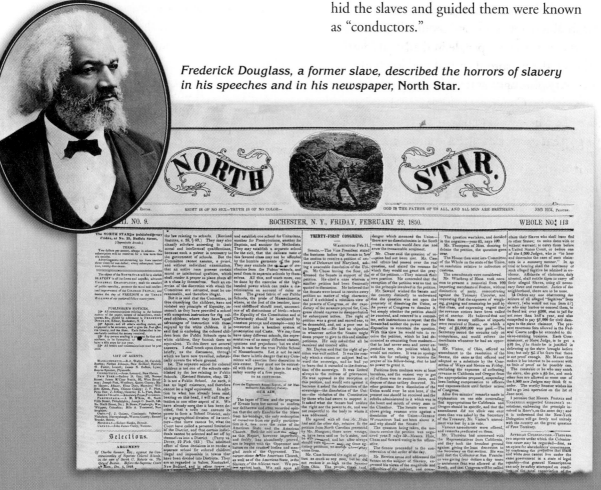

Frequency Douglass, a former slave, described the horrors of slavery in his speeches and in his newspaper, *North Star*.

One of the most famous conductors was a runaway slave who had taken the Underground Railroad to freedom herself. Her name was Harriet Tubman. In 1849, Harriet Tubman was living on a Maryland plantation when she learned that her owner had died. Such times were among the most dangerous for slaves because that was when slaves were most likely to be sold. Would families be sold together to the same buyer or would they be split up? Would the new owners be kind or would they be cruel? No one knew.

Harriet Tubman decided not to wait to find out. Late one night she went to the home of a white woman who had promised to help her escape. The woman sent Harriet to another white family a few miles away. There, the woman who welcomed her quickly gave Harriet a broom and told her to sweep the yard so that anyone seeing her in the daytime would think she was a slave. Later that night the woman's husband drove Harriet in his wagon to the next town, where still another family took her in.

In this way, hiding by day and traveling by night, Harriet made her way north until she crossed the Mason-Dixon line. That was the borderline between Maryland and Pennsylvania. Back during colonial times, when two surveyors named Mason and Dixon drew that line, it had nothing to do with slavery. But in time the Mason-Dixon line, separating the slave state of Maryland from the free state of Pennsylvania, came to have a new meaning. And now that she had crossed it, Harriet Tubman was in Pennsylvania, where slavery was prohibited. At that moment, Harriet Tubman was a free woman at last!

The next year, Harriet Tubman joined the Underground Railroad herself. Over the next ten years, she made 19 trips into the South to "conduct" slaves to freedom. During those years she led about 300 slaves to the North. She knew all kinds of tricks to help her passengers escape. She would usually start her rescues on a Saturday night, knowing that it would be Monday before the owners could spread the alarm with posters and advertisements. Traveling by night, she looked in the heavens for the North Star to find the right direction. On cloudy nights, when stars could not be seen, she would feel the bark of trees to find the soft moss because moss grows on the north side.

The slaves called Harriet Tubman "Moses" because she delivered them from slavery. In the South a reward of $12,000 was offered for her capture, but no one was ever able to collect it. Many years later, when she looked back on her work in the Underground Railroad, Harriet Tubman said, "I never ran my train off the track, and I never lost a passenger."

Harriet Tubman, standing at the far left, helped many enslaved men, women, and children escape on the Underground Railroad.

Differences Between North and South Not only were the South and the North differing more and more about slavery, but they were also growing apart in other important ways. More people lived in towns and cities in the North. Most Southerners still farmed for a living.

British mills could turn out hundreds of yards of calico cloth every day.

In the North, manufacturing was becoming more and more important. In our nation's early days, factories did not exist. Back then most families made the goods they needed by hand, whether it was chairs or candles or clothing. To make cloth, for example, the women in the family used a spinning wheel to turn raw cotton or wool into thread. They then used a hand loom to weave the thread into cloth. Using these methods, a woman could produce about a yard of cloth a day.

In those very same years, however, important changes were taking place in clothmaking on the other side of the Atlantic Ocean. In Great Britain, several men invented machines that spun cotton into thread *200 times faster* than a person using a spinning wheel. Soon after, others invented a machine that could weave the thread into hundreds of yards of cloth in a single day. Before long, British manufacturers were constructing

buildings called factories, or mills, to house the new machines. Power to run the machines came from swiftly flowing streams that turned the water wheels attached to the new machines.

With these machines, British manufacturers produced cloth faster, cheaper, and better than anyone else. The British government was determined to keep this advantage. The government would not let anyone sell the new machines to other countries or make plans for taking them out of the country. The government even passed a law that said people who worked in cotton mills were not allowed to leave Great Britain.

Keeping a secret like that, though, is like trying to hold a rainbow in a bottle. Sooner or later the secret gets out. In this case it was sooner. Several American manufacturers placed an advertisement in a British newspaper offering a reward

*Samuel Slater's mill in Pawtucket, Rhode Island,
brought British technology to the United States.*

to anyone who could build a spinning machine for them. Samuel Slater, a young employee in a British spinning mill, saw the ad. In 1789, after memorizing every part of the machine, the 21-year-old Slater disguised himself as a farm boy and boarded a ship headed for the United States.

It took Slater two years to make every wooden part of the machine by hand, but in 1791 he finished the job. The machine worked, and that year America's first cotton thread mill opened in Pawtucket, Rhode Island. Some years after, a wealthy Boston merchant named Francis Lowell and several wealthy friends built a large factory in which machines not only spun the cotton thread but also dyed it and wove it into cloth.

Soon, dozens, then hundreds of other factories sprang up. Most of these early factories were located in New England, where the rushing water of New England's many rivers and streams could be used to power the machines. Later, factories spread to other parts of the Northeast, making not only cloth but also shoes, pots and pans, clocks, guns, and many other goods.

Manufacturing brought new wealth to the North. So did the growing trade that came along with it. Canals and railroads carried clothing and household goods and farm machinery from the factories to hundreds of thousands of family farms in the North and West. Farmers paid for them by shipping their wheat, corn, barley, and other crops to eastern markets on those same canals and railroads. From there, many of those crops were sent by ship to other countries.

All this new manufacturing and trade led to the rapid growth of cities in the North. Back during the time of the American Revolution, there had been only five cities in the whole country. The largest, Philadelphia, had fewer than 40,000 residents. New York was the second largest, with fewer than 20,000. By 1850, however, nearly 100 places in the United States could call themselves cities, and nearly all of them were in the North and in what today we call the Midwest. New York alone had a half million people, and Philadelphia was not far behind. Pittsburgh, St. Louis, Chicago, and Cincinnati were also growing rapidly. In these cities, people could make a living in a hundred different ways.

The Rural South

During those same years the South had grown in a quite different direction. There were some factories in the South, but not many. The same was true for railroads. As for large cities, you could count them on the fingers of one hand. The great majority of Southerners made their living from the land. While the North was becoming more **urban,** the South remained **rural.**

Southerners, you see, believed their future lay with cotton. They were sure that the increasing demand for cotton from factories in the North and Great Britain would make the South wealthy and strong. A Northerner with money might start a new business or build a factory, but a Southerner would buy more land to grow cotton. He would also buy more slaves to work on it.

A few of these big cotton farmers—they were called planters, and their farms were plantations—owned farms a hundred times as large as the family farms of the North and West. There were thousands of large planters, each owning 50 or more slaves. These were the leaders of the South. They lived in large mansions, had many household servants, and entertained friends and relatives in the manner of wealthy people.

Of course, the great planters' grand lifestyle was built on the labor of African American slaves. So it is not surprising that at the very time Northerners were more and more turning against slavery, the leading families of the South were more and more determined to keep it. They came up with all sorts of reasons to explain why it was right to own slaves.

Back in Thomas Jefferson and George Washington's time, Southerners also had kept slaves. But in those days many of them still felt that slavery was wrong and hoped it would die out soon. Not the slaveholders of a later time, though. To them, slavery was a good thing— good for the owners, good for the slaves, good for the South, and good for the nation. They saw no reason to end it—not then, not ever.

The great majority of Southern farmers had little in common with the wealthy plantation owners. Those who owned one or two slaves instead of 40 or 50, usually worked in the field right alongside them. And most Southern farmers owned no slaves at all. They struggled to grow enough food on their small patch of poor soil for the family to live on. In fact, they grew barely enough to live on. There is no doubt, though, that many of these poor farmers dreamed of one day getting more land and owning slaves.

So by the 1840s this was the situation: Most Northerners were opposed to the spread of slavery into the territories. Most Southerners were demanding that slavery be allowed to spread. The stage was set for trouble, should the United States ever gain more territory in the West. That's just what happened as a result of the war with Mexico. The argument that followed over the spread of slavery into that new territory almost broke up the Union then and there.

A Southern plantation was a big business that depended on slave labor to make a profit.

The Big Debate For days the United States senators had been debating the question. Should slavery be allowed in the new lands won from Mexico? The question was of great importance.

As you read earlier, whatever Congress decided about allowing slavery in a territory would pretty much decide what kind of state it would later become, slave or free. In that year of 1850, there were 15 of each in the Union. But California was already asking for admission to the Union as a free state. Southerners feared that free states would soon greatly outnumber slave states, especially if Congress did not allow slavery in the new territories. When that happened, they asked, what would keep the Northerners from changing the Constitution and making all slavery illegal, even in the Southern states, where it already existed?

Tempers ran high as the argument went back and forth. Slaves are property, said the Southerners. If Northerners could bring their property into the new territories, why couldn't Southern slaveholders bring theirs? Because, said Northerners and most Westerners, slaves are people, and slavery is wrong. The soil of the new western territories had been free of slavery when Mexico owned it; it should remain free soil now. Those who believed that all the western territory should be reserved for free people came to be called "free soilers."

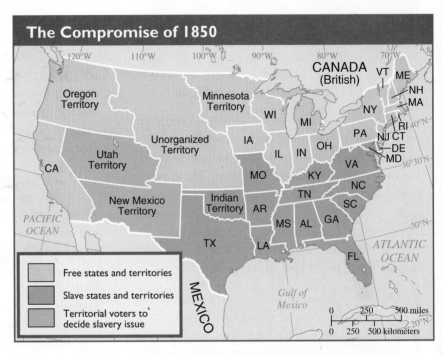

The Compromise of 1850 opened new territories to the possibilities of slavery.

Some searched for a compromise. But John C. Calhoun, the South's greatest spokesman, had no interest in compromise. On March 4, 1850, Calhoun, weak and near death, was carried to the Senate floor on a stretcher. There, he handed his speech to a younger senator to read. The North, said Calhoun, must give the South equal rights in the new territories. It must stop criticizing and stirring up trouble over slavery. It must return runaway slaves.

If Northern senators could not agree to these conditions, said Calhoun, then "say so; and let the States we both represent agree to separate and part in peace." Calhoun was saying that the

Southern states would **secede,** or pull out of the Union. His next words rang through the halls of the Senate like a clap of thunder: "If you are unwilling we should part in peace, tell us so; and we shall know what to do. . . ."

We shall know what to do. No one listening to Calhoun's words failed to understand their meaning: war!

In the end a compromise was reached, with something for each side. California was admitted to the Union as a free state. That satisfied the North. The rest of the land gained from Mexico was divided into two territories, forming New Mexico and Utah, without saying anything about slavery there. That satisfied the South.

Another part of the Compromise of 1850 made it illegal to buy and sell slaves in the city of Washington, D.C., the nation's capital. That was something the North wanted. The South got a Fugitive Slave Law that made it easier for slave owners to get back **fugitive** slaves, that is, those who had escaped to the North.

For the time being the Compromise of 1850 cooled down the argument between North and South. But could that last? Some Southerners were already saying that the South had given up too much and should secede from the Union immediately. Some Northerners, meanwhile, said they would never obey the Fugitive Slave Law and send a fellow human being back into slavery.

Uncle Tom's Cabin *helped many people recognize the evils of slavery.*

vocabulary
secede to withdraw formally from an organization or a nation
fugitive one who flees or tries to escape

Harriet Beecher Stowe

One of those Northerners was Harriet Beecher Stowe. Stowe came from a family of New England abolitionists. She decided to write a story that would show how cruel slavery was. Her book, *Uncle Tom's Cabin,* appeared in 1852 and was an immediate sensation. The most exciting part of *Uncle Tom's Cabin* tells of a young slave mother, Eliza, who discovers that her baby has been sold and will be taken from her the next day. Eliza makes a desperate dash for freedom with the child and escapes into the free state of Ohio, just ahead of her pursuers.

In its very first year, more than 300,000 copies of *Uncle Tom's Cabin* were sold. With our present population in the United States, that would be like selling *3 million* copies today. The book was translated into 20 languages and was read by millions more around the world. It was also turned into a play that was performed before large audiences all over the North.

The story and the characters of *Uncle Tom's Cabin* were soon familiar to millions of Americans. Even Northerners who had paid little attention to the abolitionists' stern lectures about the evils of slavery were deeply touched by Stowe's book. But Southerners said that the book was terribly unfair and gave a false picture of

The Kansas-Nebraska Act: 1854

Map legend:
- Free states and territories
- Slave states and territories
- Territorial voters to decide slavery issue

This map shows why the Kansas-Nebraska Act was seen as a threat by abolitionists.

slavery. If people like Harriet Beecher Stowe continued to stir up criticism of slavery and the South, they said, the Union was surely doomed.

The Kansas-Nebraska Act

Stephen A. Douglas was one of the ablest men in the United States Senate. Many thought of Douglas, a senator from Illinois, as a future President of the United States. But in 1854, Douglas made a decision that not only ended his chance to become President but also led the country toward the Civil War.

That had not been Douglas's intention, of course. He had only wanted to encourage people to move to the one remaining part of the Louisiana Purchase still unsettled. This was the huge area between the western boundaries of Missouri and Iowa and the Rocky Mountains, and from the 36°30′ latitude northward to the Canadian border.

The Missouri Compromise, you'll remember, said that no slavery would be allowed in any territory north of that 36°30′ line. And you'll also remember that a free territory now almost surely meant a free state later, which was the last thing Southern senators wanted. How, then, could Douglas win their support for his goal of settling this land?

The answer Douglas hit upon had two parts. First, the land would be divided into two territories, to be called Kansas and Nebraska. Second, the Missouri Compromise would be repealed, or canceled, and the settlers in each territory would decide for themselves whether or not to allow slavery.

To Douglas, who had no feelings about slavery one way or the other, this seemed like a perfect answer. No one expected slavery to take root in Nebraska, for it was too far north. And Kansas—well, no guarantees, but Southerners would have their opportunity to try to make it a slave territory. One for the North, one for the South. What could be fairer?

Douglas's plan opened up the argument between North and South all over again. Northerners were outraged that this plan would repeal the Missouri Compromise. Southerners were pleased that it did. After an angry debate in Congress, the Kansas-Nebraska Act, as it was called, became law.

Southerners were determined to make Kansas a slave territory and urged Southerners to move there. Antislavery Northerners were determined that Kansas would be free and urged Northerners to move there. Each group took its guns with them, and before long the two were attacking each other in Kansas. Two hundred settlers were killed before the United States Army moved in, and the territory became known as "bleeding Kansas."

The struggle over slavery in the nation's western lands had now turned to violence, and no one could say where it would all end.

Lincoln on Slavery With tensions rising over slavery, many Northerners opposed to its spread were attracted to a new political party called the Republican party. One of its leaders was a lawyer from Illinois named Abraham Lincoln.

For Lincoln, as for a great number of Americans in the North and the West, the question of whether slavery was right or wrong was quite simple. It was just a matter of putting yourself in the other fellow's shoes. "As I would not be a slave, so I would not be a master," he said. "This expresses my idea of democracy. Whatever differs from this . . . is no democracy." Lincoln once said in a private conversation, "Whenever I hear of anyone arguing [in favor of] slavery, I feel a strong impulse to see it tried on him personally."

Although he hated slavery, Lincoln was not an abolitionist. You'll remember that abolitionists—people like William Lloyd Garrison, Frederick Douglass, and members of the Underground Railroad—wanted to abolish slavery immediately and everywhere, not just in the territories of the United States but in the Southern states as well. However much Lincoln would have wished for that result, he knew that under the United States Constitution, the federal government did not have the right to interfere with slavery in the *states*. But the government could stop slavery from entering the territories, and if it did that, Lincoln hoped that slavery would gradually die out everywhere in the country.

Who Was Abraham Lincoln?

Like so many Americans in the West, Abraham Lincoln had started out in life with no special advantages. He was born in a one-room log cabin in Kentucky to a mother who could neither read nor write and a father who could barely write his own name.

That father, Thomas Lincoln, had the unfortunate knack of picking out one piece of bad farmland after another. After struggling to make a living in Kentucky, Thomas moved his family to Indiana, where he again chose land unwisely. Abraham was seven at the time. Like children everywhere on the frontier, he and his sister helped with farm chores, going to school only when they could be spared from work at home. Altogether,

Abraham Lincoln grew up in a log cabin like this one.

As a teenager, young Abe Lincoln worked his way to New Orleans on a flatboat.

Abraham probably spent less than one year in the schools of Kentucky and Indiana.

He did not miss a great deal, for frontier schools were quite poor. Children of all ages were taught at the same time in the same one-room building. With no books, the children learned by repeating after the teacher—everyone, at the same time, saying their different lessons aloud. Little wonder these schools were called "blab schools."

Tragedy struck the Lincoln home when Abraham was only nine. Abraham's mother died, leaving Thomas to care for the two children alone. A year later, Thomas married again. Abraham was fortunate, for his stepmother was a loving person. She taught Abraham to read, and, with her encouragement, he developed a strong desire to learn. The family had only a few books, but Abraham read them over and over. He was willing to travel many miles to borrow books from others. In addition, Abraham took care of all the writing for the Lincoln family. Soon he was doing the same for many neighbors as well.

However, in the hard life on the frontier, there was little time for reading. Always tall and strong for his age, Abraham did more than his share of clearing and plowing the land. His father also hired him out to work for neighbors.

Starting at age 17, Abraham began to take on jobs away from home. He worked on a ferryboat.

He built a flatboat and floated goods down the Mississippi River to New Orleans. He hired out himself and a cousin to split logs into rails for fencing. One spring the two of them split 5,000 logs, a huge amount of work, earning Lincoln the nickname the "Rail-Splitter." But through these years, Abraham seemed to have no particular goals in life. He later described himself at this time as a piece of floating driftwood.

"Floating driftwood" described the Lincoln family as well. Thomas Lincoln moved the family again when Abraham was 19, this time to Illinois. Abraham helped with the usual frontier jobs of building a cabin, clearing the land, fencing the land, and planting a crop. A couple of years later, though, when the Lincolns moved yet again, Abraham did not go with them. At 21 he was ready to strike out on his own. He went to live in the small town of New Salem, Illinois.

Lincoln on His Own

Being the newcomer in a small town was uncomfortable at first. Soon after Abe Lincoln arrived, the young men of the town challenged him to a wrestling match against their leader, a strong young man named Jack Armstrong. Lincoln, 6 feet 4 inches and rugged, defeated Armstrong. Immediately after, the two young men became the best of friends, and Lincoln was quickly accepted by all the other young men.

Lincoln did more than wrestle, however. Anxious to improve himself, he joined New Salem's debating club, read more books, and studied grammar and mathematics, all on his own.

After working for a time in a store, Abe and a partner opened a general store of their own in New Salem. However, the store did poorly, and when it closed after a year, the two partners owed large debts. When the partner died, Lincoln insisted on paying off all the money himself. It took years, but he did so—every last penny. After that, Lincoln became known as "Honest Abe."

Later, Lincoln studied law and became a lawyer. He moved to nearby Springfield, which is the capital city of Illinois. He and a young partner soon were among the most successful lawyers in town, but you would never have guessed it from the look of their office. The windows were never washed. Papers were scattered everywhere and piled high on desks and tables. On one large envelope, Lincoln wrote, "When you can't find it anywhere else, look into this." He often stuffed letters into his tall silk hat. Once when he bought a new hat, he absentmindedly threw out the old one, notes and all.

Lincoln was liked and trusted by his neighbors. They elected him to serve four terms in the Illinois State Legislature. Later he also served one term in the United States Congress, during the war against Mexico. After that, Lincoln decided to leave government and go back to his law practice.

But one thing he knew for sure—he was firmly against slavery. And as the slavery issue grew to dominate all others in American life, Lincoln knew that he could not remain on the sidelines. He decided he must take an active part in the effort to rid the nation of this curse.

After drifting from job to job as a young man, Abraham Lincoln found his calling and became a successful lawyer.

8 The Crisis Deepens

Dred Scott Bleeding Kansas left the nation more divided than ever over slavery. Things got even worse the next year, 1857, when the Supreme Court of the United States announced its decision in the Dred Scott case.

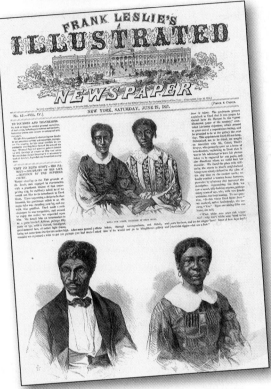

The Supreme Court's decision in the Dred Scott case was reported in a national newspaper.

Dred Scott was an African American and a slave in the state of Missouri until he was in his thirties. Then his owner, an army doctor, took him to the state of Illinois, where they lived for several years. The owner also took Dred Scott to the Wisconsin Territory for a time before finally returning to Missouri.

Some time after, with the help of several antislavery white friends in St. Louis, Dred Scott went to court to seek his freedom. Illinois, said Scott, was a free state—no slavery allowed.

Wisconsin Territory was above the 36°30′ line—again, no slavery allowed. Scott asked the court to rule that as soon as he entered the free state of Illinois and the free Wisconsin Territory, he had automatically become a free man.

The case went to the Supreme Court which decided against Dred Scott. It was true, said the Court, that no one could own a slave in the free state of Illinois. But once Dred Scott came back to Missouri, he was a slave again.

If that were all the Court said, antislavery people might have grumbled a bit and accepted the decision. But the Court went on to say that a slave was like any other property. And the Constitution of the United States says that Congress cannot just take away a person's right to his property by passing a law. Therefore, the law that had prohibited a person from owning slaves in certain territories—that is, the Missouri Compromise—had been unconstitutional all along. In other words, it had never been a proper law.

Southerners were delighted with this decision. Northerners were up in arms over it, and for the same reason. If Congress did not have the right to prohibit slavery in a territory, then there was no way to stop the spread of slavery there! Antislavery Northerners made clear that they would never accept such a situation.

The Lincoln-Douglas Debates

The next year, 1858, the people of Illinois were to choose a United States senator. Stephen A. Douglas, who had already served for many years, was running for reelection. To run against him, the Republicans chose Abraham Lincoln.

Lincoln lost the election to the Senate, but the debates with Douglas brought him national attention.

In his very first speech after being nominated, Lincoln summed up the situation facing the nation, as he saw it. "A house divided against itself cannot stand," said Lincoln. "I believe this government cannot endure permanently half *slave* and half *free*. I do not expect the Union to be *dissolved*—I do not expect the house to *fall*—but I *do* expect it will cease to be divided. It will become *all* one thing, or *all* the other." Lincoln was saying that if the spread of slavery were not stopped now and made to gradually disappear, then it would spread all through the nation. "It will become *all* one thing, or *all* the other."

In seven cities up and down the state, Lincoln and Douglas debated each other before crowds of thousands. Lincoln said that he believed black Americans were "entitled to all the natural rights . . . in the Declaration of Independence," including the right to liberty. In these rights, Lincoln said, black Americans were *"my equal and the equal of Judge Douglas, and the equal of every living man."* Stephen A. Douglas disagreed. Black people had no such rights and in no way were his equal. Lincoln went on to ask: Now that the Supreme Court had ruled that Congress couldn't keep slavery out of the territories, was there any way to stop the spread of slavery? If not, wouldn't slavery continue to spread? Not necessarily, replied Douglas. That was up to the people in each new territory. If they did not want slavery, then they wouldn't permit it.

Newspapers all over the country reported the words of these two candidates. When the votes were counted, Douglas won the election. But the campaign made Abraham Lincoln a well-known figure throughout America.

John Brown

Nestled in the foothills of the Appalachian Mountains in western Virginia (now West Virginia) is the town of Harpers Ferry. There, the United States government had built an **arsenal.** A quiet town, Harpers Ferry was not prepared for the fame that was about to come to it.

In the dark hours of October 16, 1859, a band of 19 men crossed the Potomac River from Maryland, took the arsenal by surprise, and captured it. In the attack the mayor of the town and two others were killed.

This attack was led by John Brown, an abolitionist. Brown believed he had been chosen by God to end slavery. He and his five sons had earlier lived in Kansas,

> **vocabulary**
> **arsenal** a building where weapons are stored

John Brown wanted to use the weapons stored in the Harpers Ferry arsenal to arm a slave rebellion.

where they had killed five Southern settlers during the days of bleeding Kansas.

To some abolitionists, this made Brown a hero. When he told some wealthy abolitionists in New York State that he had a plan to strike a major blow against slavery, they provided him with money. Brown's plan, which he did not reveal to the New Yorkers, was to seize the arsenal at Harpers Ferry and give the arms to nearby slaves. They would then rise up in rebellion and create a free area in the mountains of Maryland and Virginia, from which they would encourage slave rebellions throughout the South.

The plan never had a chance of succeeding. Brown himself was so disorganized that he even forgot to bring food for his men. Within a day after the attack, United States marines under the command of Robert E. Lee cornered Brown and his men in a building. When Brown refused to surrender, they stormed the building and captured Brown and seven others.

Brown was quickly tried by the state of Virginia, found guilty, and hanged. But his raid drove North and South even further apart. In the North, even while nearly all newspapers and leaders like Lincoln spoke out against Brown's violence, some leading abolitionists made him a hero. In the South, Brown's raid reawakened the nightmare of slave revolt. Those who wanted to secede from the Union now could say to their fellow Southerners, "Do you see what the North wants to do to us? And this is only the beginning. We must leave the Union now!"

The Election of 1860

As the election of 1860 drew near, it was clear to all Americans that this might be the most important election in the young nation's history. Quite possibly, it might be the last one.

The Republican party chose Abraham Lincoln as its candidate for President of the United States. Lincoln and the Republicans had often said that slavery was wrong. The South heard that. The Republicans promised to do everything they could to keep slavery out of the territories. The South heard that, too. But no matter how many times the Republicans promised not to interfere with slavery in the Southern states where it already existed, the South did not hear that. The South simply didn't trust Lincoln or any other Republican. They believed the Republicans planned to abolish slavery right away and end their way of life. Several Southern states said that if a Republican was elected President, they would secede.

That is what happened. In November 1860, Abraham Lincoln was elected President. One month later, South Carolina seceded from the Union. Over the next two months, Mississippi, Florida, Alabama, Georgia, Louisiana, and Texas also voted to leave.

At that moment the future of the United States of America looked grim. In fact, it was not clear that the United States had any future at all.

Secession Events moved swiftly. Abraham Lincoln's term as President would not start until March 4, 1861. One month before then, on February 4, representatives from the seven seceding states met in Montgomery, Alabama.

Three days later they announced the creation of a new nation, the Confederate States of America, called the Confederacy for short. The Confederacy adopted a constitution guaranteeing the future of slavery. Then the representatives from the seven seceding states chose Jefferson Davis, a cotton planter and slave owner from Mississippi, as the first president of the Confederate States of America. Davis had fought bravely in the war with Mexico and had also served in Congress as a United States senator.

Even before the new Confederate States of America was declared, each of the states that seceded had begun to take over forts, arsenals, post offices, and other United States government property in their states. All such property belongs to us, they said, because the United States no longer has any rights within our Confederate States. By the time Lincoln took over as President, only two forts in the seven Confederate States remained under the control of the United States.

Eight slave states were still in the Union when President Lincoln took office.

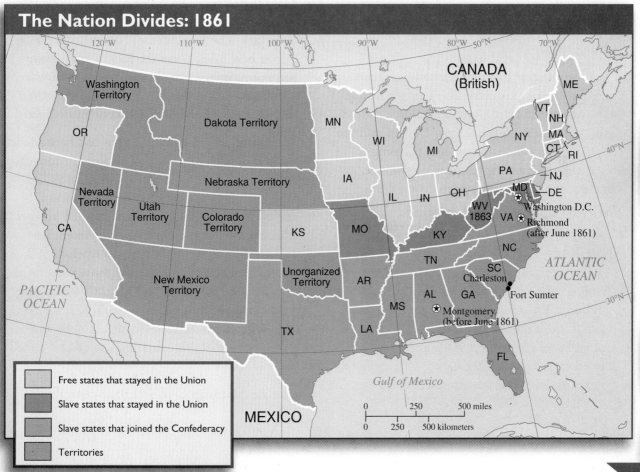

The Nation Divides: 1861

Free states that stayed in the Union

Slave states that stayed in the Union

Slave states that joined the Confederacy

Territories

Here is the problem President Lincoln faced as he began his term of office. Seven Southern states had already left the Union. Eight other slave states remained in the Union, but four of them had already warned Lincoln: If you use force against the seven states that seceded, we will join them. That would make the new Confederate States of America bigger and stronger. Yet Lincoln knew that if he did not use force, he could not make the seceding states return to the Union.

Lincoln decided to make one last appeal to the Southern states that had seceded. You probably remember that at the start of each new term of office, Presidents take an oath of office and then deliver a speech, called the inaugural address. Lincoln used his inaugural address to appeal to the South not to go ahead with secession. He reassured the South, as he had done before, that he did not intend "to interfere with . . . slavery in the States where it exists. I believe I have no lawful right to do so, and I have no inclination [desire] to do so."

> *Lincoln and the Constitution:*
> *"The Constitution will not be preserved and defended until it is enforced and obeyed in every part of every one of the United States. It must be so respected, obeyed, enforced and defended . . ."*

When it came to secession, however, Lincoln said that he had no choice. As President he had a duty to preserve the Union, to enforce its laws, and to protect its property. But, Lincoln told the South, "there will be no invasion, no using of force against or among the people anywhere." And he urged the South not to do anything hasty. "We are not enemies, but friends," said Lincoln in closing. "We must not be enemies."

Too Late for Words

The President's carefully chosen words changed nothing. It was too late for words. In South Carolina, events marched toward a showdown. One of the two Southern forts that the United States government still controlled was located on an island in the harbor of Charleston, South Carolina. This was Fort Sumter. Earlier,

South Carolina had demanded that the fort be handed over along with all the others. Major Robert Anderson, in charge of the fort, refused.

But now Fort Sumter was running short of supplies. Major Anderson told the President that unless food arrived soon, he would have to give up.

The only way to get supplies to Fort Sumter was by ships, and they would have to pass in front of the guns of the Confederate States on other islands in the harbor. President Lincoln wanted to send the needed supplies, but he didn't want to start a war over them. So he informed South Carolina that the ships he was sending to Fort Sumter carried only food and supplies—no fresh soldiers, no guns, no ammunitions. Surely, he said, there would be no reason to fire on them. President Jefferson Davis of the Confederacy decided otherwise. If supplies reached the fort, Anderson and his men could continue to hold out. Davis would not allow that. Before the supply ships could arrive, he instructed the local commander to demand the fort's surrender. When Major Anderson refused, Confederate cannons on shore opened fire. After 30 hours of shelling, Major Anderson surrendered.

That did it. Confederate guns had been fired upon the forces of the United States of America. In the eyes of the Confederacy, its gunners had struck a blow for Confederate independence. In the eyes of the Union, they had engaged in rebellion. Soon after, Lincoln called for Americans to join the army to put down the rebellion. Of course, that was the very action those other four Southern states had warned against—using force against the seceding states. Now those states, too—Arkansas, Virginia, North Carolina, and Tennessee—withdrew from the Union and joined the Confederacy.

The American Civil War had begun.

Summer Picnic A holiday mood filled the air on July 21, 1861 as people climbed into their carriages to ride from Washington into the Virginia countryside. They were heading for Manassas Junction, about 30 miles away. There, they planned to enjoy their picnic lunches while watching the first battle of the Civil War.

Five days earlier, about 35,000 Union troops had marched out of the nation's capital shouting, "Forward to Richmond!" Richmond, Virginia, was the capital of the new Confederate States of America, and the Union army wanted to capture it. After several days the Union soldiers reached Manassas Junction. A Confederate force of 25,000 was there to meet them. Newspapers in Washington reported that a battle was expected to begin shortly. This was the battle the people had come to watch.

On reaching Manassas, the sightseers spread their picnic lunches and opened brightly colored umbrellas to protect themselves from the hot sun. A few miles away, near a small stream called Bull Run, the fighting had already started. Picnickers could hear the roar of cannons and the crackle of gunfire in the distance.

Good—we're on time for the show, thought the picnickers. They were anxious not to miss this first battle of the war, for it might well be the last one also. At least, that's what most people in the North were saying. The Union army would take the field, defeat the rebels quickly, and go on to capture Richmond. The Southern states would then return to the Union, and the war would be over.

Many Southerners also expected the war to end quickly, but with a different result. As one Georgia woman later remembered, "We had an idea that when our soldiers got upon the ground and showed, unmistakably that they were really ready and willing to fight . . . the whole trouble would be declared at an end."

It didn't turn out either way. The tide of battle that day went back and forth, with neither side able to get the upper hand at first. Except for the top officers, most soldiers on each side were untrained, disorganized, and confused. They were also amazingly brave.

The picnickers were sure that the Union soldiers would win the battle and it would be a short war.

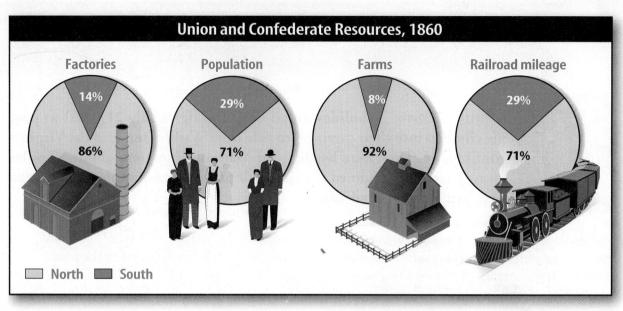

Union and Confederate Resources, 1860

Factories	Population	Farms	Railroad mileage
14% / 86%	29% / 71%	8% / 92%	29% / 71%

☐ North ■ South

The North had many advantages. But to win, it had to take the war to the South.

Late in the afternoon it appeared that Union forces might be winning. Then 2,300 fresh Confederate troops arrived by train and quickly entered the battle. That was enough to turn the tide. The half-trained Union soldiers began to retreat—first a few, then more and more until finally thousands dropped their guns and ran in panic toward the picnickers.

Now, frightened sightseers scrambled back to their carriages, leaving their tablecloths spread on the ground and their dishes and food scattered about, knocking each other over in the rush to get away. They were joined on the road by the fleeing soldiers, some of them wounded, some just weary, and all of them frightened. For hours the road to Washington was clogged. Fortunately for the Union side, the Confederate generals decided that their own troops were too tired to pursue the enemy.

Watching the men straggling back to the capital the next day, a British journalist wrote: "I saw a steady stream of men covered with mud, soaked through with rain. . . . [I asked] a pale young man who looked exhausted to death . . . where the men were coming from. 'Where from? Well, sir, I guess we're all coming out of Virginny as fast as we can, and pretty well whipped too. . . .

I know I'm going home. I've had enough of fighting to last my lifetime.'"

After the Battle of Bull Run, the hard truth began to sink in. This war would not end quickly after all. It would probably be long and bloody.

How would it end? No one could say. But the North did have many advantages. The North's population was about twice as large as the South's—four times as large if you subtract the slaves, to whom the South had no intention of giving guns. That meant the North could put four times as many men on the battlefields. With its mills and factories, the North could produce 20 times as much iron, 25 times as much railroad equipment, and 30 times as many guns as the South. With other factories producing all the clothing, blankets, tents, and medical supplies needed by the Union armies, the North didn't have to rely on European countries for these goods, as the South did. And with many more miles of railroad track, the North could move its troops and supplies more easily than the South.

Is Bigger Better?

There is more to winning a war than having such advantages, however. Remember the American Revolution? Great Britain had a far larger population. It had a bigger and better trained army. It had a larger navy. It had far more weapons than the American Patriots. But it still lost the war. Would this happen to the North as well?

Besides, at the start of the Civil War, both sides had plenty of men and supplies. The North's larger population and factory production would be a big advantage only if the war dragged on for a number of years. That's when Southern armies would feel the pinch of not having enough men to replace those killed and wounded. That's when they would find themselves short of supplies. But if the South could win enough early battles, Northerners might lose heart and quit the war before their advantages could count.

The Confederacy had its own advantages. The biggest was that it was fighting a defensive war. The South did not have to conquer an inch of Northern land to win this war. All it had to do was successfully defend its own land against Northern armies. Also, knowing that they were fighting to defend their own land and homes gave Southern soldiers an extra reason to fight hard.

In the early years of the war, the South had a second advantage. It had better and more experienced officers. Most of the generals who had trained at the United States Military Academy at West Point, New York, and fought in the Mexican War were from the South. When the Southern states seceded, most of these generals resigned from the United States Army and fought for the Confederacy.

The most brilliant of them was Robert E. Lee. President Lincoln knew Lee. He knew that Lee loved the United States and that he disliked slavery. And he knew that Lee was the best general around. That is why Lincoln asked Lee to take charge of all the Union armies.

But Lee's home state of Virginia had joined the Confederacy, and Lee, like so many others in that age, felt a deep attachment to his home state. In fact, many people at that time referred to their home state as their "country." Lee refused President Lincoln's offer, explaining, "If I owned four million slaves, I would cheerfully give them up to save the Union. But to lift my hand against Virginia is impossible. . . . [I cannot] fight against my relatives, my children, my home."

Lee's refusal was a big loss to the Union cause in the war's early years. Lee proved to be a great general, deeply respected by his men. Although his armies were usually outnumbered, General Lee used daring surprise moves to win many victories. As the war went on, however, able generals began to emerge from the test of battle for the Union side as well, and so the South lost one of its advantages.

West Point was the training ground for many officers on both sides.

11 A Brothers' War

Tragic War In their cost in human life and in their destructiveness of good and bad together, wars—even wars fought for good and noble goals—are terrible things. Civil wars are even more tragic. Countrymen fight against countrymen; friend fights against friend; and, sometimes, even brother fights against brother.

This was especially true of the American Civil War. Most people, of course, simply followed along with the thinking of their own section. Most Southerners supported the Confederate cause; most Northerners supported the Union.

But for many thousands, the decision about which side to take was terribly difficult. Yes, the Union should be preserved. But yes also, it should not use force to keep in states that don't want to be part of it any longer. Yes, slavery is wrong and should not be allowed to spread. But yes also, I love my native state—my "country," as Robert E. Lee called Virginia—and cannot bear the thought of taking up arms against it. Yes, I like the way of life of my own section of the country; but yes also, I believe more in the cause of the other section.

As a result, there were men from every one of the 11 seceding states who wore the blue of the Union army and men from every one of the 23 Union states who wore the gray of the Confederate army. David Farragut, from the Southern state of Alabama, was an admiral in the Union navy. Caleb Huse, from the Northern state of Massachusetts, served as a Confederate agent in Europe, arranging for needed goods to be sent to the South. General Winfield Scott

and General George Thomas, both Virginians, served in the United States Army.

For some, the Civil War was truly a "brothers' war." A naval officer named Percival Drayton commanded a Union gunboat, while his brother Thomas led a Confederate army. Franklin Buchanan, in command of a Confederate warship, sank a Union ship with his brother on board. One son of Senator John Crittenden of Kentucky served as a Union general, another as a Confederate general. Mary Todd Lincoln, wife of the President of the United States, had a brother, three half-brothers, and three brothers-in-law serving in the Confederate forces.

And not just brothers. Confederate General J.E.B. Stuart fought against his father-in-law, General Phillip St. George Cooke of the Union army. Edward Bates, a Missourian in Lincoln's Cabinet, had a son in the Confederate army. Robert E. Lee's cousin Samuel served in the Union navy. Relatives of the wife of Confederate President Jefferson Davis were in the Union army. Seven of the great Senator Henry Clay's grandsons fought in the war—three for the Union, four for the Confederacy. The list could go on and on.

Confederate General J.E.B. Stuart (top) fought against his father-in-law, General Phillip St. George Cooke (bottom) of the Union army.

he Scott Plan General Winfield Scott had known all along that this war would not be ended with one quick, decisive battle. The battle of Bull Run proved him right. Scott knew war. He had fought in every American war since the War of 1812.

In the war with Mexico, it was Scott who led American troops in triumph into Mexico City. After an unsuccessful run for the presidency in 1852, Scott returned to his duties as commanding general of all American forces.

A native Virginian who opposed slavery, Scott remained with the Union while some fellow Virginians, like Lee, sided with the Confederacy. But at age 75 he could no longer command troops in the field. However, he could still use his long experience to develop a winning **strategy** for the war. He got to work right after Fort Sumter fell.

Here is the plan, Scott explained to the President. The Appalachian Mountains and the Mississippi River divide the Confederacy into three nearly equal parts. We can weaken the Confederacy by cutting it up into those three parts. Gain control of the Mississippi River, and the three Confederate states on the western side of the river —Texas, Arkansas, and Louisiana—will be cut off from the rest of the Confederacy. They will be knocked out of the war.

At the same time, we can use our navy to set up a naval **blockade,** which will prevent ships from entering or

> **vocabulary**
> **strategy** the overall military plan for defeating an enemy or winning a conflict
> **blockade** a military strategy that aims to cut off supplies going in and out of an area

A naval blockade was an important part of General Scott's plan.

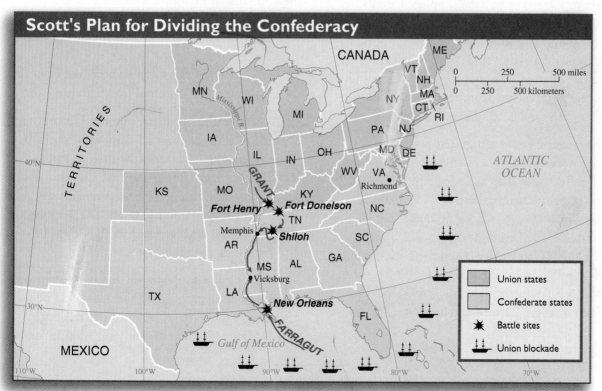

Scott's Plan for Dividing the Confederacy

CANADA

MAINE ME, VT, NH, NY, MA, CT, RI, PA, NJ, MD, DE, OH, IN, IL, WV, VA, Richmond, KY, TN, NC, SC, GA, AL, MS, Vicksburg, LA, FL, TX, AR, Memphis, New Orleans

MN, WI, MI, IA, KS, MO, TERRITORIES

GRANT

FARRAGUT

Fort Henry, Fort Donelson, Shiloh

ATLANTIC OCEAN

Gulf of Mexico

MEXICO

0 — 250 — 500 miles
0 — 250 — 500 kilometers

Legend	
■	Union states
■	Confederate states
✹	Battle sites
⚓	Union blockade

40°N, 30°N, 110°W, 100°W, 90°W, 80°W, 70°W

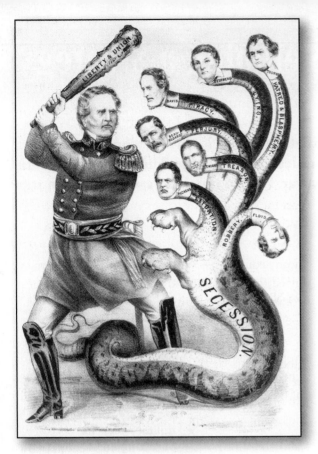

General Winfield Scott came up with a plan to defeat the Confederate "monster."

leaving the Confederacy's ports on the Atlantic and Gulf coasts.

The Confederacy will be unable to sell its cotton to Europe or buy the supplies it needs. As the Confederacy grows weaker, the Union will press its advantage in manpower and supplies. By then the Union's large armies will be experienced in battle. They will advance from the north and from the west, cut the Confederacy into still smaller parts, and crush them.

President Lincoln recognized that Scott's strategy was a sound one. Others, however, criticized it. Too slow, they said. Too timid. They ridiculed Scott's plan, calling it the "anaconda strategy." An anaconda is a long snake that kills by wrapping itself around its prey and slowly crushing it. What we need, said the critics, is a bold plan that will end the war in months, not years. Even President Lincoln worried that the nation might grow weary of a long war.

But Scott knew that the Confederate armies were not going to crumble after a few battles. They had too many fine leaders and too many brave men. The Union could win, but only after a long, hard fight. The battle of Bull Run proved him right.

The day after Fort Sumter surrendered, President Lincoln declared a naval blockade. However, in the early years of the war, the blockade was not effective. No ship can be every place at once, and the Union had only 33 ships to patrol a shoreline of 3,500 miles and 189 ports. During 1861, nine out of every ten ships that tried to "run" the blockade made it safely. However, by the start of 1862, Northern shipyards began to produce large numbers of warships, and the Union's navy was more successful. By the end of the war, the Union navy numbered 700 vessels, and the blockade was far more effective.

The *Merrimack* and the *Monitor*

For a short time in early 1862, it looked like the South might have a weapon that could shatter the Union blockade. Back at the start of the war, the United States Navy had to leave its base in Norfolk, Virginia, because Confederate forces were closing in. As the Union warships hurried out of port, one of them, the *Merrimack,* caught fire and sank in shallow waters. Later the Confederates raised the ship, cut off its burned top, and covered its sides with a double layer of 2-inch-thick iron plates. On each side were holes for five large naval guns. On its bow (the front of the ship) was a 1,500-pound iron battering ram.

All this work took many months, but on March 8, 1862, the ironclad ship, now renamed the *Virginia,* steamed out of Norfolk's harbor and took on two large Union warships. Cannonballs simply bounced off the *Virginia's* slanted sides and fell harmlessly into the water. The *Virginia* sank both ships and scattered several others before anchoring for the night.

The Union navy, however, had been building its own ironclad ship, called the *Monitor*. The next day, as the *Virginia* steamed out to destroy more Union ships, the *Monitor* was waiting for it. For four hours a battle raged as hundreds watched from the shore. Although each side claimed victory, neither ship could sink the other. For the next two months, though, fearful of the *Virginia,* Union ships steered clear of the waters off Norfolk. Then in May, as Union troops advanced on Norfolk, it was the Confederacy's turn to abandon the port. Rather than allow the *Virginia* to fall into the Union's hands, the Confederates burned the ship themselves. The Confederacy tried to buy other ironclad warships from European countries, but it was unsuccessful. Without such ships, the Confederacy had no chance of breaking the Union's blockade.

Mississippi River Ports

In 1862, Union warships commanded by Captain David Farragut made a bold move to carry out a second part of the strategy—to cut off Texas, Arkansas, and Louisiana from the rest of the Confederacy. Farragut was the commander of a fleet of 23 warships blockading the mouth of the Mississippi River. New Orleans, by far the Confederacy's biggest port, was just a short way upriver. Farragut believed that if he could take the enemy by surprise, he could capture the city. After his ships bombarded Confederate forts near the mouth of the river for five days, Farragut ordered his fleet upstream. Despite heavy fire, he captured New Orleans. Confederate ships could still sail down the Mississippi River, but they could no longer use the port at its mouth to unload goods, and they could not get to the open sea.

Meanwhile, Union armies, led by General Ulysses S. Grant, fought fierce battles in western Kentucky and western Tennessee. By the end of 1862, Grant had won several victories. But at Shiloh, near the Mississippi border, a Confederate army caught Grant by surprise. The resulting battle lasted for two days, with heavy loss of life on both sides. In the end, however, Grant drove the Confederate troops back.

So, by the end of 1862, this is how matters stood in the West: Union forces had won control of most of the Mississippi River. Confederate troops, though, still held several important ports, including Vicksburg, Mississippi. This allowed the states of Arkansas, Texas, and Louisiana to continue to help the Confederacy by sending men and supplies across the great river. Until Union forces could take those river ports, the anaconda would not be able to tighten its grip on the South.

Ironclad ships like the **Virginia** *(left) and the* **Monitor** *(right) changed naval warfare.*

Chicago Historical Society

13 The War in the East

On to Richmond In the East the Union was far less successful. There, the Union's main goal, as it had been at the Battle of Bull Run, was to capture the Confederacy's capital city, Richmond, Virginia.

Capturing the enemy's capital is often an important goal in war. It disrupts their government and often causes their people to lose heart. For the same reason, the Union side always rushed troops to defend its own capital, Washington, D.C., whenever it seemed like Confederate armies might attack it. In the case of Richmond, though, the Union would also be capturing the enemy's most important railroad center, its largest iron mill, and its largest maker of guns. Take Richmond, and the Confederacy might collapse then and there.

Three days after the defeat at Bull Run, President Lincoln changed generals. He appointed George B. McClellan to command the eastern army, which came to be called the Army of the Potomac. George McClellan was only 34 years old, very young for such a great responsibility. However, he was known as a brilliant organizer— exactly what this collection of untrained volunteers needed if it was to become an effective army.

To help McClellan train his men, Lincoln gave the general his full support. When McClellan asked for more money and supplies, he got them. When he asked for more men, he got those, too. Eventually, McClellan had 110,000 men under his command—one of the largest armies ever gathered. By the end of 1861, he was writing to his wife that he expected to "crush the rebels in one campaign."

All well and good, but as weeks stretched into months, President Lincoln wondered just when that campaign might take place. December came and went with no action, and then January. In mid-February, McClellan wrote, "In 10 days I shall be in Richmond." But still his troops had not budged. Even a message from the President telling him, "you must act" didn't get McClellan to move.

It was now clear that although McClellan talked a good game, he had little stomach for fighting. His great weakness was his caution. Every time he seemed ready to move, something caused him to think it over and delay moving his troops.

President Lincoln meets with General McClellan after a battle.

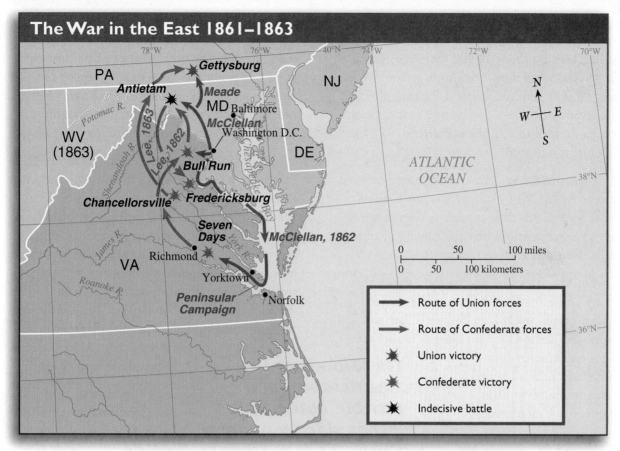

In the early years of the war, the Union forces could not take Richmond, the Confederate capital, and the South failed to invade the North.

Usually that something was a report—always inaccurate—that the enemy had more troops. Convinced he would be outnumbered, he would ask for additional troops. Lincoln's secretary of war once said, "If [McClellan] had a million men, he would swear the enemy had two millions, and then he would sit down in the mud and yell for three." President Lincoln grew so frustrated that he once remarked, "If General McClellan does not want to use the army I would like to *borrow* it."

The Peninsular Campaign

Finally, even McClellan was ready to move from his training base near Washington. Lincoln thought McClellan should march directly to Richmond. Confederate armies were ready to defend that route, however, so McClellan offered a different plan. He would take most of the Army of the Potomac by boat to the York Peninsula, which lies between the York and the James rivers in Virginia. This would be a huge task of organization, but it was exactly the kind of thing McClellan was good at. The army would then

move north up the peninsula toward Richmond, attacking it from behind. A second Union army would march south from Washington to keep Confederate troops along that route busy. The two armies would then meet and take Richmond.

It was a good plan, but to succeed, it would take daring, decisiveness, and speed—not McClellan's strong points. The first part went smoothly. In late March, McClellan floated his army of 110,000 down the Potomac River in more than 100 boats and landed them near the tip of the peninsula. But then he spent endless days organizing and reorganizing and retraining them. When he finally started north, he moved slowly and cautiously, even though there were few Confederate troops on the peninsula. Along the way he spent a whole month trying to capture a small Confederate force at Yorktown.

Confederate generals like Joseph Johnston, Stonewall Jackson, and Robert E. Lee knew how to use this time. Johnson and Lee moved their troops into position to fight against the army moving up the peninsula. Meanwhile, Jackson raced his troops through the nearby Shenandoah Valley, keeping about 40,000 Union troops busy there. And what about the Union general whose army was to join McClellan at Richmond? With Stonewall Jackson on the loose so near the capital, he decided to stay put and defend Washington instead.

Meanwhile, McClellan slowly moved forward. By the end of May, his army was just 6 miles from Richmond, close enough to see the spires of its churches and to hear the ringing of church bells. That was as far as they got.

On May 31 a Confederate force struck the Army of the Potomac hard, stopping it in its tracks. Several weeks later, Robert E. Lee and Stonewall Jackson hit hard again in battles that went on for seven days. Both sides suffered heavy losses in the Seven Days' Battle, but Union armies were driven away from Richmond. Lincoln and his military advisers now decided that McClellan's peninsular campaign, as it was called, could not succeed. The President ordered McClellan to return to Washington.

So, a year and a half after the seceding states formed the Confederate States of America, and a year after the first big battle at Bull Run, Union armies in the East had nothing to show for their efforts. Meanwhile, the South was more confident than ever that it could never be conquered.

Antietam

In the next few months, General Lee's forces handed Union armies a number of defeats in Virginia. Then, in September 1862, Lee carried the war into the North. He sent his troops across the Potomac River into Maryland, one of the slave states that had remained in the Union. A lot of Marylanders believed in the Confederate cause. If Lee could defeat the Union army there, then perhaps Maryland would join the Confederacy.

Lee planned to go even farther north, into Pennsylvania. If he could take Harrisburg, the state's capital, he would destroy the North's railroad lines, cutting off the eastern cities from the West. He could also get food and needed supplies, especially shoes, for his troops. Victories in Maryland and Pennsylvania might cause the North to lose heart and quit the war.

Lee might have succeeded but for some very bad luck. A Union soldier came upon a campsite recently used by Confederate troops, where he spotted a small bundle of cigars wrapped in paper. When the soldier unwrapped the bundle and saw what was written on the paper, his eyes must have opened wide. The paper, which was rushed to the headquarters of General McClellan, revealed General Lee's battle plans. Lee had divided his army, sending Stonewall Jackson's men on another mission. After Jackson completed that mission, he was supposed to join Lee.

McClellan now knew exactly where the enemy would be. He knew he would be able to hit Lee's smaller force before Jackson could return. "Here is a piece of paper," McClellan stated confidently, "with which if I cannot whip Bobby Lee, I will be willing to go home."

Alas for the Union, however: McClellan was still McClellan—too cautious, too worried about the enemy's strength, always finding reasons for delay. By the time he finally moved, part of Jackson's forces had returned to join Lee.

On September 17, 1862, the two sides met in battle at Antietam Creek, which is also known as the Battle of Sharpsburg. (The Union side usually named battles for natural features like creeks, rivers, and mountains; the Confederates named them for nearby towns. That's why the North called the first battle of the war Bull Run—a run is a rapidly running stream—while the South called it Manassas).

The fighting was fierce, with first one side seeming to get the upper hand, then the other. Late in the day, Union forces were making progress, when the rest of Jackson's troops arrived in time to turn them back.

> **The Bloodiest Day: Antietam was a terrible battle that neither side won and left over 23,000 troops dead or wounded.**

At the end of the day, neither side had defeated the other. But Lee had held nothing back. He had used all his men in battle, and now they were exhausted and short of supplies. McClellan still had 20,000 fresh troops. Had McClellan attacked the next day, he might have finished off Lee's army. But this was McClellan, remember. McClellan held back, which allowed the Confederate troops to cross the Potomac River and get back to Virginia.

President Lincoln was fit to be tied. He took a train to Sharpsburg and *ordered* McClellan to go after Lee. "I came back thinking he would move at once," Lincoln later wrote. "It was 19 days before he put a man over the [Potomac] river, 9 days longer before he got his army across"—remember, Lee had got his army across in one day!—"and then he stopped again."

That was the end for Lincoln. He removed McClellan from command and assigned him to sign up volunteers for the army in Trenton, New Jersey. McClellan never held another command.

Antietam was to be the bloodiest day of the entire Civil War. Altogether, 23,000 Union and Confederate soldiers were lost on that one awful day. President Lincoln had hoped for a clear and decisive victory, and not just for military reasons. He planned to make an important announcement—the most important announcement of the entire war, as you will soon read. He believed the best time to do this would be after a Union victory.

Was Antietam enough of a victory? The Union had stopped Lee's drive into the North. Certainly that was a big plus. On the other hand, you'll remember that the South didn't need to conquer Northern land to win. All it had to do was keep from getting conquered itself. And thanks to McClellan's caution, Lee's army had lived again to fight another day.

Well, perhaps Antietam was not the great victory Lincoln had hoped for, but it would have to do.

Antietam was one of the bloodiest battles of the Civil War. For the first time in history, actual photographs were made right after the battle.

Forever Free When the Civil War began, Lincoln said that the goal of this war would be to preserve the Union. Not to end slavery, but to preserve the Union. Lincoln hated slavery, as you know. Why then didn't he say that the goal of the war was to destroy slavery? He had several reasons.

Four slave states—Missouri, Kentucky, Maryland, and Delaware—had so far stayed in the Union. They came to be called the border states, because they were located on the border of North and South. If they believed the Union's goal was to end slavery, they might well join the Confederacy. And that would mean subtracting their population and resources from the Union side and adding them to the Confederacy. Furthermore, Union armies would have to conquer that much more land in order to win.

Keeping Kentucky and Maryland on the Union side was especially important. Lincoln once said, "I think to lose Kentucky is nearly the same as to lose the whole game"—that is, to lose the war. As for Maryland, you only have to look at the location of Washington, D.C., on a map. If Maryland joined Virginia in the Confederacy, the capital city of the Union would be completely surrounded by Confederate states.

There was another reason for Lincoln to say that the Union's goal was just to preserve the Union. Most Northerners agreed that saving the Union was worth a war, but they did not necessarily agree that freeing the slaves was—not at first, anyway. Being against slavery was one thing; being willing to go to war to end it was another. Abolitionists, of course, believed that ending slavery was exactly what the war should be about. However, Lincoln knew he must wait for the feelings of more Northerners to catch up to the abolitionists or else risk losing support for the war.

By the summer of 1862, President Lincoln felt that the time was ripe to announce a great change in the Union's war aims. "The moment came when I felt that slavery must die that the nation might live," said Lincoln. That summer he stayed up nights writing and rewriting a document called the Emancipation Proclamation. To *emancipate* means to "make free," and that's what Lincoln now proposed to do—to announce that as of January 1, 1863, all slaves in states that were still rebelling against the United States would be "forever free."

The Emancipation Proclamation was ready in July 1862. However, that was right after Union armies had suffered a series of defeats. Lincoln's secretary of state, William Seward, advised him, "Wait until the Union wins an important victory." Otherwise, announcing the proclamation then would look like a desperate effort to escape from defeat at the hands of the Confederacy. Lincoln waited. Antietam was not quite the victory Lincoln had hoped for, but he decided it was good enough.

On September 22, 1862, five days after Antietam, Lincoln issued his Emancipation Proclamation. From then on the war would be fought to save the Union *and* to free enslaved African Americans.

The Beginning of Freedom

It's important, though, to understand what the Emancipation Proclamation was and what it wasn't. It did not free any slaves in the border states because they were not rebelling against the United States. If Lincoln had done that, at least three border states would immediately have left the Union. That would seriously weaken the Union's chances of winning the war, and then maybe *no* slaves would be freed. The proclamation

An African American family gets the news about the Emancipation Proclamation.

freed only the slaves in the 11 Confederate states that were still rebelling against the United States. And until Union armies actually entered those states, Lincoln could say all he wanted to about freedom, but he couldn't actually free a single slave.

That's why some people said the Emancipation Proclamation didn't really mean very much. But they missed the point. After the proclamation, as long as the Union won the war, slavery was through. Slaves understood the importance of the proclamation. News of it spread through slave quarters all across the South. They knew that it was the beginning of an answer to their prayers for freedom. And in the North the abolitionist and former slave Frederick Douglass wrote, "We shout for joy that we live to record this righteous decree."

The Emancipation Proclamation was the most important American document about freedom since the Declaration of Independence in 1776. It was a step toward fulfilling the promise of that great document, that all people should have the right to "life, liberty, and the pursuit of happiness."

New Year's Day, January 1, 1863, Lincoln put his name on the Emancipation Proclamation. As he did, he said, "I never, in my life, felt more certain that I was doing right than in signing this paper."

hree Leading Generals The three most important generals during this great war were Robert E. Lee and Thomas J. Jackson for the Confederates, and Ulysses S. Grant for the Union.

Lee

Robert E. Lee came from a family of patriots and military leaders. His father was the Revolutionary War hero, Henry "Light-Horse Harry" Lee, and he himself was married to the granddaughter of Martha Washington. After finishing first in his class at the West Point military academy, Robert E. Lee went on to serve brilliantly in the Mexican War. In one battle both McClellan and Grant served under his command.

At the start of the Civil War, Lee was 54 years old and a colonel in the United States Army. You read earlier about how difficult it was for him to decide to fight for the Confederate side instead of for the Union. Lee quickly became known for his daring strategies. For example, every student

at West Point had been taught that a commander does not divide his army. That's because if you do, the enemy can pour troops between the two parts of your army, keep them from rejoining, and then defeat one part at a time. Yet Lee did that several times and got away with it—mainly because he knew the Union generals had been taught the same thing and wouldn't expect it.

Military experts also warned against going into battle with many fewer troops than the enemy, but there were times when Lee had to do just that. Usually, he came out the winner.

Lee was kind and courteous to his fellow officers and his men. He inspired confidence, and his troops were devoted to him.

The Civil War might have been shorter but for Lee's skill as a military leader.

Jackson

The second great Confederate general was Lee's partner and right-hand man, Thomas J. "Stonewall" Jackson. Jackson got his nickname in the war's first battle, at Bull Run. As Confederate troops led by Jackson held firm against a Union attack, a Southern officer shouted, "There is Jackson standing like a stone wall." The men cheered, and ever afterward the general was Stonewall Jackson.

A catchy nickname, but in fact one that did not describe this general well at all. A stone wall stands firmly in one place and is always on the defense. Jackson was a general always on the move and nearly always on the attack. This is how he described his ideas on warfare: "Always mystify, mislead, and surprise the enemy. And when you strike and overcome him never let up in the pursuit."

Like so many other generals who served the Confederacy, Stonewall Jackson had gone to West Point and later fought in the Mexican War. For nine years before the Civil War, he was a professor of mathematics and science at the Virginia Military Institute. Students remembered him as a quiet man who went about his own business without getting into anybody else's. What they didn't know was that in all those years, Jackson was also studying the strategy and **tactics** of war on his own. When war came, he knew more about strategy and tactics than anyone else on either side.

In war, being able to move forces quickly is often the key to success. No one did that better than Stonewall Jackson. He was the opposite of the cautious George B. McClellan. He would be many miles away, and the enemy would be sure he could not get to the battlefield in time to affect the outcome. But suddenly, there they were, Jackson and his troops, pitching in and swinging the tide of battle in the Confederacy's favor. Once, Jackson moved a brigade—that's

Stonewall Jackson was a brilliant general respected by both sides in the war.

> **vocabulary**
> **tactic** a method of using forces in combat

smaller than an army but still a large group—400 miles in a month. That's nearly 15 miles a day, every day, with soldiers carrying 50- and 60-pound packs on their backs.

Jackson didn't look much like a general. His clothes were usually rumpled, and at times he wore a mangy cap with its visor drawn low. Whether sitting on his favorite horse, Little Sorrel, or on a fence rail in camp, he could usually be found alone, sucking on a lemon (Jackson believed lemons kept you healthy). He was also a deeply religious man. He held a religious service almost every day. It was said that his troops were the "prayin'est" in the Confederate army. Jackson strictly observed Sunday as a day of rest, except when he was in battle. He wouldn't even mail a letter if he believed that someone would be carrying it on a Sunday.

Jackson didn't spend much time chitchatting with other officers and certainly not with his soldiers. But all of them respected him as a brilliant and daring general who figured out ways to win battles, even when outnumbered.

Grant

On the Union side, Ulysses S. Grant was the outstanding general. But if you looked at his record before the Civil War, you might have voted him "least likely to succeed." Like Lee and Jackson, Grant had graduated from West Point and fought in the war with Mexico. But there the similarities stopped. Grant was not a top student at West Point. After the Mexican War he was assigned to a lonely outpost in the West. He found the daily army duties dull and boring, and he took to drinking. As a result, he was forced to leave the army. He then tried farming in Missouri but failed. After that he tried selling real estate, but he failed at that, too.

Ulysses Grant then returned to his family in Galena, Illinois, where his father gave him a job selling harnesses in the family leather store. That's where he was working when the Civil War began.

Grant promptly volunteered to return to the army and was made a colonel in charge of a volunteer regiment. He was 39 years old at the time. In western Tennessee he developed a plan that allowed his troops to capture two Confederate forts. When the commander of one asked Grant for his terms for surrendering, Grant replied, "no terms except an unconditional and immediate surrender." This firm position brought Grant to the attention of Lincoln and others in the east. After that, people often said that Grant's initials, *U.S.,* stood for "Unconditional Surrender."

Later, some newspapers and others blamed Grant for being unprepared at Shiloh. They demanded that Lincoln remove him from command. Lincoln replied, "I can't spare this man. He fights." Lincoln could have added, and he wins.

Grant once explained his ideas about warfare this way: "The art of war is simple enough. Find out where your enemy is. Get at him as soon as you can. Strike at him as hard as you can, and keep moving on."

Grant's strategy was based on a great advantage he had over the Confederate generals. He knew that with the North's larger population and greater resources, his losses of men and guns could be replaced. He also knew that as the war went on, the other side's losses could not be. So Grant's plan was to force the Confederate armies to fight whenever and wherever he could. Sooner or later he would wear them down. And he did.

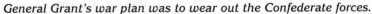

General Grant's war plan was to wear out the Confederate forces.

Fighting Men and Boys And what of the men—the common soldiers who did the fighting? What was this war like for them? At the start it was all glory and adventure. At least that's what volunteers expected when they signed up for service.

In that first year, whenever either side called for volunteers, it got all the men that they asked for, and more.

Volunteers rushed to join because they believed in the cause their side was fighting for. And they expected the war to end quickly. That was because neither side expected the other side to fight with real courage. Northerners called Southerners "Rebels," and they nicknamed the Southern soldier "Johnny Reb." Northerners were sure that once Johnny Reb had to face Northern troops, he would turn tail and run. Southerners had long called Northerners "Yankees," and the Northern soldier was "Billy Yank." Southerners were just as sure that Billy Yank would lose his stomach for fighting after one good whipping.

Rebels or Yankees, many who signed up on each side were boys rather than men. The lowest

age allowed for a volunteer was 18, and there were many of those. Some were younger still—boys of 16 or 17 who could look older and didn't want this chance for adventure to pass them by.

Since the South was overwhelmingly rural, nearly all the Southern troops were from farm families. Most had used guns all their life for hunting. The majority of Union soldiers, too, were from farm families. But some Northern troops came from towns and large cities, and few of these city dwellers had ever held a gun in their hands.

The early enthusiasm for joining did not last. Many a young man quickly learned that a soldier's life was a hard one. Often it meant marching in the worst kind of weather, without enough food and water, all the while carrying

Interest in the Civil War is so high today that many people take part in reenactments of battles, complete with the proper uniforms and weapons.

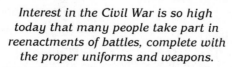

50 pounds of equipment on your back. "We have been half starved, half frozen, and half drowned," one Union soldier wrote back home. "The mud in Kentucky is awful." And a Confederate officer reported, "there is scarcely a private in the army who has a change of clothing of any kind. Hundreds of men are perfectly barefooted. . . ." Conditions were so bad that many men fell ill and died before ever seeing battle.

As word of these conditions reached home through letters, the number of volunteers started to drop. To get men to sign up, both the Confederate and Union governments started to pay cash bonuses. That brought enough men for a while. In the North, recent Irish and German immigrants saw the bonus money as a way to buy a farm when the war was over, so many of them joined the army. As a result, one in five Union soldiers was an immigrant.

Eventually, though, each side had to turn to the **draft**—that is, they had to require men to serve. This angered many people on each side. For one thing, the American government had never drafted men for any previous American war—not the Mexican War, not the War of 1812, not even the War for Independence.

In addition, the draft laws on both sides seemed unfair to the ordinary citizen. In both the North and the South, a

> ## vocabulary
> **draft** a system of selecting individuals from a group for compulsory military service

person who was drafted could get out of serving by paying a substitute to serve for him. Another way to get out of serving in the Union army was to pay the government $300. For most working people that was a whole year's income—far more than they could hope to put their hands on. In the South, big planters who owned 20 or more slaves could also be excused. No wonder so many people on both sides grumbled that this was a rich man's war but a poor man's fight.

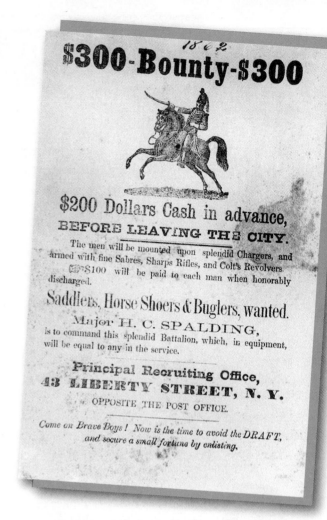

In 1862 men were offered a bonus of $300 if they enlisted in the Union army.

The Real War

Reading about the battles in a war sometimes makes it seem like the troops were busy fighting all the time. In fact, battles were few and far between, and they usually lasted only a few days. Soldiers spent most days fixing up a camp, repairing equipment, and the like. It was a boring time.

Meals were boring, too. Union troops were supplied with bacon; flour that you could make into bread; a biscuit called hardtack, which was as hard as it sounds; and coffee to dunk your biscuit into. Cattle were often brought along to supply occasional beef. Confederate soldiers received pretty much the same, except that they got cornmeal instead of wheat flour. Neither army supplied fresh fruits and vegetables, but the soldiers took care of that in their own way.

They simply took this food from the farms that they marched past.

Even at the start of the war, Billy Yank was better supplied than was Johnny Reb. As the war went on, the Confederacy's food supplies ran low, and the men often went hungry. Clothing and especially shoes were in short supply. The South did not make shoes and had to buy them from other countries. As the Northern blockade began to pinch, that became harder and harder to do.

Billy Yank always had a uniform, and Johnny Reb sometimes did not, but that doesn't mean Billy Yank was always grateful for his clothes. The uniforms were made of wool, which was fine for the winter. But in the hot summer months, the woolen uniform made Billy Yank sweat and itch.

It was boring to wait for battle, but to enter it was terrifying. Every soldier knew that that day or the next might be his last. Many soldiers spent the night before battles praying and writing home to their loved ones. Often, they said in their letters that they did not expect to live through the following days. Sadly, for far too many, their prediction came true.

Those who were wounded on the battlefield were taken to a place almost as dangerous—the army hospital. In fact, most soldiers had already spent time in an army hospital due to sicknesses not connected to battles. Many never made it out of the hospital alive. Twice as many soldiers died from disease as from battle wounds in the Civil War. That is because people at that time knew little about germs. True, they also had no modern miracle drugs. But if doctors had simply scrubbed their hands with hot water and soap before moving on to the next patient, many lives would have been saved.

In this "brothers' war," Johnny Reb and Billy Yank often got along pretty well when they were not in battle. It was not unusual for soldiers doing guard duty for each side to call out to each other. There were taunts, of course, but the men also swapped stories and traded little things. Billy usually wanted Southern tobacco, and Johnny was glad to trade it for more coffee.

Surgeons in army field hospitals worked under poor conditions.

African American Soldiers

Soon after Lincoln signed the Emancipation Proclamation on January 1, 1863, a new group of men joined Billy Yank in wearing the blue uniform of the Union. These men were African Americans. They were mostly from the North, but they also included runaway slaves who wanted to fight against the Confederacy.

Northern blacks had been volunteering to serve in the army since the war began, but the army had always turned them down. The army simply didn't want black soldiers then. After the Emancipation Proclamation, however, the army changed its mind.

Meanwhile, Frederick Douglass, the great abolitionist, urged blacks to join the army and help free the 3.5 million slaves. Douglass believed that after black Americans helped fight to save the Union, no one would dare deny them the full rights of citizenship.

Several Northern states formed all-black units. The most famous was the Massachusetts 54th Regiment, commanded by Colonel Robert Gould Shaw. In the summer of 1863, the 54th Regiment led an attack on Fort Wagner, a Confederate fort on an island in the harbor of Charleston, South Carolina. In spite of heavy cannon fire by Confederate troops, nearly a hundred soldiers forced their way into the fort. There, they engaged in hand-to-hand fighting against Confederate troops. The bravery of the 54th in the face of terrible losses won acceptance for African American soldiers everywhere. Meanwhile, in the West, blacks had fought with General Grant's forces in the campaign to take Vicksburg. They later contributed to other Union victories in Mississippi. President Lincoln wrote that "some of our commanders . . . believe that . . . the use of colored troops constitutes the heaviest blow yet dealt to the rebels, and that at least one of these important successes could not have been achieved . . . but for the aid of black soldiers."

Out of every ten Union soldiers, one was African American. Altogether, more than 180,000 black Americans served in the Union army. More than 38,000 of those gave their lives for the Union and the cause of freedom. Blacks served in the Union navy, too. One quarter of all the men who enlisted in the navy were black— nearly 30,000. More than 2,800 of them died.

The fighting record of African Americans who served in the Civil War was outstanding. Twenty-one black soldiers received the Congressional Medal of Honor for acts of bravery. This medal is our country's highest military award.

As the war went on, African Americans were allowed to enlist in the Union army.

Doing Men's Work America, remember, was still largely a nation of farms. And during the war, women and children on those farms still had all their regular tasks to perform. But they also had to do much more. For with the men off fighting, women and children had to do the men's work as well.

In the South, many women had to take charge of the farms and plantations. On the plantations there were still slaves to do the hard physical work, but remember that most Southerners didn't own slaves. In these families the women had to do all the work their husbands had done before.

Both sides in the Civil War depended on the work of women.

The same was true of farm women in the North and West. A traveler to western farm states in 1863 reported that "women were in the fields everywhere, driving the reapers . . . and loading grain." As one woman explained:

> Harvesting isn't any harder than cooking, washing, and ironing over a red-hot stove in July and August—only we have to do both now. My three brothers went into the army, all my cousins, most of the young men about here, and the men we used to hire. So there's no help to be got but women, and the crops must be got in all the same, you know.

Even without men doing their normal tasks, the farms in the North and West produced as much food as they had before the war. As a result, thanks to the hard work of women, Union troops never went hungry during the war, and workers in the cities also had plenty to eat.

In addition, women on both sides made bandages, knitted socks, and sewed clothing to send to the soldiers. They also kept up the spirits of their men with letters from home.

Women served on both sides in other ways, too. Some carried mail for the armies. Others worked as spies. One of the North's spies was Harriet Tubman, the famed conductor on the Underground Railroad. Several hundred other women managed to reach the battlefield disguised as men.

There were various other organizations that also did heroic service. One of them was the Army Corps of Nurses. About 3,000 women served as nurses during the war. When you remember that more than *3 million* men were in the two armies, that doesn't sound like a lot. But in those days, nursing was a man's job. Before the war, a woman couldn't get hired as a nurse. Once the war came, however, so many nurses were needed that women were finally accepted into that profession.

On the Confederate side, Sally Tompkins ran a private hospital in Richmond, Virginia. In this hospital she cared for both Confederate soldiers and Union prisoners. To Tompkins, a life was a life, and it didn't matter if the person wore Confederate gray or Union blue. She and her nurses saved hundreds of lives.

Clara Barton

One of the truly heroic nurses on the Union side was Clara Barton. Even before the war, Clara Barton always seemed to be breaking new ground. As a schoolteacher in New Jersey, she opened the first free school in that state—before then, parents had to pay to send their children to school. Later she became the first woman to hold a regular job in the federal government when she worked as a clerk in the United States Patent Office in Washington, D.C.

Barton always found her greatest happiness in helping others. When the Civil War broke out, she threw herself into the Union cause by helping its soldiers. Living in Washington, she provided food and comfort to the homesick soldiers who poured into that city in the war's early months. At first, Barton collected supplies herself. She wrote letters home for those who couldn't write. As news of her work spread, churches and citizens' groups sent bandages and other supplies. Soon her apartment was overflowing with boxes, and she had to rent a warehouse to store them all.

Barton was not satisfied with staying in Washington while men went into battle. She asked army officials to allow her to help the men at the battlefront. As she wrote later in the war, "My business is [stopping the flow] of blood and feeding men; my post [is] the open field between the bullet and the hospital." The officials turned down her request at first, but she kept after them until they finally said yes.

She first appeared at the battlefront in August 1862. The field hospital was almost out of dressings for wounds when Barton arrived with her mule-drawn wagon filled with supplies. An army surgeon wrote, "I thought that night if heaven ever sent out a holy angel, she must be the one, her assistance was so timely." Barton helped the surgeon bandage the wounded, and she also fed them.

After that, Clara Barton was on the scene of many battles with her wagonloads of bandages, coffee, jellies, brandy, crackers, and cans of soup and beef.

At the battle of Antietam, she was the only woman allowed at the front. She followed the cannons up to the front lines. For a long time her wagon provided the only medical supplies available.

On the battlefields, Clara Barton often worked for days with almost no sleep. She cared for the wounded in the field, and in tents, houses, churches—wherever shelter could be found. She fed them. She wrote letters home for them. She comforted the wounded and the dying.

On her return to Washington, Barton was called to serve at Lincoln Hospital. As she entered one ward, 70 men—each of whom had received her care—rose to salute her. She earned the nickname that soldiers gave her: "Angel of the Battlefield." After the war, Clara Barton founded the American Red Cross.

The war brought women like Clara Barton to the battlefields to serve as nurses.

New Year As the year 1863 began, things continued to go badly for the Union on the battlefields of the East. Just the month before, in December 1862, the Union army had tried once again to take Richmond. But before they could get there, Robert E. Lee met the Union army and defeated them in a brilliant victory at Fredericksburg.

In May 1863 a Union army of 130,000 men, the largest yet assembled, headed toward Richmond again. Lee's army, with only half as many troops, took them on at Chancellorsville, Virginia. Once again, Lee and Stonewall Jackson managed to come out on top through their daring strategy.

The South did suffer a great loss at Chancellorsville, however. In the confusion of battle, Jackson was mistakenly shot by one of his own men. His left arm had to be amputated. For a time it seemed he might recover, but then infection set in, and Jackson died.

Chancellorsville was Robert E. Lee's most brilliant victory. No one knew it then, but it was to be his last important victory.

In the West, General Grant's army had continued to gain victories in western Tennessee and Mississippi. By spring of 1863 there were only two rebel strongholds remaining along the Mississippi. The most important of these was Vicksburg, Mississippi. If Vicksburg fell to the Union army, the Union would control the entire Mississippi River. The western states of the Confederacy would be cut off from the others, and the anaconda would squeeze ever more tightly around the Confederacy.

It looked like that would happen. Just two weeks after Lee's victory at Chancellorsville, Lee learned that Grant had laid siege to Vicksburg. That means he had surrounded it and could prevent supplies and troops from going in to help the 30,000 Confederate troops who were trapped there. It seemed only a matter of time until the city fell to Unconditional Surrender Grant.

The siege of Vicksburg made Lee see that he would need to do more than fight a defensive war against invading Union troops. He would

The Union forces won Vicksburg after a long and bloody siege.

need to go on the attack. He would need to take the war into the North and win battles on Northern soil. Then the enemy might finally lose heart and agree to peace.

Lee's plan was to march across Maryland and into southern Pennsylvania. A victory there would threaten both Washington, D.C., and Philadelphia. Pennsylvania was far from his home base in Virginia, but Lee knew his army could live off the foods grown on the rich farmlands of Maryland and Pennsylvania. He would be able to seize other supplies, like desperately needed shoes, as he captured towns.

Gettysburg

And so Robert E. Lee and his Army of Northern Virginia arrived in the town of Gettysburg, Pennsylvania, on July 1, 1863. As it happened, a Union army led by General George Meade was also in the area. Lincoln had put Meade in charge of Union armies in the East only three days before.

No one had planned for a battle to take place in Gettysburg, but there they were, face-to-face. For the next three days, July 1, 2, and 3, a battle raged between the Confederate and Union armies. Again and again, Lee's forces attacked. Again and again, Union forces threw them back.

On July 3, Lee decided on one final attack, which he hoped would break the Union's resistance. At about two o'clock in the afternoon, 15,000 men under the command of General George Pickett emerged from the woods and began their advance across an open field toward the Union's line. The attack, later called Pickett's Charge, was incredibly brave, but it failed. The

Pickett's charge was a bloody event in the three-day Battle of Gettysburg.

Union army opened fire with its big guns as well as with muskets. Pickett's army, as one Confederate officer reported, "just seemed to melt away in the blue . . . smoke which now covered the hill. Nothing but stragglers came back."

With a third of his army lost, there was nothing for Lee to do now but retreat. On July 4 his exhausted, downhearted men started back toward Virginia in a pouring rain. To get there, they would have to cross the Potomac River. President Lincoln, who had been kept informed of events, realized that this was a chance to trap Lee and the rest of his army. He telegraphed General Meade, urging him to pursue Lee. But Meade, like McClellan before him, was too cautious. By the time he was ready to move, Lee's army had safely crossed the Potomac River and was out of his reach. "We had them within our grasp," complained the frustrated President. But once more, Lee had escaped.

Even so, Gettysburg was a major defeat for the Confederacy. Never again would its army invade the North. The tide of battle in the East now turned in the Union's favor. Meanwhile, in the West, Vicksburg surrendered to Grant on that same July 4, giving the Union control of the Mississippi River from its source to its mouth.

Independence Day, 1863, turned out to be a great day for the Union.

Some months later the citizens of Gettysburg held a ceremony to honor those who had died in the great battle. To give the main speech, they had invited Edward Everett of Massachusetts, known as the greatest orator, or public speaker, of that time. President Lincoln had been invited to make a few remarks, and he had come also, but he and everyone else understood that it was Everett who was to be the star of the occasion.

And Everett did, indeed, give a very fine speech, which lasted nearly two hours. Near the end of the afternoon, President Lincoln was called upon for his remarks. He spoke for just two minutes, and was done.

It's funny how things work out sometimes. Edward Everett spoke for two hours, and while he gave a fine speech, no one today remembers a word of it. Abraham Lincoln spoke for just two minutes, and his speech has become the most famous in American history. Lincoln had wanted to use this speech to explain the real meaning of the war—that it was really about the ideas found in the Declaration of Independence. That it was about liberty, and about equal rights, and about democracy. Most of the President's listeners that day didn't quite realize the importance of what he said, but Everett knew it immediately. Walking over to Lincoln, Everett said, "Mr. President, I should be glad if I could flatter myself that I came as near to the central idea of this occasion in two hours, as you did in two minutes."

Four score and seven years ago our fathers brought forth on this continent, a new nation, conceived in Liberty, and dedicated to the proposition that all men are created equal.

Now we are engaged in a great civil war, testing whether that nation, or any nation so conceived and so dedicated, can long endure. We are met on a great battle-field of that war. We have come to dedicate a portion of that field, as a final resting place for those who here gave their lives that that nation might live. It is altogether fitting and proper that we should do this.

But, in a larger sense, we can not dedicate—we can not consecrate—we can not hallow—this ground. The brave men, living and dead, who struggled here, have consecrated it, far above our poor power to add or detract. The world will little note, nor long remember what we say here, but it can never forget what they did here. It is for us the living, rather, to be dedicated here to the unfinished work which they who fought here have thus far so nobly advanced. It is rather for us to be here dedicated to the great task remaining before us—that from these honored dead we take increased devotion to that cause for which they gave the last full measure of devotion—that we here highly resolve that these dead shall not have died in vain—that this nation, under God, shall have a new birth of freedom—and that government of the people, by the people, for the people, shall not perish from the earth.

A crowd gathered at the Gettysburg battlefield to listen to President Lincoln (circled below) and other speakers honor the men who died there.

19 Confederate Problems Mount

S tates' Rights By the end of 1863, the Confederate States of America were having problems not only on the field of battle but back home as well. A lot of these problems had to do with the kind of government the Confederacy had set up.

Do you remember why the Confederacy was born? Southern states said that under the Constitution, states had certain rights that the federal government could not interfere with. If the federal government interfered with slavery in a state, for example, or if it passed a law that the people of a state didn't want, like a tax law, then the state had the right to drop out of the Union. This idea came to be called states' rights.

Naturally, when the seceding states wrote a constitution for the Confederacy, they made sure the idea of states' rights was in it. And you can be sure that any time leaders of the Southern states didn't want to do something, they cried, "Our states' rights are being violated!"

So when the Confederate Congress voted for new taxes to pay for the war, a lot of Southern governors dragged their feet in collecting them. "States' rights!" they shouted. North Carolina had plenty of uniforms and blankets, but it kept them for soldiers from its own state and refused to share them with other Confederate troops. "We don't have to contribute them to the Confederacy. States' rights," said the state's leaders. Georgia had 10,000 men in a state army but refused to let Confederate commanders give them orders. "States' rights." And South Carolina—remember that this was the first state to secede from the Union?—South Carolina at one point actually threatened to secede from the Confederacy! You can't run a war that way.

1833: Slavery was abolished throughout the British Empire.

King Cotton

The Confederacy also made a very bad prediction. Great Britain had the world's largest textile, or cloth, industry. France was not far behind. Both got most of their raw cotton from the South. Would Britain and France allow the Northern blockade to cut off their supply of cotton, forcing their factories to close and throwing their people out of work?

Not a chance, said the South. Even before secession, that's what a confident senator from South Carolina told his fellow senators from the North. "What would happen if no cotton were furnished for three years? England would topple headlong and carry the whole civilized world with her, [except] the South." That's why, this senator warned the North, "you dare not make war on cotton. No power on earth dare make war upon it. Cotton is king!"

Well, it turned out that the Southern leaders were wrong. For one thing, it just happened that when the Civil War began, Great Britain had plenty of cotton in its warehouses— much more than it needed right then. So it didn't have to buy a lot of cotton from the South right away to keep its factories going and its workers working. For another, Great Britain knew that challenging the Union's blockade might lead to war with the United States, and it didn't want that. For a third, British working people were against slavery and didn't want their government to support the last great slaveholding power in the world. Especially after the Emancipation Proclamation, they sided with the North.

So the South never got the help it expected from Great Britain. It wasn't able to sell its cotton, and it wasn't able to buy the manufactured goods and other supplies it needed so badly. As time went on, that hurt the Confederacy's chances more and more.

Jefferson Davis

Another problem the Confederacy had was with the leadership of its government. No one could blame Jefferson Davis, its president, for not being another Lincoln. Who could be? But Davis lacked certain skills that would have made him a better leader.

Oddly, he and Abraham Lincoln were born less than 100 miles from each other in Kentucky and only eight months apart. Like the Lincolns, the Davises were poor. A few years after Jefferson was born, the family moved to the Mississippi Territory. Jefferson's father proved to be better at choosing farmland than Abraham's, and the Davis family grew cotton and soon became rich.

Jefferson Davis went to West Point, and although he was not much of a student, he graduated and served in the United States Army for a number of years. When his family gave him a large piece of land along the Mississippi River, he left the army to raise cotton.

Like every big planter, Davis owned slaves. He was one of the kinder slaveholders in Mississippi. He rarely punished his slaves, and he allowed them to learn to read and write—something few owners did. But he was as firm in his belief as any other Southerner that slavery was a good thing for both blacks and whites and that it must be preserved.

As he grew older, Jefferson Davis read books on history, politics, literature, poetry, and military strategy. By the time he entered Congress in 1845, he was one of the best-educated men in that body.

Jefferson Davis left Congress to fight in the war with Mexico. He later served as a United States senator and as a secretary of war. When the Southern states formed the Confederate States of America, they chose Jefferson Davis to be president. It was a job Davis did not want, but he agreed to serve. His wife said that when he told her he had been chosen, he spoke "as a man might speak of a sentence of death."

The job was very difficult. Remember, the new government was starting from scratch—no offices,

Jefferson Davis served the United States government for many years but chose the Confederacy when the Southern states seceded.

Jefferson Davis and his cabinet listen to General Robert E. Lee explain his war plans.

no employees, no postal service. President Davis's first office—his "white house"—was in a hotel parlor. Davis worked very hard, but he kept allowing himself to get bogged down in small details that took a lot of his time. Also, he was too sure of himself when it came to military strategy. He often overruled generals, like Robert E. Lee, who were better at running a war. That was very unwise.

He interfered so much with the War Department that five different secretaries of war quit. And he just did not deal well with people. He was difficult and stubborn. Rather than try to win over those who disagreed with him, he quarreled and made enemies.

Perhaps no one could have led the Confederacy to victory. By the start of 1864, there was little chance of success left. With the fall of Vicksburg, the West was lost, and so were most of Kentucky and Tennessee. In the East, Union armies were once again carrying the fight onto Southern soil.

Also, by then, President Lincoln had found the general he had been looking for, one who would fight and fight and fight some more and never stop pursuing the enemy. That general was Ulysses S. Grant. In spring of 1864 the President put Grant in charge of all the Union armies.

Battle in the Wilderness Fight and fight some more and pursue. That is exactly what Grant did in spring of 1864. Once again the scene was northern Virginia. Once again the prize was Richmond. And once again the armies met and did battle near Chancellorsville, where one year earlier Lee had won his most brilliant victory.

But this time it was different. The fighting took place in a heavy forest known as the Wilderness. Grant's army outnumbered Lee's by nearly two to one. For five days the battle of the Wilderness raged. It was a terrible, bloody battle, and at the end, Grant had lost more men than Lee. But Grant knew that his losses could be replaced and Lee's could not.

Lee had to pull back, stopping several times to fight some more. Grant's army continued to press forward toward Richmond and Petersburg, an important railroad center near Richmond. Finally, Grant had his armies in position to begin a siege in front of the two cities. That summer, and then through the autumn and winter, Grant's army kept Lee's troops in Richmond and Petersburg from breaking out. They could only retreat and abandon the cities. All the while, Grant received fresh troops and supplies; Lee received none.

Meanwhile, General William Tecumseh Sherman, who was now in charge of Union forces in the West, prepared to tighten the squeeze of the anaconda. With an army of 90,000, Sherman set out from Tennessee toward the East. His path would take him through Alabama and then to

Georgia, where he planned to capture the important railroad city of Atlanta. Sherman didn't worry about food for his army. He would take that from the farms along the way.

In Georgia, Sherman began the practice of "total war." That meant that he not only fought the other side's soldiers but also destroyed their farms, burned their warehouses and barns, wrecked their shops, and tore up their rail lines. Sherman did whatever he could to weaken the enemy, even though he was bringing misery to people who weren't soldiers. It was a cruel way of fighting, and sadly, it has served as an example for armies in other wars around the world.

By September 1864, Atlanta had fallen to Union troops. From there, Sherman led his army on a "march to the sea," again destroying everything they came upon in a path 40 miles wide. In December the seacoast city of Savannah fell. By January, Sherman was in South Carolina. By March he was in North Carolina. Everywhere his armies went, they left behind destruction, and hatred and bitterness, too.

By this time, Abraham Lincoln had been elected to a second term in office. His opponent was none other than the general

Union troops tore up railroad tracks to weaken the enemy.

he had removed from command, George B. McClellan. McClellan said that if elected, he would end the war quickly. To people who were tired of war and sick of the terrible losses, that was very appealing.

Lincoln, who was determined to see the war through to the end in order to preserve the Union and free the slaves, could make no such promise. For a time he expected to lose the election. Then came the news of Sherman's capture of Atlanta and of several other Union victories. Northern spirits rose, and Lincoln won reelection easily.

By the time Lincoln's second term began in March 1865, it was clear that the Confederacy was doomed. Lincoln realized that it was time to get Americans to focus on the next great task before them: to reunite the nation. Would it be possible, after four years of killing and destruction, for people on each side to understand the pain and suffering of the other side? Many Northerners talked of revenge, of getting even for what the South's secession had caused. Many wanted to treat the Southerners as a conquered people.

With Malice Toward None

That was not Lincoln's way. The Union had been preserved; slavery had been ended. Enough. The job now was to get back to being one nation, the United States of America, and to fulfill its promise of greatness. President Lincoln had already announced his plan for restoring the Union. It was a plan to bring the Southern states back into the Union quickly and without harsh punishment, as you will read later. In his second inaugural address, on March 4, 1865, he urged Americans to adopt a forgiving spirit as they set about this task:

> With malice toward none; with charity for all; with firmness in the right, as God gives us to see the right, let us strive on to finish the work we are in; to bind up the nation's

wounds; to care for him who shall have borne the battle, and for his widow, and his orphan—to do all which may achieve and cherish a just, and lasting peace among ourselves, and with all nations.

All that remained was for Grant's armies to finish the job. Three weeks after Lincoln's speech, Petersburg and Richmond fell. Lee tried to gather his weary and hungry army once more, but he was pursued by Union forces. There was, finally, no way out. On April 9, Lee sent an officer with a white flag of surrender to the Union army and asked to meet with General Grant.

The surrender took place at a farmhouse in the village of Appomattox Court House, Virginia. Grant wrote out the terms of surrender. The Confederates would turn in their weapons, except for the officers' small guns. All were free to leave. And, added Grant, "let all the men who claim to own a horse or mule take the animals home with them to work their little farms." It was a generous offer, and Lee thanked Grant for it. Then Lee climbed on his horse, Traveller, looked thoughtfully over the field of Union soldiers, and rode away.

The American Civil War was over.

Confederate soldiers sadly roll up their battle flag after the surrender at Appomattox.

West Point Museum Collections

Victory, at last! News of Lee's surrender at Appomattox on April 9 quickly reached Washington. The next day, cannons boomed, fireworks exploded over the Potomac River, the Stars and Stripes hung everywhere. The celebration spilled over to the next day, April 11. That afternoon a crowd that had gathered at the White House called out, "Speech! Speech!"

John Wilkes Booth

In the audience was an actor named John Wilkes Booth. When the President finished speaking, Booth turned to a friend and snarled, "That's the last speech he will ever make."

Lincoln had seen Booth perform often at Ford's Theater, which was not far from the White House. He had enjoyed the actor's work. He did not know that, even then, Booth was his mortal enemy.

Even as a teenager, John Wilkes Booth had talked about doing great deeds some day. "I must have fame! fame!" he told friends. He said he had to do "something never before accomplished—something no other man would probably ever do."

Booth was a **racist** through and through. He believed that slavery was good and that the South's cause was right. During the war he served as a secret agent for the Confederacy. In his mind, no one was more responsible for the defeat of his beloved South than President Lincoln. And for that, Lincoln must pay.

> ### vocabulary
> **racist** one who believes that racial differences prove that a certain race is superior to others

Booth's first plan was to kidnap Lincoln, take him to Richmond, and offer to exchange him for all the Confederate soldiers who were prisoners of war. When that didn't work, he decided to kill Lincoln.

President Lincoln had received many threatening letters during his presidency, but he simply threw them away. He refused to take such threats seriously. After all, no one had ever killed an American President before. When friends urged him to use guards, Lincoln said that having guards protect him against angry Southerners "would only put the idea [of killing him] into their heads." And "as to the crazy folks, why I must only take my chances."

Lincoln Shot at Ford's Theater

On Friday, April 14—three days after the speech that Booth had heard—the President met with his Cabinet and a special guest, General Grant. Grant and his wife had been invited by the Lincolns to attend a play with them that evening at Ford's Theater. Grant had to decline the invitation, and Lincoln really didn't feel like going without him. But he knew that his wife, Mary, looked forward to going, and the people of Washington were expecting him to make an appearance. So the Lincolns went to the theater.

Sitting in the special presidential box just to the side of the stage, the President seemed to enjoy the show. Booth picked his time well. He knew the play on stage—knew every line of it. In the third act there was one line that always brought a lot of laughter. That moment—with the laughter distracting the audience—that would be the moment to strike.

Booth approached the door that opened into the back of the presidential box. The guard who was supposed to be there had left his post. Booth entered. As the actor on stage said his line and the audience laughed, Booth raised his pistol and, from 6 feet away, fired into the back of the President's head.

After shooting Lincoln, John Wilkes Booth jumped from the presidential box onto the stage.

He then moved quickly to the railing of the box, shouted "Revenge for the South," then jumped down onto the stage and shouted *"Sic semper tyrannis"*—a Latin phrase that means "Thus always to tyrants."

Booth, who had broken his leg when he landed on the stage, managed to escape. But as an actor well known to the public, he was immediately recognized. Booth avoided capture for nearly two weeks, but he was finally found hiding in a barn and was shot.

As for the wounded President, he was carried to a house across the street, where friends and a doctor tried to make him comfortable. But there was no hope that he would live. Even the most modern of medical care today could not have saved him. The following morning he breathed his last. "Now," said his secretary of war, Edwin Stanton, "he belongs to the ages."

Booth believed he was striking a blow for the South. He could not have been more mistaken. It was Lincoln who had said, "With malice toward none; with charity for all." It was Lincoln who held out the best hope for a peace without bitterness and revenge. It was Lincoln who spoke of bringing the Southern states back into the Union as quickly as possible.

And now Lincoln was gone.

Broad Streak of Ruin At the end of the Civil War, the South was a devastated land. Travelers to that region were shocked by what they saw. Wherever General Sherman's army had marched in Georgia and South Carolina, wrote one traveler, the countryside "looked for many miles like a broad black streak of ruin."

In other words, everything had been burned. Before the war, Charleston, South Carolina, had been one of the South's sparkling cities. Now, wrote one visitor, it was a city of ruins, a desolation, of vacant houses, of widowed women, of rotting wharves, of deserted warehouses, of weed wild gardens, of miles of grass-grown streets. In Tennessee, reported another, "The trail of war is visible . . . in burnt-up (cotton) gin houses, ruined bridges, mills, and factories." And in Virginia, wrote yet another, "The barns are all burned, chimneys standing without houses and houses standing without roofs, or doors or windows."

Fields that had once produced fine harvests of cotton, tobacco, and grain were covered with weeds. Small farms were destroyed, and nearly half the South's farm animals were gone. Railroad tracks were torn up, and whatever factories the South had before the war were now mostly destroyed. Many Southerners, both white and black, were without food, clothing, or any way to make a living.

The human losses were even worse. Nearly one of every six men and boys who put on the gray uniform of the Confederacy was dead by the end of the war—one of every six! Even more were wounded, some so badly they would never be the same again. Here is a number that tells you a lot about the human tragedy of this war: In 1866, the year after the war ended, out of every five dollars the state of Mississippi collected in taxes, it spent one to buy artificial arms and legs for its veterans.

As for the former slaves, the war brought them freedom, and there is no greater blessing than that. In the first months after the war, a good many black people left their old plantations just so that they could experience their new freedom. They wanted to know what it was like to go wherever they wanted, without having to get permission from an owner. One former slave told her former owner that she just could not stay and continue to cook for her. "If I stay here," she said, "I'll never know I am free."

Many freed slaves had an even more important reason for taking to the road. They hoped to find family members who had been sold and separated from them.

But most of the former slaves stayed right where they were. Does that surprise you?

Richmond, Virginia, the capital of the South, was only one of many places left in ruins.

Remember, they had to make a living. The best chance of doing that was to get hired to work on the land of their former owners or to rent some of it from them. So they stayed, and even though they were now free, their lives didn't change much.

Even while the war was going on, Congress realized it would have to help people get back on their feet. Just a month before the war's end, Congress created the Freedmen's Bureau. Freedmen were the former slaves. Actually the Freedmen's Bureau provided food, clothing, fuel, and medical supplies to needy Southern whites as well as former slaves.

The Freedmen's Bureau had its greatest success in education. It set up more than 4,000 schools, where the former slaves could learn to read and write. Northern churches sent thousands of dedicated women and men to teach in these schools. You'll remember that under slavery, slaves were usually forbidden to learn those skills. Now black Southerners flocked to these schools—not just children but adults also. Many of the adults were deeply religious people who had long yearned to read the Bible for themselves.

One thing the Freedmen's Bureau did not do, however, was give the former slaves their own land. That was a shame, because with their own land, blacks would have had a chance to support themselves and become truly independent. As one former slave said, "All I want is to get to own 4 or 5 acres of land, that I can build me a little house on and call my home." Another said, "Give us our own land and we will take care of ourselves.

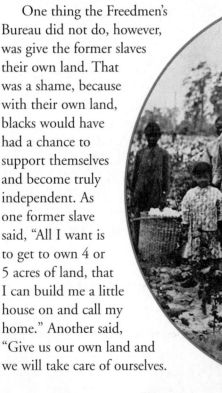

But without land, the old masters can hire us or starve us, as they please."

For a time, blacks were excited by a rumor that the government would give them 40 acres and a mule to get started in their new lives. However, that's all it was—a rumor. The only way to give land to the former slaves was to take it away from someone else, like the former slave owners. A few people in Congress were willing to do that, but most were not, and it did not happen.

Sharecropping

So most of the freed slaves continued to farm the lands of their former masters. However, a big problem had to be worked out first. When the Confederacy collapsed, all its money immediately became worthless. Southern banks also went out of business. Few Southerners had United States money. So owners of the land had no money to pay wages to their workers, and the freedmen who wanted to rent land had no money to pay for it. The problem was solved by developing a system called sharecropping.

Sharecropping worked this way: The owners let the freedmen use some of their land, gave them seed, and lent them plows, tools, and mules to work with. In return, the freedmen gave the owners a share of the crops they raised. Usually they split it half and half.

The sharecropping system was used all through the South. Nine out of ten former slave families became sharecroppers, and many poor white families did, too.

Many freed African Americans became sharecroppers on the land they had farmed as slaves.

Uniting the States For all its terrible cost in lives and money, the Civil War settled one thing for sure. No state, or any number of states, can secede from the Union. The union of states is permanent. However, a number of big questions remained.

What should be done with the states that had tried to leave the Union? Should they have to do anything to get back their full rights as states? If so, what? Should it be easy for them to return to normal statehood or should they be punished? Who had the right to decide these questions, the President or the Congress?

For President Lincoln the answers were simple. The reason for fighting the war in the first place was to preserve the Union. Therefore, the Union should be restored as quickly as possible. Of course, there were certain things the Southern states should have to do. One was that each state must ratify, or approve, the Thirteenth Amendment to the Constitution of the United States. That is the amendment that outlaws slavery. Once a state had done those things, it could write a new state constitution, elect a state government, and send representatives to Congress. It would be back in the Union, as though it had never tried to leave. Lincoln had meant what he said: "With malice toward none; with charity for all . . ." He wanted to "bind up the nation's wounds" as quickly as possible.

President Andrew Johnson

But now Lincoln was dead, and the new President was Andrew Johnson. Would Johnson have the same views as Lincoln? People looked to his background for clues as to where he might stand.

Johnson had grown up dirt poor in North Carolina and later made his living as a tailor in Greenville, Tennessee. Although he had never been to school, he taught himself the basics of

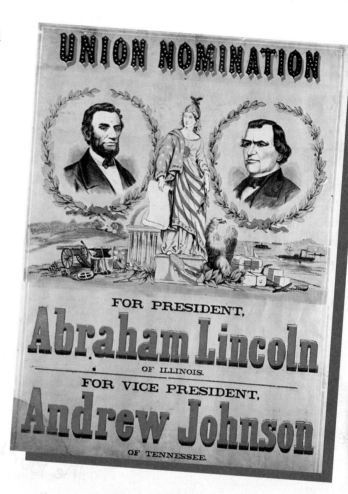

Andrew Johnson was the first Vice President to reach the presidency because of the assassination of the President.

reading and writing, and with the help of his wife, he became quite good at both.

His neighbors elected him to the Tennessee legislature, and he later served as governor, congressman, and senator from that state. Although Johnson had owned several slaves, he strongly disliked the wealthy slave-owning planters of the

South and had a strong sympathy for the common people.

Most importantly, Andrew Johnson was a strong believer in the Union. When Tennessee joined the Confederacy, Johnson refused to follow his state and remained in the United States Senate. He was the only Southern senator to do so. When President Lincoln ran for reelection in 1864, he chose Johnson to run for the vice presidency with him, even though Lincoln was a Republican and Johnson was a Democrat.

At first some of the congressmen who had opposed Lincoln's plan for restoring the Union thought that Johnson would side with them. "Johnson, we have faith in you," said one of those congressmen, "there'll be no trouble now."

Alexander Stephens, who had been vice president of the Confederacy, was one of several Confederate officials elected to the Congress immediately after the war.

However, these congressmen had guessed wrong. Johnson opposed slavery, but that was as far as it went. He believed that the Union should be restored quickly, and except for getting rid of slavery, he didn't think the South should be forced to make other major changes.

Johnson soon announced that he would follow Lincoln's plan, with a few changes. This plan to restore the Union quickly became known as Presidential Reconstruction. To reconstruct is to rebuild, or to restore. By the end of 1865, most of the Southern states had done what they were required to do and were ready to be restored to the Union. That took care of the matter, as far as President Johnson was concerned.

Congress and Radical Reconstruction

Not so far as Congress was concerned, however. They were having none of this Presidential Reconstruction business. To begin with, Congress demanded, who ever said it was up to the President to decide on Reconstruction? That should be the right of Congress, not of the President. There would be no reconstruction of the Union until *Congress* said so.

Further, Congress wanted Reconstruction to be much harder on the South than the President did. Who was it that tried to break up the Union in the first place, they asked? Who started the Civil War, anyway? Who is responsible for all the loss of life—275,000 Confederate soldiers and 350,000 Union soldiers? After all the pain they caused, Southern states should not be allowed back into the Union so easily, said Congress.

Besides, said some members of Congress, Southern states had shown no sign of regret at all about the war. Regret? Defiance was more like it. Just look at the men they had chosen to represent them in Congress. Four were Confederate generals, eight were colonels, and six had served in Jefferson Davis's Confederate cabinet. Georgia was even sending Alexander Stephens, the vice-president of the Confederacy, to the United States Senate! Why, these were some of the very people who had led the rebellion. And now they expect to be welcomed into the Congress and to share in making laws for the country!

Finally, said Congress, Southern states had shown that while they had to give up slavery, they had not changed their attitudes toward black people. Every one of the Southern states had passed laws, known as Black Codes, to keep black people down. One Southern state, for example, allowed blacks to work only on farms or as housekeepers. Another state said that blacks could not change jobs or travel from place to place. In one state they weren't allowed to own farmland. In another they weren't allowed to own a city lot.

If these states were allowed to return to the Union under the Presidential Reconstruction plan, said Congress, there would be no way to protect the rights of black people in the South.

Congress demanded a more radical plan for Reconstruction. *Radical* often means "extreme," but here it meant "getting to the root of the problem" by changing the laws of the South and the nation. Supporters of this view were known as Radical Republicans.

In December 1865, Congress blocked Presidential Reconstruction, and for the next year, Radical Republicans and President Johnson argued angrily over what to do about the South. In the spring of that year, Congress passed a Civil Rights Act. The purpose of this act was to protect the rights of the former slaves against the Black Codes. President Johnson vetoed it, but Congress passed it over the President's veto, and it became law.

The Radical Republicans then proposed one of the most important of all amendments to the Constitution, the Fourteenth Amendment. This is a long and complicated amendment, but it has a few main points. The amendment would make all former slaves citizens of the United States. (Remember Dred Scott? The Supreme Court had said that, as a black man and slave, Dred Scott could not be a citizen.) The amendment would also **prohibit** states from making any law that limits the rights of citizens of the United States— in other words, Southern states would not be allowed to limit the rights of black people. Also, the amendment would prohibit states from taking away a person's life, liberty, or property unfairly. And finally, it would require the states to treat all people equally under the law.

Radical Republicans said that this amendment would finally protect the former slaves. They said that **ratifying** it should be the price each Southern state must pay to reenter the Union. When one Southern state, Tennessee, did ratify the amendment, it was promptly readmitted to the Union.

President Johnson, though, was opposed to this amendment. He quietly told the other Southern states that once he won the struggle with Congress, they wouldn't have to ratify it. Those states took Johnson's advice and refused to ratify the amendment. It was a big mistake.

> **vocabulary**
> **prohibit** to forbid or prevent by law a particular action
> **ratify** to give formal approval to an amendment to the Constitution

When elections were held for Congress in 1866, many more Radical Republican candidates were voted into office. That finished Presidential Reconstruction. From then on, the Radicals made it clear that they would be in charge of making decisions about Reconstruction.

Who were these Radical Republicans? What did they believe? What did it mean to "get to the root of the problem"? What kind of plan did they have for restoring the Union?

Thaddeus Stevens

You can get a pretty good idea of what the Radical Republicans believed in by getting to know one of their leaders, Thaddeus Stevens. Thaddeus had grown up a poor boy in Vermont and had moved to Gettysburg, Pennsylvania, at 24. He became a very successful and wealthy lawyer, but he never lost his sympathy for the poor and the underdog. Some say that his own physical handicap (he had a clubfoot that caused him to limp badly) gave him this sympathy. Perhaps. But not everyone with a handicap devotes his life to helping the underdog.

Thaddeus Stevens felt the South should not be allowed back into the Union until black Southerners had the same rights as all American citizens.

Most of all, Stevens believed deeply in those words of Thomas Jefferson in the Declaration of Independence: "that all men are created equal," and that among their "unalienable rights" are "life, liberty, and the pursuit of happiness." Stevens lived his life by those words. He worked to get free public schools in Pennsylvania because he knew that education would help ordinary people in their "pursuit of happiness"—just as it had helped him.

The special goal of Thad Stevens's life, though, was to secure those unalienable rights for black Americans. He was an abolitionist, and he acted on his beliefs. He used his skills as a lawyer in behalf of fugitive slaves. Although he was part of a group that wrote a new constitution for the state of Pennsylvania in 1838, he refused to sign it because it did not give the right to vote to the state's black population.

So you see, Thad Stevens, Radical Republican, was no Johnny-come-lately to the cause of equal rights for black Americans. He believed, as did the other Radical Republicans in Congress, that Reconstruction would be a failure unless it raised black Southerners to equality with whites. Were the ex-slaves uneducated? Then give them schools. Did they have to depend completely on their old masters for work and do the master's bidding, as in slave days? Then give them land—40 acres and a mule. Did Southern whites deny them their rights—the right to vote, the right to be elected to office, the right to testify in court, and the right to do a hundred other things that white Southerners could do? Then make the Southern states guarantee those rights in their new state constitutions, and don't let them back into the Union until they do. And at the same time, put those rights into the United States Constitution, where they would be beyond the reach of Southerners who wanted to take them away.

Those were the ideas that Thad Stevens and the Radical Republicans held. And those were the ideas at the heart of Congressional Reconstruction. Those, and a desire to punish Southerners who had supported the rebellion against the United States.

In spring of 1867 the Congress of the United States, with the Radical Republicans in control, passed its plan for Reconstruction. Congressional Reconstruction, as it was called, began by turning the clock back to the end of the Civil War. Throw out everything done under Presidential Reconstruction—the new state constitutions, the new state governments and all the laws they had passed (including the Black Codes), the election of representatives to Congress—all of them. Congressional Reconstruction would start all over again. And, the Radicals said, this time we will do it right.

Under Congressional Reconstruction, the United States Army was to be in charge of the South until the Southern states were allowed back in the Union. And before they could get back in,

they would have to do many things. They would have to write new state constitutions again, but this time black people as well as whites must take part in writing them. They would elect new state governments again, but this time black people would be allowed to vote and to hold office. They would enjoy the same rights that whites had.

People who had supported the rebellion against the United States—that included the hundreds of thousands who served in the Confederate armies—were not allowed to take part in any of these activities. They were to have no say in writing their state's constitution, and they could neither vote nor hold office. After a state adopted its new constitution and elected a new government, it must ratify the Fourteenth Amendment to the United States Constitution.

When a state had done all these things, then and only then would it be received back into the Union. And then and only then would the United States troops leave that state.

That, said the Radical Republicans, is our plan for Reconstruction. That is what we insist the South must do. And woe be to anyone who tries to stand in our way.

The "anyone" the Radicals had in mind was President Andrew Johnson. They knew Johnson disagreed with their goals. They remembered that just the year before, he had advised the Southern states not to ratify the Fourteenth Amendment. Once, the President had told a white audience, "This is a country of white men, and by God, as long as I am President, it shall be a government for white men." During the last election campaign for Congress, Johnson had made the Radicals sound like the worst villains in the world.

African Americans voted in state elections for the first time during Reconstruction.

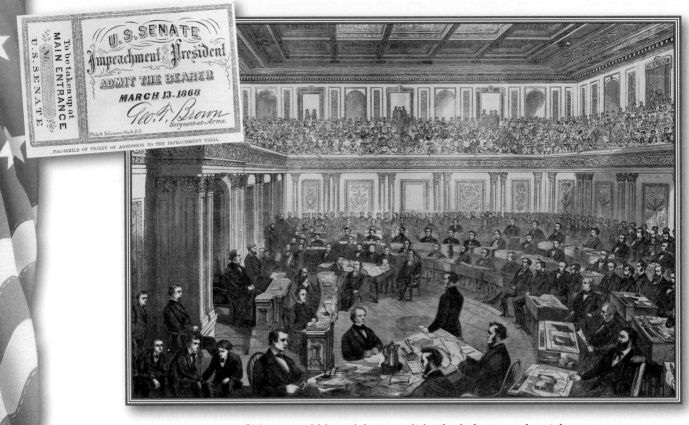

Citizens could buy tickets to sit in the balcony and watch the impeachment trial of President Johnson.

The Impeachment of President Johnson

No, the Radicals did not trust Johnson. They believed he would ruin their program if he could. So they passed several laws to limit the powers of the President.

President Johnson believed those laws were unconstitutional. He decided to ignore them. That is, he purposely violated them. When he did that, the House of Representatives voted to impeach him. To *impeach* means to "put an officeholder on trial for wrongdoing." It's a way of getting rid of an officeholder before his term is over, if that officeholder has committed some serious offense. Under our Constitution it is the job of the House of Representatives to impeach a President who is thought to be guilty of serious wrongdoing. If the House votes to impeach— that is, to bring charges against—the President, then he is put on trial before the Senate of the United States. Then, if two thirds of the senators find the President guilty of the charges brought against him, he is removed from office.

Some Radical Republicans like Thaddeus Stevens had been wanting to impeach Johnson for a long time. But they couldn't impeach the President just because they didn't like his proposals. They needed a better reason than that. Now that Johnson had ignored the laws, they had one.

The impeachment and trial of President Johnson lasted for two months in early 1868, and while it lasted, it was the best show in town. The government printed tickets of admission, and people fell all over each other to get them. To no one's surprise, the House voted to impeach the President. The case then moved on to the Senate. There, it would take 36 senators to vote "guilty as charged" in order to reach the two thirds needed to remove Johnson from office. The vote was close, extremely close. But the final count was 35 in favor of guilty, 19 in favor of not guilty—one vote short of the number needed to remove the President from office. So by that slim margin, Andrew Johnson was able to finish his term.

New Governments Even though President Johnson escaped removal from office, he was powerless to stop Congressional Reconstruction. All over the defeated South, Southerners—this time black Southerners as well as white—began the job of writing new constitutions, holding elections, and starting up their state governments again. It took several years.

Congressional Reconstruction led to big changes in the South. In each of the former Confederate states, blacks were elected to serve in their state legislatures. In a few states, blacks were elected to higher offices, like lieutenant governor. Several African Americans were elected to serve in the United States House of Representatives and the United States Senate.

Half of these black officials had been free persons before the war. Some of them were well-educated Northerners who had moved to the South after the war ended. But about half of them had been slaves only a few years before. What an amazing turnaround that was!

Even though there were many black officials and lawmakers, don't think that African Americans actually controlled these Southern states. They didn't. Even under Congressional Reconstruction, most officeholders in the South continued to be whites.

Some of the white lawmakers and officials in the new Southern governments actually were Northerners who had gone south after the war. They went south for various reasons: to start farms or businesses, to help the freedmen as teachers and ministers, or just to see if they could make money from the South's troubles.

During Reconstruction, African Americans served as members of Congress for the first time.

The woman in this cartoon is a symbol of the South, which is being crushed by the carpetbagger who is protected by soldiers.

White Southerners hated these Northern whites. They had an insulting name for them. They called them carpetbaggers. A carpetbag is a cheap suitcase—a bag, really—made of pieces of carpet. Southerners said these people came to the South with all their belongings in a carpetbag, which they hoped to fill with riches.

Most whites in the new governments, though, were people who had lived in the South all their lives. Some had never been in favor of secession. Some were business leaders. A good number were poor whites who were getting their first chance to gain power over the big planters who ruled the South for so many years. All of them thought the South would be better off if it changed some of its old ways.

Southerners who wanted to stick with the old ways had an insulting name for these people. They called them scalawags. That was the name Southerners gave to small, worthless farm animals.

The insults didn't matter. Serving together, the black and white officials brought many improvements to their states. They rebuilt roads, railroads, and buildings that had been destroyed during the war, and they helped the Southern economy to recover little by little. Perhaps any Southern government would have done that. But they also built hospitals and orphanages.

Probably most important, they started the first public school system in the South. There had been a few public schools in the South before the Civil War, but not many. In several of the Southern states, there were no public schools at all before the war. Now, in South Carolina alone, 120,000 children went to public schools.

These black and white officeholders, acting together, did one more thing, too. They ratified another amendment to the United States Constitution. This was the Fifteenth Amendment. The Fifteenth Amendment says that no state can keep a person from voting because of his race or color. However, the Fifteenth Amendment did not give either black or white women the right to vote. They did not get the right to vote until many years later.

Radical Republicans never reached their goal of full equality for black Americans, as you will see. For many years, those who wanted to keep African Americans from voting found ways to get around the Fifteenth Amendment. But the Radical Republicans made an important start. The journey to reaching the goal of equal rights for all would be long and difficult, and even today it is not yet finished. But we are much closer to reaching it today than ever before. And all Americans owe a debt of gratitude to the Radical Republicans for having started us on that road.

The End of Reconstruction

Congressional Reconstruction lasted for only a few years because most white Southerners hated the new state governments. They felt these governments had been forced upon them against their will.

They were outraged that people who were once their slaves were now voting and holding office and making laws. They opposed paying taxes for public schools that would educate black children—even though those schools were educating their own children. They just couldn't accept the idea of a society in which white and black people had equal rights.

Southerners who felt this way were determined to win back control of their states and put an end to these changes. A number of them formed secret societies such as the Ku Klux Klan. Wearing white sheets and hoods, members of the Ku Klux Klan rode through the countryside on horseback, spreading terror. They beat up black people to "keep them in their place" and to warn them not to vote. They whipped white people who were friendly with blacks. Sometimes they burned schools and churches and homes and barns. And they killed a number of people. Other secret groups sprang up with the same goal of restoring "white supremacy"—which is the racist idea that whites should rule and be supreme over nonwhite groups in society.

Finally, the federal government sent troops to stop the Ku Klux Klan and other secret groups like it. The government was successful, and the Klan almost disappeared. No one at that time

The Ku Klux Klan and other white supremacist groups worked to deny African Americans their rights by any possible means.

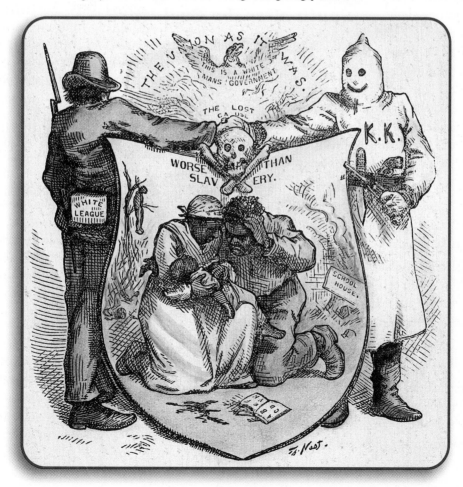

knew that it would appear again more than 30 years later, preaching its message of hatred against even more groups of Americans. The Klan is with us still.

Putting an end to the Klan, though, did not mean putting an end to white resistance to Congressional Reconstruction. Southerners formed other groups—not secret societies but societies that operated right out in the open—to keep blacks from voting. They warned that blacks who voted would lose their jobs and not be able to buy goods on credit in the farm stores. They also threatened violence.

On election days a few white thugs with rifles hanging around the voting places sent a message to black voters: Go ahead and vote, if you are ready to risk your life.

Those who wanted to get rid of the Reconstruction governments in the South finally succeeded in doing so. People in the North had their own concerns. They were growing weary of hearing about the trouble in the South and of being asked to do something about it. Strong leaders like Thaddeus Stevens were gone. After a few years the United States government gave back the vote to those who had served in the Confederate army. At the same time, white Southerners continued to use threats and violence to keep blacks from voting.

You can figure out what happened. In one Southern state after another, carpetbaggers, scalawags, and blacks were voted out of office. They were replaced by whites who wanted to return to the old ways. In 1877 the United States government removed the last troops from the South. With that, Reconstruction was over.

Over the next 20 years, black Americans in the South lost nearly every right they had won during Reconstruction. During the days of slavery, there had never been a question about black people—even free blacks—mixing with whites. That had changed during the short time of Reconstruction. But with Reconstruction over, states passed segregation laws. These are laws that require the separation of white and black people from each other. Black people could no longer use the same restaurants, hotels, streetcars, theaters, and other public places that whites used. Or if they could, they had to sit in separate sections. These laws were known as Jim Crow laws. Segregation was practiced in much of the North, too, even though few Northern states had Jim Crow laws.

The end of Reconstruction also marked the end of fair trials of black persons in the courts. And although the Fifteenth Amendment said that no state could deny persons the right to vote on account of their race or color, Southern states found ways to get around that. They passed laws that made it nearly impossible for blacks to vote. One such law required everyone who wanted to vote to pay a tax of two dollars. This kind of tax is called a poll tax. For many poor blacks, and for poor whites, too, a two-dollar poll tax was nearly one week's wages!

Another law said that in order to vote, people had to pass a test to prove they could read and understand the state's constitution. It was up to a local official to decide who passed the test and who didn't, and that local official was a white man who was determined to keep blacks from voting. So no matter how well a black person could read, he often was not allowed to pass the test. When a white person couldn't read, he was usually allowed to vote anyway.

And for any black person still thinking about casting a vote, there remained the threat of violence or of losing one's job. Before long there were few black voters in the South and no black officeholders.

Black Americans would have to wait many more years before they would really enjoy the equal rights that the Declaration of Independence and the Fourteenth and Fifteenth Amendments to the Constitution promised them.

A Date to Remember: The reconstruction of the South after the Civil War ended in 1877.

abolitionist a person opposed to slavery and in favor of ending it right away

arsenal a building where weapons are stored

blockade a military strategy that aims to cut off supplies going in and out of an area

compromise a settlement of differences between two or more sides reached by each side giving up some of what it wanted

draft a system of selecting individuals from a group for compulsory military service

fugitive one who flees or tries to escape

prohibit to forbid or prevent by law a particular action

racist one who believes that racial differences prove that a certain race is superior to others

ratify to give formal approval to an amendment to the Constitution

rural having to do with the countryside and agriculture

secede to withdraw formally from an organization or a nation

strategy the overall military plan for defeating an enemy or winning a conflict

tactic a method of using forces in combat

urban having to do with cities or towns

Westward Expansion
After the Civil War

Contents

Gold Fever In 1858 the North and the South were moving closer and closer to war. But tens of thousands of people had other things on their minds. These were the people who had gone to California after gold was discovered there. They talked of nothing but gold, gold, gold. They dreamed of becoming fabulously rich.

Most of the eager gold-seekers found nothing but disappointment in California. Then, in the summer of 1858, came news that gold had been found near Pikes Peak, in present-day Colorado. In less than a year, about 100,000 people, most of them from California, rushed into the Rocky Mountains, many of them crying out "Pikes Peak or Bust!"

"Pikes Peak and Bust" would have been more accurate. It turned out that there was actually little gold or silver there, and what little there was had been quickly mined out before most of the newcomers arrived.

This item is reproduced by permission of The Huntington Library, San Marino, California.

Omaha, Nebraska, was a starting point for travelers going to Pikes Peak.

Among the disappointed miners at Pikes Peak were two Irish **immigrants,** Pete O'Reilly and Pat McLaughlin. The next year, 1859, these two fortune hunters moved on to the Sierra Nevada Mountains in present-day Nevada. There they staked a claim to land in a place called Six Mile Canyon. A man named Henry Comstock talked the two immigrants into letting him become their partner.

One day Pete O'Reilly and Pat McLaughlin dug up a chunk of heavy, blue rock. They had never seen anything like it before, so they showed the rock to a couple of rich Californians. The Californians, who knew something about mining, quickly realized that this rock was silver ore. That's not what they told O'Reilly, McLaughlin, and Comstock, though. Instead, they just offered to buy the land that the rock had come from for a few thousand dollars. Comstock told his immigrant partners to let him deal with these fellows. With his experience, he assured them, he'd get a lot more than a few thousand out of those rich Californians. And he did. The final price was $11,000. Split three ways, that came to nearly $3,700 each. Later on, Comstock bragged to everyone about the terrific deal he had made. But, as it turned out, the joke was on him.

In the next 20 years, that piece of land the three partners sold for $11,000, and the area around it, produced $500 million worth of silver and gold for its owners! The rich silver deposit was named the Comstock Lode, after the partner who had made the deal. Probably, though, had Henry Comstock been given the choice, he would rather have had the money than the fame.

As was always the case, news of the find traveled quickly, and thousands of miners rushed to the region. And as was always the case, hardly a dozen of them became rich. The others soon found that most of the silver ore in Six Mile Canyon was too deep in the ground to dig out with simple pickaxes and shovels. It took large mining companies with expensive machinery to do that. Before long, most of the miners who had gone to Six Mile Canyon to seek their fortunes were working for such mining companies.

Mining Towns

And so it went all through the West—in present-day Nevada, Colorado, Idaho, Arizona, Montana, and Wyoming. The last great gold rush of the mining frontier was in the Black Hills of present-day South Dakota in 1874. Some of these finds, like the one at Pikes Peak, yielded little gold or silver. Others, like the Comstock Lode, produced incredible riches. Whenever a "strike" was reported or even rumored, hundreds of miners rushed to stake claims to the land. Mining camps sprang up on every nearby hillside. These camps brought together people from many places and from all walks of life. There were farmers and city people, poor workers and the sons of rich families, southern whites and northern blacks, native-born Americans and newly-arrived immigrants. The one thing they had in common was the dream of instant wealth.

Some did not care how they got it. One person wrote that in the mining camps, "hordes of pickpockets, robbers, thieves, and swindlers were mixed with men who had come with honest intentions." Daring thefts and cold-blooded murders were a common part of life in these unruly camps. There were no laws or police in the mining camps to deal with outlaws and thieves, so honest miners made their own laws and formed committees to enforce them. This system of justice came to be known as "vigilante justice" or "frontier justice." It was often very harsh. Those declared guilty of crimes were likely to be hanged. Sometimes they didn't even get a trial.

Most mining camps remained a collection of tents on a hillside. But a big strike could turn a

Helena, Montana, shown here in 1865, later became the capital of the state.

mining camp into a booming town in no time at all. Within days, merchants would arrive and put up a string of wooden stores along a main street to sell tools, clothing, and food to the miners. A good many of them became far richer than their customers. Every mining town had its gambling houses and saloons. In time, a number of them also had banks, hotels, newspaper offices, and even theaters. The mining frontier was mostly a male world, but there were also women who ran small hotels, boarding houses, and laundries.

The richest of these western mining towns was Virginia City, in Nevada. Samuel Clemens, who would later become known to the world as the great American writer Mark Twain, was at that time a young newspaper reporter living in Virginia City. This is how he described life in that boom town: The sidewalks swarmed with people. . . . The streets themselves were just as crowded with . . . wagons, freight teams, and other vehicles. . . . Money was as plenty as dust. . . . There were . . . fire companies, brass bands, banks,

hotels, theaters, . . . wide open gambling places, . . . street fights, murders, . . . riots, a whiskey mill every fifteen steps.

Settling the Mining Frontier

Some mining towns grew into lasting cities. Last Chance Gulch, for example, became the city of Helena, Montana. But most blazed brightly for a short time and then, like comets in the sky, were gone. For when the gold or silver was mined out, the miners moved on. Empty buildings gathered dust, and the towns became the ghost towns of the West.

Still, the mining frontier brought people to the West. And while most miners did move on, some stayed. So did many of the men and women who ran the stores, farmed the land, raised cattle, and started schools and churches. They raised families and built up the country. Remember those thousands who headed for Pikes Peak, only to find no gold there? Many found work in the nearby town of Denver and helped to build up that town. In that way, mining helped to settle the present-day states of Colorado, Nevada, Montana, Idaho, Washington, and South Dakota.

The whole mining frontier lasted for only about 25 years, from the great gold rush in California in 1849 until the strike in South Dakota in 1874. There was still plenty of gold and silver in the West, but it lay deep below the earth's surface, where only the expensive machinery of the big mining companies could get it. By the 1880s the lone prospector—the person with a pickaxe, shovel, and pack mule—could still be seen wandering the West in search of that one lucky strike, but his day had passed. And the rowdy, get-rich-quick days of the mining frontier had passed as well.

This man is "panning" for gold, trying to separate gold dust from rocks and pebbles.

Hard Work Imagine cutting through solid rock with only a hammer and a chisel. Now picture digging a tunnel through a mountain that way. Imagine carrying heavy pieces of wood and iron rails all day in temperatures over 100 degrees. Or in temperatures below 0 degrees.

In the 1860s, thousands of men did just those things, and more, in building the nation's first transcontinental railroad—the first railroad to connect the Atlantic and the Pacific coasts of America.

Soon after the Civil War started, Congress passed a law to build this transcontinental railroad. At the time, railroads already reached as far west as Omaha, Nebraska, so the new line would only have to go from there to the Pacific coast. *Only* was still a distance of 1,800 miles—longer than any railroad line ever built!

Congress named two companies to construct this railroad line. One, called the Union Pacific Railroad Company, would build westward from Omaha. The other, called the Central Pacific, would build eastward from Sacramento, California. The two would connect somewhere in between.

To help these companies, the United States government gave each company a gift of 10 square miles of land alongside each mile of track they built. The idea was that once the railroad was built, that land would become valuable and the railroad could sell it. The government also lent each company money to help pay for the construction. With that kind of encouragement, each company raced to put down as many miles of track as it could.

Spanning the Continent

The transcontinental railroad was the grandest construction project of the age. In size and in difficulty, it dwarfed any other building project of that time. The two companies employed more than 20,000 people to build the railroad. No other organization, except the army, had ever brought together so many people to work on one project. No

Horse-drawn carts carry away earth dug up by construction crews in the long, slow process of building a railroad.

other single railroad project had even come close to building a line 1,800 miles long. No other project had to face a task as difficult as building over, around, and through tall mountains. Just getting together all the necessary supplies to get started was a major job in itself. For example, no one in California manufactured iron rails or locomotives. That meant the Central Pacific company, which was starting from California, had to get nearly all its supplies from the East by sea—an 18,000-mile voyage that took at least six months. The men had to do their work in all weather. One winter there were 44 storms. Most of the workers on the Central Pacific were Chinese immigrants. They had come to California hoping to find riches in the gold fields. Now they did the backbreaking and dangerous work of laying railroad tracks through the Sierra Nevada Mountains. The head of the Central Pacific Railroad Company said, "Without them it would be impossible to complete the line on time."

At first, working in gangs of 30 each, they labored 12 hours a day, 6 days a week. They chopped trees and cut them into **railroad ties.** They built railroad bridges. Hardest of all, they dug through mountains. Remember, this was before the days of steam shovels, bulldozers, giant cranes, and drilling machines. Workers had only hammers, chisels, pickaxes, shovels, and wheelbarrows. Only after reaching flatter land on the other side of the mountains did the work get any easier.

At first, workers on the Union Pacific line were mainly Irish immigrants, but the railroad company also hired Mexican Americans, African Americans, and Native Americans. After the Civil War ended in 1865, army veterans from both the North and

the South joined the work crews. While these workers also had to lay track across some mountains, most of their building stretched across the Great Plains. Laying track across flat prairie land was certainly easier than cutting through mountains, but it had its own difficulties. Winter temperatures on the plains can be brutally cold, with winds that feel like they can cut right through you. Just to stay alive, the shivering men sometimes had to use precious railroad ties to build bonfires. In addition, the Union Pacific was building on lands that for centuries had been home to Native American tribes. The farther onto those lands the railroad pushed, the greater the danger of attack by Native American warriors. After a number of such attacks, the railroad company called on the army to protect its work crews. Most of the railroad, in fact, had to be built under military protection.

Driving the Golden Spike

Year after year, under blazing summer sun and in below-zero winter cold, the work went forward. Finally, on May 10, 1869, the two lines met at

Chinese workers used simple tools to build trestles like this through the western mountains.

Promontory Point, Utah. Leland Stanford, Jr., president of the Central Pacific, was given the honor of driving the final spike into the last railroad tie. To celebrate the occasion, the spike was made of gold.

Success at last! The two railroads met at Promontory Point and opened the West to more settlement.

With each swing of Stanford's hammer, the telegraph flashed the news to a waiting nation: "One, two, three—done!" and cheers rang out all over America. (To be accurate, the telegraph message should have been, "one, two, three, *four*—done!" On his first swing, Stanford had missed everything. You can imagine the howls of laughter from the working crews who were watching the ceremony.)

Four more transcontinental railroads were built in the next 25 years, two farther north and two farther south of the first one. From one coast to another, gleaming ribbons of track now tied the nation together.

Railroads Help Develop the West

The new transcontinental railroads helped to open the West to more and more settlement. It's easy to understand why. Before the railroads there were only three routes you could take to reach California from the East. Two were by sea, either going all the way around the tip of South America or going as far as Panama, cutting across through the jungle, and then taking a ship north. The third was by railroad to Omaha, and then by wagon, horseback, or on foot across the plains and through the mountain passes. Each of these trips could take about half a year. However, after the golden spike was driven into the track in Utah that day in May 1869, you could make the trip from Omaha to San Francisco, California, *in less than four days!*

Also, the railroad companies did everything they could to encourage people to move west. The more people who did, the more tickets the companies sold. More settlers meant more crops, and that meant more business for the railroads that carried the crops to the East. Railroads advertised, telling of the inexpensive land people could get in the West. They even advertised in many of the port cities in Europe.

Railroads also helped cities to grow. News that a railroad company was going to build its line through a town brought cheers from the townspeople. It's not hard to understand why. Railroads brought prosperity. Farmers from nearby areas needed to rent storage space while waiting to load their grain onto railroad cars. Cattle ranchers bringing their animals to town for shipment to market needed to buy feed. Passengers spending the night needed restaurants to eat in and hotels to sleep in. New jobs were created in countless ways.

Towns where two or more railroad lines met and crossed became especially prosperous. That's why many a town did all it could to persuade a railroad company to choose it for one of these crossing points. For example, one railroad company had to choose between Kansas City, Missouri, and Fort Leavenworth, Kansas, two towns of about the same size. The railroad company chose Kansas City. In the 30 years that followed, Kansas City became a large city, while Fort Leavenworth remained a small town. Chicago was already a growing city when it became the chief railroad center in the nation. After that, Chicago increased greatly in size and became the country's second largest city.

ature's Gift Even before that historic joining at Promontory Point, large numbers of Americans had already been drawn to the West. Some, as you read earlier, were lured there by the hope of finding scarce gold and silver. Others hoped to become rich from something far more ordinary, something found wherever you looked on the western plains.

That something was grass—millions and millions of acres of it. In the end, many more people became rich from ordinary grass than from precious gold. For it was grass that made possible the rise of a great cattle industry in the West. The story of that industry begins nearly 300 years earlier, when a ship from Spain arrived in Mexico with a few head of cattle. Unlike in Spain, where they had been fenced in, the cattle in Mexico were allowed to roam freely, finding their own grass and water. Over the centuries that followed, the cattle wandered into northern Mexico and southwestern Texas.

And they multiplied. By 1860 there were about 5 million head in just one small corner of Texas, between the Rio Grande and the town of San Antonio. Because the horns could be as much as 7 feet across, the cattle came to be called longhorns.

These longhorns belonged to no one. They were anyone's for the taking. Yet few bothered to do so. They were so numerous that no one in Texas would pay more than $3 or $4 a head for them. That was hardly enough to pay the cost of rounding them up and keeping them on a ranch.

The market for Texas longhorn cattle was in the East.

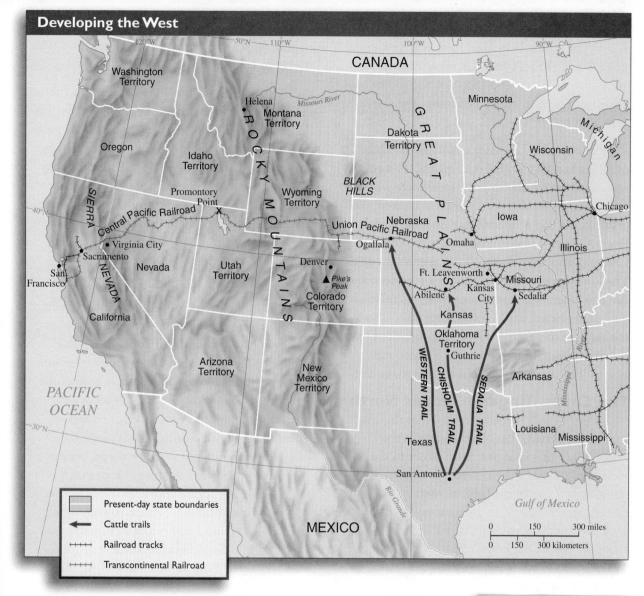

Texans knew there was a profitable market for beef, but it was in the far-off cities of the East. And they knew that if they could just find a way to get their cattle there, they could easily get $30 or $40 a head.

The obvious solution to their problem was the railroad. But there was no railroad line between southern Texas and the East, and it might be many years before one would be built. Until then the nearest railroad connecting to the East was in Sedalia, Missouri, a good thousand miles away.

Soon after the end of the Civil War, several clever ranchers figured it out: if they couldn't bring the railroad to the cattle, maybe they could bring the cattle to the railroad. They could herd the cattle to Sedalia, letting them **graze** on grass as they went. It would take maybe three months to get

there, and no one knew what problems might occur along the way. But if they succeeded, they would make a fortune.

The Long Drive

From this bright idea sprang the "long drive." In spring 1866, ranchers brought their herds together and set out for Sedalia. Unfortunately for them, they chose a poor route. Much of the trail led through wooded areas where it was difficult to control the herd. Parts of the trail crossed fenced-in farms, and other parts ran through Indian territory. At times heavy rains turned the trail into mud. Most of the 260,000 cattle that

> **vocabulary**
> **graze** to feed on the natural grass or plants of an open area, as cattle graze on the range

started out on the long drive died or were lost or stolen along the way. Still, for every animal that made it to Sedalia, the owners got $35. They knew right then that they had found the way to their fortune.

The next year Texas cattle ranchers chose a route farther west, on the open plains. This route was called the Chisholm Trail. Here there were no trees or farms or mud—only endless acres of grass. At the end of the trail lay Abilene, Kansas. From Abilene, a new railroad line ran directly to Chicago. This time nearly all the animals made it. The long drive to Abilene was a huge success, and Abilene became the first "cow town." As railroads pushed westward, cattle ranchers set out on trails farther west to new cow towns that rose up. Over the years about 10 million cattle plodded their way to these towns from Texas for shipment east.

The Cattle Kingdom Moves North

In time, cattle ranchers learned that the animals could survive the colder winters farther north. Since that land was much closer to the railroad line, and since the United States government, which owned the land, allowed cattle to graze for free, many ranchers took their herds north. This saved them the cost of the long drive. Soon the cattle kingdom stretched from Texas northward to Montana and from Kansas westward to the Rocky Mountains. For a time, cattle ranchers made huge fortunes. But the good times did not last. For one thing, the cattle ranchers soon faced competition from sheep herders for the use of the free grass. Sheep nibble grass close to the roots, leaving little or nothing for cattle. Bitter warfare between cattle ranchers and sheep herders often flared up.

The work was hard, and most cowboys were young men.

Then, as you will read in the next lesson, farmers began to arrive on the open range in large numbers, plowing up the land and fencing it off. Cattle ranchers added to their own problems by increasing the size of their herds too much. They raised more cattle than the buyers wanted. Prices began to fall.

Nature delivered the final blow in the 1880s. Two terrible winters and a hot, dry summer that killed grass and dried up streams destroyed more than 80 percent of the cattle. After that, ranchers saw they could no longer depend so completely on the grass of the open range to feed their herds. So they fenced in their cattle and raised enough feed to take care of them through the winter.

The Cowboy

The cattle kingdom gave America its most colorful character, the cowboy. And not just America, for there is probably no country where the American cowboy is not known, and where children have never played at being cowboys. And who has never seen a movie or a television show about cowboys? Oddly, if cowboys of the 1870s could see most of these TV shows or commercials, they would probably not recognize themselves. For one thing, nearly all cowboys on TV are white Americans. In fact, one in every three or four cowboys was Mexican. (It was the Mexican *vaquero,* or cowboy, who taught the American cowboy all his skills, from riding to roping.) And of the American cowboys, a good number were African Americans who had left the South after the Civil War, and others were Native Americans. For another thing, TV cowboys are usually grown men. In real life, most were young, and a great many were still in their teens. By the time most cowboys reached the age of 30, they had sold their saddles and turned to other work.

Also, the real cowboy did not lead a life of constant excitement and adventure. The picture of the cowboy with two guns slung low on his hips, chasing outlaws or rescuing women in distress, is mainly fiction. Few cowboys carried even one six-shooter, let alone two. At most, a few of them carried rifles in their saddle bags for hunting. The real cowboy's job was pretty much what the name says it was: to herd cows. His life was mainly one of dull routine. He was a hired hand, not the independent hero who rode where he wished and did what he wanted. For eight or nine months of the year, what he mainly did was "ride the line" between his boss's ranch and the neighbor's, trying to keep his cattle from wandering away.

Twice a year, cowboys from all the ranches joined in a cattle roundup. In the spring they branded newborn calves with the owner's special mark. After that the animals were allowed to graze once again on the open plains. In the fall, cowboys separated those cattle ready for market from the rest of the herd.

Working on the Long Drive

Then came the hardest part of the cowboy's work—the long drive. For two or three months, seven days a week, in all kinds of weather, cowboys spent up to 18 hours a day in the saddle, riding alongside, behind, and ahead of the herd. Only mealtimes broke up their long, weary days. Sitting cross-legged on the ground, they ate the same boring food day after day. At night they bedded down on the hard prairie, with their saddles for pillows.

The cowboy's greatest worry was a cattle stampede. Lightning, thunder, even a tiny sound like a small animal moving in the brush or a cowboy striking a match could frighten and set off the cattle. Then, for a few terrifying hours, the

cowboy had all the adventure he could handle. The trick to ending the stampede was to force the animals to run in a wide circle until they tired and calmed down. All of this, often took place in the dark of night, perhaps with neither moon nor stars to help the rider see the ground ahead of him. It was dangerous work, and if the cowboy did not do it skillfully, he could lose his life.

Little wonder, then, that when cowboys arrived at the end of the trail, they were ready to blow off steam. They gambled, they drank whiskey, and they got into fights. Unwisely for them, some of these fights were gunfights. Many a cowboy went to an early grave because he thought he was as skillful at gunslinging as he was at herding cattle.

Like the mining frontier, the great age of the cowboy lasted only about 25 years, from the late 1860s to 1890. By then, as you will read in the next lesson, farmers had taken up much of the land on the plains. Also, when the cattle kingdom moved north, there was no longer any need for the long drive. Many ranches were hardly a day's drive from the railroads. Finally, following the terrible winters that led ranchers to move their herds off the open range, there were no more spring and fall roundups, either.

With these changes, the cowboy of old passed from the scene. He now became simply a ranch hand, who spent more time digging holes for fence posts than riding horseback and herding cattle.

Having a hot meal was important to a cowboy on a cattle drive.

The Great Plains For America's first 200 years, the country's frontier had moved steadily westward as settlers opened up fresh land for farming. Then, around the 1840s, it suddenly stopped. Farm families were no longer willing to move on to the next land closest to the frontier. To understand why, you'll need to know something about the geography of the United States.

Stretching 1,500 miles across the middle of our country is a plain, or flat area. Standing at almost any point on this plain, one can see straight out to the horizon, where sky and land seem to meet without a single rise in the land to interrupt the view.

This vast plain has two major parts. The first, called the Interior Lowlands, lies between the Appalachian Mountains and roughly 100 degrees west longitude, which passes through North Dakota, South Dakota, and Nebraska. This area receives 30 to 40 inches of **precipitation** a year. Together with its rich soil, this made it perfect for farming. The second part of this plain, running from 100 degrees west longitude to the Rocky Mountains, is called the Great Plains. Winters on the Great Plains are very cold, and summers are very hot. Here, precipitation drops sharply, to as little as 10 or 15 inches a year. In some years the Great Plains receive far less. As a result, even though the soil is rich, there are almost no trees on the Great Plains. Maps of the 1840s called this part of the plains the Great American Desert.

Farm families considering a move to the Great Plains took one look at the short grass turning brown in the summer sun and decided that this was no place for them. That is why, in the 1840s, the tide of western settlement leaped nearly 2,000 miles

across the Great Plains all the way to Oregon. Beginning in the late 1860s, however, Americans and European immigrants swarmed onto the Great Plains and started farms. So many were there that in the 20 years between 1870 and 1890, farmers opened up more land for farming than the size of England and France combined.

Why did farmers change their minds about living on the Great Plains? The main reason was a change in the weather pattern. For eight years in a row, the Great Plains received higher than normal rainfall. Many believed that this must be a permanent change in the climate. (They were wrong, but they did not find that out until some years later.)

> **vocabulary**
> **precipitation**
> moisture that falls to earth in the form of rain, snow, sleet, or hail

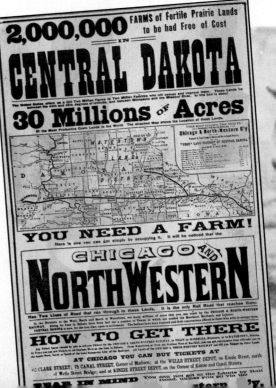

Posters such as this one lured many settlers to the Great Plains.

At the same time, great land bargains became available. Some of these bargains were offered by the railroads. Remember that the United States government gave railroads a large amount of land as a gift to encourage them to build in the West? The railroads were now offering to sell this land to farmers at low prices. All over the United States, and in Europe too, railroads advertised on posters with letters so large they practically shouted to the reader: "MILLIONS OF ACRES—IOWA AND NEBRASKA LANDS FOR SALE ON 10 YEARS CREDIT." To make the offer even more attractive, the railroad invited you to come out West and have a look at the land yourself. If you decided to buy within 30 days of your purchase of a ticket, the railroad would fully refund your fare. You can see why the railroad would offer this deal. It would make money two ways. One, it would get money right away from the buyers, and two, it would make money later on when the buyers started farms and used the railroad to ship their crops to market.

An even bigger land bargain was offered by the federal government. In 1862, Congress passed the Homestead Act. This law gave 160 acres of land free to anyone who would settle on it and farm for five years. Not only Americans but also immigrants were able to receive homesteads. In Europe many farm families were eking out a living on only three or four acres of worn-out land. Here was an opportunity to get fresh land, and 160 acres of it. What a country this America was!

In the next 40 years, the United States gave away 80 million acres of land under the Homestead Act. That was about a half million farms! One aim of the Homestead Act was to help poor people to start family farms. However, even with free land, a really poor family could not afford all the other costs of starting a farm, such as fencing, plows, animals, a barn, and seed. Therefore, most people who "homesteaded" on the plains were people who already were farmers and had saved some money.

Still, some poor people did manage to homestead. Among them was a group of African Americans from the former slave states of the South. Thousands of these former slaves gathered their belongings and set out for Kansas. Using a term from the Bible, they called themselves Exodusters, because they were making an Exodus, or departure, from their homes.

After the Civil War, African American families also went west to settle on the Great Plains.

Hard Life Farm families settling on the Great Plains found a climate and land different from anything they had known in the East or in Europe. Temperatures in the summer went as high as 110 degrees; in the winter they often fell below 0. Strong winds swept across the treeless plains.

Settlers were used to building log cabins and heating them with wood fires, but without trees, that was impossible. Yet families managed. With little wood or stone available, they built houses of sod, which is the top layer of grassy soil, complete with its tangled roots. On the sunbaked plains this sod was almost as hard as rock. After a rain or melting snow softened it, farmers cut it into long, flat bricks and made walls by piling the bricks one upon another, two to three rows thick. The roof was made of what little wood they could find, with another layer of sod piled on that. Sod houses were surprisingly tight. The thick walls kept the inside warm in winter and cool in summer. Better-off farmers even had glass windows. However, they were very small. In a letter to friends back in New England, a woman who had moved to the Kansas frontier wrote, "We have but one room, in which we all eat, drink, and sleep, and that is not as large as your

kitchen." Also, dirt was forever crumbling from the walls and ceiling. Insects, snakes, and small animals came through the walls. And while rain was always welcome on the Great Plains, it meant leaky roofs and walls for days afterward.

Getting water for daily needs was a big problem. One way was to drill a well 200 to 300 feet deep and build a windmill to pump the water up. Farmers could count on the strong winds that swept the plains to provide power for the windmill. However, digging wells and building windmills was costly. Few farmers could afford to get their household water that way. Most got their water from a nearby pond or spring, the way this woman's family did:

This prosperous ranching family had a large sod house and a windmill.

The spring, about a half mile or more distant, was the nearest source of good water. . . . A yoke was made to place across the shoulders, so as to carry at each end a bucket of water, and then water was brought a half mile from spring to house. Both father and mother carried water thus from day to day.

As for fuel, farmers on the plains learned to burn corncobs.

Perhaps the hardest thing about life on the Great Plains was the loneliness. Farms were far apart, and there might not be even a small village nearby to visit. Farm families might go many days without seeing another person. A well-known author of a hundred years ago named Hamlin Garland grew up on a farm on the prairies of northern Iowa. After he became famous, he wrote his own life story. In it he tells how lonely much of farm life was. Plowing was an especially lonely job:

> It meant moving to and fro hour after hour, day after day, with no one to talk to but the horses. I cheered myself in every imaginable way. I whistled. I sang. I studied the clouds . . . and I counted the prairie chickens.

Learning New Ways of Farming

The different environment of the plains created new problems for successful farming, too. As on every farm, the farmer had to plow the land before planting. But here the sod was so tough that the farmer's iron plow often broke on it. The shortage of water, of course, was a big problem. So was the absence of wood for the fencing needed to keep cattle from trampling young crops. Three inventions helped the farmers succeed on

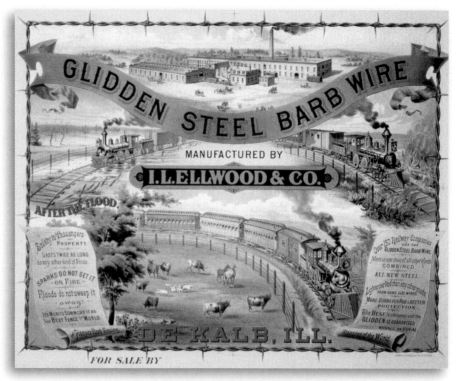

The widespread use of barbed wire changed the use of the land on the plains from ranching to farming.

the Great Plains. One was the lightweight steel plow, which cut through the tough sod. Another was barbed wire, which is a type of wire that has sharp points every few feet. Farmers now needed only enough wood for the fence posts to hold the long strings of barbed wire.

The third invention, a new method of farming called dry farming, is still used in parts of the world today. In dry farming, when rain finally comes, you capture the water in shallow ditches on each side of the growing plants. Then, as soon as the rain stops, you turn over the soil again in those ditches. This moves the wet soil underneath, closer to the roots of the plants, and keeps it from drying out through **evaporation.** Farmers also switched to new kinds of wheat and other crops that needed less water.

There was one problem that farmers could do

> **vocabulary**
> **evaporation** the process in which moisture is drawn away from the surface of the earth in the form of vapor

311

nothing about: grasshoppers. These insects appeared on the plains every few years, in such numbers that they devoured everything in their path. Can you imagine what it must have been like to be standing in your farmyard, filled with pride as you looked out at the tall corn ripening in the sun. This year, for sure, you would say to your husband or wife, there will be a good harvest. We can pay off our debts, buy another piece of farm machinery, and maybe have a bit left over for . . . then suddenly you hear a faint humming noise in the distance. Soon the hum swells into a deafening roar. The sky darkens as millions upon millions of grasshoppers block out the sun. The insects drop down upon your cornfield, and you watch helplessly as your hopes for this year's

crop vanish. One settler, to whom this happened in 1873, wrote: "So thick were the grasshoppers in the cornfield of which both of us had been so proud, that not a spot of green could be seen. And within two hours of the time that they had come not a leaf was left in all that field."

Despite all the hardships, farm families continued to move onto the Great Plains. Nothing could turn back the tide. Not the grasshoppers. Not the cattle ranchers, who complained about the farmers' barbed wire fences. Not even the return of dry weather, which caused many a farm family to give up and go back East. By the end of the 1800s, the Great Plains had become the nation's chief producer of grain.

Farmers tried many methods to save their crops from swarms of grasshoppers, sometimes even starting smokey fires from the bodies of dead grasshoppers.

Moving West In its nearly 400-year history, America has had many "Wests." To the first English colonists, the West was anywhere west of their small settlements on the Atlantic coast. A hundred years later the West had become the land leading up to the Appalachian Mountains, where mostly Scots-Irish immigrants settled before the American Revolution.

After Daniel Boone crossed the Cumberland Gap in 1769, there was a new West—the land west of the Appalachians, up to the Mississippi River. With Lewis and Clark's amazing journey of exploration, the whole huge area between the Mississippi River and the Rocky Mountains became America's newest West.

The West also came to mean the frontier—that line that marked the farthest edge of western settlement. Americans watched with pride and wonder as that line moved steadily, relentlessly westward all through the 1800s.

Even those who at first opposed the rapid expansion of the frontier changed their minds in time. One of them was Horace Greeley, editor of an important newspaper, the *New York Tribune*. In 1843, when several hundred Americans were about to set out across the Great Plains for Oregon, Greeley wrote that their plan was "foolhardy" and amounted to "insanity." So sure was he that many would die of starvation or in attacks by angry Native Americans that he predicted 90 percent would never reach their destination alive.

But when nearly all not only reached Oregon but also sent back reports on their happy lives there, Horace Greeley changed his mind. He soon became a strong supporter of westward movement. To his readers he advised, "Go West, young man, and grow up with the country." Greeley himself took a trip to the West just before the Civil War, and as a result he became even more enthusiastic about the region.

Oklahoma Land Rush

Americans didn't really need Horace Greeley's advice. They had been moving west since the earliest days of their country, gobbling up huge amounts of land. Their hunger for more never seemed to be satisfied. As farmers swarmed over one area of the Great Plains after another, however, there was one that they could not touch—at least at first. That was the area known as Indian territory, which is present-day Oklahoma. Back in the 1830s the United States government had moved eastern Indians there—do you remember the Cherokee "Trail of Tears"?—promising that they would be able to live there without interference by white settlers. Settlers, however, pressured their government to allow them to have this land as well. Therefore, the United States forced the Indian tribes to sell back 2 million acres. This land was then divided into homesteads of 160 acres and given to the settlers. Even this, however, was not enough to satisfy land-hungry westerners. The government then announced that, starting at noon, April 22, 1889, a large part of western Oklahoma—land long promised to the Indians—would be given away to settlers. First come, first served.

That morning of April 22, the Oklahoma border was a madhouse. About 100,000 people on horses, in wagons, on bicycles and on foot, lined up at the border as if getting ready to start a race. In fact, that's just what it was—a race to get the best land. At noon the starter fired his gun, giving the signal to begin. The mad rush for land was on! Settlers devoured the land like grasshoppers descending on a field of corn. In just two hours nearly every homestead had been claimed. This is how incredible the whole event was: before the starter fired his gun at noon on April 22, the town of Guthrie, Oklahoma, did not even exist. Before the sun had set that same day, Guthrie had a population of 15,000!

The Closing of the Frontier

In 1890, just a year after the Oklahoma land rush, there came an announcement from the United States **Census** Bureau that startled some and left others with an uneasy feeling.

The Census Bureau announced that the frontier was no more. You'll remember that the frontier was an imaginary line that marked the farthest edge of settlement. Not that there was no more unsettled land in the West. There was plenty of it.

But most of it was in areas too dry for farming without large-scale irrigation. What the Census Bureau was saying was that the edge of settlement had reached the end of land that could be farmed with normal rainfall.

The Census Bureau's announcement did not mean the end of homesteading. There were millions of acres far behind the frontier, in states like Kansas, Nebraska, Colorado, and North and South Dakota, where settlers could still get free land from

Thousands of settlers raced to stake their claims to Oklahoma land.

the government to start farms. And they did. In fact, more homesteads were started *after* the 1890 announcement than before.

And certainly, the closing of the frontier did not mean the end of opportunity for Americans or the end of the chance to make their fortunes. There were opportunities throughout the land, not just in the West but in all sections of the country, and especially in its growing cities.

Still, the announcement was significant. For many Americans it marked the end of an era. The frontier was gone.

Western Legends

Gone, maybe, but definitely not forgotten. In fact, it seemed that the more westerners settled down to the day-to-day business of making their living, the more the easterners pictured the West as a place of gunfighters, rugged cowboys, and endless adventures—the "Wild West." But few easterners ever saw the West. Where, then, did they get their ideas of what the West was like? Partly their ideas were shaped by the newspapers. These newspapers carried many stories about real-life western characters, but the stories were often wildly exaggerated.

There really was an outlaw named Billy the Kid. And there really was an outlaw named Jesse James. Some eastern newspapers, however, went way beyond the truth in their stories about these men. These outlaws were made out to be clever men, which they really weren't; and they were made out to be Robin Hoods, stealing from the rich and giving to the poor—which they really weren't, either. In reality Billy the Kid was a skinny little fellow who was not very skillful with a gun. He began his career of horse stealing, jail-breaking, and killing at age 15. Jesse James, who had fought with the Confederates in the Civil War, was older when he started his life of crime. He held up banks, stagecoaches, and trains in broad daylight in half a dozen different states.

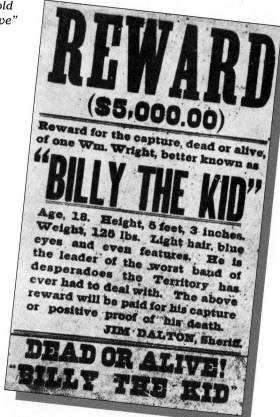

He was also a cruel killer who, without giving it a second thought, murdered anyone who stood in his way. Both these outlaws came to violent ends. Billy the Kid met his at the hands of a lawman, while Jessie James was gunned down by a member of his own gang for reward money.

Shaping Opinions About the West

The reasons some newspapers exaggerated in those days are the same as the reasons some newspapers exaggerate today. Exciting stories sell newspapers. The day-to-day struggle of western farm families to survive may have been what the West was really about, but that would not attract as many readers as would wild stories of western outlaws and gunfights.

Americans also got their ideas about the West from writers of adventure books. In the last part of the 1800s, the "dime novel" became very popular. Writers of these paperback adventure stories quickly found that stories about the West sold well. For just ten cents, kids in Boston or Baltimore or Chicago—and their parents too—could read exciting tales of cowboys and outlaws. Publishers produced more than 2,200 of these stories, in which taking on a half-dozen gunfighters at a time was all in a day's work for make-believe heroes like Arizona Joe, Denver Dan, and Lariat Lil. Even when the stories were about characters who really did live, the adventures they described were usually made up.

Finally, Americans' ideas about the West were shaped by a new popular entertainment called the Wild West show. Long before the frontier had disappeared, some westerners came up with the idea that they could make money by putting on shows about the West for eastern audiences. The Wild West shows became hugely popular, and by the 1880s there were about 50 such shows traveling among the cities and towns of the East.

The most popular Wild West show featured "Buffalo Bill" Cody. William F. Cody—that was his real name— had worked as a pony express rider, a scout, a cowboy, and a buffalo hunter. He was already known to many easterners through several dime novels. In

1883, Buffalo Bill Cody created an outdoor western show that played to audiences of up to 20,000, twice a day! The show featured riding and shooting contests, a stagecoach robbery, lots of gunfighting, and plenty of "dangerous" Indians. The Indians included the famous Indian chief Sitting Bull, about whom you will read later. One of the stars of the show was Annie Oakley, a young woman who had been born in Ohio and had never seen the West but shot a rifle with the most amazing accuracy.

After performing to big crowds in the United States for several years, William Cody packed up the show, buffalo and all, and took it to Great Britain. There, he, Annie Oakley, and the others thrilled audiences of many thousands—including Queen Victoria herself!

Buffalo Bill Cody's Wild West show continued to give performances well into the early 1900s. By that time the real frontier had long since passed into history. But it was kept alive in the minds of Americans by the newspapers, dime novels, and traveling Wild West shows that gave their audiences a taste, even though an exaggerated one, of life in the great Wild West.

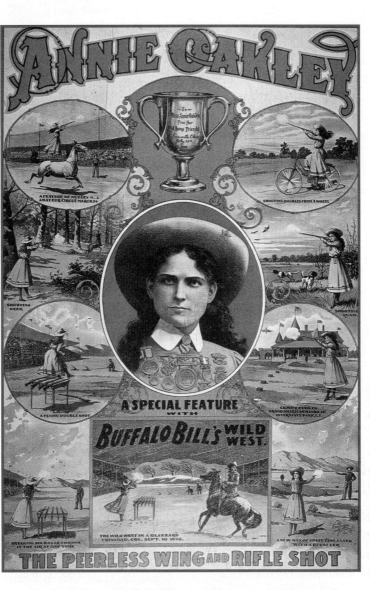

Annie Oakley, Buffalo Bill, and dime novels presented an exaggerated and often unrealistic picture of the West.

Northern Icebox After the United States gained all of the Southwest from Mexico and half of Oregon from Great Britain, the land hunger of most Americans seemed to be satisfied.

However, the United States was to gain one more piece of the North American continent. That was the huge area of land to the west of Canada known as Alaska. This time there were no voices shouting "Manifest Destiny!" There were no would-be settlers pushing across borders. In fact, there was very little interest in Alaska at all. Most Americans then knew less about Alaska than we know about Antarctica today. And they were no more interested in moving to Alaska than we are in moving to Antarctica.

How, then, did Alaska become part of the United States? The story goes back to the early 1700s, when Russia, having sent a handful of people to explore this unknown area, claimed the territory as its own. That's what European nations did in those days. They would send explorers to lands where Europeans had not been before, and after a month or even a few days there, the explorers would claim the land for the country that sent them. That's what Columbus did for Spain when he arrived in the Americas. That's what Jacques Cartier did for France in Canada. That's what Henry Hudson did for the Netherlands in New York. (Of course no one ever asked the people already living in these areas how they felt about this.)

The Russian government set up a trading company, which traded with the native peoples for fur. For 100 years or so, the Russian company made a lot of money at it. However, by the mid-1800s most of the fur-bearing animals were gone. The company began to lose money. That's when the Russian government started to think about selling Alaska. The Russians were also worried that if they ever went to war against Great Britain—and it

Many people made fun of the purchase of Alaska. This cartoon shows President Johnson and Secretary Seward welcoming "native Alaskans."

looked as if they might—the British navy would simply take Alaska from them, and they'd get nothing for it. And then there were those land-hungry Americans. True, none were talking about Manifest Destiny and Alaska in the same breath so far. But one never knew when that cry might be raised.

In 1867 the tsar of Russia told his representative in the United States, a man named Edouard de Stoeckl, to see if the Americans were interested in buying Alaska. "I won't take less than $5 million," the tsar told Stoeckl, "but see if you can get more."

The American secretary of state at that time was William Seward. Seward told Stoeckl that he was indeed interested. The two bargained back and forth over price for a number of days and finally settled at $7.2 million. What followed then was quite unusual. After checking back with the tsar, Stoeckl stopped off at Seward's home one evening with the good news: the tsar had approved the deal. "Let us meet at your office in the Department of State tomorrow," Stoeckl suggested, "and write up the treaty." Seward pushed away the card table in front of him, rose, and the two men had the following exchange:

Seward: "Why wait till tomorrow, Mr. Stoeckl? Let us make the treaty tonight."

Stoeckl: "But your department is closed. You have no clerks, and my secretaries are scattered about the town."

Seward: "Never mind that. If you can [get your people] together, before midnight you will find me awaiting you at the department, which will be open and ready for business."

And that is how it happened that the treaty to buy Alaska was written by the flickering oil lamps in William Seward's office in the wee hours of a morning in March 1867, and signed by the two men at 4:00 A.M.

This was a treaty, so of course the Senate had to approve of it by a two-thirds vote. Because it also required spending money, the House of Representatives had to approve it too. There was some grumbling in Congress and in several newspapers about this plan to buy Alaska. "Seward's Polar Bear Garden," one called it. To others it was "Seward's Ice Box" and "Seward's Folly," and a bad bargain at that.

Most, though, realized that Seward had made a wise deal. They believed there was great potential in this huge territory. The timber might some day become very valuable, and the fish were so plentiful that American fishermen could make a living from them for years. At less than two cents an acre, it was a very good bargain indeed. Both houses of Congress voted in its favor by large margins, and Alaska became part of the United States.

Seward and Stoeckl work out the final arrangements for the purchase of Alaska. Seward is seated with papers on his lap. Stoeckl stands in the foreground, with his hand on the globe.

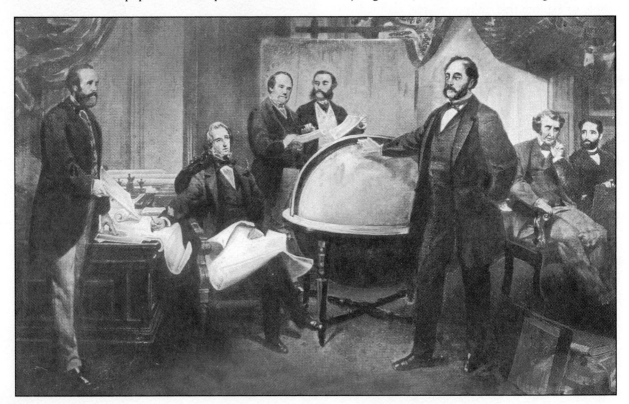

census a count by a government of the number of people living in its country

evaporation the process in which moisture is drawn from the surface of the earth in the form of vapor

graze to feed on the natural grass or plants of an open area, as cattle graze on the range

immigrant a person who comes from one country to live in another one

precipitation moisture that falls to earth in the form of rain, snow, sleet, or hail

railroad ties thick wooden timbers that support iron rails and keep them in line

Thaw Collection, Fenimore Art Museum, Cooperstown, NY

Native Americans:
Cultures and Conflicts

Contents

Westward Expansion Even before Europeans arrived in what we now call the United States, there were people living here. These were the Native American peoples, or Indians. There were many different groups of Indians. Some organized themselves as large nations, others as smaller tribes, and some remained bands. However, each had a distinct way of life.

During the 1800s Native Americans living on lands west of the Mississippi River faced dramatic changes. Their **cultures** were disrupted and sometimes even destroyed by white Americans who relentlessly pushed westward. What were some of the major Indian cultural groups whom the whites encountered, and how did their lives change?

First, let's look at the Indians who lived in the Great Basin of the American West.

A Challenging Environment

The Great Basin is like a big bowl that encompasses what is now Nevada and parts of California, Idaho, Oregon, and Utah. The "sides" of the bowl are ranges of the Rocky Mountains (to the east) and the Sierra Nevada (to the west). Inside the bowl is a desert, with streams that only occasionally have a little water. When the sun beats down during the day, the basin becomes extremely hot; but nights can be very cool, even cold. Temperatures can reach 120°F on a summer's day and -20°F on a winter's night. The Great Basin includes Death Valley, which is the hottest place in the United States, and the desolate salt flats around the Great Salt Lake.

> **vocabulary**
> **culture** the attitudes, customs, and beliefs of a group of people

But much of the Great Basin is not quite so barren. With great ingenuity, native peoples learned to survive there. In many places there are fruits and vegetables that can be eaten, including pine nuts, cactus fruits, and roots, and there are a few animals as well: insects, snakes, mice, rabbits, and other rodents. Most of us today would not find these the most desirable sources of food, but if you have to live off the land of the Great Basin, you will eat just about anything you can catch.

Life in the Great Basin

The Great Basin has never been an easy place to live. Yet various Indian tribes who live there—including the Bannocks, the Shoshonis, the Utes, and the Paiutes (pye YOOTS)—created cultures that have endured for thousands of years.

Like other Native Americans, Great Basin people such as the Paiutes

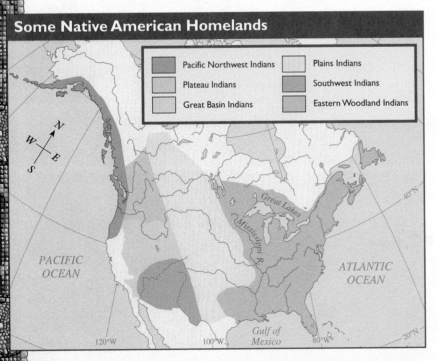

Some Native American Homelands

Pacific Northwest Indians
Plateau Indians
Great Basin Indians
Plains Indians
Southwest Indians
Eastern Woodland Indians

PACIFIC OCEAN

ATLANTIC OCEAN

Great Lakes

Mississippi R.

Gulf of Mexico

120°W   100°W   80°W

40°N   20°N

For several of the major cultural groups that lived west of the Mississippi River, settlers pushing west were a catastrophe. This was especially true for Indians in the Great Basin, Plateau, Plains, and Northwest.

No plants or animals live on the dramatic salt flats that are part of the Great Basin.

traditionally believed that the world was filled with mysterious natural forces, or "powers." Their **myths** explained how their lives were affected by these powers. According to these myths, the awesome things that people saw in nature, like thunderstorms, wind, and snow, were living spiritual forces. Myths also told about animals—with names like Wolf, Coyote, and Rabbit—that could speak and act as we do. These mythical animals, which lived before humans, created the world and its people. They taught people how to organize themselves into families and bands, how to gather food, and how to live moral lives.

Traditionally, Paiutes and most other Indian peoples believed that certain men and women had special abilities to communicate with the spirits inhabiting the natural world. Such people were known as **shamans.** People did not necessarily try or even want to become shamans. Often, natural spirits would make themselves known to an Indian, and it was dangerous to refuse their power. Indians sought a shaman's guidance when they were ill or when their tribe or band was hungry.

The Paiutes and other Great Basin Indians lived in groups—parents, children, aunts or uncles and their families, and grandparents. These small bands hunted game and looked for edible plants.

They had no agriculture, although in some places they could get enough water to irrigate naturally growing plants in order to increase their yield.

Hunting and gathering were vital parts of Paiute life. Although they had to cover a huge amount of territory in their never-ending quest for food, Great Basin peoples never wandered aimlessly. They knew that there were certain places where food was likely to be found at different seasons, and they returned to these places year after year.

Until the Paiutes got a few guns and horses from the Spanish, in the late 1700s, they depended on **corrals,** clubs, and knives in their hunts. (Bows and arrows were useful only for killing larger animals, like antelope.) The men would build a corral by stringing nets between large cactuses, and then they would patiently maneuver a jackrabbit into the trap. When the animal was caught, women would quickly use a bone knife to kill and skin it.

Paiute women and children tried to find as many edible plants as possible, as well as insects and small rodents. They never overlooked poisonous vegetation that could be made edible by special treatment. It took great skill to tell what could be safely eaten. Because women provided so much of the food that Indians ate—jackrabbits and snakes couldn't always be found—they were as important as men in traditional Great Basin society.

Great Basin Indians knew that they must not waste anything. For example, a jackrabbit's muscles were used to tie sharpened stones to arrows, and its bones became needles and knives. From rabbit fur, Indians made garments for the cold winters, when several bands would huddle together in camps where they built simple shelters.

Harvest Time

The best time to join the Indians of the Great Basin is in the fall, when larger numbers of small bands come together. They share stories about the past year, they dance and play, they seek spouses, and they hunt jackrabbits. However, the main purpose of their gathering is to harvest pine nuts. But isn't this a desert? Well, yes, but a few areas of green forest do exist, and there Paiutes gather each year to find their staple food.

It is not easy to harvest pine nuts. The Indians have to gather just before the nuts ripen. If they are a day or two late, the pine cones will have opened and animals will have gotten the nuts first. The men pull pine cones off the trees while women and children fill hundreds of baskets with them—baskets that the women make. Then the pine cones have to be roasted, which helps open them up so the nuts can be shaken out. The nuts are then roasted until their fuzzy shells can be cracked and the edible inner kernels released.

The roasted nuts are delicious, and the Great Basin Indians eat their fill during harvest time. However, they need to preserve most of the harvest. The nuts can later be ground and mixed with water to make soup.

You can see how the Great Basin's environment forced Indians like the Paiutes to make use of every possible resource, to hold animals, plants, and natural forces in great respect, and to keep their social organization as simple as possible. Families were seldom large, nor was the Indian population of the Great Basin ever very numerous. It was a harsh existence, but peoples like the Paiutes did whatever they had to do in order to survive. Their myths and their traditions gave them strict rules of morality, all of which were dictated by the natural conditions under which they lived. They carefully taught these rules to their children, along with the complex skills needed to find food, water, and shelter in the Great Basin.

National Anthropological Archives, Smithsonian Institution

Two Paiute women gather pine cones for the pine nuts that their families will eat. They wear hats to keep the pine gum out of their hair.

Living by the Seasons Just a few hundred miles north of where the Paiutes roam, we find the Plateau region. This region includes portions of the present states of Idaho, Oregon, Washington, California, Montana, and adjacent areas in Canada.

Indian tribes who live in this region include the Kutenais (KOOT en ayz), the Walla Wallas (WAH lah WAH lahz), the Coeur d'Alenes (kur del AYNZ), the Cayuses (KYE yoos uz), and the Nez Percés (nez PUHRS).

The weather on the plateau is similar to that in the Great Basin—hot summers and cold winters—but there is a lot more water and more abundant plants and animals. Like the Great Basin Indians, Plateau peoples were **hunter-gatherers** who traveled from place to place according to the availability of food at different sea-sons. Also like the Paiutes, Plateau Indians were highly skilled in living off the land. Men, women, and children all had special jobs to perform as groups worked together to find food. Like all other Native Americans, Plateau Indians regarded nature with religious reverence. Compared to what Great Basin Indians could find, however, Plateau peoples could draw on a much wider range of food sources.

> **vocabulary**
> **hunter-gatherers** a people who belong to a culture that does not practice agriculture, but instead feeds itself by hunting, fishing, and finding edible plants

In 1805, about 6,000 Nez Percés, or Nimipu (NEE me poo), Indians lived in the plateau area. Here is how they would have spent a year:

Spring

The snow has not yet melted, and all the dried food the Nez Percés have saved for the winter is gone. Now they must seek food. Those in the large villages break into smaller groups. Some Nez Percés put on snowshoes to hunt deer, bear, or caribou in the valleys. Other Nez Percés paddle their canoes down the Columbia River to catch the first salmon

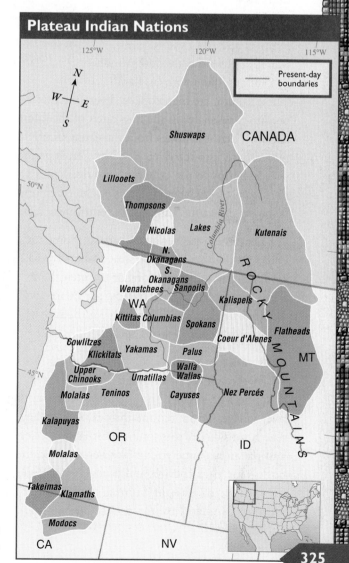

Plateau Indian Nations

Many different Indian tribes lived in the Plateau region.

of the year as the fish travel upriver to spawning areas. Here, salmon is king—and also sacred.

The Indians of the plateau know that their lives depend on the salmon. They eat it fresh, and they dry large amounts of it for trading and for eating during the coming months when they leave the rivers and head for the mountainsides. Salmon is so important that every man, woman, and child who is not sick or off hunting deer and caribou joins in the salmon hunt. For the Nez Percés this is more than just a hunt. It is a religious ritual that brings thousands of Nez Percés together into river villages to catch and process these fish.

A shaman wades gingerly into the river and from the gurgling waters chooses the first few salmon by catching them with his hands. These salmon are then cooked. Everyone eats a little piece and shares in the first catch of the salmon season. Then, the bones from the eaten salmon are placed back into the river. The Nez Percés perform this ceremony to pay tribute to the river spirit and the salmon spirit; they believe that the ceremony will ensure that the salmon will return next year.

Then the hunt begins in earnest. Some Nez Percés fish with a hook and line; others try to spear salmon with harpoons or to catch them with traps and nets. Afterwards, the people work together to clean the fish and hang them on racks to dry, so they won't spoil.

Summer

By the middle of summer, the Nez Percés break up into smaller groups and move from the river villages to the mountainsides. There, they search for wild carrots, onions, bitterroot, celery, and parsnips. Some young Nez Percés scout the bushes for huckleberries and blueberries. While the men are off on long hunting and trading journeys, women have the primary responsibility

In the 1700s, the Plateau Indians began to use horses for transportation. Nez Percé women still take pride in raising them.

to find, harvest, and preserve plant foods. The life of the entire group depends on the women drying enough food for the winter months.

Autumn and Winter

In late summer and early fall, the Nez Percés return to the rivers to catch more salmon as new fish make their way back downstream to the Pacific Ocean. The Nez Percés also harvest the last of the year's roots and berries, preparing for the winter. They remain in groups of only about 20 to 30 people as the winter approaches.

Some of the Nez Percés build special homes to use in winter. They dig a pit in the ground deep enough so that, if they stand up, they can barely see over the top of the pit. The pit is from 10 to 40 feet in diameter. Next, they build a cone-shaped frame above the pit, covering it with brush and earth. The builders leave a hole in the top that allows smoke to escape and is also used for entering and exiting the earth lodge. There is a ladder or notched log inside the dwelling so that residents can climb in and out of the home.

The earthen pit is the perfect place to sit by the fire and listen to the older people tell stories and myths in which animals, plants, rocks, rivers, and even stars come to life. Coyote, the "trickster," is a popular character. He is always getting into trouble or into odd situations. The Plateau Indians often tell stories about Coyote to teach lessons to the children.

During the winter, baskets will be made and nets mended or woven. These will be used the following spring—again, for the salmon. This is a time to gather one's energy while waiting for another spring.

Here's a tale a Plateau child might have heard about one Coyote tricking another Coyote.

A Coyote Tale

Two Coyotes were crossing a field, but one had not met the other before. They heard an Indian yell, "There's a Coyote in the field!" The first Coyote turned to the other and told him to run! They both started to run for the trees when they heard the man yell, "And there goes another one!"

Finally, both Coyotes made it to the cover of the trees and introduced themselves. "I never saw you before. My name's Wanderer. I am a Coyote like you."

The other Coyote looked at him oddly and said, "My name's Sleek, but I am not a Coyote like you."

"Yes you are," said Wanderer.

"Oh, no I am not," replied Sleek.

"Look, my friend, you're confused. Your ears are like mine, your tail is like mine, your fur is the same as mine, our snouts are the same, everything is the same. You are just like me and we are both Coyotes."

"Listen, let's run across the field again and you will see," challenged Sleek.

So off they ran. First went Wanderer and again the Indian yelled, "There goes that Coyote!" Then Sleek took off, and the farmer yelled, "And there goes another one!"

When the two Coyotes reached the other side of the field, they ducked into the woods. Wanderer turned to Sleek and said, "There! Didn't you hear the man? He called us both Coyotes."

Sleek look disappointed with his confused friend and said, "Yes, I heard the man call you a Coyote, but he called me 'Another One.'"

That just goes to show that we shouldn't let others tell us who we are.

When the two Coyotes reached the other side of the field, they ducked into the woods.

From Farmers to Hunters Think very carefully about this: What are two things you could not live without—without them, your life would change completely? Did you say a house? television? stereo? computer? car? refrigerator? microwave oven? Keep your answers in mind as you read.

As you have learned, the Indians of the Great Basin and Plateau regions were hunter-gatherers. They traveled to find food and take advantage of weather. Mostly, they traveled by foot or sometimes by canoe. They crossed mountains, valleys, gorges, rivers, and hillsides.

However, many of the Native Americans living in the Plains region were *not* hunter-gatherers, at least not at first. The Plains are grasslands extending from central Canada south to Mexico and from midwestern United States westward to the Rockies. Plains land is flat and dotted with trees. The Indians who lived on these plains were farmers for centuries. They grew most of their own food. They also gathered wild fruits and nuts and occasionally hunted bison (a type of buffalo)— always on foot. But at the end of the hunting trip, they would always return to the same home they lived in year-round.

Some Plains Indians, like the Hidatsas, Mandans, and Arikaras in North Dakota, always kept their agricultural life. The Missouri River gave enough water for them to remain successful farmers. But around 1750, other Plains peoples' lives changed forever because a new animal became available to them— the horse.

Horses

Ancestors of horses had existed on this continent, but they had been wiped out during the Ice Age, and perhaps by the earliest hunters who entered the continent. So the horse was unknown to North and South American Indians when Spanish soldiers invaded Mexico in the 1500s. They brought horses with them. The Spaniards lost some of their horses, and these

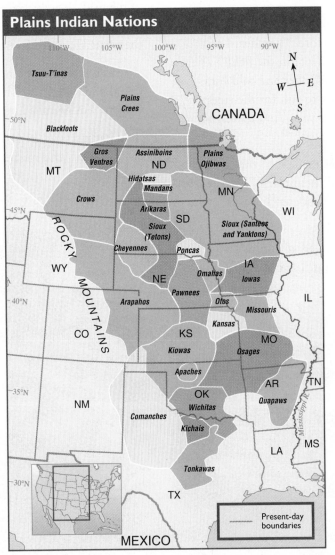

Plains Indian Nations

In the early 1800s, there were about 250,000 Indians living on the Great Plains.

animals multiplied into wild herds that migrated northward to the Plains.

The arrival of horses on the Great Plains changed American history. How? Remember the two things that you couldn't live without? Well, for Plains Indians those two things were the horse and the bison. To learn about these two animals and the role they played in the lives of these Indians is to understand a major part of American history.

Bison Become King

Remember how salmon was king to the Plateau Indians? Well, with more than 30 million bison roaming North America, bison was king on the plains. To the Plains Indians—such as the Arapahos (uh RAP uh hohz), Blackfoot Cheyennes (shye ANZ), Osages (oh SAYJZ), and Sioux (soo) —the bison was excellent and plentiful food. But these people also used the bison to supply just about every other need they had.

The Plains Indians once hunted bison the way Paiutes hunted rabbits—by building corrals and herding a few animals into them. On foot it was tiring and very hard work. Many people were needed to bring down just one animal. But when the horse arrived, everything changed. With the horse, the bison hunters could supply hundreds of people with all they needed. During such a hunt, one man could kill one or two bison, and a skilled hunter could take as many as four or five. Twenty skilled hunters, then, could kill up to 80 bison *in one day!*

The Plains Indians, though, never hunted more bison than they could use. They thanked the Great Spirit for the abundance of food and never thought of wasting it.

Hunting for Bison

Plains Indians quickly became highly skilled riders. The most widely used hunting method was known as the chase. Once a herd was found, each rider rode his horse toward it. When the bison realized the danger, they scattered. Each Indian rider would bear down on a single target.

When he was as close as possible to the bison, the rider shot an arrow, aiming just behind the last rib. That's where a bison was most vulnerable. Often, though, the first arrow only slowed

the animal down. But the horse could keep up the chase, and after a few more shots, the bison was killed.

Now, as skilled riders and hunters, Plains Indians could ride long distances for food. They could carry many things with them—food, tepees, tools, clothing, and cookware. They didn't have to stay in one place and raise crops. They stopped being farmers and became primarily hunters and traders. Plains Indians now had extra food and goods made from bison. They could trade those things for items they didn't have, such as metals, beads, tools, and agricultural products, which as we have seen, some Plains people continued to raise and sell. At first they traded with other tribes; later they began to trade with the white men who had begun to appear on the frontier. From the white man the Indians acquired another item that changed their lives—the gun. Guns made shooting bison even easier.

Uses of Bison

hides	tepee coverings, clothing, robes, moccasins, arrow quivers, medicine bags, shields, drums, saddles, stirrups
hair	pillows, ropes, ornaments
horns	cups, spoons, ladles
bones	awls, knives, shovels, war clubs
dung	fuel

Horses and War

The horse brought much good to the Plains Indians. It has been said that the horse didn't just *change* the Plains Indians—it *created* them. On the other hand, horses now made it easier for Plains Indians to wage war on each other.

Before the horse, Plains farmers were very busy people. They cleared the land, tilled the soil,

Plains Indians learned to be skilled riders and how to use the bow and arrow to hunt for bison.

planted seeds, watered plants, and harvested and preserved the crops. The coming of the horse did not change the Plains Indians' basic value systems, but it did bring them into conflict with more distant rivals. Tribes waged war to drive rivals away from good hunting grounds, to keep them from taking too much food, to steal horses, or to control trade and gain access to resources.

But tribes and individual Indian warriors also fought simply for glory. To Plains Indians, battles were fought not just to kill enemies (though there was plenty of killing), but even more to shame them with displays of superior bravery and skill.

The word *coup* (coo) is a French word that means "touch" or "blow," as in striking someone. Often, Plains Indians' object in fighting was to *count coup*—to see who could achieve the bravest deeds and win the greatest glory. Warriors' reputations depended on how many coups they could count. Striking an enemy with a stick, taking his gun, or stealing his horse were bigger coups than killing him.

From Childhood to Adulthood

Indian boys listened to stories of how warriors gained glory. Parents and other respected adults spoke of tribal heroes and traditions, passing on

the Indians' strong sense of justice and honorable behavior. Playing with bows and arrows, learning to handle horses, and hunting small game prepared boys for adult life. Accompanying adult males on bison hunts, joining war parties, and going through initiation rites marked a teenager's gradual entrance into manhood, with tribal ceremonies celebrating their accomplishments.

As adults, men continued displaying their skill, bravery, and fortitude not just in hunts and warfare, but also in self-torturing rituals like the annual "sun dance." Through such rituals they gained spiritual "power" by enduring pain.

Like all Indians, Plains peoples depended on women's skills, too. Women turned bison hides into fur robes and tepees. They gathered edible plants and, among agricultural tribes, took care of crops. They cooked, did sewing and beadwork, and were largely responsible for moving encampments during the hunting season. Girls learned these skills from their mothers and other older women, and they had their own rituals to mark their coming of age. So vital was women's contribution that in many Plains tribes (and other Indian societies) people traced their descent not from their father's ancestors but from their mother's.

Indians of the Northwest Now, let's travel to a fourth area and visit an Indian group very different from the ones we've seen so far. We're heading for the Pacific Northwest. This region extends from southern Alaska and along Canada's coastline to Washington, Oregon, and northern California.

The Indians who lived in the Pacific Northwest included the Tlingets (TLIHNG gihts), Salishes (SAY lihsh uz), Haidas (HYE dahz), Kwakiutls (kwah kee OOT elz), and other tribes. These people were hunter-gatherers too, but of a different kind.

Land of Forests and Rivers

Northwest Coast Indians lived in a rugged, windy region along the coast, with towering, majestic mountains on the eastern side and the crashing waves of the Pacific Ocean on the western side. This area is about 100 miles wide and 1,000 miles long, with over 2,000 miles of jagged shoreline.

In the Pacific Northwest the weather is mild. The area doesn't have the extremes of temperatures that occur in the Great Basin, Plateau, and Plains regions. The temperatures generally range from 35°F to 45°F in January and from 55°F to 65°F in July.

The Pacific Northwest is also moist. In some areas, 150 inches of rain falls every year. That's enough rain to make a 12-foot-deep swimming pool overflow! All those rainstorms, along with fogs and moist winds, make for lush forests teeming with plants and animals. Redwood and cedar trees tower many stories above the land, and these trees provided the Northwest Coast Indians with building supplies and other natural resources.

The Indians of the moist, lush, and relatively densely populated Pacific Northwest got so much food from their environment that they never had to develop agriculture. Their tribes were sharply divided into chiefs, nobles, ordinary people, and slaves (usually war captives). The society and value systems of these peoples, who were the most status-conscious of all Native Americans, revolved around acquiring and displaying property—and giving it away! The more things that an Indian could give away, the more respect and aid he would be owed. And the best way to acquire power through giving things away was to hold potlatches and erect totem poles.

*Look at me friend!
I come to ask
for your dress
since there is nothing
you cannot be used for.
I come to beg you for this,
Long-life Maker!*

This is a Kwakiutl prayer to the cedar tree.

All families belong to one of two totems: The frog shows that the family belongs to the Raven totem. The bear clan belongs to the Eagle totem.

Potlatches and Totem Poles

Potlatches were great ceremonies that lasted days, even weeks. Anywhere from 50 to several hundred people might attend. There were dances, stories, games, singing, gift-giving—and food galore! The purpose was not just to have fun, but to strengthen the bonds that held Northwest Coast Indian society together.

Some potlatches were held to honor a dead chief, some to celebrate a new house. In fact, Northwest Coast Indians celebrated many of the same events we do: marriage, a child's birth, the naming of a child, coming of age, a wedding anniversary. Let's imagine we've been invited to a potlatch to celebrate a marriage.

We approach this village from the ocean side. Lining the coast are large houses, called long houses, built of cedar planks. The village stretches for over a mile and is home to about 900 Indians. This is unusual, though. Most villages are home to about 30 to 50 Indians

who live in only one or two long houses.

As we walk up from the beach, we notice that these houses are beautifully painted with signs and symbols of ravens, bears, eagles, wolves, or other animals. These animals are symbols for different families, or totems. Each group of Northwest Coast Indians is a member of one of two totems: Raven or Eagle. Within each totem there are various clans. If you belong to the Raven totem, then you could be a member of a Frog, Goose, Owl, Salmon, or Sea Lion clan. If you belong to the Eagle totem, you could be a member of a Bear, Shark, Whale, or Wolf clan.

Since these Indians have no written language, they carve their tribal legends and family histories into tall posts of cedar wood, called totem poles. The totem pole serves as the emblem of a family or clan and as a reminder of its ancestry. The symbols represent not only a clan but also the power and characteristics of individuals in the clan. Each clan's totem has a history, and each totem has power based on a particular animal's abilities. For example, the bear represents strength and courage, while the wolf symbolizes perseverance and guardianship. An individual in these clans is thought to possess the same qualities as the totem.

This potlatch has taken over a year to prepare. Why? First of all, potlatches were used to display treasures and important momentos of the party-giver's family. So lots of things needed to be gathered—things that showed wealth, such as blankets, robes, tools, and plaques of pounded, decorated copper. Elaborate songs recounting family history needed to be created and rehearsed —and that took time. Food had to be prepared. And most important, the totem pole had to be designed, sculpted, and painted.

Welcoming the Guests

Standing before one of the bigger, nicer houses is the groom's father. He is in his best clothes: An intricately woven goat-hair blanket and a hat decorated with ermine. We know he is an important member of the Raven Totem because a raven is painted on the brim of his hat. He also carries a fancy staff inlaid with mother-of-pearl and whale-bone. He is ready and eager to greet his guests.

As a drum starts beating, we turn around and see many canoes offshore. The canoes are decorated with Bear and Wolf and Eagle totems. The groom's father greets his guests with a flowery and elaborate speech. The guests, in turn, sing their own songs and make their own speeches. One by one the guests come ashore, in order of rank, which basically means that the richest man comes first, then the next richest, and so on.

We enter the father's house. He has built a fire so large that sparks fly through the hole in the roof. Some of the beams in the ceiling are scorched. Once again, this is for show. What the host is really saying is, "I am rich enough to build such a large fire that my house could burn down and it wouldn't matter!"

More speeches follow, and what seemed to be a normal party starts becoming—well, unusual.

The host talks about his family and its history and at the same time insults each and every one of his guests! He points to one chief and says, "There are too few chiefs in your family. You are not worthy to sit next to me." He points to another and declares, "Your clothes are so ragged and cheap. How dare you show up here." Then the guests start insulting the host.

Why all these insults? Status is very important in these tribes, and pretending to be the most important and the richest is part of a Northwest Coast Indian's life. The host and his guests are unoffended by the insults; they recognize them as part of the ceremony.

The host then has slaves carry in a canoe filled with food and sets it before a guest. "You and your family are so skinny," he says, pointing to someone from the Bear clan and insulting him. "You must never have enough to eat. Here,

Many guests were invited to a potlatch. Typically they traveled by canoes to the celebration.

eat this." The family then feels obligated to eat all the food in the canoe; if they cannot do so, the failure will shame them.

On the second day, the chief breaks up his best canoe and burns it. This is his way of saying, "I am so rich I don't need this canoe. I can afford to have another one built." The insulting, eating, and flaunting go on for a few days, leading up to the two great moments of a potlatch: the "giving away" (which is what the word *potlatch* means), and the raising of the totem.

To the chief ranking second to him, the host gives 6,000 blankets. People of low rank get only strips from torn blankets. Then guests give gifts to the host. Giving and accepting gifts obligates both parties to help each other in the future.

Raising the Totem

Now, we are led outside to the front of the house. Lying on its side, but covered, is the potlatch totem pole. The totem pole tells a story in pictures about the party-giver. Slaves uncover the pole and raise it with rope until its base rests in a hole.

All of us marvel at its beauty. The totem pole tells the story of the host's son's marriage. Because the host and his son belong to a Raven clan, a raven totem is carved at the top. The wife is from the Wolf clan, and so the raven is shown perched on the wolf's back. More carvings show a raven with a bear's claw in its beak. This tells about a time when a Raven clan defeated the Bear clan in a battle. Many stories are told on this totem pole. It will stand for many years to honor this marriage. Then it will rot away. The Raven chief doesn't care. When it does rot away, he will host another potlatch and raise another totem pole.

Now you have some idea of how some Native Americans lived long ago and for hundreds, maybe even thousands, of years. In the next few lessons, you will learn how they were threatened and even destroyed by white settlers as they moved farther west across America.

A totem stands in front of each house in this Northwest Coast village. Each totem pole tells the story of the family who lives there.

Government Policy Uneasy relations between Americans and Indians can be traced all the way back to the days when the first European settlers arrived. Already in those early days, there were successes and failures.

Many people are familiar with the story of how the Indians helped the Pilgrims through their first difficult winter in Massachusetts. But for each example of cooperation, there were many violent clashes, including wars and mass slaughters. Indians traded with the newcomers, but trade also caused intertribal rivalries and devastating battles among Native American peoples, as well as between Europeans and their Indian allies. Unfortunately for the Indians, their bodies often could not resist the germs that Europeans and Africans brought to the New World and spread from their settlements and trading posts. Disease killed native peoples in great numbers.

As a result, throughout the colonial period the Indian population of eastern North America declined. The colonists pushed the remaining Native American population across the Appalachian Mountains. After 1783, when the Treaty of Paris ended the Revolutionary War and recognized American independence, the United States government decided to treat the Indians living beyond the Appalachians as a sovereign, or separate, people. It used **diplomacy** in its dealings with them, just as it did in its relations with France, Spain, or Great Britain.

For example, in the Northwest Ordinance of 1787, Congress expressed this policy:

The utmost faith shall always be observed towards Indians; their lands and property shall never be taken from them without their consent; and in their property, rights, and liberty, they shall never be invaded or disturbed, unless in just and lawful wars authorized by Congress; but laws founded in justice and humanity shall from time to time be made, for preventing wrongs done to them, and for preserving peace and friendship with them.

Diplomacy Fails

But traditional diplomacy would soon prove to be a doomed effort. Here's an example of why:

Imagine that someone comes to your neighborhood. He spots a neighbor of yours, one who seems rich or important. This visitor then offers your neighbor some money to buy *all* the houses in the area and gives your neighbor a house elsewhere. Your neighbor says, "Sure! That sounds good." He then sells the neighborhood. When you come home and learn what has happened, you are indignant. "How dare he sell my land!" you cry. "He has no right!" When the buyer shows up to take possession, you refuse to leave. Arguments and fights soon break out.

Something like this happened with the Indians. You see, American officials had appointed people to represent the American government. An official might come to an Indian "neighborhood" and talk to someone who seemed important, maybe a chief of some sort. A treaty would be written and signed. The government would give this leader money

> **vocabulary**
> **diplomacy** the management of relations between nations

and land somewhere else in the country. The treaty would also say that he and the rest of his group must leave in a certain amount of time. That was because white people wanted to settle there. This was diplomacy in the traditional European sense: I give you this (money and land somewhere else), and in return, you agree to leave peacefully before a certain date.

The official goes back to Washington and tells his supervisors that the treaty was signed and should now be sent to Congress for approval. Meanwhile, white people hear that the government has bought this area of land and are anxious to move there. They bring all their goods over hundreds of miles, over mountains and through rivers. When they get to the area, *both* Indians and settlers are surprised—to say the least.

The settlers say, "Your leader signed a treaty and took money for this land. You agreed to move. You're not supposed to be here."

The Indians say, "Someone may have signed a treaty, but we didn't. The one who signed that treaty doesn't speak for us. He does not even own this land. You must leave!"

What happened next would be one of these things: The Indians would threaten the settlers, who would return east; the settlers would refuse to leave, and the Indians would reluctantly move; the Indians and settlers would fight each other; or United States troops would be sent to settle the issue. None of these "solutions" was really ideal.

Diplomacy failed because Americans didn't understand tribal leadership. Indian groups did not belong to one central government. They could not be treated like independent nations such as England or France. As a result, an agreement made with one group of Sioux had no meaning to other Sioux and certainly had no meaning to Cheyennes.

Nor did Americans understand how fiercely independent most Indians were—they often ignored their own leader's words. If a tribe had chiefs at all (some didn't), they weren't like a United States President who represents all Americans. An Indian might be a chief because he had shown bravery or good sense or was respected by others in the group. But that didn't mean his word was law. This was not disobedience but an Indian way of life.

The Growth of a Country

After the Revolutionary War, Americans were full of pride and thought their way of living was the best. And why not? Hadn't they just fought a war to secure their natural rights and beaten the greatest military power in the world?

Many treaties failed because Americans didn't understand the Indian way of life.

Then another important event happened. The French emperor, Napoleon Bonaparte, was fighting wars in Europe and needed money. France owned huge amounts of land west of the Mississippi River from the Gulf of Mexico to Canada. Napoleon sold this land, known as the Louisiana Territory, to the United States in 1803. The Louisiana Purchase doubled the size of the United States! (Of course, no one asked any of the many Indians who lived in this area if the land could be bought or sold.)

In 1803, President Thomas Jefferson authorized an expedition to explore the huge region. When the Lewis and Clark expedition—as it came to be called—got under way, Captain Meriwether Lewis spoke to the Osage Indians in the Missouri Valley:

> We are all now of one family, born in the same land, and bound to live as brothers; and the strangers from beyond the great water [the British Army] are gone from among us. The Great Spirit has given you strength, and has given us strength; not that we might hurt one another, but to do each other all the good in our power. Our dwellings indeed are very far apart, but not too far to carry on commerce and useful [discussions]. . . . Let us employ ourselves then in mutually accommodating each other.

Again, the hope for peaceful cooperation was expressed, but the brotherhood and unity that Lewis wished for proved difficult to realize.

The United States government set up Indian reservations such as the one shown here. Reservations were usually much smaller than the lands that the Indians had lived on.

Why? Remember what you have learned about Indians in the previous lessons as you read the rest of this lesson.

Removal and Assimilation

As we have seen, Americans were flush with pride after winning their independence. They believed they had found the best way to live. Americans at the time believed that farming and ranching were excellent occupations. Some Americans also liked working in the ever-growing cities. Most were Christians. Most had homes they lived in all the time. Most believed that making money and increasing their wealth was very desirable. Most believed land should be owned and used in certain ways—to grow food and build homes on.

The general feeling (and hope) was that Indians would eventually live the same way as white people. All white people had to do, they thought, was teach Indians how to farm, ranch, or work in cities. Teach them to read, write, and speak English. Teach them to believe in Christianity. Teach them the value of a dollar and that hard work would be rewarded with money and comfort. Teach them to forget their old ways and become more like white farmers. Once Indians became like the whites—once Indians became **assimilated**—Americans were convinced they could all live together.

Americans believed that the best way to do this was to encourage Indians to move away from their traditional lifestyle and settle down on particular pieces of land. If they could put Indians onto land that was *reserved* just for the Indians, they could begin to teach the Indians how to live as the whites did. Meanwhile they could be isolated from whites. That's how reservations got started. The United States government adopted a policy of removing the Indians to reservations across the Mississippi River. The plan was so successful that by 1860, a great majority of the tribes had been relocated and isolated. But it did not happen without a struggle.

When Indians wouldn't sign treaties that sent them to reservations, or when they signed treaties but wouldn't move, the United States Army forced them under gunpoint to move. Sometimes Indians moved peacefully; sometimes they did not. White people were shocked when Indians resisted what seemed to them a good deal, and so more troops would be sent to remove the Indians.

> **vocabulary**
> **assimilate** to become like the people of a nation in customs, viewpoint, values, and so on

The Trail Where They Cried

In the 1830s, no Native American people was making faster progress toward adopting white ways than the Cherokees of the southeastern United States. They created an alphabet, published a newspaper, learned to farm, and acquired black slaves. Their ancestral land was especially suitable for cultivating cotton—the crop that was making many white Southerners rich. And there was gold in their mountains! Whites, including President Andrew Jackson (a veteran Indian fighter from Tennessee), viewed the Cherokees as successful rivals and wanted to seize their lands before the Indians succeeded any more.

In 1832 the United States Supreme Court ruled that the Cherokees could keep their lands. But Jackson ignored the Court's ruling and had the army begin driving the Cherokees far to the west, to what is now Oklahoma. In 1838 the government ordered 9,000 soldiers to build stockades and fill them with Cherokees and other Indians.

An eyewitness remembered: "Families at dinner were startled by the sudden gleam of bayonets in the doorway. . . . Women were taken from their spinning wheels and children from their play." Whites ransacked Cherokee homes and graves, looking for gold.

The army herded about 15,000 Cherokees into the stockades and then force-marched them on an 800-mile journey to Oklahoma. Hunger, summer heat, and winter cold killed about 4,000 of them in the stockades or on the march. They could not even bury their dead. This tragedy is known in American history as the Trail of Tears. The Cherokees called it *Nuna-da-ut-sun'y,* "The Trail Where They Cried."

The Carlisle Indian School

Moving Indians onto reservations was a short-term solution to the Indian problem. Adult Indians for the most part were so used to living as Indians that there was little hope of their adopting white people's ways. Experience proved this to be true. A Plains Indian used to hunting bison did not want to return to the confining life of the plow and hoe. That was a lifestyle his ancestors had given up not so long ago, when the horse had brought the joys of the chase.

The forced removal of Cherokees from their homelands during the Trail of Tears was a dark time in American history.

A man named Richard Henry Pratt, an officer of the 10th Cavalry, commanding a unit of African American "Buffalo Soldiers" and Indian scouts, hoped he had an answer: If the older Indians would not adopt white ways, then the Americans should try to assimilate *young* Indians. On October 6, 1879, Pratt opened Carlisle Indian Industrial School, in Carlisle, Pennsylvania, with 82 Indian children whose parents had given their consent.

School life was modeled after military life. Boys wore army-style uniforms and girls wore dresses. Shoes, no moccasins. Short, not long hair. Students marched to and from classes and dining halls. As far as language was concerned, the rule was English only, please. Reading, writing, and arithmetic in the mornings were followed by metalworking and carpentry (for the boys) or cooking and laundry (for the girls) in the afternoon. Music was also taught.

To hasten assimilation, students were not allowed to go home for vacations. Instead, they worked in non-Indian homes so they would continue learning white ways. With the best intentions, Pratt wanted to "kill the Indian, save the man"—to "kill" the Indians' non-Christian lifestyle and "save" them as white men.

Despite the seemingly harsh routine, some Indian parents recognized that Carlisle School was teaching young Native Americans useful skills and knowledge. Its popular sports program produced Jim Thorpe, one of the greatest athletes in American history. Other schools were created on its model. But at school Indian children were exposed to germs their bodies were not able to fight, and the resulting high death rates naturally frightened parents. After taking in 12,000 Indian children over a 39-year period, Carlisle School closed, and most of the other schools failed, too.

Carlisle School was only one of many attempts to assimilate young Indians. As far back as 1744 the Virginia legislature offered free tuition at the College of William and Mary to six Iroquois youths. An Iroquois spokesman, Canasatego, explained why the offer of a college education was declined:

The top picture is of new students at Carlisle School in 1886. The bottom picture shows some of the students three months later. What changes do you see in these "before" and "after" photographs?

Several of our young people were formerly brought up in the colleges of the Northern provinces. They were instructed in all your sciences. But when they came back to us, they were bad runners, ignorant of every means of living in the woods, unable to bear either cold or hunger, knew neither how to build a cabin, take a deer, nor kill an enemy, spoke our language imperfectly, were therefore neither fit for hunters, warriors, nor counselors. They were totally good for nothing.

The Iroquois did say that "if the gentlemen of Virginia shall send us a dozen of their sons, we will take great care of their education, and instruct them in all we know, and make men of them." The Virginians politely declined, too.

The Invisible "Guns" Up until the 1500s, Indians lived their entire lives without ever seeing a white person. Indians had lived completely isolated from the rest of the world. They had never been exposed to diseases like measles, smallpox, influenza, pneumonia, and dysentery, so they had no resistance to them.

They had no vaccinations and no medicines to fight these diseases. An Indian might visit a trading post and shake hands with a white person who had one of these diseases. The white person might become ill but would recover because he had been exposed to the disease before. The Indian, though, would return to his tribe, fall ill, and, in all likelihood, infect other members of his tribe.

Once a disease was introduced into an Indian village, Indians began dying. Sometimes 50 to 90 percent of the people would die. Worse, all the people would get sick at the same time. That meant there were few left to hunt, tend crops, and nurse the sick.

Smallpox hit Indians in the Northeast in 1633, causing a 95 percent mortality rate among some villages along the Connecticut River. In 1620, Huron Indians numbered around 20,000 people. By 1640, disease had slashed that number in half.

In the Pacific Northwest, diseases killed nearly one out of three Indians. Between 1780 and 1820, half the Native Americans living in the northern Rockies died.

The winter of 1839–1840 was especially devastating. It became known as the "smallpox winter." Estimates say that 8,000 Blackfoot Indians, 2,000 Pawnees, and 1,000 Crows died from smallpox that winter.

> *If the Great Spirit sent the smallpox into our country to destroy us, it was to punish us for listening to the false promises of white men. It is a white man's disease, sent to punish them for their sins.*
>
> —Neu-mon-ya,
> Paxoche tribe (Ioway Indians)

For the most part these infections were accidental and unconscious. There was nothing anyone could have done about them. However, there were some exceptional cases in which white settlers used disease as a weapon against the Indians.

During a siege of a British fort in 1763, the fort's commander invited some Delaware Indians, who had been staging the attack, to a truce in order to talk peace. As a greeting, the commander presented the Delawares with a handkerchief and two blankets that he knew were infected with smallpox. In the next few months, hundreds of Indians in the Ohio Valley died.

Continuing Growth

While the number of Indians decreased, the number of European settlers increased. Throughout the 1800s, everything that Europeans heard about the United States and Canada was "wonderful," "marvelous," and "dazzling." They were told that America offered limitless opportunity to anyone who worked hard. The Swedish dairyman, the French peasant, the Irish farmer, the English storekeeper, the German butcher, and others all believed that they could come to the United States and make a better life for their families. True or not, such tales lured immigrants to America's shores *by the millions*. These new waves of immigrants needed land. And they were going to get it!

With little regard for the consequences, white hunters aboard the railroads that cut across the Plains killed bison by the hundreds of thousands as sport.

After the Revolutionary War and the Louisiana Purchase, United States territory reached far beyond the Mississippi River. Spain held on to Florida and the southernmost parts of Georgia and Mississippi until 1819. Then those lands became part of the United States as well.

The United States continued to grow. Texas was annexed in 1845, and although it had won its independence from Mexico nine years earlier, this move touched off the Mexican-American War from 1846 to 1848. That war ended with the Treaty of Guadeloupe Hidalgo. With this treaty, Mexico gave to the United States lands that would become New Mexico, Arizona, Nevada, Utah, and California. The final "puzzle piece" was put into place in 1846 when Great Britain agreed that lands south of the 49th parallel (now Washington, Oregon, and Idaho) would belong to the United States. The lands that would become the United States were now open to white settlement.

Although white America was pleased by the expansion of the lands of the United States, they were disappointed in their attempts to assimilate the Indians. They had hoped that Indians would abandon their traditional ways of living and become farmers, ranchers, and store clerks, like white people.

Some Indians did try to assimilate; others refused. But all regarded whites' attempts to seize their lands as theft. Their resistance angered white Americans.

With a dwindling Indian population and increasing white population, with white military superiority, with a lack of a central Indian leadership to bring the many tribes together as a force, the consequences were obvious.

Internal and External Conflicts

All the land west of the Mississippi River was supposed to belong to Native Americans "forever." But even this agreement caused major problems: The Plains Indians who lived there didn't really want to share their hunting grounds with the Indians removed from the East. As you remember, Plains Indians depended on bison for many of their needs. But the arrival of new tribes and American settlers had a dramatic influence on the bison population. Americans often killed these animals for sport, shooting them from trains. Estimates place the bison population in 1800 at 40 million. By 1850 the number was cut in half. By 1875 the number of bison was reduced to about a million, and by 1895 there were fewer than a thousand bison in the United States. Less food and more competition for the food led to intertribal wars.

Gold was discovered on reservation land, and white settlers were soon crossing the Mississippi River in search of riches as well as homesteads. Many battles and skirmishes were fought between settlers, United States forces, and Indians.

Wars in the West

After 1860 most of the fighting between the United States military and Indians took place west of the Mississippi River. United States forces were determined to gain control over the huge western territory and to clear routes for American immigrants to move west. But the battles became more intense and even involved **massacres.** During some of the battles, Indians did terrible things to white settlers and to soldiers. But some of the darkest, saddest, and most tragic atrocities in United States history were committed by whites on Native Americans.

> **vocabulary**
> **massacre** the cruel and violent killing of a large number of people

The Sand Creek Massacre

In November 1864 the United States was still being torn apart by the Civil War. In five long and bloody months, General Robert E. Lee would surrender to General Ulysses S. Grant, and the Civil War would be over.

Imagine that you and your family are living in the new and thriving city of Denver, Colorado, in the winter of 1864.

The Civil War is distant to you. You're more concerned with the shouting in the streets that has awakened you and your parents. Your feet hit the icy floor as you run to the window and throw it open. You hear your father shout from your front door, "What's all the ruckus?"

One of the people in the street shouts back, "Indians killed a miner's family. They got the bodies out for us to look at. Really horrible. We're gonna teach them Indians a lesson!"

Your parents refuse to dishonor the dead by viewing their bodies "like linens at a general store." You ask them, "Which Indians did such a thing?" and they reply, "No one knows for sure who killed these people. No one knows if it even was Indians."

Later, a loud and rapid knocking on the front door startles you and your family. Your father answers, and a breathless stranger blurts out,

"We're gonna get them Indians. There are 700 of us ready to ride out with Colonel Chivington at sunrise tomorrow. Come on and join us!"

Your father shakes his head and quietly and slowly closes the door behind him. "Frontier justice," he sighs. "Drunks and amateurs and Indian haters all out to be judge and jury against people who may or not be guilty. God have mercy on all our souls."

At dawn the next day, you're again awakened, this time by 700 horses mounted by 700 men riding out southeast of Denver to give a taste of frontier justice to some Indians.

A few days later, you see a headline as your father reads the *Denver News:* "Colorado Soldiers Have Again Covered Themselves With Glory!"

"Father, what has happened?" you ask.

"A massacre," he replies, his voice choked with anger and sadness.

The Investigation

Colonel Chivington's actions to "contain the dangerous Indians" made him an instant hero. But only briefly. Within the year, the United States Congress ordered an investigation into what was being called the Sand Creek Massacre. Not until the investigation did the citizens really know what happened that day in November. Colonel Chivington would no longer be considered a hero but a villain.

Earlier, in the summer of 1864, Governor Evans of the Colorado Territory had asked all Indians who were friendly to whites to go to the nearest military post for protection. Soldiers were soon going to be sent out to deal with Indians who were acting hostile to settlers. Indians not under the protection of a military post would be considered unfriendly and could be attacked.

Two groups of Cheyennes led by Black Kettle and White Antelope, and one group of Arapahos led by Left Hand voluntarily entered Fort Lyon and declared their friendliness to white people. They gave up their weapons and in return were given protection and food—for a time.

Mysteriously, after a while they were told that rations would no longer be provided and that they must leave the fort to hunt and find food for themselves. Major Anthony, commander of Fort Lyon, recommended that Black Kettle, White Antelope, and Left Hand leave with their people and head for Sand Creek, some 35 miles away. Major Anthony returned the Indians' weapons to them.

On the morning of November 28, 1864, Colonel Chivington arrived at Fort Lyon with 700 mounted soldiers and two cannons. He joined Major Anthony who had 125 soldiers and two cannons. They left for Sand Creek that evening.

Just after daybreak, Chivington and Anthony and their troops approached Sand Creek. They counted 100 Cheyenne lodges and 8 to 10 Arapaho lodges. Chivington and Anthony estimated there were about 550 Indians and, grazing nearby, 500 to 600 horses.

Chivington sent some troops to capture the Indians' horses, as he knew how fearsome the Indian warriors were on horseback. Some of the horses broke away and ran into the village, alerting the sleeping Indians. The people ran from their lodges. Chief Black Kettle quickly hung an American flag along with a white flag of truce on his lodge. He wanted to make sure the soldiers understood that he and his people were friendly.

Chivington and Anthony ordered an attack. In just two hours, 123 Indians were dead. One hundred of them were women and children, including infants.

In his final report to Congress, the head of the investigation, Senator Benjamin F. Wade, wrote: "It is difficult to believe that beings in the form of men, and disgracing the uniform of the United States soldiers and officers, could commit or countenance the commission of such acts of cruelty and barbarity. . . ."

Near the end of his report, Senator Wade continued: ". . . the truth is that he [Chivington] surprised and murdered, in cold blood, the unsuspecting men, women, and children on Sand Creek, who had every reason to believe they were under the protection of the United States authorities. . . ." The report ends by recommending severe punishment for Chivington and others, including removal from office.

Unfortunately, these men were never punished. The only people who suffered as a result of this event were the Cheyenne and Arapaho Indians who died in the massacre.

This painting shows an artist's version of the Sand Creek Massacre, an event that shocked the nation. Colonel Chivington ordered the brutal killing of all the Indians. Even babies were killed.

7 The Indian Wars

Indian Conflicts After the massacre at Sand Creek, violence became a way of life as settlers continued to move across the new frontier and into Indian territory. Although their records were incomplete, the Bureau of Indian Affairs reported 65 skirmishes and wars between 1782 and 1890. This bloody period of conflict has become known as the Indian Wars Period.

In the Southwest (Arizona, New Mexico, Texas, and Mexico), Apaches had long resisted Spanish and American colonization of their homelands. They were willing to die fighting to preserve their way of life. In 1846 a 17-year-old warrior, Geronimo, had been admitted to the warriors' council. Embittered by the death of his mother, wife, and children at the hands of Mexicans in 1858, he took leadership of a band of warriors and led successive raids of vengeance on Mexicans.

During the 1860s, disputes between settlers and the Paiutes in the Great Basin Territory of Nevada increased. The settlers reported Paiutes stealing or killing their cattle. Sarah Winnemucca, a Paiute interpreter who spoke English, Spanish,

and three Indian languages, was called upon to be a peace negotiator. She felt that white settlers were starting the battles in order to make money. When troops arrived at the settlements, they would buy the settlers' products.

Near the West Coast, the Modoc War of 1872–1873 broke out when a band of Modoc Indians refused to stay on their reservation. The Modoc, natives of northern California and southern Oregon, could barely survive on the poor land they were given. The band of about 50 Indians, led by Captain Jack, hid in the lava beds of northern California and fought off more than 1,000 soldiers. Eventually, the Modocs were forced to surrender. The army hanged Captain Jack and several of his warriors for murder.

Native Americans Battle for Their Land

On the Plains

Plains Indians fought hard to keep their lands. Unlike Indians east of the Mississippi, the Plains Indians owned horses and were praised by their enemies as "the best fighters the sun ever shone on." The Sioux Indians massacred hundreds of settlers in Minnesota before army forces stopped them. In the 1860s, Chief Red Cloud and other strong chiefs chased out all white people who dared to enter Sioux territory.

In 1866, Sitting Bull, a Hunkpapa Sioux, respected for his courage and wisdom, became a leader of the northern Sioux. In 1868 he and some of the Sioux agreed to the Second Treaty of Fort Laramie, making peace with the United States government. This treaty guaranteed the Sioux a reservation until the end of time in what is now southwestern South Dakota. The treaty recognized the nearby Black Hills mountains as the sacred hunting grounds of Sioux and Cheyenne Indians.

The peace was only to last a few years, however. The discovery of gold in the Black Hills in 1874 caused a rush of white prospectors and miners to invade the sacred hunting grounds of the Sioux and Cheyennes. The Sioux, under Chiefs Sitting Bull and Crazy Horse, retaliated against the prospectors and miners.

The United States government directed that all Indians must move onto reservations by January 31, 1876. Otherwise, they would be thought of as unfriendly. Officials sent regiments under the direction of

General George F. Crook (perhaps the army's best Indian fighter), General Alfred H. Terry, and Lieutenant Colonel George A. Custer. Their mission was to stop the warfare and move the Indians back to their reservations. The Sioux were disheartened to discover that the troops were not sent to enforce the United States treaty with the Indians but to protect the encroaching gold miners. Outraged by attacks from United States forces, Chief Sitting Bull declared, "We are an island of Indians in a lake of whites. . . . These soldiers want war. All right, we'll give it to them!"

On June 17, 1876, Sioux warriors surprised Crook's troops and defeated them in the Battle of the Rosebud in southeastern Montana.

Battle of the Little Bighorn

A week later, on June 24, Lieutenant Colonel George A. Custer and his regiment spotted a group of Sioux and Cheyenne warriors on the Little Bighorn River. Custer led one column of a planned two-part attack under the command of General Terry. Terry's column was to join him in two days. But instead of waiting for Terry, "Long Hair" (as the Indians called Custer) decided to attack the next day.

Custer was unaware that he was up against the largest fighting force ever assembled on the Plains, between 2,500 and 4,000 warriors. Of the more than 200 men who followed Custer into battle, not one lived to tell the story of what happened during that one

Chief Sitting Bull was at the Battle of the Little Bighorn when the Sioux defeated the cavalry led by Lt. Col. George Custer, shown on the right.

345

fateful hour on June 25. A single horse, Comanche, survived. For many years afterwards, Comanche appeared in 7th Cavalry parades, saddled but riderless. The Battle of the Little Bighorn has become known as Custer's Last Stand.

In reaction to Custer's death, the defeat at the Little Bighorn, and Crook's losses, white Americans demanded more military action. The Sioux continued to emerge victorious in their battles with United States troops. But even though they won battle after battle, the Indians could not stem the rising tide of white settlement. The bison they depended on were dwindling in numbers, and hunger led more and more Sioux to surrender.

In May 1877, Sitting Bull led his remaining followers across the border into Canada. However, the Canadian government could not be responsible for feeding United States Indians—Canadians had their own Indians to deal with. After four years, Sitting Bull returned to the United States, with a promise of **amnesty**. He was placed in prison for two years and then returned to the reservation.

The Nez Percé War

During the time when Sitting Bull and his followers were making a new home in Canada, Chief Joseph and a band of Nez Percé Indians were being forced to move from their home in the Wallowa Valley of Oregon to a reservation in Lapwai, Idaho.

In 1877, Chief Joseph and his people were ordered to move to the Idaho reservation by General Oliver O. Howard. Chief Joseph persuaded Howard to agree that the Nez Percés had never signed a treaty giving up their homeland. Although he understood Joseph's arguments, Howard had to face the facts. First, he recognized that Americans were settling this part of Oregon and wide-roaming Indians just wouldn't survive. Second, he was under orders to move the Indians to the reservation. Most of the Nez Percés reluctantly complied. Unfortunately, some warriors in Joseph's group attacked and killed some white ranchers.

In spite of his sympathies toward the Indians, Howard didn't wait a moment to send his troops against the Nez Percé warriors. And so the Nez Percé War began.

Now Joseph and his band of Nez Percés were outlaws and were pursued by federal troops. About 1,000 Nez Percés—carrying all the worldly goods they could—retreated, trying to reach a safe haven in Canada and to join up with the Sioux led by Sitting Bull. Over the next few months, the Nez Percés trekked some 1,500 miles over rugged mountains and through forested passes, fighting the troops following them.

On September 30, 1877 —at Bear Paw Mountain, 40 miles from the Canadian border—U.S. troops and the Nez Percés clashed for the last time. A few days later, Chief Joseph surrendered, hoping to save the 400 fellow Nez Percés who remained.

"I will fight no more forever."
—*Chief Joseph*

Joseph himself had lost his daughter, a brother, and many relatives.

Chief Joseph said at the formal surrender:

> I am tired of fighting. Our chiefs are killed. . . .The old men are all dead. . . . It is cold, and we have no blankets. The little children are freezing to death. My people, some of them, have run away to the hills, and have no blankets, no food. No one knows where they are—perhaps freezing to death. I want to have time to look for my children, and see how many of them I can find. Maybe I shall find them among the dead. Hear me my chiefs! I am tired. My heart is sick and sad. From where the sun now stands, I will fight no more forever.

When Chief Joseph surrendered, General Howard spoke loudly and clearly, unsuccessfully arguing that the Nez Percés be allowed to return to their homes. Chief Joseph and the Nez Percés were confined to Fort Leavenworth in Oklahoma. Joseph made appeals to the military, to President Rutherford B. Hayes, and to the American people in general. He asked the government to allow his people to return to their ancestors' lands. Chief Joseph never saw his homeland again. Not until 1885 were 268 Nez Percés permitted to return to the Plateau region.

Apache Battles Continue

In 1874, United States authorities forcibly moved some 4,000 Apaches to a reservation at San Carlos, a wasteland in east-central Arizona. Many Apaches could not tolerate reservation life. Also, they were short on **rations**. They turned to Geronimo and other leaders, who led them off the reservation to continue their resistance to whites.

In 1882, General Crook went after Geronimo and his band of Apaches. Geronimo surrendered a few years later, only to escape from the San Carlos Reservation a second time. Crook recaptured Geronimo ten months later in the state of Sonora, Mexico. As he neared the United States border, though, Geronimo and his followers feared they would be killed once they crossed into United States territory. Geronimo and his Apaches escaped once again.

> **vocabulary**
> **ration** a fixed share or portion, especially of food

No fewer than 5,000 soldiers and 500 Indian volunteers were employed at various times in trying to find Geronimo's small band. Five months and 1,645 miles later, Geronimo was tracked to his camp in the Sonora Mountains. At a conference in September 1886, Geronimo surrendered one last time. Occasional raids by other Apache bands continued until the 1890s. Meanwhile, even the Apaches who helped the United States army fight Geronimo were exiled from their native land.

For 25 years, Geronimo led Apache warriors in their fight against white settlers.

New Hope? The on-again, off-again war that was waged between Indians and whites saw much blood shed over the centuries. But more than lives were lost. Indians lost homelands their families had lived on for hundreds of years. Their parents and ancestors were buried on lands they could no longer visit.

Those lands, as you have learned, were the life source for all their worldly needs. The reservations they were forced to live on were often barren and **inhospitable**.

On the plains reservations, grasshoppers and drought prevented the Indians from growing gardens. Treaties promised **subsistence** rations, but many times the promises were not honored. Sometimes the Indians received only half of the food they needed to survive. The Indians were faced with famine and death.

By the late 1880s, in spite of increased resistance and significant military victories over white forces, most Native Americans felt conquered and in despair. Many were ready to hear any message of hope that could be given. That message came first as a whisper and then as a great shout from a Paiute leader in the Great Basin—Wovoka, called Jack Wilson by the white people.

> **vocabulary**
> **inhospitable** not offering protection, shelter, food, or other necessary things
> **subsistence** the barest means of food, clothing, and shelter needed to live

Traditional Indian cultures valued spirituality. Indians relied on a Great Spirit to speak to them through signs and symbols, even dreams and visions. During a delirious fever on New Year's Day in 1889, Wovoka claimed to have had such a vision.

I went up to heaven and saw God and all the people who had died a long time ago. God told me to come back and tell my people they must be good and love one another, and not fight, or steal, or lie. He gave me this dance to give my people.

Wovoka became a spiritual leader, calling himself "the Messiah." Wovoka claimed that in his vision, he saw all his dead ancestors "engaged in their old-time sports and occupations, all happy and forever young." He claimed that the dance he had seen in his vision would bring dead and living Indians together in their old homelands. The bison would return as well. The whites would go back to the land where the sun rose. The dance he spoke about came to be called the Ghost Dance.

In order for these visions to come true, though, Wovoka told his people they must live quietly and honestly. He spoke of nonviolence. He preached of shunning the white man's ways, especially drinking alcohol. However, he did urge Indians to adopt farming, schooling, and Christianity.

By the fall of 1889, leaders of certain other tribes had journeyed to the Great Basin to hear Wovoka's message and to dance the large circle dances he taught

them. They took his message and his dances back to their people. Some tribes danced the Ghost Dance nightly.

But some tribes—such as the Sioux—only heard what they wanted to hear: The good days will return; yes, but only if the white man is gone.

In less than a year, the Ghost Dance was embraced by many Plains Indians. They even wore Ghost Shirts—cotton shirts decorated with feathers and drawings of eagles and bison—that they thought would protect them from soldiers' bullets.

New Religion

The Ghost Dance inspired some Indians, but it made many whites fearful. White military officials became edgy with what they perceived as the new Ghost Dance religion. The Indians seemed obsessed with the dance and its promise.

A frightened Indian agent at Pine Ridge (now in South Dakota) wired officials in Washington, "Indians are dancing in the snow and are wild and crazy. . . . We need protection and we need it now. The leaders should be arrested and confined at some military post until the matter is quieted, and this should be done now."

Finally, in November 1890, white officials banned the Ghost Dance in Dakota Territory. When the dances continued, troops were called into the area—just in case. The military was sure that trouble was brewing.

Suspecting that the great Sioux leader Sitting Bull might be the one to lead a rebellion, the Bureau of Indian Affairs agent at the Standing Rock Reservation wrote: "[Sitting Bull] is the chief mischief maker, and if he were not here, this craze so general among the Indians would never have gotten a foothold at this agency."

Orders for Sitting Bull's arrest came. As Indian police tried to arrest the former leader, a scuffle broke out and Sitting Bull was accidentally killed. Big Foot, Sitting Bull's half brother, was next on the soldiers' arrest list.

The Battle of Wounded Knee

When Big Foot heard of his half brother's death, he fled with his band south to the Pine Ridge Reservation. Many of Sitting Bull's followers fled to join Chief Big Foot, who had been one of those who was leading Ghost Dancers. On December 28, 1890, a group of about 500 soldiers caught up with Big Foot's group—106 warriors and about 250 women and children. Ill with pneumonia and facing insurmountable odds, Big Foot was persuaded to lead his people to Wounded Knee Creek where they would be disarmed before proceeding to the Pine Ridge Reservation.

The next morning, December 29, soldiers under the direction of General Nelson A. Miles entered Big Foot's camp to gather all

The Ghost Dance offered hope that the Indians of the Great Plains would return to their old ways of life.

At the Massacre of Wounded Knee, Chief Big Foot (pictured here) and hundreds of men, women, and children were left dying in the snow. For the Plains Indians, their old way of life would never be the same.

firearms. Few of the Indians would comply. Their tepees were searched, yielding about 38 rifles. Then, the Indians were asked to open the blankets draped about them against the cold. A young warrior, Black Coyote, raised his hidden rifle over his head and shouted that he would not give it up. As soldiers wrestled with Black Coyote, the rifle fired.

The soldiers, already extremely nervous and fearing that they would be slaughtered, opened fire immediately. From above the camp, the army fired its Hotchkiss cannon into the camp. The Sioux men, women, and children ran for their lives.

By noon, 300 Indians, including Big Foot and many women and children, lay dead. Fifty were wounded. Troops continued hunting Indians who had gotten away. Small groups of slain Indians were found miles away from the camp. The army casualties were 25 dead and 39 wounded. Many army deaths were caused by "friendly crossfire"—one soldier shooting at an Indian but hitting a soldier on the other side of the camp.

Viewing the scene later in the day, the Oglala Sioux chief Black Elk said, "I wished that I had died too, but I was not sorry for the women and children. It was better for them to be happy in the other world."

Later, an army investigator concluded: "There is nothing to conceal or apologize for in the Wounded Knee Battle. The Indians brought on their own destruction as surely as any people ever did." Nineteen soldiers who fought at the Battle of Wounded Knee received the Congressional Medal of Honor, the country's most distinguished military honor.

Scattered fighting between United States forces and the Indians continued. But the Battle of Wounded Knee stopped the Ghost Dance religion and, for the most part, ended the Indian Wars.

amnesty a pardon for political offenses against the government

assimilate to become like the people of a nation in customs, viewpoint, values, and so on

corral an area enclosed on three sides and open only at one end, used to contain animals

culture the attitudes, customs, and beliefs of a group of people

diplomacy the management of relations between nations

hunter-gatherers a people who belong to a culture that does not practice agriculture, but instead feeds itself by hunting, fishing, and finding edible plants

inhospitable not offering protection, shelter, food, or other necessary things

massacre the cruel and violent killing of a large number of people

myth a story that expresses basic ideas about human values that are held by the people of a certain culture

ration a fixed share or portion, especially of food

shaman in traditional cultures like those of the Native Americans, men and women who are believed to be gifted with special abilities to communicate with the spirit world

subsistence the barest means of food, clothing, and shelter needed to live

Geography
of the
United States

Contents

xploring the United States of America The United States stretches about 3,000 miles from coast to coast. Because of its great size, it is often divided into smaller geographical areas, or regions. The states in each region share many things, such as geography, climate, and natural resources.

Regions of the United States

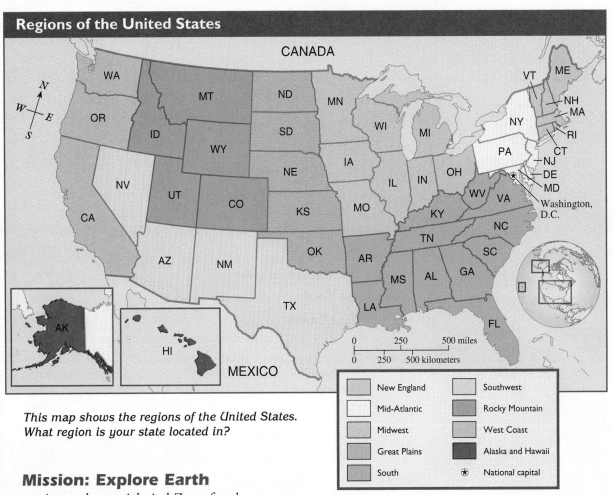

This map shows the regions of the United States. What region is your state located in?

New England | Southwest
Mid-Atlantic | Rocky Mountain
Midwest | West Coast
Great Plains | Alaska and Hawaii
South | ⊛ National capital

Mission: Explore Earth

As you know, Admiral Zorg, for almost a year the spaceship that I command has been exploring the planet known as Earth. Exploring Earth has been fun and exciting. We have discovered it to be very different from our planet Proteus. We have observed its interesting physical features and life forms and reported our observations to you. Now our year of exploring draws to a close. There is one last place we have to see and describe—the United States of America.

After we explore each area of the country we will send you a report. In each report, we will answer questions, such as: Which states make up each **region**? What does the land look like in this region? What

> **vocabulary**
> **region** an area of land whose parts have one or more common characteristics

sort of plants and animals live there? What is the weather like? How do the people make their livings? What do they eat and drink? How do they enjoy themselves?

We decided that we would send you a report from each region of the United States. These are the regions we will report from: New England; the Mid-Atlantic; the South; the Midwest; the Great Plains; the Rocky Mountains; the Southwest; and the West Coast. There are also two states which don't belong to a region, because they are not connected to any other state. They are called Alaska and Hawaii. We will send a separate report from these two states.

We will gather information for our reports by looking at things. When we have questions we will talk to some of the people we meet. (Of course, we will always remember to be disguised as human beings!)

Right now, as I record this audio message, we are flying over a huge body of water called the Atlantic Ocean. The next land we see will be the United States of America.

A Vast and Varied Country

The United States of America is reported to be a huge country. Earthlings in other places have described it as having a great variety of **landforms** and life forms. I have heard, too, that it is full of many different kinds of people. This is because people have traveled from all over the world to live there.

> **vocabulary**
> **landform** a feature of the earth's surface created by nature

Before we left the last country we visited, we remembered to buy some maps of the United States. These will help us find the places we want to go. They will also help us to identify the different areas of this vast country.

You remember, Admiral, that Earth is shaped like a globe, or sphere. Earthlings divide their world into two half-globes, or hemispheres.

They speak of an Eastern Hemisphere and a Western Hemisphere.

The United States is in the Western Hemisphere, on the continent called North America. A continent is a big landmass that sometimes has islands off its shores. On the mainland of North America, the northernmost country is called Canada. The southernmost country is called Mexico. And, in the middle of the continent, there is the United States of America.

Looking at our maps, we see that the United States stretches all the way across the continent of North America—a distance of about 3,000 miles. On each side of the country, there is a huge body of water called an ocean. On the west side, the United States borders on the Pacific Ocean. On the east side, it borders on the Atlantic Ocean.

Lieutenant Koola just informed me that she's sighted land below us. She's pretty sure that it is the state of Maine, in the northeastern United States. Our map shows that the country is divided into 50 smaller units, or states. I bet that's why they call it the United States!

Each of the 50 states has its own government and its own capital city. This is because the United States is a democracy. In other words, it has a system of government in which the people rule through elected representatives. The head of the national government, or all 50 states, is called the President. He lives in a place called Washington, D.C., which is the capital of the United States.

Now, we are flying low over the coast of Maine. Through the spaceship's porthole I can see huge, gray waves crashing against tall cliffs, which are covered with evergreen trees. We will look for a place where people live and land there. We are all very excited to meet our first Americans. In my next report, I hope to have plenty to tell you about this interesting country.

I've given the order to turn on the invisibility shield and start our descent.

Exploring New England This region is in the north-eastern part of the United States. It is made up of six states—Maine, New Hampshire, Vermont, Massachusetts, Connecticut, and Rhode Island. The Atlantic Ocean is a boundary to all of these states except one—Vermont.

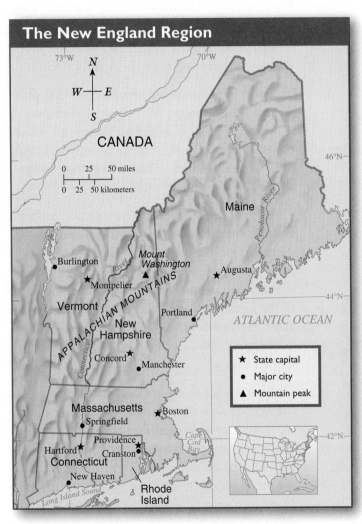

The Appalachian Mountains, a major feature of this region, are among the oldest mountains on Earth.

In my last message, Admiral, I told you how we arrived in the state of Maine. After flying over the coast for a while, we located a town. Lieutenant Koola landed our ship in a forest outside the town. The town had lots of wooden houses and a small harbor with sailboats. The people we met were friendly.

We were hungry because we hadn't eaten since taking off from the other side of the ocean. So we asked someone to tell us where a restaurant was. As you know, one of the things we like to find out about a place is what sort of food the people who live there eat.

When we were all seated in a nearby restaurant, we said we wanted to try one of the special foods of the area. The waiter said, "What about some lobster?" Since we had never heard of lobster, we thought we'd give it a try.

Imagine our surprise when the waiter brought each of us what looked like a gigantic red bug! It had long antennae and big mean-looking claws. By talking to the waiter, we figured out that lobsters come from the sea, so they aren't really bugs. We were relieved to hear that!

Lobster traps are piled high on the shore of a Maine town. To the right, a lobsterer removes his catch from a trap.

The waiter mentioned that many people in this part of Maine make their living by catching lobster. We asked him where we could go to find out more about the area. He said, "You could try the public library." We didn't know what a public library was, but we were curious. The waiter gave us directions, and after we left the restaurant we went looking for one.

Learning at the Library

The library turned out to be a brick building on the main street. When we went inside, we realized that we had made a great discovery. A public library, Admiral, is a place full of books that people can come to read without paying anything. Most public libraries also have computers, and between the books and the computers, you can find information on any subject.

In America, there are thousands and thousands of these libraries. Almost every town or city has at least one. As soon as we found this out, we realized that we had a wonderful new way to find information. We decided that every time we came to a new place, we would spend some time in the public library, gathering facts.

Here are some of the things we learned about Maine. You remember, Admiral, that Maine is in the northeastern part of the United States. It is one of six northeastern states that make up the region called New England. The others are New Hampshire, Vermont, Massachusetts, Connecticut, and Rhode Island.

In terms of **climate**, New England has four very different seasons. It has a cool spring, a warm summer, a crisp fall, and a long, cold, snowy winter.

> **vocabulary**
> **climate** the pattern of weather in a place over a long period of time

You may wonder why the area is called New England. It is because in the 1600s, people from the European country called England crossed the Atlantic Ocean and settled in the area. They also settled further south, all the way down the Atlantic coast.

Then, in the late 1700s the English who had settled in America decided they wanted to break away from England, which was now called Great

Britain. They wanted to set up a country of their own. In the year 1776 they declared their independence from Great Britain. The new country was called the United States of America.

The ruler of Great Britain tried to keep the Americans from breaking away. He sent troops to fight the American army. After several years of war, which the Americans call the Revolutionary War, the United States defeated Great Britain. It established itself as an independent country. But the Americans still kept some British ideas and customs. Most important, they kept the English language, which is spoken by almost all Americans today.

After a few days of studying in the library, we were anxious to begin exploring again. But we knew that we would miss the little Maine town and its kind people. Even more, we would miss the delicious lobster.

Mountains and Skyscrapers

After taking off, we turned the ship southwest, toward the mountainous states of New Hampshire and Vermont. Flying low over the mountains, we were greeted by a spectacular sight. Because it was Earth's season of autumn, the green leaves of the trees had changed color.

Spectators come from all over the world to enjoy the brilliantly colored leaves of autumn in New England.

Some of the trees were gold, some red, some purple. Every hillside was ablaze with different colors.

As we flew down for a closer look, Lieutenant Koola pointed to some of the most brilliantly colored trees. "Do you see those trees?" she asked. "A book I was reading said that those were sugar maples. A sweet sauce that is called maple syrup is made from the sap of those trees." You really have to hand it to the Americans, Admiral. They seem to be able to make tasty food out of almost anything— even tree sap and big bugs from the ocean!

From Vermont, we flew south, across the western part of the state of Massachusetts, where we enjoyed the sight of more rolling hills and colorful trees. But we were eager to see the city of Boston, which we knew was the capital of Massachusetts as well as the biggest city in New England. So we turned back east, toward the coast.

Boston looks nothing at all like the small town we visited in Maine. It is a huge, bustling city, full of the tall modern buildings that Americans call skyscrapers. But parts of it are very old. In fact, Boston was the first important city in the United States. When we went to the public library to study, we discovered that it was the oldest public library in the United States. We also learned that there is a local university called Harvard, which was the first college founded in America. Today, Boston is famous as a center of education, with dozens of colleges scattered around town.

Boston is also a city full of history. The Revolutionary War broke out in the Boston area. When we walked through the city on the Freedom Trail, we saw many places important in the story of the Revolution.

We visited Faneuil Hall, an old brick building where the revolutionaries gave speeches against the British. We also saw the house of Paul Revere, one of the heroes of the Revolution. When British troops invaded, he rode out in the middle of the night to warn people that they were coming. A famous old poem talks about "the midnight ride of Paul Revere."

We could have spent much more time in Boston, but we knew we had to fly on to explore the region known as the Mid-Atlantic. So we returned to our ship and headed south and west. Right now we're over the two southern states of New England—Rhode Island and Connecticut. We can see from our map that Rhode Island is by far the smallest of the 50 states, less than 50 miles across. Both Connecticut and Rhode Island have **port** towns as well as some larger cities.

> **vocabulary**
> **port** a place on a river, lake, or ocean where ships can safely unload and load supplies

But speaking of cities, Admiral, the crew is getting excited because our next stop is the biggest city in the whole United States— New York, New York.

Villagers awake to the sound of Paul Revere's midnight call in this painting, "Midnight Ride of Paul Revere" by the American artist, Grant Wood.

The Mid-Atlantic Region

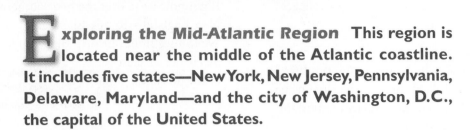

Exploring the Mid-Atlantic Region This region is located near the middle of the Atlantic coastline. It includes five states—New York, New Jersey, Pennsylvania, Delaware, Maryland—and the city of Washington, D.C., the capital of the United States.

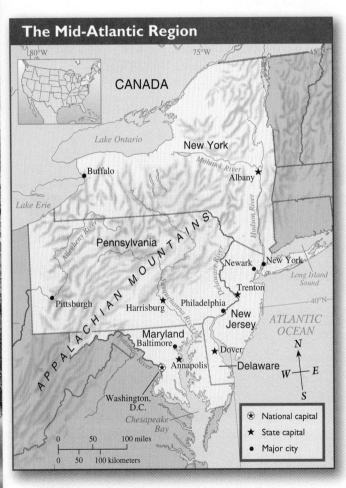

The Mid-Atlantic Region

CANADA

Lake Ontario

New York

Buffalo

Mohawk River

Albany

Lake Erie

Allegheny River

Pennsylvania

Hudson River

APPALACHIAN MOUNTAINS

Newark

New York

Long Island Sound

Delaware River

Trenton

40°N

Pittsburgh

Harrisburg

Susquehanna River

Philadelphia

New Jersey

ATLANTIC OCEAN

Maryland

Baltimore

Dover

Potomac River

Annapolis

Delaware

N

W — E

S

Washington, D.C.

Chesapeake Bay

| 0 | 50 | 100 miles |
| 0 | 50 | 100 kilometers |

⊛ National capital
★ State capital
● Major city

There are many port cities in the Mid-Atlantic region. Two of these port cities—Philadelphia, Pennsylvania and Trenton, New Jersey—are located on the Delaware River.

As you recall from my last message, Admiral, we flew from Boston in Massachusetts to the state of New York. New York is a large state, which stretches all the way from the Atlantic to what are called the Great Lakes. It has lots of green countryside and several large cities. But the place we most wanted to see in New York was the city with the same name. New York City is the most populated city in America and one of the most populated in the world.

The first thing we noticed about New York City is how many tall buildings it has. There are so many skyscrapers packed so closely together that when you walk between them, you can hardly see the sky itself.

New York is very, very crowded. Many people come to visit and to live in this famous city. Most of the time the sidewalks are packed with people and the streets are packed with cars. Everyone seems to be in a hurry.

A large wave of people came to live in New York City in the 1800s. These immigrants came from countries all around the world. Sometimes they came because they were looking for a better way of life. You see, Admiral, the United States is a country of immigrants. Since the country's beginning, people have come from all the continents of Earth to make their homes in America.

Usually, the first thing the immigrants saw when they sailed into New York Harbor was a

*Tall skyscrapers crowd the island of Manhattan in this historic
photograph of the Port of New York in 1923.*

gigantic metal statue called the Statue of Liberty. This statue is in the shape of a woman holding up a torch. This statue is supposed to stand for the freedom that Americans enjoy. We took a ferry out to the statue and discovered that you can walk up inside it. By the time we got to the top of the 354 steps, we were worn out!

Things to Do in Manhattan

When people came to New York from all over Earth, they brought along the different kinds of food they ate back home. So in New York you can get almost any kind of Earth food imaginable. The crew enjoyed sampling all these different dishes. In the area called Chinatown, we ate several of the crispy snacks called egg rolls. In Little Italy, we picked up some sweet treats called cannoli. At a hot-dog stand, we had Polish sausages called kielbasa.

But there's more to do in New York than eat. Lots more! New York is full of cultural attractions —concert halls, theaters, and museums. Broadway is a street lined with famous theaters where you can watch musicals and plays.

I especially liked visiting the Metropolitan Museum of Art, where you can see some of the most famous art earthlings have ever made. Because she's so interested in plants and animals, Lieutenant Koola preferred the Museum of Natural History. She showed me the big skeletons of some extinct Earth animals called dinosaurs.

Of course, we also went to the library. We found the New York Public Library in an impressive building guarded by two stone lions. We spent some time there looking up facts about New York and the other states of the Mid-Atlantic region. We found out, for example, that the area has a climate pretty much like New England's. However, the summers are hotter and the winters aren't quite so cold.

We also found out that the states of New York, New Jersey, Pennsylvania, Delaware, and Maryland are among the most heavily populated states in the country. Their many large cities are centers of industry and government.

In fact, the headquarters of the national government is in a place called Washington. Washington is in the southern part of the region. We decided to make Washington our next stop.

Exploring the Capital

Washington is the only American city that is not in a state. Since it is the capital of the whole country, it cannot be part of any one state because that state would hold too much power. So the city is in its own district, the District of Columbia. That's why Washington is often referred to as *Washington, D.C.*

On the way to Washington, we flew over some of the other interesting cities in the area. In Pennsylvania, we flew over Philadelphia. In Maryland, we flew over Baltimore.

We also flew over a big body of water called the Chesapeake Bay, which was covered with hundreds of small fishing boats. We had read that wonderful seafood came from this bay. Chesapeake Bay is especially famous for its crabs, which are supposed to be sort of like lobsters, but smaller and rounder.

When we arrived in Washington we noticed the city has broad, straight avenues. There are a lot of grand buildings where the people who run the government work. Maybe the grandest building is the U.S. Capitol, with its big white dome. This is where the Congress comes up with America's laws. The Congress is made up of elected lawmakers from every state.

To the west of the Capitol is a long grassy field called the Mall. Usually, when Americans talk about a mall, they mean a shopping center full of stores. But this Mall is definitely not a shopping center! Instead, it is a place where Americans gather for different kinds of big celebrations.

Right in the middle of the Mall is a huge stone obelisk more than five hundred feet tall. An obelisk is a four-sided shaft that tapers to a pyramid-like point. This one is called the Washington Monument. It was put up in honor of America's first President, George Washington.

At the far end of the Mall is the Lincoln Memorial, which honors another great American President, Abraham Lincoln. Inside is a big statue of Lincoln, three or four times the size of a real human being. He is seated in a chair, and looks very serious and commanding.

Near the Mall is the house where today's President lives. When we saw it, we thought he was lucky to live in the elegant white house with tall pillars in front of the door. Americans call the President's home the White House.

When it was time for some studying, we went to the Library of Congress. This is the biggest library in the United States. There, we looked up facts about the next region we'd be visiting—the South.

The Mall in Washington, D.C. is lined with famous attractions and historical buildings. The Capitol building, shown below, is located at one end of the Mall.

Exploring the South The South is a large region with a diverse geography, including mountains, rivers, valleys, and sandy beaches. The twelve states that make up the South are Virginia, North Carolina, South Carolina, Georgia, Florida, West Virginia, Kentucky, Tennessee, Alabama, Mississippi, Arkansas, and Louisiana.

The South Region

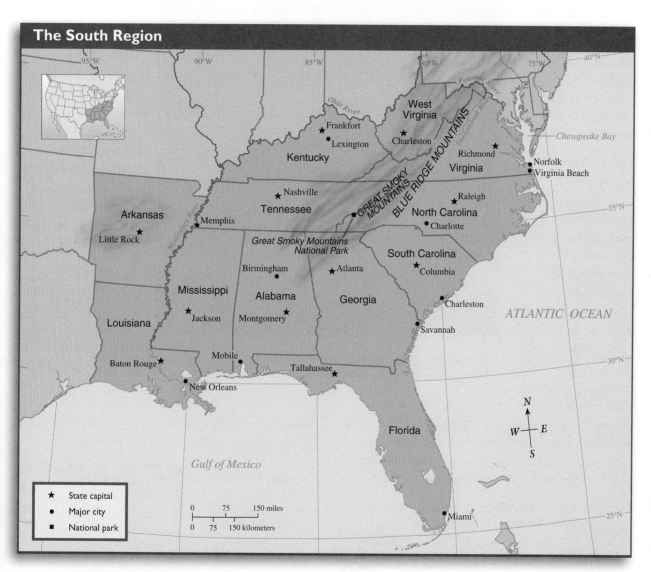

Two large bodies of water border this region, the Gulf of Mexico and the Atlantic Ocean.

The South is a big region of the United States. It includes all the states on the Atlantic coast south of Maryland: Virginia, North Carolina, South Carolina, Georgia, and Florida. It also includes the seven states of West Virginia, Kentucky, Tennessee, Alabama, Mississippi, Arkansas, and Louisiana.

The South has a different climate from the northern states we've been reporting on. Especially in the summer, it is much hotter and more humid. So on Southern farms, they grow different crops from the ones they grow on Northern farms.

In the 1800s, the two most important crops for Southern farmers were cotton and tobacco. These crops had to be picked by hand. This was terribly hard work, which most people didn't want to do. So the Southern planters had people brought over from Africa to work the farms. But the people who came over didn't come willingly. They were kidnapped from their homes and were enslaved. Then they were sold to the people who owned the **plantations**.

In the Northern states, many people disapproved of slavery. For this and other reasons, there was conflict between the North and the South. Then, in 1861, eleven of the Southern states broke away from the United States and declared that they were now a different country. They called themselves the Confederate States of America.

For the next four years, a bloody war was fought between the North and the South. This Civil War ended with the defeat of the South. The Southern states came back into the Union, and the slaves were freed. When we learned that Abraham Lincoln was President during the Civil War, we understood why his statue in Washington had such a sad, serious expression.

The Shenandoah River twists its way through the Shenandoah Valley in Virginia's Blue Ridge Mountains.

Most of today's African Americans are descended from the enslaved people who worked on Southern plantations. Since the late 1800s, African Americans have moved all over the United States. But many still live in the South. You can see the African-American influence everywhere in Southern culture, especially in the food and music.

The South is a region of great geographic diversity. We flew south and west to a mountainous area shared by the states of West Virginia, Virginia, and North Carolina. The scenery here is very wild. The mountains are part of the great Appalachian chain, which reaches all the way up into New England.

In the South the Appalachians are known by different names. In Virginia they are called the Blue Ridge Mountains, and in North Carolina, the Great Smoky Mountains.

> **vocabulary**
> **plantation** a big farm where cotton and/or tobacco were grown

We landed our ship in a place the map called the Great Smoky Mountains National Park. After landing we found a man wearing an odd round hat. He explained that he was a park official, or ranger. He told us that a national park was a place the government had set aside so that people could come and enjoy nature. This was only one of dozens of national parks, he explained. We asked why the mountains here were called Smoky. The ranger explained that sometimes the mountains seemed to be smoking because of the fog on their tops. We spent several peaceful hours walking through the woods that cover the hills.

Enjoying the Southern Coast

Next we flew back east, to the coast. The coast of Virginia, North Carolina, and South Carolina is covered with sandy beaches. We enjoyed walking in the fresh sea-air and observing the behavior of the people on the beach.

The most famous beaches on the East Coast are farther south, in the state of Florida. This state is a long peninsula. It juts out between two bodies of water—the Atlantic Ocean on the east side and the Gulf of Mexico on the west side. One of the reasons why people go to the beaches in Florida and the other Southern states is that the water is warm enough to swim in. The water is warm partly because of a stream of warm water that flows through the Gulf of Mexico and up the East Coast. It is called the Gulf Stream.

Florida is even warmer than the rest of the South. In fact, it stays warm all year round in parts of Florida. Because of the warm weather, farmers in Florida can grow fruits that can't be grown in the North, such as oranges. Most of America's oranges are grown in Florida.

After visiting an orange farm, we flew on to Florida's most famous city, Miami. Many people come to Miami to visit the beaches nearby. But it is also a big modern city, with a diverse population. We found that Miami was full of immigrants from Cuba and other islands in the Caribbean

Sea. The Caribbean is the sea off Florida's southern coast. On the streets of Miami, lots of people spoke Spanish, the language of Cuba.

After leaving Florida, we headed north again, to visit the states of Kentucky, Tennessee, and Arkansas. In Kentucky, we visited a farm where horses are raised to run in races. The most famous horse race in America is called the Kentucky Derby.

In Tennessee, we stopped off in Nashville and Memphis, two cities famous for music. In Nashville, we went to see musicians play what's called country music. In Memphis, we heard an African-American form of music called the blues.

The Deep South

Heading south again, we visited a peach farm in Georgia. We also cruised above Georgia's capital city, Atlanta. Atlanta was burned down in the Civil War and then rebuilt. Today, it is the most important business center in the South. Georgia, Alabama, and Mississippi are part of what some people call the Deep South. When exploring this area, we found that life seemed to move at as slower pace than in the rest of America.

The last Southern city we visited was New Orleans, in the state of Louisiana. We especially liked the part of town called the French Quarter, which is full of old houses. Pretty little fences made of black iron surround the houses, and their balconies were covered with potted flowers. Just like Memphis and Nashville, New Orleans is famous for music, especially jazz, another kind of music invented by African Americans. When you walk around, so much music is coming out of the buildings it makes you want to dance in the streets. In fact, New Orleans is known for a once-a-year party when people *do* dance in the streets. It is called Mardi Gras.

New Orleans is located on the biggest river in the United States, the Mississippi. This broad brown river runs all the way down from the state of Minnesota in the northern United States. It is the most important river in the whole country for transporting goods by boat.

Exploring the Midwest This region includes eight states—Ohio, Michigan, Indiana, Illinois, Wisconsin, Minnesota, Iowa, and Missouri. Rivers and lakes are major features of this region.

The Midwest Region

★ State capital
● Major city
◆ National monument

Three mighty rivers cut through the Midwest region. They are the Mississippi River, the Missouri River, and the Ohio River.

Hundreds of miles north of New Orleans we came to another large city on the banks of the Mississippi River. The map said it was St. Louis, in the state of Missouri. Missouri is in the area in which Americans call the Midwest. Also part of this region are the states to the north and east— Ohio, Michigan, Indiana, Illinois, Wisconsin, Minnesota, and Iowa.

We stopped for a while in St. Louis. There, we took a ride on the river in a big white wooden boat with a couple of smokestacks. The boat was built to look just like a paddlewheeler, one of the boats that used to travel up and down the Mississippi in the 1800s.

The most interesting thing we saw from the paddlewheeler was a huge shiny arch of steel standing on the riverbank. The guide on the boat called this the Gateway Arch. She said that it was the tallest monument in the United States—even taller than the Washington Monument.

Reading about the Midwest in the library, we found out that the area has always been very important for agriculture. In Iowa and Illinois, we saw many farms where they grow crops like corn and soybeans.

The cornfields were an especially impressive sight, with their thousands of tall green stalks laid out in neat rows. Later, we found out that most of the corn is actually not used as food for people. Instead it is used to feed animals, like hogs, which are raised for their meat.

Midwestern farmers raise animals for other things, too. North of Iowa and Illinois is the state of Wisconsin, which is called America's Dairyland. It seems as if everywhere you go in Wisconsin you see cows. We heard that there are as many cows as there are people in this state. These dairy cows are raised for their milk, which is one of the favorite drinks of Americans. The

Cargo ships move through ice on Lake Superior, near Duluth, Minnesota. Large Coast Guard ships help break the ice so the cargo ships can deliver iron ore to a steel mill.

milk is also turned into other foods—like cheese and butter.

But don't think that the Midwest is all corn-fields and dairy farms, Admiral. It also has a number of big cities that are centers of commerce and industry. Cleveland, Ohio, and Milwaukee, Wisconsin, are important manufacturing cities. Detroit, Michigan, is the headquarters of the auto-mobile industry. In fact, one nickname for Detroit is Motor City.

Cleveland and Detroit are located on the shores of the huge bodies of water that are called the Great Lakes. There are five of these lakes: Lake Superior, Lake Michigan, Lake Huron, Lake Erie, and Lake Ontario. Rivers connect the lakes to the Atlantic Ocean, so goods from the Midwest can be shipped all over the world. But the most amazing thing about the Great Lakes, Admiral, is their size. They weren't kidding when they called them great. When we flew over them, they just went on and on—more like seas, really, than lakes. We measured Lake Superior on the map and saw that it was more than 350 miles

long. Later, we read that it is the largest freshwater lake on Earth.

Visiting the Windy City

Chicago, Illinois, is located on the southern shore of Lake Michigan. It is the biggest city in the Midwest. Chicago is a center of transporta-tion, where railways from both sides of the United States come together. It is also one of the major port cities in the United States.

Chicago is the third most populated city in the United States. Los Angeles, in California, is number two, and New York, as I said before, is number one. When we went there, Chicago kind of reminded us of New York. It is a big, crowded city full of skyscrapers. In fact, we learned that the first skyscrapers in America were built in Chicago, back in the late 1800s.

Today, Chicago has the tallest skyscraper in the country. It is called the Sears Tower. We rode an elevator up to the top. Since the tower is al-most 1,500 feet tall, we were glad we didn't have to walk up, as we did at the Statue of Liberty. When we got to the top, the view was inspiring.

We looked down on the huge lake, blue and sparkling in the sun.

Later we walked along the shore of the lake. Wind from the water whipped against us, making us chilly even though the sun was shining. We had heard that Chicago was called the Windy City, and now we knew why. Or so we thought. Later, studying in the public library, we found out the *real* reason for the city's nickname.

Long ago a newspaper writer from New York called Chicago the Windy City. He did so because he believed the people there were always boasting about how great their city was. You see, Admiral, when Americans think someone talks too much they call him or her a windbag.

We didn't notice people from Chicago boasting any more than other Americans. But they did seem very proud of their city. For one thing, they're always talking about their sports teams. You see, Admiral, in America the big cities play against each other in sports. Three main sports in America are baseball, basketball, and football. In Chicago, we went to an old stadium called Wrigley Field to watch a game of baseball. We enjoyed eating hot dogs, drinking sodas, and yelling along with the crowd.

When we left Chicago, we flew over the northern parts of Michigan, Wisconsin, and Minnesota. The land was covered with forests. Not many people live in this area. Lieutenant Koola had been reading about the animals of the region. She told us about the animal called the wolf, a kind of wild dog, which used to live in many parts of the United States. But over the years hunters have killed so many wolves that now northern Minnesota is one of the very few places where wolves still live. Lieutenant Koola said that if we looked closely into the forests, we might also see moose and bears. We had no such luck. But, we were still in good spirits on our way to the next region—the Great Plains.

Wrigley Field in Chicago, Illinois, looks much the same today as it did in 1939, as seen in this historic postcard.

Exploring the Great Plains This region is located near the center of the United States. It includes five states—North Dakota, South Dakota, Nebraska, Kansas, and Oklahoma.

The states of Oklahoma, Kansas, Nebraska, South Dakota, and North Dakota make up the region known as the Great Plains. As you know, Admiral, a plain is a flat area without hills or mountains. Flying over it, we were amazed at just how flat most of this region is. We noticed, too, that there aren't as many big cities here as there are in the East or the Midwest. Instead, the land is covered with farms and ranches.

Flying over the eastern part of the Great Plains, we saw huge fields of wheat. So much wheat is grown in this area that it is called America's Breadbasket. In the western part of the region, we saw big cattle farms, where much of the country's beef is raised. Another important product of the region is oil. Oil is turned into gasoline to run the millions of cars that Americans drive.

Early Life on the Great Plains

When we read about the history of the Great Plains, we learned how much the region has changed in the last 200 years. We learned that if we had flown over the plains in the early 1800s, we would have seen thousands of animals called bison. The Native Americans who lived in the region hunted the bison for food. Native Americans—also called Indians—are the people who have lived in America since long before the European settlers arrived.

In the 1800s, European settlers began moving into the Great Plains, taking over land that had belonged to the Native Americans. They also hunted the bison, and they killed so many that soon the great herds had almost vanished. The Native Americans fought the settlers who were taking their land and killing off the bison. Then, troops from the U.S. army came west to support the settlers. After years of fighting, the army defeated the Native

The Great Plains Region

CANADA

North Dakota
Grand Forks
BADLANDS
Bismarck

South Dakota
BLACK HILLS
Rapid City
Pierre
Mount Rushmore
Sioux Falls

Nebraska
Omaha
Lincoln

Kansas
Topeka
Kansas City
Wichita

Oklahoma
Tulsa
Oklahoma City

TORNADO ALLEY

Red River of the North
Missouri River
Arkansas River
Red River

N
W—E
S

0   100   200 miles
0   100   200 kilometers

★ State capital
● Major city
◆ National monument

A major characteristic of the Great Plains region is the flatness of the land.

Americans,
who were forced
to move to special
areas called reservations.
Although defeated, the Native
American culture survived. Today,
many Native Americans still live
in Oklahoma.

People have always had to be tough to
survive on the Great Plains. The region has
little water and a harsh climate, with fiery
summers and freezing winters.

In the Great Plains spring is tornado
season. A tornado is a special kind of very
destructive storm. Most of the tornadoes
on Earth happen in a part of the
Great Plains called Tornado Alley.
Tornadoes are clouds that funnel
down to the ground at winds
more than 100 miles an hour.

In the northern part of the
region, the winter weather is
especially harsh. This might

be a reason
why the states
of North and South
Dakota have so few
people. North Dakota is
bigger than the state of New
York, but New York has more
than 20 times as many people.

In South Dakota, we visited
an area called the Badlands. There
we saw colored hills of rock carved
into different shapes by erosion. Early
Americans called this land bad because it
was dry and barren.

In a national park near the Badlands, four
gigantic faces stare down from the side of a hill.
The sculpture is called Mount Rushmore and it is
of four American Presidents: George Washington,
Thomas Jefferson, Theodore Roosevelt, and
Abraham Lincoln. Each face is almost 60 feet
tall. As we flew on to the next region, the image
of these men stayed with us for a long time.

*A tornado touches down on
a town in the Great Plains.*

Exploring the Rocky Mountain Region The Rocky Mountains form a long range that runs through all of the states in this region. These five states are Colorado, Wyoming, Montana, Idaho, and Utah.

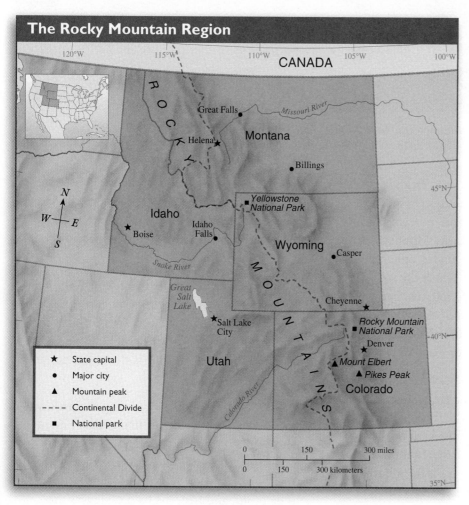

The Rocky Mountain Region

The Continental Divide runs through the center of this region. It is a line of mountain ridges that separates rivers that flow eastward, like the Missouri River, from those that flow westward, like the Snake River.

Flying west from the Great Plains, we were greeted by a dramatic sight—a huge wall of tall mountains, stretching from north to south. Our map told us that this was the great range called the Rocky Mountains, which runs from Canada to New Mexico, and through the states of Colorado, Wyoming, Montana, Idaho, and Utah.

We noticed right away how different these mountains were from the ones in the Appalachians, the big mountain range in the eastern United States. Most mountains in the Appalachians have gentle slopes and rounded tops covered with trees. Mountains in the Rockies are more likely to have steep, craggy sides and jagged, rocky tops. Noticing how many of the mountains had snow on their peaks, we guessed that the Rockies were much taller than the Appalachians, too. It turns out we were right. The tallest mountain in the Appalachian range is only around 6,000 feet high. But the Rockies have dozens of peaks towering more than 14,000 feet.

Rocky Mountain National Park, in Colorado, contains many peaks over 10,000 feet high. Longs Peak, shown here, is over 14,000 feet high.

After the flatness of the Great Plains, we were eager to explore this mountainous region. Our map showed that Colorado had more and taller mountains than any other Rocky Mountain state, so we headed there first. We landed our ship in a park in the city of Denver, which the map said was Colorado's capital. We found out that it was a big modern city, the largest in the whole Rocky Mountain region. It is called the Mile-High City because of its high altitude, or height.

As usual, we went to the public library to find out some facts about the region. I wondered what made people settle in the Rockies during the 1800s. After all, most of the land in the mountains was too steep to farm. I found out that the early settlers mostly came to mine valuable metals that were discovered in the mountains. Among the metals they mined were copper, lead, and the most valuable of all, gold and silver.

Today, people who live in the Rockies work in many different kinds of business and industry. One of the most important industries is tourism. People come from all over the country to admire the beauty of the mountains and to visit its famous national parks. People also come to ski.

Skiing is a kind of sport practiced in many places in the Rockies. People go up to the snowy mountaintops. There, they strap long boards on their feet and slide downhill over the snow.

A Day at Yellowstone

From Colorado we flew north to Wyoming. This is the state with the fewest people in the whole United States. We flew over lots of wild, empty country on our way to Yellowstone National Park. Yellowstone is the oldest national park in the world.

In the day we spent wandering the park, we saw more amazing animals than we had in our whole time in the United States. Lieutenant Koola showed us big birds called eagles soaring in the sky. She told us that because it was supposed to be proud and free, the bald eagle was the national symbol of the United States.

Then she pointed out a herd of shaggy animals with horns and humped backs. "Remember the bison we read about when we studied the Great Plains?" she said. "That's what those animals are. They were almost killed off by hunters in the 1800s, but then the government decided to protect them in parks like this. Now there are thousands of them in Yellowstone."

In another field, Lieutenant Koola showed us some animals that looked like deer but were much bigger. On their heads were gigantic antlers, or horns, that branched out into many sharp points. Lieutenant Koola said that they were elk. Lieutenant Koola also told us about grizzly bears. "Grizzlies," she said, "usually stay hidden in the woods, but if they smell food, they come looking for it. People who camp overnight in Yellowstone hang their food from high tree branches so it won't attract the bears."

Later Lieutenant Koola took us to a place where a sign said Old Faithful. We wondered what Old Faithful was—another kind of animal, maybe? But there weren't any animals around. Lieutenant Koola said, "Just wait." Suddenly a huge jet of steaming water came bursting out of the ground and shot at least a hundred feet into the air! Lieutenant Koola said, "*That's* Old Faithful. It is the world's most famous **geyser**."

We asked her what made the hot water shoot out of the ground like that. She explained that deep inside the earth there is a layer of hot liquid rock called magma. In a few places on Earth, like Yellowstone, the magma is especially close to the surface, and it heats the rocks just under the ground. When water from the ground seeps into the hot rocks, it boils and starts to turn into steam.

Brown bears, such as this one, can be found in Yellowstone National Park.

> **vocabulary**
> **geyser** a hot spring that ejects water and steam

Pressure builds up, and the water and steam burst out of the ground together—and that is what's called a geyser. I said it sounded as if we were standing on top of a giant teakettle.

After leaving Wyoming, we flew north to Montana, another state with lots of magnificent scenery and very few people. In the northwestern part of the state we flew over mountains and valleys that had been carved out tens of thousands of years ago by glaciers—huge slow-moving rivers of ice.

Then we turned west and south and flew over the mountains of Idaho. I said to a crewmember, "Guess what Idaho is most famous for." He said, "I don't know—mountains, maybe?" I said, "No—potatoes!" I explained that Idaho grows more potatoes than any other state.

We flew further south, to the last of the Rocky Mountain states, Utah. I had read that most people living in this state belonged to a religious group called the Mormons. They had come here in the middle of the 1800s because their religious ideas were unpopular in the rest of the country. They wanted to practice their faith in peace. Today, Mormons live all over the United States. But the headquarters of their church is still in Salt Lake City, which is also the capital of the state.

Utah is only partly a mountainous state. West of Salt Lake City, the mountains end and the desert begins. But I think I'll wait until my next message to describe the American desert. I hear there's *lots* of desert to describe in the region we're heading to next—the Southwest.

Exploring the Southwest This region is in the south-western part of the United States. The four states that make up this region are Texas, New Mexico, Arizona, and Nevada.

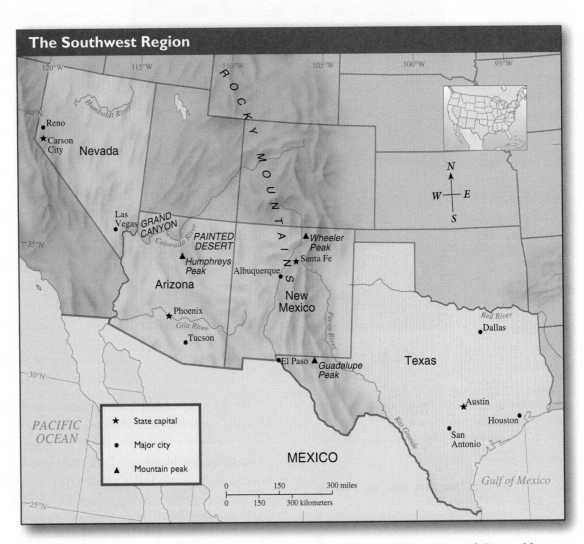

The Southwest Region

The Southwest is home to the Grand Canyon, one of the natural wonders of the world.

Our next job was to explore the southwestern states of Texas, New Mexico, Arizona, and Nevada. First, we had to backtrack a little, flying east to Texas. This is a huge state—the map showed that it was more than 700 miles wide.

Later, we found out that Texas is the second largest state in size, after Alaska. It is also the second largest state in population, after California. We certainly saw a lot of really big things in Texas—big cities, big oilfields, and big ranches.

In fact, we found out that there's a ranch in Texas that's bigger than the whole state of Rhode Island!

Texas raises more cattle than any other state. The cowboy, a person who takes care of cattle, is a symbol of Texas. In the late 1800s, Texas cowboys used to drive large herds of cattle hundreds of miles to market in the northern states. It was hard, dangerous, adventurous work, so many people thought of cowboys as heroes. But over time the cattle business changed so that there was less need for cowboys. Today, there aren't as many cowboys in Texas. There are, however, many Texans that still dress like cowboys. They wear cowboy boots and a kind of tall cowboy hat they call a ten-gallon because it looks as if it could hold that much water.

Another symbol of Texas is the oil well. Texas produces more oil than any other state. Oil was first discovered near the city of Houston in the early 1900s.

Today, Houston is the biggest city in Texas. The American space program has one of its largest facilities in Houston. One man told us that *Houston* was the first word spoken on the moon. He explained that when an American became the first human to land on the moon in the 1960s, the first thing he did was radio back to Houston.

In our exploration of Texas and the other southwestern states, we heard people speaking Spanish, the same language we had heard spoken a lot in parts of Florida. When we studied the history of the Southwest, we understood this better. A couple of hundred years ago this region wasn't part of the United States at all. Instead, it was part of Mexico, the country just to the south of the United States, where people speak Spanish. But in the early 1800s, American settlers started moving into the region.

In the 1830s the American settlers in Texas broke away from Mexico. Then, in the 1840s, Texas joined the United States. At the same time, a big war broke out between Mexico and the United States. Mexico was defeated and forced to give up the land that became parts of Texas, New Mexico, Arizona, Nevada, Utah, Colorado, and California.

Mexican culture still has a heavy influence on this region. Lots of the cities here have Spanish names like San Antonio, El Paso, and Santa Fe. Today, the region is home to millions of Mexican Americans, many of whom speak Spanish as well as English. Mexican influence is especially strong in the state of New Mexico.

One of the best things about traveling in the Southwest is the wonderful Mexican food you can buy everywhere. Many Mexican dishes are

Modern-day cowboys drive cattle near the city of Dallas, Texas.

375

made with a kind of thin pancake called a tortilla. I especially liked the enchiladas—soft tortillas filled with meat or cheese and covered with a spicy sauce called salsa.

Much of the Southwest is desert—dry, sandy land with few trees. The desert begins in western Texas and covers much of New Mexico, Arizona, and Nevada. Very little rain falls in the desert. In the summer it gets hotter than any other part of the United States—temperatures of 115 or 120 degrees Fahrenheit aren't uncommon.

The desert gets so hot in the summer that it isn't safe to walk around in. Luckily, we were visiting in the winter, so we were able to put our ship down in southern Arizona and have a look. The desert was very different from most of the other landscapes we'd seen. We almost felt as if we were on another planet. Instead of trees, we saw cactuses—plants covered with sharp spines. Some of the cactuses were short and round. Others were very tall, with thick "arms" sticking upward from their trunks.

The Colorado River cuts through Canyonlands National Park and continues to wind through the Grand Canyon.

Suddenly we saw something strange—a little bird with long legs running quickly across the sand. We'd never seen a bird run before. Lieutenant Koola explained, "That's a roadrunner. He can fly, but he'd rather run." She went on to say, "You know, a lot of people think there's no life in the desert, but that's not true. Look—there's a jackrabbit." We saw a large brown rabbit hop out of a bush. Then I said, "Wow! I've found a little lobster." When we looked down, I saw something that did look like a tiny lobster, except that it had a long tail that curled over its body. Lieutenant Koola yelled, "Don't touch that! It is a scorpion. It has a poisonous sting in its tail, and if it stings you, you'll get very sick." When I heard that, I jumped back a couple of feet.

After we'd explored the desert for a little while, I decided that we should get back in our ship and fly to northern Arizona. There was a deep, wide hole in the ground that I wanted to see—the Grand Canyon. The Grand Canyon is one of the great natural wonders of America. It is a gigantic **gorge** carved out by the Colorado River, a mile deep and 18 miles across. If you peer over the edge, you can see the silver river glistening far, far down at the bottom. The walls of the canyon are all different colors—red, brown, white, and yellow. The colors vary because they are made of layers of different kinds of rock. Like most visitors to the canyon, we just stood there for a long time, looking at it in awe.

Exploring the West Coast This region is made up of three states that border the Pacific Ocean. These states are Washington, Oregon, and California.

After flying over Nevada, we headed west again toward the Pacific Ocean. The part of the United States that borders on the Pacific is known as the West Coast. There are three states on the West Coast—California, Oregon, and Washington. California is by far the biggest of the three, covering two-thirds of the coast. It also has more people than any other state.

We decided to begin our exploration of California in Los Angeles, the biggest city in the state. Flying over the city, we were amazed by just how big it was. It spread out as far as the eye could see in every direction. We learned that big roads called freeways tie this sprawling city together. Los Angeles is so spread out that people sometimes spend hours every day in their cars, driving from home to work and back again. Since almost everyone has a car, there are too many cars on the roads, and traffic gets jammed. Americans call the times they drive to work in the morning and back home at night rush hour.

Los Angeles is home to people of many different backgrounds. For example, there are European Americans, Asian Americans, African Americans, and Hispanic Americans, to name a few. As you wander around L.A.—as the people who live there call it—you hear not only English and Spanish, but also languages such as Japanese and Korean.

Los Angeles is famous for its beautiful sandy beaches. On summer days the beaches are packed with people who have come there to enjoy themselves. We were there in the winter, so there weren't as many people on the beach. But we did get to see some people surfing. A surfer paddles out into the water with a long board. He waits for a big wave

The West Coast Region

130°W 125°W 120°W 115°W 50°N

CANADA

Puget Sound
Seattle
Olympia ★
Washington

Portland ●
Salem ★
Columbia River

CASCADE MOUNTAINS

COAST RANGES

Oregon

45°N

PACIFIC OCEAN

SIERRA NEVADA

40°N

★ Sacramento
San ● Francisco

▲ *Mount Whitney*

California

N
W — E
S

★ State capital
● Major city
▲ Mountain peak

Los Angeles ●
MOJAVE DESERT

35°N

0   150   300 miles
0   150   300 kilometers

A long chain of mountains, called the Coast Ranges, extends along the coast from northern Washington to southern California.

The Hollywood sign sits high in the hills of Los Angeles, California.

to arrive. Then, he actually *stands up* on the board and glides down the wave—a little bit like the skiers we saw gliding down the snowy hillsides in Colorado.

Los Angeles is also famous for being the world capital of the movie business. As you know, Admiral, earthlings are very fond of sitting in pitch-black rooms and looking at the flickering pictures they call movies. The best-known actors and actresses who appear in these movies are called stars. Americans almost seem to worship them. In fact, I saw something very odd in a part of L.A. called Hollywood, where thousands of movies have been made. It was a place where movie stars had stuck their hands and feet in soft cement so that when the cement hardened, people could come to see their handprints and footprints.

Los Angeles is in the southern part of California. Flying north to explore the rest of the state, we saw some very different landscapes. To the north, the California coast becomes rocky rather than sandy. Tall cliffs plunge down to the ocean, and huge waves explode against the rocks.

Mountains, Valleys, and Steep Hills

Flying inland from the coast, we crossed a range of mountains. Then, we came to a long valley that stretches all the way down the center of the state. When we flew low over the valley, we saw that it was covered with farms. Later, we learned that this is one of the most important food-growing regions of the United States.

Flying further east, we came to a range of tall mountains, which the map calls the Sierra Nevada. According to the map, the tallest mountain in the range is Mount Whitney. Later, we learned that this is the tallest mountain in the United States outside of Alaska. As beautiful as the mountains were, we were eager to see California's other famous city, San Francisco. So we turned our ship back toward the coast. San Francisco is very different from Los Angeles. San Francisco is full of elegant new skyscrapers as well as lovely old houses. Its parks are lush and green, displaying interesting trees and flowers collected from all over Earth. The city sits beside a beautiful blue bay. Spanning the bay is the famous Golden Gate Bridge. The bridge's two towers are 70 stories tall, and they're connected to the bridge by great swooping cables.

Much of San Francisco is built on steep hills. At the end of each day's exploring, we were worn-out and aching from all that climbing up and down. We learned that over a hundred years ago, someone felt sorry for the horses that had to haul heavy wagons up the steep hills. He felt so sorry for them that he invented a new way to haul things in San Francisco. It was a kind of little train, called a cable car, which was pulled along by an iron rope set in the ground. Today, people come from all over the world to ride the cable cars up San Francisco's hills.

After leaving San Francisco, we flew north to explore the states of Oregon and Washington, which make up the area called the Pacific Northwest. From the air we noticed a long mountain range which runs through both states from north to south. The map said that these were called the Cascade Mountains. Later we found out that these mountains were very important to the climate of the region.

When winds blow in from the Pacific, they pick up lots of moisture from the sea. When the air rises to cross the mountains, it cools off. Since cold air holds less moisture than warm air, the moisture falls as rain—*lots* of rain. The western part of Oregon and Washington is one of the rainiest areas in the United States.

We were amazed by how wet the area was—it drizzled almost the whole time we were there. But we were also surprised at how green it was. All that rain has helped give life to great forests full of towering trees. Lots of people in this region make their living by logging—cutting down trees to use for building or to make products like paper. But many of the trees are protected from cutting and set aside in national parks for people to enjoy.

After leaving the park we flew off to visit Seattle, Washington, which is the biggest city in the Pacific Northwest. Maybe because it rains so much, Seattle is full of coffeehouses. The most famous building in Seattle is known as the Space Needle. It is a tall tower with a funny-looking round top shaped sort of like the toy that Americans call the yo-yo. The tower is known as the Space Needle because the top is supposed to look like the sort of spaceship that aliens from another planet might use to visit Earth. Of course, it looks nothing like a real spaceship. We all had a good laugh over this. Earthlings can be so funny!

From the top of the 605-foot-high Space Needle, spectators can see a magnificent view of the city of Seattle.

Exploring Alaska and Hawaii Alaska and Hawaii are states that border the Pacific Ocean. Alaska is the largest state in the United States. Hawaii is made up of a chain of 8 small islands and 124 even smaller islands. The most southern point of the United States is in Hawaii.

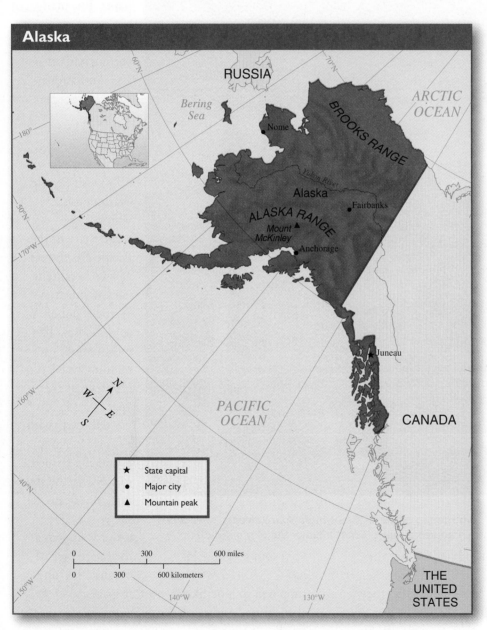

Alaska

RUSSIA

Bering Sea

Nome

ARCTIC OCEAN

BROOKS RANGE

Yukon River

Alaska

ALASKA RANGE

Fairbanks

Mount McKinley ▲

Anchorage

Juneau

PACIFIC OCEAN

CANADA

★ State capital
● Major city
▲ Mountain peak

0   300   600 miles

0   300   600 kilometers

THE UNITED STATES

Although Alaska is a part of the United States, it is closer to Russia and Canada than to the continental United States.

Well, Admiral, we've described our journeys through the 48 connected states of the United States. "Wait!" I hear you saying. "Didn't you say there were 50 states?" You're right, there are 50. But two of them, Alaska and Hawaii, aren't connected to the rest. Alaska is located 500 miles to the north of Washington State. To get there, you have to fly or drive across the country of Canada. Hawaii is located 2,000 miles west of California, in the middle of the Pacific Ocean. To get there, you have to fly or sail across the sea.

Alaska and Hawaii were the last two states to become part of the United States.

Sunrays reflect on the snow as a dogsled team runs in the Iditarod Race near Nome, Alaska. The Iditarod Race is an annual dogsled competition that covers 1,160 miles from Anchorage to Nome.

Alaska is the biggest American state by far. Two Texases could fit inside it. Yet few people, under a million, live in this vast space. Most of the people who do live there live in the biggest city, Anchorage. Much of the rest of the state is wild, rugged land—forests, rivers, lakes, and especially mountains. Boy, does Alaska have mountains. Seventeen of the 20 tallest mountains in the United States are located there, including the tallest of them all, Mount McKinley.

Alaska is so far north—just under Earth's North Pole—that it gets freezing cold in the winter. Temperatures often go down to 40 degrees below zero Fahrenheit. As we flew around, the mountains and glaciers of the state looked magnificent in their sparkling white robes of snow. Yet we wish we could have seen Alaska in the summer. Then, Lieutenant Koola tells us, the hills, forests, and streams are full of wildlife—such as moose, bears, beavers, otters, eagles, wolves, and mountain goats. She says that if you stand by the sea you can sometimes see a huge whale come to the surface.

The Islands of Hawaii

From Alaska, Hawaii was a long, long flight over the ocean. When we arrived, it was as if we were in another world. The state of Hawaii is made up of more than a hundred islands in the middle of the sea. Some of the islands are very small. Most people live on a few of the biggest islands. The islands are covered with forests, which are green even in the middle of winter. When we flew low to get a better look, we saw that the forests were full of brightly colored flowers. Then we saw something truly amazing—a red river of liquid fire running down the side of a mountain!

Lieutenant Koola explained that the mountain was a **volcano**, and that the liquid fire was lava. "Remember in Yellowstone, when I told you about the liquid rock called magma? Well, when a volcano erupts and the magma comes to the surface, it is called lava." Lieutenant Koola said that the whole Hawaiian chain of islands was formed long ago by erupting volcanoes. Some of them are still active, pouring out streams of lava.

> **vocabulary**
> **volcano** a mountain created by the eruption of lava from the earth

From there we flew off to the island called Oahu. We landed our ship in Honolulu, the biggest city of the islands. When we got out, we were amazed at how warm the air was. People were crowding onto the white sand beaches around the city. We noticed surfers in the water,

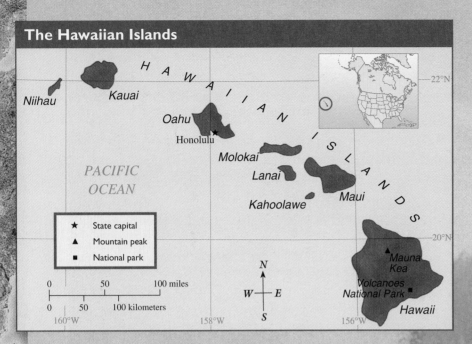

The Hawaiian Islands

The state of Hawaii is a string of islands located in the Pacific Ocean.

Niihau

Kauai

H A W A I I A N

I S L A N D S

Oahu

Honolulu

PACIFIC
OCEAN

Molokai

Lanai

Kahoolawe

Maui

22°N

20°N

★ State capital

▲ Mountain peak

■ National park

Mauna Kea

Volcanoes National Park ■

Hawaii

0   50   100 miles

0   50   100 kilometers

N
W — E
S

160°W   158°W   156°W

and someone on the beach told us that surfing was invented in Hawaii.

In the library in Honolulu, we learned that Hawaii was first settled about a thousand years ago by people who came from islands further west in the Pacific. These first Hawaiians had their own culture, language, and religion.

Today, however, most people who live in Hawaii are Asian American or European American. Hawaii is the only state that has an Asian American majority. Only a small minority are native Hawaiians. Few people speak the Hawaiian language. But some old Hawaiian traditions are still alive.

One night we went to a traditional Hawaiian dinner called a luau. One of the things we ate there was a kind of

In 1986, and again in 1993, the volcano Kilauea erupted in Hawaii Volcanoes National Park, creating lava flows as shown here.

porridge called poi. You eat poi with your fingers. We also enjoyed the main dish, which was roast pork. The dessert was fresh pineapple. Most of America's pineapples come from Hawaii.

After dinner, we watched some Hawaiian women perform a traditional dance called the hula. Afterward, the dancers put chains of flowers around our necks. These flower-chains are called leis. They're given to visitors as a way of saying "welcome."

Hawaii was a friendly and beautiful place. But we knew that it was time to head home to Proteus. Right now, our ship is leaving Earth's atmosphere.

As I look back at the blue planet, I think of everything we've seen and learned in our year and a half of exploring. America, we learned, is big crowded cities and vast, empty deserts. It is towering mountains and deep canyons. It is forests and farmland, beaches and swamps. It is Hawaii's rivers of fire and Alaska's rivers of ice. The people of America are just as diverse as its landscape. They come from every corner of the earth, so that America has a culture that is made up of many different cultures.

I am still wearing the lei that the Hawaiian hula dancers gave me. It reminds me of something I learned from some people who spoke Hawaiian. They told me that there is one Hawaiian word that every visitor to the islands learns. It is *Aloha*. It means both "hello" and "goodbye." I like that. I think what it means is that saying hello and saying goodbye should give you the same happy feeling. After all, it is good to visit a new place, but it is also good to go home. If you liked the new place, there is always a chance you will visit it again.

I am signing off now, Admiral. I will see you soon. For now, I will just say: "Aloha, America! Aloha, Earth!"

Glossary

climate the pattern of weather in a place over a long period of time

geyser a hot spring that ejects water and steam

gorge a deep passage with steep rock sides

landform a feature of the earth's surface created by nature

plantation a big farm where cotton and/or tobacco were grown

port a place on a river, lake, or ocean where ships can safely unload and load supplies

region an area of land whose parts have one or more common characteristics

volcano a mountain created by the eruption of lava from the earth

Index

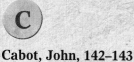

Credits

COVER: *top left to top right, counterclockwise:* Seaver Center for History Research, Los Angeles County Museum of Natural History. Trustees of the Royal Watercolour Society, London, UK/The Bridgeman Art Library. Hirmer Fotoarchive. Library of Congress. Bettmann/Corbis. The Granger Collection. Culver Pictures, Inc. SuperStock. Pearson Learning. Earl & Nazima Kowall/Corbis.

WORLD LAKES
Photos: *Unit Opener: bkgd.* PhotoDisc, Inc. *frgd.* Luis Marden/© National Geographic Society Image Collection. 4: © M. Bertinetti/Photo Researchers, Inc. 5: Luis Marden/© National Geographic Society Image Collection. 7: T. P. Nagle/Gallery Graphics. 9: Medford Taylor/© National Geographic Society Image Collection. 11: Andris Apse/Bruce Coleman Incorporated. 12: Sovfoto/Eastfoto/PictureQuest. 14: David & Peter Turnley/Corbis.
Maps: 3, 6, 8, 13: Mapping Specialists, Ltd.

THE MAYA, AZTEC, AND INCA CIVILIZATIONS
Photos: *Unit Opener:* Schalkwijk/Art Resource. 19: Richard A. Cooke/Corbis. 20: Laurie Platt Winfrey/Carousel Research, Inc. 21: North Wind Picture Archives. 22–23: Stone. 24: Bodliean Library. 25: Art Resource. 26: Biblioteca Nacional, Madrid, Spain/The Bridgeman Art Library. 27: Robert Frerck/Odyssey Productions. 28–29: Schalkwijk/Art Resource. 30: The Granger Collection. 31: Wolfgang Kaehler/Corbis. 33: William Allard/National Geographic Society. 34: The Granger Collection. 35: Tony Morrison/South American Pictures. 37: Robert Frerck/Odyssey Productions. 38: North Wind Picture Archives.
Maps: 18, 36: Mapping Specialists, Ltd.
Border and Initial Capital Art: Gary Torrisi.

THE RENAISSANCE
Photos: *Unit Opener:* Scala/Art Resource, NY. 42: The Bridgeman Art Library. 44: Dennis Massico/Corbis. 46: The New York Public Library at Lincoln Center. 48: Scala/Art Resource. 49: Peter Willi/The Bridgeman Art Library. 52: Archivo Iconografico, S.A./Corbis. 53: Boltin Picture Library. 54: Hugh Rooney/Eye Ubiquitous/Corbis. 57: Burstein Collection/Corbis. 58–60: Wood River Gallery/Eyewire. 61, 62: Scala/Art Resource, NY. 63: The Bridgeman Art Library. 64: Erich Lessing/Art Resource, NY. 65: Scala/Art Resrouce, NY. 66, 68: The Bridgeman Art Library. 69: British Library, London/Art Resource, NY. 69: The Bridgeman Art Library. 70: Chris Hellier/Corbis.
Maps: 45, 67: Mapping Specialists, Ltd.
Border Art: Dorothea Fox and Cathy Pawlowski.

THE REFORMATION
Photos: *Unit Opener:* The Granger Collection. 74: Library of Congress. 75: Giraudon/Art Resource. 77: Bettmann/Corbis. 79: David Lees/Corbis. 80–81: The Granger Collection. 82: Archivo Iconografico, S.A. /Corbis. 84: *l.* National Gallery of Scotland, Edinburgh/The Bridgeman Art Library. 84: *r.* Library of Congress. 85: Historical Picture Archive/Corbis. 86: Portrait by Hans the Younger Holbein/The Bridgeman Art Library. 87: Index/The Bridgeman Art Library. 88: Snark/Art Resource. 89: Scala/Art Resource. 90: Library of Congress. 91: The Kosciuszko Foundation. 92: The Granger Collection. 93: Bausch & Lomb Inc. 94: Private Collection/The Bridgeman Art Library.
Illustration: 76: Gary Torrisi.
Border Art: Michael Storrings/Artville/PictureQuest.
Initial Capital Art: Aridi Computer Graphics Inc.

ENGLAND: GOLDEN AGE TO GLORIOUS REVOLUTION
Photos: *Unit Opener: bkgrd.* Silver Burdett Ginn. *frgd.* Bedfordshire, Woburn Abbey/A.K.G. Berlin/SuperStock, Inc. 98: Carousel Research, Inc. 99–100: North Wind Picture Archives. 101: Carousel Research, Inc. 102: North Wind Picture Archives. 103–104: The Granger Collection. 106: *l.* Victoria & Albert Museum, London/ Art Resource, NY. *r.* The Granger Collection. 107: *t., b.* Art Resource, NY. 108: The Granger Collection. 109: North Wind Picture Archives. 110: Leeds Museum and Galleries, UK/The Bridgeman Art Library. 111: The Granger Collection. 112–113: Robert Harding Picture Library. 113: *t.* Carousel Research, Inc. 114: North Wind Picture Archives. 115: The Bridgeman Art Library. 117: North Wind Picture Archives
Border and Initial Capital Art: Gary Torrisi.

THE AGE OF EXPLORATION
Photos: *Unit Opener:* Buddy Mays/Corbis. 123: Arne Hodalic/Corbis. 124: British Library, London, UK/The Bridgeman Art Library. 126: FPG International. 127: Fred Maroon/Photo Researchers, Inc. 128: Dave G. Houser/Corbis. 130: Private Collection/Index/The Bridgeman Art Library. 131: Bojan Brecelj/Corbis. 133: A.K.G. Berlin/SuperStock, Inc. 134–135: J.P. Cowan/Photo Researchers, Inc. 136: North Wind Picture Archives. 138: Bettmann/Corbis. 141: Library of Congress. 142: Bettmann/Corbis. 144: Joel W. Rogers/Corbis. 145: Bettmann/Corbis. 146: *l.* Corbis; *r.* Bettmann/Corbis. 147: Bettmann/Corbis. 149–152: Bettmann/Corbis. 153: Library of Congress. 155: Bettmann/Corbis.
Maps: 122, 129, 132, 156, 158: Mapping Specialists, Ltd.
Border Art: Michael Storrings/Artville/PictureQuest.
Initial Capital Art: Gary Torrisi.

EARLY RUSSIA
Photos: *Unit Opener: bkgd.* Artbeats Software, Inc.; *frgd.* Scheufler Collection/Corbis. 163: The Bridgeman Art Library. 166: Novosti Photo Desk/Sovfoto/Eastfoto. 168: RIA-Novosti/Sovfoto/Eastfoto. 169: Sovfoto/Eastfoto. 170: SuperStock, Inc. 171: *t.* Sovfoto/Eastfoto; *b.* The Granger Collection. 172: Culver Pictures. 173, 174: Sovfoto/Eastfoto.
Map: 162: Mapping Specialists, Ltd.
Border and Initial Capital Art: Gary Torrisi.

6488013